More to the Story

THE LEGACY AND PROMISE OF LUTHERAN PENSION AND BENEFIT PLANS

by Lowell G. Almen

Lutheran University Press
Minneapolis

More to the Story
The Legacy and Promise of Lutheran Pension and Benefit Plans

by Lowell G. Almen

First Edition

Cover photograph and design: Stephen Mitzuk

Published under the auspices of:
> The Board of Pensions
> The Evangelical Lutheran Church in America
> 800 Marquette Ave, Suite 1050
> Minneapolis, MN 55402-2892

12 11 10 09 1 2 3 4 5

Library of Congress Cataloging-in-Publication Data

Almen, Lowell G., 1941-
  More to the story : the legacy and promise of Lutheran pension and benefit plans / by Lowell G. Almen. — 1st ed.
      p. cm.
  Includes index.
  ISBN-13: 978-1-932688-47-4 (alk. paper)
  ISBN-10: 1-932688-47-1 (alk. paper)
  1. Evangelical Lutheran Church in America. Board of Pensions—History. 2. Lutheran Church—United States—Clergy—Pensions—History. I. Title.
  BX8048.3A635 2010
  331.25'291284135—dc22
                          2010008077

Lutheran University Press, P.O. Box 390759, Minneapolis, MN 55439.
Manufactured in the United States of America.

In honor of John G. Kapanke
for his untiring and distinguished
leadership as president of the
Board of Pensions of the
Evangelical Lutheran Church in America

Contents

In Gratitude

You have in your hands the result of research that surveyed an era of more than two centuries. Emerging from that research is this account of the unfolding history of Lutheran pension plans and especially the Board of Pensions of the Evangelical Lutheran Church in America throughout its first 20 years. Although this research was commissioned by the Board of Pensions, what follows does not represent an "official" history, whatever that might mean for a survey of nearly 250 years of U.S. Lutheran endeavors for the care of clergy and their families.

Given the span of the story, a vast company of individuals might have been cited by name for their valuable contributions. Comparatively few are mentioned in these chapters. This was done to ensure a reasonable length for this historical overview.

Special gratitude is expressed for the assistance of Ms. Nancy L. Batsell from the staff of the Board of Pensions. She examined the records of the Board of Pensions and prepared numerous subject files for my review. Likewise, Mr. Andrew Walter worked in the Archives of the ELCA during the summer of 2007 to gather historical documentation. He was a student at the time at Augustana College in Rock Island, Ill. Both devoted enormous amounts of time to extensive research in support of this project. In addition, Mr. Joel A. Thoreson, chief archivist for management, reference, and technology in the Archives of the ELCA, was most helpful in guiding me in my search for particular documents. Likewise, Mr. David G. Adams, vice president for products and services of the Board of Pensions, was generous in giving his time to a careful review of the manuscript. He offered numerous suggestions that were salutary for refining the text in the pursuit of clarity and accuracy. Further, Mr. Terrance G. Mencel, who oversees communications for the Board of Pension, and his colleagues provided specific aid in aspects of this project. I am grateful to all of them and others for their assistance in this project. In addition, I express my thanks to my wife, Sally, who was a careful reader of various drafts of the manuscript. She offered valuable suggestions and encouragement along the way.

Great effort has been made to ensure accuracy. Careful readers, however, will find inconsistencies in style, especially related to punctuation and the capitalizations of various words. That is because the style used in original documents was followed in their quotation. To preserve the record, changes were not made for the sake of consistency. Decisions also had to be made on what material to include, what to summarize, and what to leave out of this survey. What remains, I hope, will be helpful to readers who wish to recall the first two decades of the work of the Board of Pensions of the ELCA and also to remember the efforts of forebears throughout many generations whose dedication brought us to this place.

Obviously, official minutes, numerous exhibits, reports for meetings and assemblies, and various news articles were crucial sources of information and are cited in footnotes. Especially significant were the "Core Pension Strategy" document from 2000 and the "Philosophy of Benefits" document from 2004. Both were prepared by staff of the Board of Pensions of the ELCA. Those documents, where quoted directly, are cited in footnotes. Information from them also was adapted to the narrative style of this volume and used extensively where relevant to the story. The two documents themselves, however, are not repeatedly cited in footnotes, except for direct quotations.

Some relevant details are repeated in various chapters. The overlap in such details was deliberate. That was done to outline thoroughly various issues in the development of the ELCA's Pension and Other Benefits Program. At the same time, some of those same details contribute to a more complete picture of the pension and benefit programs of the predecessor American Lutheran Church and Lutheran Church in America.

Footnotes are more detailed than what is the general pattern for such works. For clarity, the citation, *ibid.*, is not used in the footnotes. Rather the specific document is cited, albeit in an abbreviated manner after the first reference in a given chapter.

To all who contributed time and effort to the development of this history, abiding gratitude is expressed. And for all those who demonstrated throughout the past 250 years profound commitment to the care of "superannuated ministers" and their families, we give thanks to God.

The Reverend Lowell G. Almen

October 7, 2009
Day of Commemoration of Henry Melchior Muhlenberg,
patriarch of North American Lutheranism

Forebear Not Only in Faith But Also in Family

We now can explore the unfolding saga of more than two centuries
of Lutheran care for pastors, church workers, and their families
in pension and benefit plans

Paging through a nearly century-old ledger book of the aid fund in the Augustana Lutheran Church, I found a forebear not only in the faith but also in the family. The Rev. L. G. Almén. Same initials. Different name. His: Lars Gustaf. Mine: Lowell Gordon. He was a brother of my great grandfather.

Lars Gustaf Almén was born at Tössö in Dalsland, Sweden, on March 30, 1846, to Per Persson and Maria Andersdotter Persson. He likely was given the name "Almén" while in the Swedish army, perhaps by one of the French Hugenot military officers who became leaders in the Swedish army after emigrating from France. The name previously existed in various forms in both France and Germany. When Lars left the army, he kept the name, and most of his brothers also adopted it, because the name Persson was so common in Sweden, and later its Americanized versions of Petterson and Peterson were widespread throughout Scandinavian settlements in the United States.

Lars emigrated from Sweden in 1870 at the age of 24. He worked for a couple of years as a laborer and on railroads in Minnesota and Wisconsin before attending Augustana College and Seminary, first in Paxton, Ill., and then in his final year of 1875-1876 in Rock Island, Ill., where the school had relocated. He was ordained on June 25, 1876, at Jamestown, N.Y. That day, coincidently, marked the 346th anniversary of the first public reading of the Augsburg Confession, the basic doctrinal statement for Lutherans throughout the world.

Pr. Almén served various parishes and worked in starting new congregations as immigrants spread throughout the Upper Midwest. He also carried out responsibilities from 1904 to 1909 as a fund raiser for Gustavus Adolphus College in St. Peter, Minn. He is credited with the inception of the endowment fund of Gustavus Adolphus College. After serving as a board member and seeing the needs of the college, he resigned from his parish to work full time in seeking the initial goal of $100,000 for the endowment fund. Before he returned to parish ministry, two-thirds of that goal was achieved in gifts and pledges.

He and his wife, Elizabeth Christina (Johnson) Almén, were the parents of 10 children, including two who became pastors, the Rev. Alphonse Peter Almén and the Rev. Carl Wilhelm Almén.

The ledger page of the Augustana aid fund with his name concludes abruptly in 1912. Written at an angle across the bottom of the page was this notation: "Died December 5, 1912." He was 66.

Pr. L. G. Almén died while serving a parish in Carthage, S.D. Since there was no long-term pension for survivors, his widow, Elizabeth, and three dependent children moved to a farm near the rural Sillerud Lutheran Church at Balaton, Minn. The farm had been purchased in the 1890s when Pr. Almén sold land in North Dakota that had been homesteaded for him by his brothers. Son Carl Almén took responsibility with some other siblings for the support of their mother and the younger children. Thus, Carl's seminary studies were delayed and he was not ordained until he was 35. Carl worked during his seminary years in construction and played semi-professional basketball to support his wife, Agnes L. (Hedeen) Almén, and their two children, Elizabeth and Louis Theodore.

Their son, Louis, was ordained on June 11, 1950, and served as a parish pastor, college professor, church executive, and Thiel College president in Greenville, Pa., before his retirement. Coincidentally, I also was ordained on June 11, St. Barnabas Day, but in 1967, 17 years after Louis's ordination.

My paternal grandfather, Mr. L. G. Almén, also was named Lars Gustaf. He was an immigrant farmer in northeastern North Dakota. When I was born on September 25, 1941, my parents wanted to acknowledge the family heritage with the same initials, but different name.

The tale of Pr. Lars Gustaf Almén and the plight of his surviving widow and dependent children are only small pieces of a much broader story of struggle and difficulty for pioneer clergy and their families. That longer, more complicated story is the saga of how U.S. Lutherans sought over the centuries to care for pastors, other church workers, and their families.

We may take for granted the scope of Lutheran pension and benefit plans today. That can be true only because multiple generations before us demonstrated dedication and courage. Emerging from their vision and commitment was the Pension and Other Benefits Program of the Evangelical Lutheran Church in America. For that, we can be grateful now and in the years to come.

CHAPTER 1

An Unfolding Drama
of Vision and Courage

The roots of the Board of Pensions of the Evangelical Lutheran Church in America (ELCA) reach deep into the experience of Lutherans in North America. Although those roots stretch to colonial days, the ELCA's Board of Pensions only came into operational existence on January 1, 1988. With its formation, the amazing saga of Lutheran concern for pastors, other church workers, and their families entered a new stage of significant challenge and growth.

Tracing the history of Lutheran pension and aid programs is complicated. Begun by Lutherans more than 225 years ago, the first efforts on behalf of "superannuated ministers, their widows, and orphans" were intended as a means of support for the destitute. Grants in aid were provided, not a regular pension. The primary focus of the earliest aid plans was on widows and orphans. The expectation was that clergy would continue to serve until they—in some instances—actually "died in the pulpit." That is, they were expected to function as pastors throughout *all* their years.

For the ELCA's Board of Pensions, there is much more to the story than the efforts of Lutherans to address the retirement needs of pastors, church workers, and their dependents. The ELCA Pension and Other Benefits Program also encompasses health insurance for members and their dependents, disability coverage, survivor-benefit insurance, and options for tax-deferred contributions by plan members. About 50,000 individuals are served through the program.

With the passing years, the Board of Pensions of the ELCA has grown into a $6.8 billion pension fund in the United States of America.[1]

The story of faithful service for the well-being of pastors and other church workers has unfolded in manifold ways. What emerges from that history is a chronicle of dedication, vision, and, at points, great courage.

---

[1] This was the total in 2007. When the Board of Pensions of the Evangelical Lutheran Church in America was established in 1988, the amount was $1.5 billion.

A complex history

The history of the Board of Pensions is complex, given the substantial number of separate Lutheran church bodies that existed at one time or another.[2] Gradually, Lutherans came together through a series of mergers. In fact, the 11,000 congregations that were brought together into the ELCA had been part of a score of different Lutheran churches at one time or another just in the twentieth century alone.

The ELCA as a church body was constituted in 1987 by uniting three church bodies: (1) the Lutheran Church in America (LCA), with a history in North America through predecessor church bodies beginning in the mid-1700s; (2) The American Lutheran Church (ALC), with a history through predecessor church bodies from the 1800s; and (3) the Association of Evangelical Lutheran Churches (AELC), which involved a small number of congregations that broke away from The Lutheran Church–Missouri Synod in 1976.[3]

Built on the past for the present

Major Lutheran church mergers had taken place in 1917, 1918, 1930, 1960, and 1962.[4] Thus, through successive mergers, eventually the ELCA

---

[2] For a brief summary of the waves of Lutheran immigration and the formation of various early synods, see *One Great Cloud of Witnesses* by Lowell G. Almen (Minneapolis: Augsburg Fortress, Publishers, 2006), pp. 76-85.

[3] This account of the development of Lutheran pension and benefit plans deals only with the Evangelical Lutheran Church in America and its predecessor church bodies. It does not describe the history of The Lutheran Church–Missouri Synod since the formation of that church body in 1847, nor is the development of the pension and benefits programs of the LCMS and the various smaller U.S. Lutheran churches recounted in this narrative.

[4] In 1917, three Norwegian immigrant churches merged to form the Norwegian Lutheran Church of America (the name was changed after World War II to Evangelical Lutheran Church). The General Synod, United Synod South, and General Council constituted the United Lutheran Church in America in 1918. Merging synods (Joint Synod of Ohio, Iowa Synod, Texas Synod, and Buffalo Synod) established the American Lutheran Church in 1930.

Coming together in The American Lutheran Church of 1960 (a capital letter was used officially on "The" to distinguish it from the 1930 ALC) were the: (1) American Lutheran Church of 1930, with German roots; (2) Evangelical Lutheran Church of 1917, with Norwegian roots; (3) United Evangelical Lutheran Church of 1896, with Danish roots; and (4) Lutheran Free Church of 1897, with Norwegian roots that joined the ALC in 1963.

The Lutheran Church in America brought together four churches: (1) American Evangelical Lutheran Church of 1878, with Danish roots; (2) Augustana Lutheran Church of 1860, with primarily Swedish roots; (2) Finnish Evangelical Lutheran Church (Suomi Synod) of 1890; and (4) United Lutheran Church in America, the largest and oldest of the four, which traced its earliest roots to the formation by German immigrants of the first synod in colonial America in 1748.

was formed. The Pension and Other Benefits Program of the ELCA was built upon the patterns in predecessor church bodies but the program also was refined substantially over the years to meet current needs.

Lutheran attempts to create pension and insurance programs for pastors and their families did not escape controversy in the nineteenth and early twentieth centuries. An issue of biblical application complicated adoption of such programs. Many folks in frontier America suspected that efforts for ministerial relief reflected a failure to live by faith and an unwillingness to depend on the charity of congregations. Or, if lacking such support, the families of elderly clergy and their widows were expected to bear responsibility for their welfare. This interpretation of "living by faith" did not apply just to clergy. Thus, the establishment in the early twentieth century of Lutheran fraternal benefit societies offering life insurance for members of congregations was, in a way, revolutionary.

Attempts to create viable annuity and relief programs were affected both by internal church struggles and the external context of economic and social life. Devastating was the experience of the Great Depression in the 1930s. For several years in its aftermath, investment policies for many programs tended to be extremely conservative. Lutheran pension plans only slowly adjusted to the significantly changed economy in the two decades following World War II.

A major development for clergy income in retirement occurred in the 1950s. Through an amendment of the Social Security law, coverage for ordained ministers was permitted as of January 1, 1955. Unlike employees of companies, however, clergy were required to pay Social Security taxes as self-employed individuals. That stipulation was intended to maintain the principle of separation of church and state. It proved to be an increasingly strange quirk in the law since, in practice, many congregations provided a Social Security supplement to pastors, although such money had to be treated as additional income for tax purposes.

To address concerns about pension plans in general, the U.S. Congress passed a law in 1974, known as the Employee Retirement Income Security Act. That act commonly is called ERISA. Given what were projected at the time as substantial costs for compliance by church plans, various churches advocated and were granted an exception from the requirements of ERISA. Although exempt from the federal reporting requirements and other aspects of ERISA, the principles reflected in ERISA generally guided the operation of many church pension plans.

Creation of Board of Pensions

Within the list of basic purposes for the ELCA's churchwide organization is the obligation to maintain a program for pensions and other benefits.[5] That purpose is underscored in the section dealing specifically with the Board of Pensions, declaring that the board shall "manage and operate the Pension and Other Benefits Program" and "provide pension, health, and other benefits exclusively for the benefit of eligible members working within the structure of this church [meaning the whole ELCA] and other organizations operated exclusively for religious purposes."[6]

This language in the ELCA's governing documents establishes the overall objectives of this church's provision for pensions and other benefits. In so doing, the framers of the ELCA's program sought to (1) encourage uniform treatment for all clergy and other church workers, (2) facilitate mobility, (3) achieve economies of scale, and (4) relieve congregations, synods, and other employee entities of the need to manage local or regional programs for benefits.

The uniform pattern was designed to avoid the matter of pensions and other benefits becoming a factor in the "call" process for pastors and lay rostered church workers. That is, the program was the same whether the person was serving in Hawaii or North Dakota or Florida. Further, the benefits were portable. A member did not have to enroll in a new plan with different coverage depending on where the individual served in the ELCA. The same benefits were available and applied wherever a person lived.

The ELCA program for pensions and other benefits was "designed for the whole church to share care and concern for the welfare of all its employees wherever they may serve. As a common program for lay employees and ordained ministers, it reflects the distinctive histories and philosophies of the benefit programs of the uniting churches and includes the breadth of coverage" of those programs.[7]

Key principles

Five supporting principles were formulated in the middle 1980s for what would become the ELCA Board of Pensions. Those five principles dealt

---

[5] Provision 11.21.m. in the *Constitution, Bylaws, and Continuing Resolutions of the Evangelical Lutheran Church in America* (2007 edition), p. 86.

[6] Continuing resolution 17.61.A05.a. and b., *Constitution* (2007 edition), p. 136.

[7] "Proposed Pension and Other Benefits Program," *Report and Recommendations of the Commission for a New Lutheran Church*, August 1986, p. 172.

with (1) plan participation, (2) level of benefits, (3) a bundled program, (4) contribution policy, and (5) the sharing of health-care costs.[8]

Plan participation: The underlying conviction is that all pastors and other church workers should be sponsored in the ELCA Pension and Other Benefits Program. The ELCA's churchwide office, the Board of Pensions itself, synods, and ELCA seminaries as employing entities were required to provide such coverage. In this way, they set an example for the whole church in sponsoring all employees, lay as well as clergy, in the program. Further, synodical bishops and staff, in dealing with the call process for pastors and other rostered persons, encourage congregations to participate. About 94 percent of ELCA pastors serving congregations are in the ELCA Pension and Other Benefits Program. This widespread participation has fostered equal treatment for pastors, rostered church workers, and lay employees.

Level of benefits: The benefits program of the Board of Pensions was designed to provide adequate financial protection in the event of illness, injury, disability, retirement, or death. Benefits were designed to compare favorably to those available to individuals serving in other church bodies as well as in non-church employment.

Bundled program: Four plans were offered from the beginning in the ELCA as a package—retirement pension, health, disability, and survivor benefits. Bundling helped ensure consistency of benefit coverage and avoided gaps in that coverage. The pattern also was intended to discourage congregations from seeking lower-value health or disability coverage, thereby maintaining high participation that protected the financial integrity of the plans.

Contribution policy: The program was designed as an employer-paid model. Therefore, the monthly cost of the program was to be affordable and paid entirely by the congregation or other sponsoring employer. This helped maintain consistency of benefits and was deemed appropriate in view of the comparatively low salaries of many pastors and church workers. For retirees, pension benefits represented not only retirement support, but also deferred compensation from their years of active service.

---

[8] "Report on the ELCA's Philosophy of Benefits" was prepared for the trustees of the Board of Pensions of the ELCA in August 2004. The report was affirmed by the trustees in Action Number PN04.08.31, *Minutes*, Board of Trustees of the Board of Pensions of the ELCA, August 4-6, 2004, p. 16.

Sharing of health costs: Employers of greater means were expected to pay more in order to help employers of lesser means participate fully. This reflected the ELCA's principle of interdependence of congregations, synods, and churchwide ministries and helped keep the health plan affordable for congregations of very limited means.

Defined-contribution plan

The ELCA's pension plan is a defined-contribution plan, not a defined-benefit plan.[9] The plan defines the contributions to be made, not the resulting benefits. Therefore, actual levels of income in retirement cannot be predicted precisely.

From the beginning, the goal of the ELCA's pension plan was "to provide retired church workers with a replacement income including Social Security at a level to assist them to maintain their pre-retirement standard of living."[10] The plan's purpose was to build and preserve income for retirement. To reach the level of their pre-retirement standard of living, members needed to participate in the plan for at least 35 years and also draw Social Security benefits. Those with fewer years of ELCA service received, in effect, a "pro-rata portion" of a "full-career" pension benefit. The individual account system in the defined-contribution plan qualified as a tax-sheltered annuity under the Internal Revenue Service Code, Section 403(b)(9).

The minimum employer-paid contribution for each plan member is determined on the basis of a percentage of the member's defined compensation. That minimum percentage for most plan members now is 10 percent of defined compensation for pension purposes.

---

[9] In a *defined-contribution plan*, the amount of an individual's eventual pension income in retirement depends on the total amount contributed by or for the individual and the investment experience for growth of those funds during the individual's active service. This differs from a defined-benefit plan. In a *defined-benefit plan*, the amount of an individual's pension income in retirement is determined by a formula set by the board of the organization that established the plan. Forms of defined-benefit plans were in place in some Lutheran churches in the nineteenth century and the first decades of the twentieth century, but contributions and investments did not yield sufficient funds in those defined-benefit plans to provide even a modest income for pastors in retirement or adequate support for their widows and orphans.

[10] *Report and Recommendations . . .* , August 1986, p. 173.

For pastors, annual defined compensation includes (1) the base salary before any pretax benefit contributions are deducted,[11] (2) the amount of any Social Security tax allowance paid to the pastor, and (3) the total amount of any cash housing allowance paid to the pastor. If the pastor lives in a church-provided parsonage, an additional 30 percent is calculated on the amount of the pastor's base salary and any Social Security allowance, plus any allowances paid to the pastor for household furnishings or utilities.[12]

For rostered lay persons and lay employees, the annual defined compensation refers to the base salary prior to any deductions for pretax benefit contributions.

Impact of fluctuations in the market

In a defined-contribution plan, several factors affect an individual's eventual pension benefit. Those factors include: (1) the level of contributions related to the member's compensation over an entire career, (2) the length of service in the plan, (3) the types of funds that a member selects from among those offered by the Board of Pensions, and (4) the actual performance of those funds over the years. With ups and downs, fluctuations in the market will have an impact on a member's accumulation of funds for retirement.[13]

Members regularly were informed of the importance of understanding "how the underlying assets of each ELCA fund are invested and how the investment performance of those underlying investments will affect the amount of the pension benefit you ultimately will receive."[14] As explained in descriptions of the ELCA pension plan regarding retirement benefits, "When determining how much can be paid per month, the actuary uses,

---

[11] "Pretax benefit contributions" refer to member pretax contributions to the ELCA Retirement Plan, member pretax contributions to another eligible retirement plan, and pretax contributions to eligible reimbursement accounts for health care, dependent care, or transportation expenses.

[12] *Summary [of] Pension and Other Benefits Plans*, Constituting Convention of the Evangelical Lutheran Church in America, Columbus, Ohio, April 30–May 3, 1987, Part A-4, p. 10. Excluded from defined-compensation calculations are the costs of any employer-provided utility payments, employer contributions made to the ELCA Retirement Plan or another retirement plan, housing equity contributions made to the ELCA Retirement Plan, and non-taxable reimbursements or expense allowances, such as for automobile expenses, vestments, books, continuing education, or other professional expenses.

[13] "Pension Equity Report," *Minutes*, Appendix VI.C., Section 3A, Board of Trustees of the Board of Pensions of the ELCA, February 28–March 2, 2003, p. 6.

[14] *Summary [of] Pension and Other Benefits Plans*, 1987, Part A-7, p. 13.

among other elements, an interest assumption. To the extent that the actual experience differs from this assumption, your pension will be adjusted. . . ."[15]

From predecessor plans

The ELCA pension plan carried forward elements of predecessor plans, but the ELCA program included more options for members.

In the ALC pension program, two plans existed, one for clergy and one for laity. Each of the ALC pension plans provided a balanced fund and offered no investment choices to individuals. The ALC's pension contribution rate varied between eight percent and 12 percent of defined compensation and was employer-paid for ordained ministers.

Originally in the LCA, only a high quality bond fund was available, known as the Fixed Income Pension or FIP. An equity fund, called the Variable Income Pension (VIP), was added in 1967. The contribution rate in the LCA pension plan was 12 percent of defined compensation, with four percent paid by the member and eight percent submitted by the congregation or employing entity.

The design of the LCA plan followed closely the program of TIAA-CREF,[16] the giant retirement system used by most U.S. colleges and universities. With the development of the second fund in the LCA, participants were given an annual opportunity to move investments from the bond to the stock fund. At retirement, they could reverse course, given the prevailing wisdom at the time that they should be invested more conservatively in retirement.[17]

No withdrawal of funds was permitted in either the ALC or the LCA plans. The only distribution option was a cash-refund annuity upon retirement. That was designed so that the sum of annuity payments would be equal at least to the amount used to provide the annuity.[18]

---

[15] *Summary [of] Pension and Other Benefits Plans*, 1987, Part A-21, p. 27.

[16] TIAA is the acronym for Teachers Insurance and Annuity Association and CREF for College Retirement Equities Fund.

[17] David G. Adams, "A Survey of Developments for the Pension and Benefits Plans of the ELCA," Continuing Education Seminar for Staff of the Board of Pensions of the ELCA, transcript prepared and edited January 9, 2008. Mr. Adams is an actuary who served as vice president for products and services of the Board of Pensions of the ELCA.

[18] Adams, January 9, 2008.

The AELC did not operate its own pension plan in the manner of the ALC or LCA, but purchased services from The Travelers Companies. Under the terms of the AELC's plan, which was created in January 1977, the contribution rate for congregations or employers was set at six percent of the pastor's or church worker's defined compensation. At the same time, contributions to the plan by pastors or church workers could range from one percent to no more than ten percent of defined compensation.[19] Cash withdrawals of the participant's contribution were permitted under the AELC pension plan.[20] Retirement benefits could be drawn in the form of a lump sum pay-out or an annuity available under the group annuity contract issued by The Travelers Companies.[21]

Like the ALC and LCA programs, the AELC plan included accidental death and disability benefits as well as health insurance.

Decisions on "old" and "new" money

When the ELCA plan was created, the annuity pattern and "cash-refund" approach were maintained, but a retiree had to make separate decisions on the "old" money in a predecessor plan and the "new" money in the ELCA plan. Because those predecessor plans were continued following the formation of the ELCA, each had its own set of annuity options, as did the ELCA plan. With the passing of years, that process was simplified.

By the end of 1996, individuals who already had retired with annuities from a bond fund or a stock fund were encouraged to move their annuity to a balanced fund. The shift was intended to improve the returns on the annuity funds so that retirees likely would have a higher income. That had to be an "all or nothing" step. For *future* retirees, annuities no longer were paid from the funds that the members had prior to retirement. Instead, all the money, upon annuitization, was transferred to a balanced fund. That balanced fund for annuity payments used a crediting-rate process that was designed to smooth the lows and highs of the markets. The goal was a moderate but steady increase in annuity payments. Obviously, constant growth could not be guaranteed. Growth could be impeded by any significant recession and, as a result, be unattainable for a period of time.

The "cash-refund" pattern for annuities was eliminated at the end of 1996 for future annuitants. That pattern had provided that total

---

[19] Association of Evangelical Lutheran Churches Retirement Plan, January 1977, p. 7.

[20] AELC Retirement Plan, p. 11.

[21] AELC Retirement Plan, p. 17.

payments would never be less than the amount annuitized, even in the event of early death. Instead, a 10-year minimum payout was adopted, effective January 1, 1997.[22] Later that was shifted to a 15-year minimum pattern.[23]

Debate on contribution rate

Because of the different fund patterns and the past underlying assumptions on rates of return, leaders of the ALC and LCA debated at length prior to the merger what should be the appropriate contribution rate for the new ELCA plan. The ALC argued for nine percent; the LCA, 12 percent. The theory behind the argument suggested that more aggressive investment practices favored by some ALC leaders would ensure that a nine percent rate could provide for adequate retirement benefits. More conservative investment practices supported by some in the LCA pointed toward a need for the 12-percent rate. A compromise of sorts was reached for the ELCA plan. A higher than nine percent contribution rate was established for plan members who were age 35 or older at the beginning of the ELCA plan. Thus, in 1988, for those ages 35 to 44, the minimum was set at 10 percent; 45 to 54, 11 percent; and 55 and older, 12 percent.[24] (Notwithstanding the stair-step formula, several synods in their call procedures required a contribution rate of 12 percent for all participants. That was possible under the program.)

In 1988, about one-fifth of the plan participants were at the nine percent contribution rate. Specifically, participant rates were: 19.1 percent at nine percent; 16.6 percent at 10 percent; 14.2 percent at 11 percent; 43.1 percent at 12 percent; and 3.6 percent at greater than 12 percent. The other 3.4 percent of participants were employed in social-service institutions in

---

[22] Exhibit B-4, *Minutes*, Board of Trustees of the Board of Pensions of the ELCA, August 1-2, 1996. The change meant that if the member "and contingent annuitant" died with the 10-year span, a pension payment would "continue to the member's beneficiary for the remainder of the 120-month period" (1997 *Summary Plan Description of the Board of Pensions*, p. 15).

[23] PN00.11.50, *Minutes*, Board of Trustees of the Board of Pensions of the ELCA, November 3-5, 2000, p. 21. See also *Minutes*, Board of Trustees of the Board of Pensions of the ELCA, August 2-4, 2000, pp. 10-12.

[24] Section 4.02, *Pension and Other Benefits Plans*, *Constituting Convention of the Evangelical Lutheran Church in America*, Columbus, Ohio, April 30–May 2, 1987, pp. 11-12. See also *Summary [of] Pension and Other Benefits Plans*, Part A-4, p. 10; Action Number ELCA 87.02.56, *Minutes*, Constituting Convention of the Evangelical Lutheran Church in America, pp. 69-70.

which the rate was less than nine percent.[25] Clearly, the formula established only the minimum in each age category. The actual contribution rates, if beyond the minimum, were set by the calling or employing entities.

Discussion of the minimum contribution rate did not fade. A trustee-initiated resolution emerged in October 1990 that called for raising the minimum pension-contribution rate to 12 percent for all participants. A one percent increase was proposed for every two years, beginning January 1, 1992, so that a uniform rate of 12 percent would be reached by 1996.[26] The claim was made that the nine percent level unfairly discriminated against younger plan members and that a rate of 11 percent to 12 percent really would be needed to achieve—with Social Security—the goal of full income replacement in retirement. The resolution was submitted by pension trustees to the Church Council; in response, the council called for further study. Some argued for continuing the nine percent rate, but urged greater promotion of balanced fund investments as a way of achieving an adequate pension income for retirement. Others believed a wise course would be a higher minimum contribution.

Wrestling with the issue, the Church Council asked "that the Board of Pensions prepare information on the financial implications on congregations, synods, and the churchwide organization of the recommendation to increase the contribution rate to a uniform 12 percent."[27]

Discussion in the pension board's Executive Committee and observations offered by some members of the Church Council suggested that implementation of a higher minimum contribution rate be delayed either (1) one year to 1993, with biennial increases of two percent thereafter to 12 percent or (2) two years to 1994, with annual increases of one percent to 12 percent per member, regardless of age. This revised schedule for increases, some suggested, would give congregations more time to adjust for budget purposes. Trustees of the Board of Pensions indicated their willingness to

---

[25] "Report of the Board of Pensions," 1989 Reports and Records, Vol. 2, First Churchwide Assembly of the Evangelical Lutheran Church in America, Rosemont, Ill., August 23-30, 1989, p. 381.

[26] Action Number PN90.10.79, Minutes, Board of Trustees of the Board of Pensions of the ELCA, October 20-21, 1990, p. 15.

[27] Action Number CC91.04.34, Minutes, Church Council of the Evangelical Lutheran Church in America, April 13-15, 1991, p. 39. Cited also in "Report of the Church Council," 1991 Reports and Records, Vol. 2, Second Churchwide Assembly of the Evangelical Lutheran Church in America, Orlando, Fla., August 28–September 4, 1991, p. 848.

consider an altered schedule, hoping that the 12 percent rate could be achieved by 1996.[28]

Half-point increases in the minimum contribution rate took place in 1993 and 1994, moving the minimum rate from nine percent to 10 percent of defined compensation for the pension plan. The Church Council approved those changes in April 1992.[29] Later studies indicated that the additional steps toward a contribution level of 12 percent would not be needed if the long-term asset allocation mix in a balanced fund were shifted toward about 60 percent equities.[30] Therefore, subsequent increases in the minimum contribution rate beyond 10 percent were not implemented.

Five fund options at first

At the beginning of 1988, with the start of operation by the ELCA's Board of Pensions, the ELCA Regular Pension Plan had five funds:

(1) Bond Fund;

(2) Balanced Fund;

(3) Equity Fund;

(4) Social Purpose Bond Fund; and

(5) Social Purpose Equity Fund.

The first three funds essentially replicated the funds of the two predecessor plans (the ALC balanced fund and the LCA bond fund and equity fund). New ground, however, was being broken in the creation of the Social Purpose Bond Fund and the Social Purpose Equity Fund for plan members. Then, beginning January 1, 1990, a Social Purpose Balanced Fund was added. Those funds offered similar risk-and-return characteristics of the unscreened funds, but they provided social-purpose investment objectives.

Both the ALC clergy and lay balanced fund plans and the LCA FIP and VIP plans were maintained at the start of 1988. But, at that point, no new contributions to those plans were accepted. Future contributions would go into the newly created ELCA plans: (1) a regular pension plan

---

[28] Action Number PN91.04.36, *Minutes*, Board of Trustees of the Board of Pensions of the ELCA., April 5-7, 1991, p. 18.

[29] Action Number CC92.04.11, "Report of the Church Council," *1993 Reports and Records*, Vol. 1, Part 1, Third Churchwide Assembly of the Evangelical Lutheran Church in America, Kansas City, Mo., August 25–September 1, 1993, p. 423.

[30] *1993 Reports and Records*, Vol. 2, p. 537.

for employer contributions; and (2) an optional pension plan for member contributions and for any additional contributions by employers.

The ELCA Regular Pension Plan was managed by staff of the Board of Pensions in the form of bond, balanced, and stock funds. By contrast, the Optional Pension Plan had five commercial mutual funds. Use of mutual funds grew out of legal advice on the risks of investment of member contributions.

The greatest proportion of contributions in 1988 went into the Bond Fund, followed closely by the Balanced Fund. The percentages at that time by fund were: Bond Fund, 38.2 percent; Balanced Fund, 35.7 percent; Equity Fund, 16.8 percent; Social Purpose Bond Fund, 5.2 percent; and Social Purpose Equity Fund, 4.1 percent.[31]

The default fund—the fund to which contributions were credited in the event that the member did not make an investment choice—was the unscreened Bond Fund. That conservative investment default remained in place into the mid-1990s, when the Balanced Fund was made the default fund.

As the final decade of the twentieth century began to unfold, steps were taken toward consolidation and simplification. The predecessor church plans were merged in 1991 into the ELCA's plan. The predecessor investment funds themselves, however, were still kept in separate trusts, although the clergy and lay funds were combined. Finally, in the mid-1990s, the remaining balances in the predecessor bond, balanced, and equity funds were merged into the ELCA bond, balanced, and equity funds, thereby reducing costs and providing greater efficiency for the money under management.

Creation of new funds

Amid the intense divestment debates of that era, additional funds were developed. By mid-1991, a total of 12 funds were being offered (four bond, four balanced, and four stock funds). Among the 12 funds were three new "South Africa Free" Funds that had no investments in any companies doing business in South Africa, but did not have other social screens attached to them.[32] The Social Purpose Funds also were continued with the South Africa screen as well as various other social screens.

---

[31] 1989 Reports and Records, Vol. 2, p. 380.

[32] See Chapter 5 for greater elaboration on the debates and steps the led to creation of the "South Africa Free" Funds.

Unscreened funds were managed by the ELCA Board of Pensions in accordance with the "equivalency policy" in effect at the time—a policy that had been inaugurated in the ALC. The 1980 ALC General Convention received a report that declared, "Only in those cases where economic considerations are equal as between two or more securities issues under study may the investment decision be based on social considerations." The equivalency policy directed that whenever the conditions of risk and return were equal in the choice among stocks and bonds held on behalf of plan members, or available for purchase, companies doing business in South Africa would be avoided.[33] That approach was affirmed by the ALC's 1982 convention.[34]

Interest crediting

Market value and interest crediting became complicating factors for the different ELCA pension funds.

The account value of the bond funds in the ELCA Regular Pension Plan were reported using an interest-crediting approach. That practice cushioned the lows for member balances and moderated the highs in the market. The formula was complicated but basically involved the annual market return and a five-year rolling average of the market to determine the annual percentage credited to the member accounts. For the balanced funds, no formula existed; rather, the crediting depended on analysis and judgment by the investment staff, with the final decision being made by the trustees. Pure equity funds were reported at market value. Because of

---

[33] *Reports and Actions of the Ninth General Convention of The American Lutheran Church*, Minneapolis, Minn., October 1-7, 1980, p. 200. The 1980 ALC convention voted (GC80.4.58) to affirm "divestiture" as "the most legitimate strategy in opposing apartheid and the most effective consequence of a declaration of *status confessionis*" by the church. At the same time, the convention urged that such "disinvestment take place in a prudent manner that is consistent with legal requirements" (*Reports and Actions*, 1980, p. 985). The ALC Board of Trustees in May 1981 adopted a resolution that said, ". . . in the buying and selling of securities, where, in the judgment of the Board of Trustees, the economic considerations are equal as between two or more securities issues under study, the Board of Trustees will, where applicable, choose in favor of the company not doing business in South Africa. . . ."

[34] *Reports and Actions of the Tenth General Convention of The American Lutheran Church*, San Diego, Calif., September 6-12, 1982, p. 176. The 1982 ALC convention voted (GC82.11.116) to advise "the Board of Trustees that its efforts to divest stocks in corporations doing business in South Africa" were deemed "an adequate response to the 1980 American Lutheran Church General Convention resolution (GC80.4.58), and to commend the board for its efforts" (*Reports and Actions*, 1982, p. 1213).

those differing crediting patterns in the various funds, the ELCA Regular Pension Plan initially had very limited transfer options.

Both the ELCA and the predecessor plans were amended to modify the method of allocating excess interest for participants retiring after 1988, so that excess interest would be distributed uniformly in all plans. What was termed "excess interest" consisted of the credited interest of the various bond and balanced funds beyond the assumed interest rate for pensions of 4.5 percent. Thus, for retirees after 1988 under the amendments adopted that year, most of the excess interest was used to purchase permanent increases in the monthly pensions in each year that the investment funds earned more than 4.5 percent. That was a change from the previous pattern of distributing the total excess interest to pensioners in a single year. In the ALC, the amount had been distributed as a single payment, a thirteenth check, while in the LCA, one-twelfth of the "dividend" had been added to each monthly check.[35]

For 1988, the interest-crediting rate for ALC Clergy and Lay Balanced Funds was 10 percent, while the LCA Fixed Income Pension (FIP) Fund crediting rate was 9.7 percent for those retired and the AELC's was set at 9.41 percent. The new ELCA Bond, Balanced, and Social Purpose Bond Funds were credited at 8.5 percent. That rate was lower because those funds were new and the predecessor funds contained at that time some higher-yielding securities. Credited to participants in the stock funds were: (1) LCA Variable Income Pension (VIP) Fund, 13 percent; (2) ELCA Equity Fund, 8.3 percent; and (3) ELCA Social Purpose Equity Fund, 9.9 percent.[36]

Returns during 1989 on the equity funds ranged between 26 percent and 29 percent, while the bond funds returned 10 percent to 14 percent. The balanced funds gained about 17 percent in that year.[37] By contrast, equity funds in 1990 decreased between 4.5 and 5.8 percent, while the bond funds grew between 8.6 and 9.9 percent for the year.[38] Significant growth resumed in 1991, with the ELCA balanced funds returning about 25 percent and the ELCA bond funds, 15.4 to 16.3 percent.[39]

---

[35] *1989 Reports and Records*, Vol. 2, p. 381.

[36] *1989 Reports and Records*, Vol. 2, p. 386.

[37] *Annual Report*, 1989, Board of Pensions of the Evangelical Lutheran Church in America, p. 3.

[38] *Annual Report*, 1990, Board of Pensions of the Evangelical Lutheran Church in America, p. 5.

[39] *Annual Report*, 1991, Board of Pensions of the Evangelical Lutheran Church in America, p. 4.

Earnings credited in 1992 to member accounts ranged between 7.8 and 8.5 percent for the bond funds, 9.1 to 10 percent for balanced funds, and 7.8 to 9.6 percent for the equity funds.[40] While the rate of inflation remained at about three percent in 1993, the returns credited for the ELCA bond funds ranged between 8 and 8.5 percent, the ELCA balanced funds between 9.5 and 10 percent, and the ELCA equity funds between 12.3 and 15.4 percent.[41]

Changes in the experience of the various funds were reflected later, as in the 1994 crediting pattern for the funds available at that time: (1) South Africa Free Bond Fund, 7.7 percent; (2) Social Purpose Fund, 7.7 percent; (3) Bond Fund, 7.5 percent; (4) LCA FIP, 7.5 percent; (5) South Africa Free Balanced Fund, 10 percent; (6) Social Purpose Balanced Fund, 10 percent; (7) Balanced Fund (unscreened), 10 percent; (8) ALC Balanced Fund, 10.4 percent; (9) LCA VIP, 2.1 percent; (10) ELCA Equity Fund, 2.0 percent; (11) ELCA Social Purpose Equity Fund, 1.8 percent; and (12) ELCA South Africa Free Equity Fund, 0.8 percent. The smaller size of the Social Purpose Equity Fund and the South Africa Free Equity Fund affected the rate return for those funds.[42]

Domestic stocks in 1995 posted the highest return rates since 1958 and the sixth highest in the previous 70 years. As a result, the returns on the ELCA equity funds ranged from 30 to 30.9 percent, while the ELCA balanced funds were credited with earnings from 9 to 9.4 percent. At the same time, the bond funds were credited at rates of 6.5 to 6.8 percent.[43]

The bull market continued to run when, for example, the social-purpose stock funds grew by 19.8 percent in 1997, while the unscreened stock funds increased 19.4 percent. In the same year, screened balanced funds gained 15.8 percent and the unscreened balanced funds experienced growth of 17.1 percent. The rates of return on the bond funds ranged from 8.2 to 8.7 percent (screened and unscreened, respectively).[44] A similar but slightly

---

[40] *Annual Report*, 1992, Board of Pensions of the Evangelical Lutheran Church in America, pp. 4-5.

[41] *Annual Report*, 1993, Board of Pensions of the Evangelical Lutheran Church in America, p. 6.

[42] "Report of the Board of Pensions," *1995 Pre-Assembly Report*, Vol. 1, Fourth Churchwide Assembly of the Evangelical Lutheran Church in America, Minneapolis, Minn., August 16-22, 1995, p. 159.

[43] *Annual Report*, 1995, Board of Pensions of the Evangelical Lutheran Church in America.

[44] *Annual Report*, 1997, Board of Pensions of the Evangelical Lutheran Church in America, p. 4.

more modest pattern was set in 1998 (stock, about 18 percent; balanced, 12 percent; and bond, 7 percent).[45]

By the end of the decade in 2000, the ten-year rate of return on the unscreened stock fund was 16.8 percent and 15.6 for the social purpose stock fund. The unscreened balanced fund experienced growth for the decade of 13.6 percent and the social purpose balanced fund, 12.6 percent. During the same period, the unscreened bond fund increased 7.9 percent, while the social purpose bond fund grew by 7.7 percent.[46]

As the operation of the Board of Pensions moved into its second decade, $4.2 billion was managed in the ELCA Regular Pension Plan, $111 million in the ELCA Optional Pension Plan, $68.2 million in the ELCA Institutional Pension Plan, and $35.7 million in the ELCA Institutional Savings Plan.[47]

The phenomenal growth experienced throughout many years in the 1990s ended amid the market downturn in 2001 and beyond. That market slide occurred in the aftermath of the terrorist attacks on September 11, 2001, and also as a result of the bursting of the "tech bubble" in the sharp decline in technology stocks. The change in the economic climate had a dramatic impact. Funds in the ELCA Regular Pension Plan decreased from $4.8 billion in 2000 to $3.8 billion in 2002.[48] The total climbed in succeeding years to surpass earlier levels for a few years.[49]

Another bear market hit in 2008, substantially driving down returns in a severe economic recession. The "credit bubble" burst, drastically affecting housing, banking, automobile sales, and the overall economy (see Chapter 14).

---

[45] *Annual Report*, 1998, Board of Pensions of the Evangelical Lutheran Church in America.

[46] *Annual Report*, 2000, Board of Pensions of the Evangelical Lutheran Church in America, p. 7.

[47] "Report of the Board of Pensions," *1999 Pre-Assembly Report*, Sixth Churchwide Assembly of the Evangelical Lutheran Church in America, Denver, Colo., August 16-22, 1999, p. 130. These amounts represented the total market value of the various plans as of December 31, 1998.

[48] "Report of the Board of Pensions," *2003 Pre-Assembly Report*, Eighth Churchwide Assembly of the Evangelical Lutheran Church in America, Milwaukee, Wis., August 11-17, 2003, p. 115.

[49] *Annual Report*, 2007, Board of Pensions of the Evangelical Lutheran Church in America, p. 29.

Shift to market value

To increase flexibility for plan members, the Bond and Balanced Funds were shifted in 1997 from the practice of interest crediting to being reported at market value. The timing of that shift was delicate. The change could be made only if the market values were greater than the account values based on interest crediting. It would not have been possible to make that change under conditions that would have reduced an individual's account value. So trustees and staff of the Board of Pensions watched closely the year-end market in 1996, even in the midst of a long bull or upward market. If there had been a sudden decline, which some anticipated in the up-and-down market cycles, one or more of the funds might have fallen below the account value. A contingency plan was in place—namely, the change would be postponed until the market values recovered. Fortunately, that backup plan was not needed.

Because the ELCA Optional Pension Plan had involved commercial mutual funds, the member balances always had been reported at market value—that is, fluctuating with the ups and downs of the equity and bond markets.

With all funds being reported at market value, transfers could be permitted between funds. That meant members could move money out of bond funds, where they had been locked in place under the crediting system, to equity or balanced funds.

Through a change in the plan that was approved in late 1995 for implementation in 1997, members could select from a wide range of funds or they could choose the Standard Investment Choice. That "standard" fund basically was a balanced fund with 65 percent stocks, 20 percent bonds, 5 percent high-yield securities, and 10 percent real assets.

Another change in the pension plan in 1997 added an option for partial withdrawals. Individual members of the plan, beginning at age 60 or upon separation from ELCA service, could withdraw each year the greater of $10,000 or 10 percent of the account balance at the beginning of the year. A one-time withdrawal was permitted at a rate of $20,000 or 20 percent of the account. The withdrawals, for instance, could assist a pastor who had lived in a parsonage throughout her or his pastoral ministry to obtain funds for a down payment on a dwelling. The option also offered flexibility to members in financial planning for retirement.

A further step for retirement planning was the development in 1998 of a "bridge" fund, known initially as the Transitional Pension Fund. With the bridge fund, members at age 60 or older could shift funds away from the volatile, fluctuating markets toward the likelihood of greater assurance of a steady rate of return in the months or years immediately prior to a member's commencement of pension benefits.[50] The transfer could only be one way. A member could not shift funds back into any of the other funds. The fund itself was renamed in 2000 the Participating Annuity Bridge Fund. It was a valuable tool for members who wanted increased stability in moving toward partial or full annuitization of their pension accumulations for retirement income.

Annuitization not required

Required annuitization upon the retirement of plan members was eliminated in 2000.[51] Retirees could take limited withdrawals instead and maintain active participation in the various fund options. This new approach created greater flexibility for retirees and those planning for retirement. If they chose, they could annuitize only a portion of the funds, rather than the total amount when retiring.

This was a significant change from the past. Previously, annuitization had been required in the ELCA plan, both predecessor church-body plans, and most other traditional church plans. For the first time, plan members could choose whether to annuitize or take limited withdrawals from their individual accounts (or opt for a combination of both methods). The change gave members the opportunity, in retirement planning, to consider their own financial and health circumstances. For example, members with substantial account balances and those with poor health or family-health histories were found to be less likely to annuitize. Because of federally mandated distribution requirements, all members are required to annuitize or start to withdraw a certain minimum amount at age 70½, beginning at about four percent of their pension accumulation.

When a member converted all or part of the accumulations to an annuity, the designated amount was moved from the investment funds into the ELCA Participating Annuity Fund, a "pooled fund" from which pension payments were paid. The member thereby was assured of a monthly pension payment until death. In essence, the member traded individual "ownership" of her or his accumulations for a lifetime stream of income.

---

[50] In 2005, the eligibility age for the Participating Annuity Bridge Fund was lowered to 55.

[51] The effective date of the change was August 1, 2000.

The annuity, however, was not guaranteed. Further, the amount of the annuity payment in any given year could increase or decrease depending on how market conditions affected the ELCA Annuity Fund.[52]

Indeed, the ELCA Participating Annuity Fund, like other investments, experienced the gains and losses of the markets. With a long-term investment philosophy, the ELCA Board of Pensions had sought over the years to strike a balance for steady growth from returns on equities and bonds. That strategy worked well until drastic declines in the markets hit in 2008.

The ELCA Participating Annuity Fund, including the Annuity Bridge Fund, was almost $860 million below projected benefit obligations as of December 31, 2008.[53] In the two subsequent months, the fund sank even deeper "under water" until markets began to climb in early March 2009. Clearly, drastic action was needed. The prolonged health of the ELCA Participating Annuity Fund was at stake. Therefore, in a monumental decision, the ELCA Participating Annuity and Bridge Fund was closed in April 2009 to new retirees. Various possibilities were explored for future retirees (see Chapter 14).[54]

At start of new century

The dawn of a new century saw far greater options being offered to plan participants. The number of investment funds expanded from six to 20 funds in 2003. In addition to employer contributions, members could make

---

[52] Members were advised in various Web-based documents and other materials of the ELCA Board of Pensions, "You should carefully consider the investment objectives, risks, charges, and expenses of any fund before investing in it. All funds, including the ELCA Annuity Fund, are subject to risk. Past performance cannot be used to predict future performance." Further underscored was the fact that funds managed by the ELCA Board of Pensions "are not insured or guaranteed by the Federal Deposit Insurance Corporation or any other government agency. Fund assets are invested in multiple sectors of the market. Some sectors, and therefore the funds, may perform below expectations and lose money over short or extended periods. With respect to the annuity fund, the goal of the Board of Pensions is to increase a member's annuity income over time. However, substantial or extended losses or underperformance in the markets could cause a reduction in monthly annuity payments" (*Annual Report*, 2008, Board of Pensions of the Evangelical Lutheran Church in America, p. 1).

[53] *Annual Report*, 2008, Board of Pensions of the Evangelical Lutheran Church in America, p. 10.

[54] Action Number PN09.04.22, *Minutes*, Board of Trustees of the Board of Pensions, April 23, 2009, p. 3. The action of the management of the Board of Pensions on April 3, 2009—in closing the ELCA Participating Annuity and Bridge Fund, after consultation with an ad hoc committee of the board of trustees—was confirmed in a special meeting of the full board of trustees, held by conference call.

voluntary contributions on a salary-reduction (pretax) basis to enhance their pension accumulation for their retirement.[55]

Six balanced funds now were offered (40 percent equities, 60 percent, or 80 percent), each with unscreened and social-purpose versions. Included, too, was the S&P 500 Index Fund,[56] which had been the most popular fund in what had been the optional plan. The optional plan at that point was merged into the regular pension plan, thereby discontinuing the use of commercial mutual funds.

The ELCA funds offered in the expanded program were:
(1) 80e Balanced Fund;
(2) Social Purpose 80e Balanced Fund;
(3) 60e Balanced Fund;
(4) Social Purpose 60e Balanced Fund;
(5) 40e Balanced Fund;
(6) Social Purpose 40e Balanced Fund;
(7) Global Stock Fund;
(8) Social Purpose Global Stock Fund;
(9) Non-U.S. Stock Fund;
(10) Social Purpose Non-U.S. Stock Fund;
(11) U.S. Stock Fund;
(12) Social Purpose U.S. Stock Fund;
(13) ELCA S&P 500 Stock Index Fund;
(14) Social Purpose Stock Index Fund;
(15) Small- and Mid-Cap Stock Index Fund;
(16) Real Estate Securities Fund;
(17) High-Yield Bond Fund;
(18) Bond Fund;
(19) Social Purpose Bond Fund; and
(20) Money Market Fund.[57]

The additional fund options gave even greater flexibility to members for determining their investment choices and planning for their retirement income. Funds one through six were known as the "Select Series Funds" and seven through 20 as the "Build Your Own Series Funds."

---

[55] "Pension Equity Report," 2003, p. 5.

[56] "S&P 500" is a trademark of the McGraw-Hill Companies Inc. and was licensed for use by the Board of Pensions of the ELCA. The ELCA S&P 500 Stock Index Fund was not sponsored, endorsed, sold, or promoted by Standard & Poor's.

[57] *Annual Report*, 2006, Board of Pensions of the Evangelical Lutheran Church in America, pp. 5-6.

Health benefits

From its start, the ELCA Medical and Dental Benefits Plan was designed to "protect employees from suffering a financial disaster because of health problems by keeping out-of-pocket costs at manageable levels."[58] Initially, the per-person deductible was set at $250 and the per-family deductible at $500 a year. In addition, a co-payment resulted in a maximum out-of-pocket limit at $1000 per person or $2000 per family a year. Those amounts were adjusted over the years, especially in relation to the move into managed care in point-of-service (POS) and preferred-provider-organization (PPO) patterns (see Chapter 3). Further, the shift to separate benefits related to medical, dental, behavioral health, and pharmacy needs meant the end to a single out-of-pocket limit.

The sharing of costs for the health plan—as well as disability coverage and the survivor benefit—resulted from the premiums being determined as a percentage of compensation. That approach was unique, particularly for health-benefit plans. Originally, the contribution rate for the health plan involved a single percentage of compensation for all sponsored members, with a minimum and a maximum contribution amount. Eventually, the plan moved to a three-tier rate structure—member only, member plus spouse *or* children, and member plus spouse *and* children. Somewhat later, six rate classes were set so that contributions were aligned more closely with the expected costs of coverage in particular areas. As a result, sharing was taking place within each synod rather than across the entire medical plan.

For the ELCA Pension and Other Benefits Program, the average age of members represented a challenging factor. By the turn of the century, the U.S. population had an average age of 39. Yet, at the same time in the ELCA Pension and Other Benefits Program, two-thirds of all pastors were 45 years of age or older. Health-care costs tend to be higher for older members of the plan, thereby putting greater pressure on the medical and dental rates paid by congregations and other employers.

The average age for ordination had risen from 29 in 1980 in the ELCA's three predecessor churches to 41 for the ELCA in the early years of the twenty-first century. That change meant that the total number of years of active service for many pastors would be considerably less than the span of 35 to 40 years needed for what could be seen as an adequate pension, with Social Security, for a fiscally comfortable retirement (see Chapter 4).[59]

---

[58] *Report and Recommendations* . . . , August 1986, p. 172.

[59] *Minutes,* Board of Trustees of the Board of Pensions of the ELCA, November 5-7, 1999, pp. 8-9.

Other benefits

In addition to the pension plan and health coverage, the ELCA provided through the Board of Pensions a Survivor Benefits Plan and a Disability Benefits Plan.

The ELCA Survivor Benefits Plan replaced the survivor benefits plans of the predecessor churches as of January 1, 1988. Survivor benefits for individuals who died prior to 1988 remained subject to the terms of the plans of the predecessor churches. Under the ELCA Survivor Benefits Plan, a lump sum is paid that ranges from $6,000 to $50,000, based on the member's age at death and the defined compensation of the member during the 12 months prior to death or retirement. The plan also supplements the income of the surviving spouse, paying a specified percentage of defined compensation that varies by the member's age and years of participation in the plan. In addition, the plan provides a monthly benefit for children under age 21. As of May 1, 1997, no benefit payments were reduced as a result of the remarriage of the surviving spouse.

The ELCA Survivor Benefits Plan is funded by employer-paid contributions, calculated as a percentage of the defined compensation of each member. The ELCA Disability Benefits Plan is funded in the same way.

Three types of benefits are part of disability coverage under the ELCA plan: (1) a monthly disability income benefit equal to two-thirds of the member's prior monthly defined compensation (less Social Security and other governmental disability benefits); (2) continued pension retirement contributions; and (3) continued coverage for health and survivor benefits. The benefits are paid for plan members who are totally disabled due to injury or physical or mental disorder and also for plan members who are partially disabled due to certain neurological diseases.

Formation of trusts

To protect the assets of each of the benefit plans managed by the Board of Pensions, nine trusts were created. That pattern of trusts was carried forward from The American Lutheran Church when the ELCA was formed. Established were the: (1) ELCA Retirement Trust; (2) ELCA Medical and Dental Benefits Trust; (3) ELCA Survivor Benefits Trust; (4) ELCA Disability Benefits Trust; (5) ELCA Master Institutional Retirement Trust; (6) ELCA Master 457(b) Deferred Compensation Trust; (7) ELCA Continuation of the ALC Major Medical-Dental Trust for Retired Participants; (8) ELCA Benefits Contribution Trust; and (9)

ELCA Supplemental Retirement Trust. All nine were formed under the Minnesota statute that provides for such trusts.

Testing the principles

In 2003 and 2004, steps were taken to test support for the guiding principles in the program of the Board of Pensions.

Synodical bishops and other church leaders affirmed the practice of encouraging widespread participation in the ELCA Pension and Other Benefits Program. Some noted that the compensation agreement for clergy and rostered lay persons, which normally accompanies Letters of Call, expresses unequivocal support for participation, even though it is not mandatory for congregations. They also viewed the current level of benefits as appropriate. At the same time, they were reluctant to envision offering choices in levels of benefits, fearing that many congregations would choose the benefits with the lowest costs rather than adequate coverage. Specifically, they observed, pastors who serve congregations of lesser means, likely with lower compensation, would be the most likely to receive lower benefits if such options were offered. Furthermore, if benefits varied from congregation to congregation, the level of benefits could become a complicating issue in the process of calling pastors or lay rostered church workers.

Support continued to be expressed for the bundled program. While many of those interviewed acknowledged that the high cost of health care is a significant issue, they also felt that the step of allowing a member to waive ELCA coverage when included in a spouse's program helped to minimize that issue. Recognized, too, was the fact that bundling served well to discourage some congregations from seeking lower-price (or lower-value) health or disability coverage for younger pastors and church workers.[60]

Retaining the requirement that employers pay the full monthly cost of benefits was affirmed, especially by synodical bishops. They expressed concern, however, that rapidly rising costs of health benefits were adversely affecting salary increases for pastors. Possible adjustments in co-payments, through which some of the costs would be shifted to employees, received support from about 20 percent of the synodical bishops in their responses in 2003 and 2004.

---

[60] Maintaining the bundled approach for the ELCA Pension and Other Benefits Program was affirmed again in 2008 following a study by the consulting firm Hewitt Associates of Lincolnshire, Ill. The report was submitted to the May 3-4, 2008, meeting of the Board of Trustees of the Board of Pensions.

The cost-sharing principle in the health plan gained unqualified endorsement in responses from synodical bishops. As one bishop said, "This is what it means to be the body of Christ and not just individual congregations."[61]

In a profound sense, that statement aptly characterizes all the efforts of the past two and a quarter centuries for the care of pastors, other church workers, their spouses, and dependents. Beginning in their early days in North America, Lutherans sought to provide support for "superannuated ministers, their widows, and orphans." That concern has not changed, but, as we shall see, the methods and systems for showing care and providing support have changed significantly over the decades and centuries. Thus, through the Board of Pensions of the Evangelical Lutheran Church in America, the Pension and Other Benefits Program continues to evolve in courageous and creative ways in these early years of the twenty-first century.

---

[61] "Philosophy of Benefits Report," Board of Pensions of the ELCA, August 2004, p. 6.

CHAPTER 2

No Simple
Path To Change

The massive challenge of operating the new pension and benefits
program of the Evangelical Lutheran Church in America (ELCA)
demanded all-consuming attention. Immediate tasks involved fulfilling the
obligations of the predecessor pension and medical plans. In the medical
plans alone, the backlog of unpaid claims towered over the desks of staff
in the early months of 1988. At the same time, differing elements in the
predecessor pension plans had to be understood and administered properly,
even while the new ELCA plans were being implemented.

The complexity of the operation was evident in the listing of the diverse
plans administered by the ELCA's Board of Pensions in the initial years:

(1)   ELCA Regular Pension Plan;

(2)   ELCA Optional Pension Plan;

(3)   ELCA Medical and Dental Benefits Plan;

(4)   Survivor Benefits Plan;

(5)   Disability Benefits Plan;

(6)   Government Chaplaincy Plans;[1]

(7)   Master Institutional Regular Pension Plan;

(8)   Master Institutional Savings Plan;

(9)   Institutional Welfare Benefits Program;

(10) Survivor Benefits Plan for Seminarians;

---

[1] Two plans for government chaplains—an ELCA Pension Plan for Government Chaplains
and an ELCA Welfare Plan for Government Chaplains—were designed: (1) to offset benefit
losses or reductions when government chaplains were unable to become fully vested under a
government retirement plan prior to termination of service as a result of reduction in force,
being passed over for promotion, or resignation of commission; and (2) to make medical,
dental, and other benefit coverages available at cost to particular chaplains who did not
receive such benefits from the government agency they served (*Annual Report*, 1988, Board
of Pensions of the Evangelical Lutheran Church in America, p. 4).

(11) Medical Benefits Plan for Seminarians;

(12) Continuation of the Medical-Dental Plan for Retired Participants from The American Lutheran Church (ALC);

(13) Continuation of the Ministerial Health Benefits Plan for Retired Members from the Lutheran Church in America (LCA);

(14) Continuation of the ALC and LCA Minimum and Non-Contributory Pension Plans; and

(15) Retirement Plan of the Association of Evangelical Lutheran Churches.

Prior to the ELCA's formation, the LCA Board of Pensions had managed about $800 million in member assets, while the ALC pension operation was responsible for $600 million in member assets. The AELC had some $9 million in member assets insured through The Travelers Companies.[2]

Early stages of ELCA program

Enrollment for the ELCA program of all non-retired plan members was required because participation in the predecessor church plan was terminated as of December 31, 1987. Moreover, new options for coverage, beneficiary designations, and pension contributions became available January 1, 1988, under the ELCA plans.[3]

The initial "mission statement" of the ELCA's Board of Pensions declared that the board was to:

> Administer responsive, efficient, and competitive pension and other benefit coverages, as adopted by the Churchwide Assembly, within a cost structure that is manageable by ELCA churches and church-related entities.

In so doing, the Board of Pensions was to (1) emphasize "quality and service;" (2) provide "prompt processing of all benefits;" (3) prepare "timely and accurate communication to plan members;" and (4) pursue "low administrative costs."[4]

Reflecting on the initial days of operation of the ELCA's Board of Pensions, President John G. Kapanke observed that "we dealt with new challenges every day" in 1988. "Almost everything we did was new. The pension and benefits plans were new, the information system was new,

---

[2] *Annual Report*, 1988, Board of Pensions of the Evangelical Lutheran Church in America, p. 7.

[3] *Annual Report*, 1988, Board of Pensions of the Evangelical Lutheran Church in America, p. 9.

[4] *Annual Report*, 1988, Board of Pensions of the Evangelical Lutheran Church in America, p. 3.

the accounting system was new. We were always plowing new ground, and because we were so busy keeping up with the immediate needs of our members, there was rarely time to plan ahead."[5]

Following the initial stage of operation for the ELCA's pension and other benefits program, President Kapanke and others on the staff of the Board of Pensions recognized the need for longer term planning and potentially significant changes. They also understood that no simple path to those changes existed.

To assist in the process, a consulting firm known as Strategic Decisions Group (SDG) was retained in 1992. Before approving that step, the trustees struggled with the significant cost for that contract, but in the end they decided to proceed with SDG of Menlo Park, Calif.[6] The SDG fee was nearly $300,000, and other expenses for the project amounted in the final tabulation to another $130,000, for a combined total $430,000, some $70,000 under the $500,000 originally budgeted for the whole effort.

The project proceeded with the appointment of strategy teams to address what were deemed three major challenges facing the Board of Pensions at that time: (1) pension and investment concerns; (2) the design of the medical and dental plan; and (3) issues of governance.

Each strategy team followed the six-step process of the SDG consultants. They sought to: (1) assess the "business" situation; (2) develop alternative strategies, information, and values; (3) evaluate the potential risk and return of possible strategies; (4) decide among various strategies; (5) plan for change; and (6) implement the chosen strategy.

A key decision for moving forward was the adoption in July 1993 of a new mission statement for the Board of Pensions. The statement read:

> The mission of the Board of Pensions is to provide pension, health, and other benefits and related services that will enhance the lives of pastors, rostered lay persons,[7] lay employees, and their

---

[5] *Annual Report*, 1988, Board of Pensions of the Evangelical Lutheran Church in America, p. 7.

[6] Action Number PN92.10.61, *Minutes*, Board of Trustees of the Board of Pensions of the ELCA, October 16-18, 1992, p. 15. Prior to the recommendation, President John G. Kapanke, trustee Fred B. Renwick, and staff members Michael L. Troutman and David A. Lecander met with the principals of Strategic Decisions Group at SDG's headquarters in Menlo Park, Calif., to discuss the project. Subsequent to that meeting and with the endorsement of the Executive Committee of the Board of Trustees, a workshop for six trustees and nine senior staff members was convened in September 1992 in Minneapolis to begin the process.

families, and support the well-being of congregations and institutions of the Evangelical Lutheran Church in America.[8]

Related to the statement of mission was a summary of values of the Board of Pensions: "We will: (1) act with integrity; (2) treat everyone with care and respect; and (3) excel in our work."[9]

The planning initiative guided by the Strategic Decisions Group resulted in the 1994, 1995, 1996 strategic plan that superseded a more limited, staff formulated five-year plan from 1991. The SDG experience set in motion a triennial planning calendar with subsequent plans developed for 1997-1999, 2000-2002, 2003-2005, 2006-2008, and 2009-2011.

Foundation for major changes

Clearly, from the perspective of subsequent developments, the SDG process produced fruitful results for the operation of the Board of Pensions in moving forward. That planning process laid the foundation for major changes in the years to come.

The pension and investment strategy team reported finding "numerous potential opportunities for improving the financial efficiency" of the pension plan's design. Trustees in July 1993 urged the team to: (1) refine proposed strategies; (2) investigate knowledge gaps for possible proposals; (3) explore transition issues, including those related to medical plan changes; and (4) undertake analysis of customer service and retirement plan patterns.[10]

Emerging from the work of the pension and investment strategy team were changes that added flexibility to the pension plan so that members could customize their payout options. Previously, a plan member would work full time until a specific "retirement date." At that point, the individual's salary would be replaced by an ELCA pension annuity payment and Social

---

[7] In its original form in 1993, the term "associates in ministry" was used in place of "rostered lay persons." "Associates in ministry" initially was the omnibus term in the ELCA for the lay rostered ministries inherited from the three predecessor church bodies as well as persons certified for lay rostered ministry by the ELCA. The 1993 Churchwide Assembly of the ELCA acted on recommendations of the ELCA's Study of Ministry. In so doing, the voting members of the assembly determined there would be three separate categories of "rostered lay persons," specifically, associates in ministry, deaconesses of the ELCA, and diaconal ministers. Thus, the terminology of the board's mission statement was adjusted in accordance with the assembly's action.

[8] Action Number PN93.07.28, *Minutes*, Board of Trustees of the Board of Pensions of the ELCA, July 16-18, 1993, p. 6.

[9] *Minutes*, Board of Trustees of the Board of Pensions of the ELCA, May 29-30, 1997, p. 3.

[10] Action Number 93.07.30, *Minutes*, Trustees, July 16-18, 1993, pp. 9-10.

Security benefits. By the mid-1990s, that rigid formula served fewer and fewer members. Some continued to work, at least part time, beyond a customary retirement age. Others had greater needs for financial resources in the early years of retirement, such as obtaining housing after living in parsonages throughout their pastoral ministry.

In adding flexibility, safeguards were envisioned to ensure that pension accumulations would be used for retirement security. As the team reported to the board, "Congregations and other sponsoring employers make contributions on behalf of their pastors and other employees with the understanding that they are fulfilling their obligation to help these persons maintain their standard of living after employment ends."[11]

An option for limited withdrawals was embraced. Members were permitted to obtain a one-time withdrawal of 20 percent of an individual's accumulation. In addition, 10 percent of the existing balance in a given year could be withdrawn, under changes approved in November 1995 and made effective January 1, 1997.[12]

Medical and dental changes

The four primary goals identified in the 1993 medical-dental strategy report were efforts to: (1) reduce the cost escalation in the plan; (2) maintain high participation; (3) improve financial integrity undergirding the plan; and (4) prepare for future changes (see Chapter 3).[13]

The trustees voted to revise the ELCA Medical and Dental Benefits Program, effective January 1, 1995, to include:

(1) a point-of-service (POS) arrangement phased into operation over a three- to five-year period, with initial implementation in the Minneapolis-St. Paul area and in Chicago;

(2) a "managed indemnity" arrangement for those not covered by the point-of-service arrangement, which would include additional review of inpatient pre-certification and use, large-case management, and a simplified reimbursement schedule for chiropractic, out-patient psychotherapy, and major dental care;

(3) elimination of the supplement option for the Medical and Dental Benefits Plan;

---

[11] "Pension and Investment Strategy Report," Board of Pensions of the Evangelical Lutheran Church in America, May 1995, p. 13.

[12] *Minutes*, Board of Trustees of the Board of Pensions of the ELCA, November 4-5, 1995, p. 8.

[13] *Minutes*, Trustees, July 16-18, 1993, pp. 6-7.

(4) operation of both the point-of-service and managed-indemnity arrangements under the same national ELCA health plan;

(5) continued bundling of the Medical and Dental Benefits Plan with the other ELCA pension and benefit plans;

(6) in-network benefits of the POS arrangement reimbursed at 90 percent of eligible expenses or 100 percent with a small co-payment per physician office visit, while out-of-network benefits would be reimbursed at 70 percent of eligible expenses after a deductible;

(7) a single-rate structure for all congregations and employers; and

(8) contributions from congregations and other employers calculated on a percent of salary basis but with a subsidy of family rates and a surcharge on member-only rates phased in over a period of years. A low-income subsidy was maintained for health coverage.[14]

Governance

In regard to governance, four primary concerns were identified through the SDG process: (1) continuity of leadership within the board of trustees; (2) continuity of leadership in the staff; (3) changes in roles and responsibilities within the board of trustees and between the board of trustees and staff; and (4) the relationship of the Board of Pensions to plan members and other stakeholders.

Some trustees expressed concern that, under the ELCA's churchwide nomination and election process, trustees could serve only one six-year term, thereby limiting continuity on the board. Others believed that election of the trustees by the Churchwide Assembly—which included the possibility of nominations from the floor by voting members—did not guarantee that the board would have trustees with the necessary expertise to oversee the plans and carry out their fiduciary duties. Ongoing changes in senior leadership of the Board of Pensions as the operation evolved also raised anxiety on the part of some trustees concerning continuity in administration. The strategy team wrestled with those concerns and sought to address them.

Concerning continuity of leadership among trustees, the team did not recommend a change in the six-year, one-term pattern for trustees, nor did the team suggest alteration in the nomination process. Acknowledged was the possibility of having individuals with particular expertise serve with the

---

[14] Action Number 93.07.29, *Minutes*, Trustees, July 16-18, 1993, pp. 8-9.

trustees in an advisory capacity. Further, the importance of trustees identifying apt potential nominees for consideration by the assembly was underscored.

Regarding delegation of responsibilities to staff, the board's need to focus on strategic and audit issues was highlighted, as well as the duty of making strategy and policy decisions. While key policy decisions were to be made by the full board, committees of the board were empowered to reach particular decisions in keeping with board-approved policy.

To assist the trustees in their policy and oversight roles, a decision was made to meet quarterly. (That pattern later was adjusted to three meetings a year—mid-winter, late summer, and early November, thereby dropping what had been a trustee meeting in May.) A personnel and compensation committee also was established, but later that committee's responsibilities were shifted to the board's Executive Committee. The various committees were to "advise and audit staff decisions" and provide recommendations to the full board.

Meanwhile, staff members of the Board of Pensions were directed to undertake an operational planning process to: (1) develop an annual corporate plan; (2) monitor the "business" plan results quarterly; and (3) shift trustee meetings to more strategic decisions with daily operational management to be performed by staff.

The need to build a strong "backup-succession" plan for key management positions was underscored. Endorsed, too, was the shift of some consulting functions from external contracts to internal positions.[15]

Face-to-face visits

Emerging from the SDG planning process was greater face-to-face contact with key "stakeholders" and plan members. Annual visits with bishops and synodical staff members were inaugurated. Those visits provided an opportunity to outline forthcoming changes in the pension and other benefits program. At the same time, concerns identified by synodical leaders were gathered to help guide future plans.

Representatives of the Board of Pensions also attended synodical assemblies and some conferences for pastors and other church workers. They were available to answer questions of members and convey information for retirement planning. Through technology, these "on-the-road" opportunities allowed staff to consult with individuals on their accounts and explore possible scenarios for drawing benefits.

---

[15] *Minutes*, Trustees, July 16-18, 1993, p. 4.

A toll-free telephone number offered added convenience to members in their contacts with staff of the Board of Pensions. Begun as a pilot program in April 1995, the toll-free service was available nationwide by the end of that year.[16]

The launching of a Web site in 1998 represented another step toward greater accessibility. The new Web site gave members 24-hour access to information and materials, including a main e-mail address for the Board of Pensions. Through www.elcabop.org, members could check online the status of their accounts.

Evolving vocabulary

During the mid-1990s, a careful observer would have noticed a change in vocabulary for the operation. The shift was reflected in meetings of the trustees and deliberations of staff members. While leaders of the Board of Pensions remained mindful that the board was a unit of the ELCA's churchwide organization, terms from the corporate or business world were employed increasingly in planning and administration. Talk of "customers" rather than members, "customer service," "corporate plan," "business decisions," "products," "benchmarks," "brand," "promotion," "marketing," "roll out," "critical success factors," "measurable objectives," "desired state," and other terms could be heard during meetings of the trustees and staff. The terms did not emerge only through the SDG experience, but also developed in the subsequent cycles of three-year, iterative planning processes. Reflected in this narrative are those "business" terms in the description of the board's evolving development throughout the closing years of the twentieth century and the early years of the new century.

The vocabulary pointed to what may have seemed at times the paradox of operating a pension investment and insurance "business" as part of the structure and ministry of a church body. That reality required staff and trustees of the Board of Pensions to balance their fiduciary and "business" endeavors with the opportunity and obligation to serve as part of the mission of the ELCA. The skills required for a well-run business were exercised with conscientious stewardship within the context of the church. One proverbial foot was in the business world and the other in the arena of churchwide ministry. In that way, the Board of Pensions functioned well for the sake of plan members and their dependents.

---

[16] "Report of the Board of Pensions," 1995 Pre-Assembly Report, Vol. 1, Fourth Churchwide Assembly of the Evangelical Lutheran Church in America, Minneapolis, Minn., August 16-22, 1995, pp. 157-158.

Major directions identified in 1994 for 1995 and 1996 were shaped by the fruits of the SDG process. As outlined for the trustees by President Kapanke, the "critical success factors" in that plan called for the Board of Pensions to:

(1) provide high quality benefits and services to plan members at below market costs;

(2) maintain a fiscally sound operation by establishing appropriate levels of reserve funds;

(3) instill confidence in the work of the Board of Pensions for plan members and the various expressions and related entities of the ELCA, including congregations, synods, churchwide units, and institutions and agencies;

(4) maximize long-term investment returns while controlling investment risk;

(5) attract and retain competent people with high ethical standards and integrity, providing a challenging work environment that recognizes the value of each individual;

(6) communicate effectively with plan members and other outside entities;

(7) anticipate and respond to changing member needs, regulations, and benefit delivery systems;

(8) coordinate policy planning for the operation of the Board of Pensions in various sections, including benefits, investment, financial reporting, and information technology;

(9) maintain interactions with other parts of the ELCA's churchwide organization, recognizing the interdependence among churchwide units; and

(10) identify and offer services, where appropriate, to other expressions of the ELCA.

The particular initiatives identified for 1995 were:

(1) effective implementation for phase one of the point-of-service medical plan changes;

(2) more complete development and implementation of the pension and investment strategy project;

(3) elimination of the South Africa Free Funds, as no longer needed;

(4) implementation of nationwide "800 number" telephone service;

(5) creation of a "business recovery" plan;

(6) evaluation of retiree health plans;

(7) implementation of alternative contribution crediting procedures for the Institutional Pension Plans;

(8) implementation of an internal investment portfolio management accounting system;

(9) pursuit of enhanced access to health and enrollment data;

(10) review of the performance-management process;

(11) review survivor-plan design with appropriate changes;

(12) ongoing development of affirmative action and diversity plan; and

(13) staff training and development.[17]

"Customer Service Strategy"

The key initiative undertaken in 1996 was the Customer Service Strategy. Recognized were certain "realities" facing congregations and the whole church as well as individuals. Those "realities" included these facts:

(1) Congregations were experiencing budget pressures. Low salaries for pastors merited attention. Demographic changes were occurring. The needs of second-career pastors required consideration.

(2) The circumstances of plan members were diverse and required a balance between costs and benefits. Members also were demanding greater choice and flexibility. Plan sponsors and members sometimes reflected differing priorities.

(3) The Board of Pensions had to administer complex products, seeking prudent use of resources and enhanced efficiency while struggling with rising costs. Commitments to maintain and expand products and services were affirmed. In that regard, clear communication was viewed as essential.

The goals of the Customer Service Strategy included building customer trust and loyalty as well as the prudent management of resources. Pursued was the vision of improved lives of members, exceptional service to them, and the apt addressing of their needs.

At the time, the "current state" of the board's operation was seen as chiefly member-focused, with minimal attention to sponsors. Questions

---

[17] *Minutes*, Board of Trustees of the Board of Pensions of the ELCA, November 6, 1994, pp. 3-4.

were raised on whether the organizational structure was designed to support the board's 1993 statement of mission to "enhance the lives" of plan members and "support the well-being of congregations and institutions" of the ELCA.[18] The "desired state" for the Board of Pensions was seen as an organization structured to meet customer needs, with a focus on the member, while also having the ability to develop and nurture lifetime relationships in meeting their needs. Commitment was made to "attract and retain service-oriented employees" of the Board of Pensions and to "learn from failure and celebrate success."[19]

Steps were undertaken for greater two-way communication with members. To do so, a "knowledge warehouse" was proposed to target individuals and groups with information related to their particular needs. Discovering the concerns of members at specific points in life was a key part of such focused communication.[20]

Elements of the Customer Service Strategy were influenced by the experience of two staff members who attended a Malcolm Baldridge Quality Conference early in 1996. Advice obtained at that conference underscored the need to: (1) set a compelling goal; (2) seek to know one's customers; (3) "benchmark" best practices; (4) operate with an effective governance system; and (5) remember that "good enough, never is."[21]

Therefore, to nurture within the Board of Pensions a "culture of service," initiatives were embraced to: (1) integrate the vision and values of the board into all aspects of the organization; (2) promote an environment of trust, respect, integrity, excitement, and commitment; (3) improve continually; (4) value differences and the contributions of all employees; and (5) provide support, training, resources, and opportunities for employees.[22]

Identified as factors for success in the Customer Service Strategy were initiatives to:

(1) improve the benefits and services offered by the Board of Pensions while maintaining competitive costs;

---

[18] As noted earlier in this chapter, that 1993 statement had replaced the original statement of mission for the ELCA's Board of Pensions that was adopted in 1988.

[19] *Minutes*, Board of Trustees of the Board of Pensions of the ELCA, November 2-3, 1996, p. 3.

[20] *Minutes*, Trustees, November 2-3, 1996, pp. 4-5.

[21] *Minutes*, Board of Trustees of the Board of Pensions of the ELCA, August 1-2, 1996, p. 4.

[22] Minutes, Trustees, August 1-2, 1996, p. 4.

(2) understand customer needs and establish communication that enables them to utilize effectively the products and services of the Board of Pensions;

(3) anticipate, respond, and adapt quickly to changing customer needs, regulations, and benefit-delivery systems;

(4) integrate planning and resource allocation to meet in the best ways possible customer needs;

(5) increase the number and types of customers served by the Board of Pensions;

(6) attract and retain staff focused on customer service by providing them with a rewarding work environment that uses the strengths of each individual;

(7) maintain a fiscally sound operation;

(8) maximize long-term investment returns while controlling investment risks; and

(9) build partnerships and relationships with ELCA-related entities.[23]

Problems on "bridge to the future"

For the 1997-1999 strategic planning process, an image of a "bridge to the future" was used. Various problems were identified. Those problems metaphorically were called "burning platforms" that threatened the integrity of the symbolic bridge.

Among the "burning platforms" were these:

(1) Customer expectations were rising.

(2) Pricing was a strong concern.

(3) Use of technology by others had grown substantially while the Board of Pensions was struggling with outdated technology and problems in new developments.

(4) Increased competition was evident.[24]

Cited as an example of such "competition" was the fact that representatives of Aid Association for Lutherans and Lutheran Brotherhood (later merged and known as Thrivent Financial for Lutherans) were trying to get pension-plan members to roll withdrawals from pension funds into their products, while ignoring the possibility of long-term tax problems members could face.

---

[23] *Minutes*, Trustees, May 29-30, 1997, p. 4.

[24] *Minutes*, Board of Trustees of the Board of Pensions of the ELCA, November 8-9, 1997, p. 5.

In the context of the time, staff of the Board of Pensions assessed the culture and structure of the organization. They charted a course toward providing even greater customer service, including regional customer service teams to be available over an expanded number of hours, given the various U.S. time zones.

A comprehensive communication plan was put into place to speak to the needs and concerns of members. The plan was designed to strengthen relationships with plan members and foster knowledge for a lifetime with them. As part of that "lifetime" relationship, a pilot program was initiated to assist in financial planning.

Surveys showed significant increases in member satisfaction from 1997 to 1998 among both active and retired individuals, including in areas of responsiveness and resolution of problems.

Result of review

A well-planned "bridge to the future" was being "constructed" for the operation of the Board of Pensions. In the aftermath of the 1997 review of the program, the pattern of employer-paid benefits was maintained. That decision reflected the original principles that guided the development of the ELCA Pension and Other Benefits Program. For pensions, 10 percent of defined compensation was retained as the minimum for those employers whose sponsorship was either "required" or "encouraged." (Eventually, however, the option of a six percent minimum was opened for employees whose sponsorship was deemed "discretionary," particularly non-rostered lay employees of congregations.[25] That followed the practice that already existed in the institutional plans for social ministry organizations.)

Concern for individuals who experienced "service interruptions" was addressed. That issue related particularly to ordained ministers who served under contract rather than an official Letter of Call as interim pastors as well as other rostered individuals who had periods of being "on-leave-from-call" for a variety of reasons, among them parenting responsibilities. Extension of health coverage and availability of disability protection were recognized as needs for such individuals.[26]

---

[25] Action Number PN05.08.50, *Minutes*, Board of Trustees of the Board of Pensions of the ELCA, August 3-5, 2005, p. 24.

[26] Action Number PN97.08.38, *Minutes*, Board of Trustees of the Board of Pensions of the ELCA, July 31–August 1, 1997, p. 8. The action was consistent with the requirements of the U.S. Health Insurance Portability and Accountability Act of 1996.

Consistent with the guiding principles of the Board of Pensions, changes were made to enable participation in the program by rostered laypersons serving in non-ELCA organizations as well as clergy serving non-sponsoring employers.[27] Sponsorship of ELCA clergy serving congregations of other church bodies through the ELCA's full-communion relationships also was opened.[28]

Planning process

The strategic planning process for 1997, 1998, and 1999 identified three crucial areas:

(1) *Health-care:* Were there alternatives to the current health-care strategy of the Board of Pensions that would lead to an increase in customer satisfaction, a reduction of cost, or both?

(2) *Customer Focus:* What were the characteristics of products and services in the "defined-contribution marketplace?" What were the opportunities and challenges for serving ELCA-related institutions? Were there opportunities for serving unmet benefit needs of lay employees in congregations?

(3) *Sharing of Benefit Costs:* Was the method in place for determining contributions to the ELCA health plan consistent with the objectives of the church? Was there a need to supplement pensions for low-income retirees, pastors serving at low salaries, or second-career pastors?[29]

Several options were identified in each area. For health-care concerns, the course chosen to reduce costs and increase member satisfaction was engagement of a preferred provider organization (PPO) in areas that had not been covered previously by the point-of-service networks. Improvements were sought through

---

[27] Action Number PN97.05.23, *Minutes*, Trustees, May 29-30, 1997, pp. 7-8.

[28] Action Number PN98.08.38, *Minutes*, Board of Trustees of the Board of Pensions of the ELCA, August 5-7, 1998, pp. 8-9. A full-communion, church-to-church relationship was established by the 1997 Churchwide Assembly of the ELCA with the Presbyterian Church (U.S.A.), Reformed Church in America, and United Church of Christ. The agreement permitted the exchange of clergy for temporary service in parishes of the participating church bodies. Two years later, in 1999, similar full-communion agreements were established between the ELCA and The Episcopal Church as well as the ELCA and the Moravian Church. Then, in 2009, such a full-communion relationship was established with the United Methodist Church.

[29] *Minutes*, Board of Trustees of the Board of Pensions of the ELCA, November 6-8, 1998, p. 3.

"more aggressive management" of the medical and dental plan. Promotion of a wellness and health emphasis also was instituted (see Chapter 3).[30]

Organizational values

Five core organizational values were embraced in the corporate plan that was implemented in 1999. Those values were practiced in a variety of ways throughout subsequent years:

1. *Integrity*, meaning act with honesty, sincerity, and accountability; communicate fully and openly; and serve in the best interest of sponsors, employees, and the whole ELCA.

2. *Excellence*, meaning continual commitment to improve the quality of service; encouragement and recognition of leadership, innovation, and personal responsibility; and steadfast attempts to understand what customers expect and strive to exceed the expectations.

3. *Respect*, meaning valuing individuals and their diverse contributions and styles; treating everyone with dignity and respect; and striving to create a work environment of openness and trust.

4. *Stewardship*, meaning embracing the board's mission within the whole ELCA to serve those who serve; managing responsibly the resources entrusted to the Board of Pensions; and providing financial security and support for the well-being of those served.

5. *Collaboration*, meaning working together to achieve common goals; placing the goals of the organization above departmental and individual goals; and supporting one another in facing challenges and celebrating successes.[31]

From high transaction to high relationship

A new statement of vision emerged in the evolution of the Board of Pensions. Incorporated into the three-year strategic plan for the years 2000 through 2002 was the vision that:

> We are the *first place to call* when you need a caring and responsive partner to meet your health care and retirement needs. *Technology at our fingertips* enables us to assist members with knowledgeable, supportive services. We are *advocates* to

---

[30] *Minutes*, Trustees, November 6-8, 1998, p. 4.

[31] *Minutes*, Trustees, November 6-8, 1998, p. 7.

ensure that the ELCA benefits programs meet the needs of the entire church.[32]

The revised statement of vision sought to underscore the transition in the Board of Pensions from being a high-transaction, limited-service organization to a relationship-based organization. The operation was moving from being a "production shop" to a "service center." Clearly the change required investment in people, service, products, and technology.[33]

The shift from "transaction processing" to "service" involved several steps, including outsourcing health-claims processing in 2000 and engaging Mellon Employee Benefits Solutions (later known as ACS HR Solutions) for pension administration and record keeping of the institutional plan in July 2002 and the ELCA's Regular Pension Plan in January 2003. These changes required "transforming" (1) *people* by developing new skills, (2) *processes* by focusing on advocacy rather than transactions, and (3) *technology* by providing data management and access.[34]

Expanded use of the Internet was a significant element for service. Members could obtain daily reporting of market valuations of their funds. They also had opportunity to make changes through the Internet in their investment allocations and obtain other services for ongoing participation and retirement planning.[35]

Five strategic objectives were identified as the core for the 2000-2002 strategic plan:

(1) To develop and maintain a benefit-plan structure that would be flexible enough to meet the ever-changing needs of the customers.

(2) To provide a health-care plan that would be priced as competitively as possible, while fully supporting the mission of the ELCA.

(3) To undertake a pension-plan strategy that would support the retirement needs of all of the customers.

(4) To create an infrastructure for the Board of Pensions for the focus on customer relationships.

---

[32] *Minutes*, Board of Trustees of the Board of Pensions of the ELCA, November 5-7, 1999, p. 6. Italic emphasis is shown as in the original citation.

[33] *Minutes*, Trustees, November 5-7, 1999, pp. 6-7.

[34] *Minutes*, Board of Trustees of the Board of Pensions of the ELCA, November 2-4, 2001, pp. 5-6.

[35] *Minutes*, Trustees, August 3-5, 2005, p. 5.

(5) To develop further the ability to attract, retain, and equip staff within the Board of Pensions to meet customer needs.[36]

Strategic objectives for 2003-2005

Building on the developments of the previous three-year plans, the strategic objectives identified for the period of 2003-2005 were:

(1) To keep the ELCA health plan affordable while maintaining adequate benefits for members and promoting health and wellness throughout the ELCA.

(2) To deliver a consistent, high-quality level of personalized service and advocate for members, congregations, and other sponsoring organizations.

(3) To increase participation in the retirement plan and in the amount of managed assets.

(4) To develop retirement and other financial products to meet more effectively the needs of members, congregations, and other sponsoring organizations.

(5) To develop a benefit-plan structure flexible enough to meet the ever-changing needs of members, congregations, and other sponsoring organizations.[37]

Carried forward from 2002 were some ongoing elements, including: (1) aggressive health-care management; (2) flexibility in the plan design; and (3) customer service and advocacy. Identified as new were: (1) a partnership with the Mayo Clinic for the promotion of healthy practices as part of the continuing emphasis on wellness; (2) expanded efforts for growth in the pension program; and (3) exploration of possible "new products." Greater collaboration with denominational partners was envisioned for the health-care plan. Furthermore, the organizational structure of the Board of Pensions was reshaped for greater customer service and interaction.[38]

---

[36] Action Number PN99.11.62, *Minutes*, Trustees, November 5-7, 1999, pp. 14-15 and 18.

[37] Action Number PN02.08.23, *Minutes*, Board of Trustees of the Board of Pensions of the ELCA, July 31–August 2, 2002, pp. 15-16.

[38] *Minutes*, Board of Trustees of the Board of Pensions of the ELCA, March 1-3, 2002, pp. 4-6.

"Faithful to your well-being"

The "brand" for the Board of Pensions—"Faithful to your well-being" —was put into practice by encouraging clergy and other plan members to lead healthier lives and seek greater financial security. In operating a benefits program for the whole ELCA in all its expressions, the Board of Pensions fostered such "well-being" in manifold ways, including working to: (1) lower costs through economies of scale; (2) improve opportunities for mobility of pastors and other church workers; and (3) free congregations and other employers from the need to establish and implement employee-benefit plans on their own.

The Board of Pensions offered "value added" service for members through: (1) superior long-term investment performance; (2) a full array of investment choices; (3) flexible lifetime distribution options; (4) tax benefits for pastors with use of the clergy housing allowance; and (5) a proven program of social purpose funds.[39]

New statement of mission

In preparation of the strategic plan for the 2006-2008 triennium, trustees and staff reexamined the "mission," "vision," and "values" of the ELCA's Board of Pensions. "Mission" was defined as "a statement of corporate intent that was informed by both values and vision." "Vision" was viewed as an exercise in "predicting a future and the board's role in it." And a declaration of "values" was seen as "a statement of who we are."[40]

The dozen-year-old mission statement of the Board of Pensions was studied.[41] From that review emerged a new mission statement that declared:

> We will provide retirement, health and related benefits and services to enhance the well-being of those who serve through the Evangelical Lutheran Church in America and other faith-based organizations.[42]

---

[39] *Minutes*, Trustees, August 3-5, 2005, pp. 5-6.

[40] John G. Kapanke, "Report of the President," Board of Trustees of the Board of Pensions of the ELCA, February 27-29, 2004, p. 9.

[41] The statement of mission from 1993 read: "The mission of the Board of Pensions is to provide pension, health, and other benefits and related services that will enhance the lives of pastors, rostered lay persons, lay employees, and their families, and support the well-being of congregations and institutions of the Evangelical Lutheran Church in America."

[42] Action Number PN04.08.24, *Minutes*, Board of Trustees of the Board of Pensions of the ELCA, August 3-5, 2004, p. 14.

Significantly, for the long-term, the statement reflected a potentially expanded scope of services in the reference to "other faith-based organizations."

The vision statement for the operation of the Board of Pensions also was revised. The new vision statement read:

Those we serve lead healthy lives and achieve financial security.[43]

The key "values" that had been in place since 1999, however, were maintained without revision. Those values were: (1) integrity; (2) excellence; (3) respect; (4) stewardship; and (5) collaboration.

The 2006-2008 strategic plan had three objectives: (1) to strengthen the health plan; (2) to expand the "business;" and (3) to enhance operational excellence of the Board of Pensions. The "outcomes" sought in relation to the health plan included cost containment, financial protection of the plan, and a strong focus on health and wellness. Increasing assets under management, control over retirement-plan expenses in operation, and leveraging of core competencies were seen as part of expanded "business" possibilities. Improved infrastructure to meet more effectively the needs for high-quality service to members was viewed as an ongoing need.[44]

Iterative processes

The iterative planning processes of the Board of Pensions continued in 2008 to determine the strategic plan for the triennium of 2009-2011. Identified as the strategic objective for the triennium were efforts to "attract new and retain existing customer groups on a sustainable basis by enhancing customer experience and strengthening engagement." The term "customer groups" included plan members as well as congregations and other sponsoring entities and institutions.[45]

Several initiatives were identified for a highly satisfactory "customer experience" on the part of members and sponsors. These included efforts to

---

[43] Action Number PN04.08.26, *Minutes*, Trustees, August 3-5, 2004, p. 15. A much longer vision statement previously had been in use that read: "We are the first place to call when you need a caring and responsive partner to meet your health care and retirement needs. Information at our fingertips enables us to assist members with knowledgeable, supportive service. We are advocates to ensure that the ELCA benefit programs meet the needs of the entire church."

[44] *Minutes*, Trustees, August 3-5, 2005, p. 6.

[45] *Minutes*, Board of Trustees of the Board of Pensions of the ELCA, October 31–November 2, 2008.

improve the readiness of members for their retirement decisions. In addition, increased use by members of the Mayo Clinic health-assessment resources was envisioned. At the same time, emphasis was placed on decreasing the number of avoidable medical problems through fostering changes in the behavior of plan members and their dependents. This commitment to health and wellness was seen as crucial for the financial viability of the ELCA Medical and Dental Benefits Plan.

Another goal in the plan focused on asset and customer retention and growth. Members were encouraged to increase contributions to their pension accounts. In addition, members were urged to roll other retirement funds into their ELCA plan.

Excellence in the quality of the service offered by staff of the Board of Pensions also was emphasized in the 2009-2011 strategic plan.

In a major change from past strategic planning documents that sometimes filled 40 pages with statements of strategy and listings of tactics, the 2009-2011 plan was distilled into a concise, one-page format. The format followed the "best practices" pattern identified by the Malcolm Baldrige National Quality Award. The plan embraced the acronym SMART, including specific, measurable, attainable, relevant, and timely goals to provide greater clarity and focus for the responsibilities of individuals as well as the whole organization.[46]

Each evolving plan reflected the ongoing, unfolding history of the Board of Pensions of the Evangelical Lutheran Church in America.

Manual on governance

A separate but related step in the planning processes was the development of a "Policy Governance Manual." The manual, which was adopted in 2005, reflected the "Carver Model," a pattern of governance developed by John and Miriam Mayhew Carver.[47] The manual defined a process for (1) governance, (2) executive responsibility, (3) the relationship of the board and the chief executive officer, and (4) "ends," declaring that "through a deliberate planning process designed to support the

---

[46] John G. Kapanke, "Next Strategic Plan Has Four Areas of Focus," *Boardwalk*, October 2008, p. 2.

[47] See "Policy Governance Model" at www.carvergoverance.com/model.htm. John and Miriam Carver outlined the model on a Web site and in several books and seminars. Among the books are *Basic Principles of Policy Governance* and *The Policy Governance Model*.

mission of the ELCA, plan members of the ELCA and other faith-based organizations" will be "able to lead healthy lives and attain financial security at a competitive cost."[48]

The pattern of governance by the trustees, as envisioned in the manual, called for (1) a strategic outward vision rather than a focus on administrative detail, (2) encouragement of a diversity of viewpoints and perspectives in reaching consensus, (3) a clear distinction between the role of the board of trustees and the chief executive officer's responsibilities, (4) collective rather than individual decisions, (5) a view toward the future rather than the past or present, and (6) proactive rather than reactive practice.[49]

Past as prologue

The significant developments for the ELCA's Board of Pensions throughout the final years of the twentieth century and the early years of the twenty-first century proved to be a prologue for continuing development. As the ELCA's Board of Pensions entered its third decade of operation, a comprehensive evaluation of the business practices and operations was undertaken.[50] The focus continued to be this—to help members of the ELCA Pension and Other Benefits Program achieve greater health and financial security for the present and the future.

---

[48] *Policy Governance Manual*, Board of Pensions of the Evangelical Lutheran Church in America, pp. 2 and 17.

[49] *Policy Governance Manual*, p. 3.

[50] *Annual Report*, 2007, Board of Pensions of the Evangelical Lutheran Church in America, p. 3.

CHAPTER 3

Challenge of Escalating
Health-Care Costs

The enormous increases in medical costs throughout the United States in the late 1980s and early 1990s hit hard the congregations of the ELCA as they sought to provide insurance for their pastors, church workers, and their families. As a result, major changes were needed to maintain viability in the health plan provided by the Board of Pensions of the Evangelical Lutheran Church in America (ELCA).

The geographic distribution of those covered largely reflected the concentration of ELCA members. Three-fourths of the members of ELCA congregations lived in 14 states,[1] yet the health plans provided for church workers by the Board of Pensions had to serve members in all U.S. states as well as Puerto Rico and the U.S. Virgin Islands.

During 1988, more than 200,000 medical and dental claims were processed. Payments amounted to $46 million in the four plans operating at that time: (1) the ELCA Medical and Dental Benefits Plan; (2) the ELCA Continuation of the ALC Medical-Dental Plan for Retired Participants; (3) the ELCA Continuation of the LCA Ministerial Health Benefits Plan for Retired Members; and (4) the ELCA Medical Benefits Plan for Seminarians.[2]

Because the new software for the medical and dental claims in the ELCA health-benefits program was not operational until late February 1988, the backlog of unprocessed claims had reached eight weeks, lagging far behind the goal of processing a claim in 10 days or less. The length of

---

[1] About 75 percent of the ELCA's membership is concentrated in Minnesota, Pennsylvania, Wisconsin, Ohio, Illinois, North and South Dakota, Iowa, Michigan, Nebraska, California, New York, Texas, and Washington.

[2] *1989 Reports and Records*, Vol. 2, First Churchwide Assembly of the Evangelical Lutheran Church in America, Rosemont, Ill., August 23-30, 1989, p. 382.

time for processing a claim grew even longer in succeeding months to 11 weeks. That was cut, however, to two weeks by mid-August 1988.[3]

In its first year of operation, claims exceeded income by more than $1.6 million. The deficit occurred because the rate for 1988 was set too low in 1986 and because of high increases in costs for medical care during that period.[4] Originally, the premiums for the medical and dental plans in 1988 established the minimum at $1,200 and the maximum of $3,000 per year.[5] Rates had to be adjusted in 1989 through 1991 to make up the deficit and cover existing claims in those years. For instance, the rate was adjusted from 8.1 percent of defined compensation in 1988 to 9.9 percent in 1989.[6] Escalating costs required continuing increases in the premiums. For instance, rates were raised in 1999 as much as 16 percent over the rates of the previous year.[7]

The five-year period between 1987 and 1991 witnessed annual increases in U.S. health-care costs between 18 and 20 percent. The higher costs were caused by (1) medical-care inflation, (2) greater use of health-care services, (3) advances in medical technology, (4) new treatment patterns, (5) shifts in patterns of public-health reimbursement, (6) an aging population, and (7) greater assigning of costs of the uninsured to group-health plans.[8]

Challenge of processing claims

Increased medical costs affected, of course, the total ELCA medical and dental benefits paid in 1989 and 1990. In those two years, benefits paid exceeded $110 million.[9] The next biennium saw a slower rate of increase; even so, benefits paid in 1991 and 1992 amounted to $120 million.[10] In

---

[3] *Annual Report*, 1988, Board of Pensions of the Evangelical Lutheran Church in America, p. 10.

[4] *1989 Reports and Records*, Vol. 2, pp. 381-382.

[5] *Summary [of] Pension and Other Benefits Plans*, Constituting Convention of the Evangelical Lutheran Church in America, Columbus, Ohio, April 30–May 3, 1987, C-10, p. 70.

[6] *Annual Report*, 1988, p. 13.

[7] *Annual Report*, 1998, Board of Pensions of the Evangelical Lutheran Church in America, p. 6.

[8] *Annual Report*, 1988, p. 5.

[9] "Report of the Board of Pensions," *1991 Reports and Records*, Vol. 1, Part 2, Second Churchwide Assembly of the Evangelical Lutheran Church in America, Orlando, Fla., August 28–September 4, 1991, p. 690.

[10] "Report of the Board of Pensions," *1993 Reports and Records*, Vol. 1, Part 2, Third Churchwide Assembly of the Evangelical Lutheran Church in America, Kansas City, Mo., August 25–September 1, 1993, p. 244.

1993 and 1994, some 800,000 medical and dental claims reached $135 million.[11]

"Reasonable and customary" fee guidelines were instituted by the Board of Pensions in 1992. Under that system, the costs for health-care services were compared to those of other health-care professionals in the same geographic area and were reimbursed accordingly. The pattern resulted in claim savings of 3.4 percent in that year.[12]

President John G. Kapanke was able to report to the trustees that the health plan was in a better financial position at the end of 1993 than in previous years. Said Mr. Kapanke:

> A slowdown in the trend of medical inflation and plan changes involving implementation of a mail-order prescription drug program combined to generate a year-end 1993 surplus position of approximately 25 percent of prior year incurred claims in the ELCA medical and dental plan. Just as the phenomenon of rising health care costs in previous years was not unique to the ELCA, a slow-down in the trend rates is an industry-wide situation.[13]

The slowdown coincided with discussions of potential forms of a government-mandated health-care program. After heated debate in Washington in 1993 and 1994, such a plan did not materialize at that time.

At the request of participants, a supplemental plan was put into place in 1988 to reduce the deductible in the medical plans by half and provide reimbursement for the 10 percent co-payment amount. With subsequent changes and the move to managed-care plans, the supplemental plan was eliminated in 1995.

Effective January 1, 1990, the rate structure of the ELCA medical and dental benefits plan was changed. A separate rate was established for the person under call or employed from the rate for spouse or spouse and children. Members could specify coverage for (1) member only, (2)

---

[11] "Report of the Board of Pensions," 1995 Pre-Assembly Report, Vol. 1, Fourth Churchwide Assembly of the Evangelical Lutheran Church in America, Minneapolis, Minn., August 16-22, 1995, p. 157.

[12] Annual Report, 1992, Board of Pensions of the Evangelical Lutheran Church in America, p. 6.

[13] John G. Kapanke, "Management Report," Agenda, Section IV, Board of Trustees of the Board of Pensions of the ELCA, March 3, 1994, p. 1.

member and spouse, (3) member and children, or (4) member, spouse, and children. The change was made to minimize dual coverage in instances where a spouse received benefits from another employer.

Members were given the option to waive medical and dental coverage under the ELCA Pension and Other Benefits Program while still participating in the disability, survivor benefit, and pension plans, provided they had or could obtain health coverage through another employer-provided group plan, such as a spouse's coverage.[14] At the beginning, to obtain this exemption, employers were assessed a two percent fee, based on the individual's defined compensation. That fee was eliminated at the end of 2000.

In the face of sharply increasing costs, the Board of Pensions joined with 15 denominations in 1990 to form the Church Healthcare Network. The purpose of the network was to explore ways to negotiate and purchase jointly, at reduced rates, health-care services.[15] While the network did not yield immediate results, such ecumenical cooperation would prove crucial for achieving substantial savings in the coming years.

In 1993, four primary goals were identified in an emerging strategy for the board's medical-dental benefits plan. The goals were these: (1) reduce the cost escalation in the plan; (2) maintain high participation; (3) improve financial integrity undergirding the plan; and (4) prepare for future changes.[16]

"Clout with providers"

The most substantial change in the overall health plan in the 1990s was the shift to managed care. "The health-care environment . . . dictated . . . change . . . to keep our plan viable and solvent," President Kapanke said in 1994. Like the predecessor church bodies, the board operated "a traditional indemnity plan that was self-insured and self-administered." Therefore, the board "had no contract or clout with providers," but "simply reimbursed for services using reasonable and customary guidelines," Kapanke explained. By paying full rates, the board's medical plan was subsidizing other plans that had negotiated for lower rates. "It became obvious that we needed to move into managed care," he said.[17]

---

[14] *Annual Report*, 1994, Board of Pensions of the Evangelical Lutheran Church in America, p. 15.

[15] *Annual Report*, 1990, Board of Pensions of the Evangelical Lutheran Church in America, p. 6.

[16] *Minutes*, Board of Trustees of the Board of Pensions of the ELCA, July 16-18, 1993, pp. 6-7.

[17] *Annual Report*, 1994, pp. 12-13.

Therefore, the ELCA Medical and Dental Benefits Plan was revised—effective January 1, 1995—to include:

(1) a point-of-service arrangement phased into operation over a three- to five-year period, with initial implementation in the Minneapolis-St. Paul area of Minnesota and in Chicago;

(2) a "managed indemnity" arrangement for those not covered by the point-of-service arrangement, which would include additional review of inpatient pre-certification and use, large-case management, and a simplified reimbursement schedule for chiropractic, out-patient psychotherapy, and major dental care;

(3) elimination of the supplement to the Medical and Dental Benefits Plan;

(4) operation of both the point-of-service and managed indemnity arrangements under the same, national ELCA health plan;

(5) continued bundling of the Medical and Dental Benefits Plan with the other ELCA pension and benefit plans; and

(6) in-network benefits of the point-of-service arrangement reimbursed at 90 percent of eligible expenses or 100 percent with a small co-payment per physician office visit, while out-of-network benefits would be reimbursed at 70 percent of eligible expenses after a deductible.

Move to "Point-of-Service"

Some 11,400 individuals in 18 different areas—about 33 percent of plan members—were included in the first phase of the ELCA managed-care program that started January 1, 1995. The point-of-service (POS) arrangement was administered by Aetna. In the second phase, which was implemented a year later, an additional 12 percent of plan members in 20 areas were covered under the POS program.[18] That was followed by the third phase being implemented on January 1, 1998, with about 800 plan members and their families in 29 network areas being enrolled at that time.[19]

Initially, in the POS network, members had a $15 co-payment for an office visit with their primary care physician, $15 for a visit with a specialist, and $50 for an emergency room visit. For those covered under the POS

---

[18] *1995 Pre-Assembly Report*, Fourth Churchwide Assembly of the Evangelical Lutheran Church in America, Minneapolis, Minn., August 16-22, 1995, p. 157.

[19] *Minutes*, Board of Trustees of the Board of Pensions of the ELCA, November 2-3, 1996, p. 6.

network who sought treatment from physicians not in the network, the plan reimbursed 70 percent of all eligible reasonable and customary charges after a $500 deductible for individuals and $1,000 for families. In this way, members were encouraged to use the POS network, but they still had a choice.[20]

A medical-use management firm, Healthmarc, was retained to work with members and physicians in reviewing the medical necessity of proposed care as well as ongoing case management.[21]

Savings from the managed-care system and a slower rate of escalation in U.S. health-care costs resulted in smaller increases in premium rates in 1995. Savings through the managed-care system in that year alone amounted to some $9 million. The favorable experience on costs permitted the building of more adequate reserves for the continuing operation of the health plan.[22]

"Outsourced" in 2000 was the processing of health-benefit claims for standard benefits in the ELCA health plan as well as the ELCA Medicare supplement plan. Seabury & Smith, Inc., in Des Moines, Iowa, was contracted for that service.[23]

Shift to PPO

A gradual shift began in the late 1990s from the POS pattern to benefits under the preferred provider organization (PPO) of Blue Cross and Blue Shield of Minnesota. The PPO program offered more cost-effective health-care options and greater savings to plan members.

Like the POS arrangement, the PPO contracted with a network of medical doctors and hospitals to deliver services at discounted prices. The PPO differed, however, from the POS arrangement in that the PPO networks tended to be broader and referrals were not required prior to seeking the care of a specialist. Initially, the PPO benefits covered 85 percent of the charges after a $240 deductible.[24]

---

[20] *Annual Report*, 1993, Board of Pensions of the Evangelical Lutheran Church in America, pp. 19-20.

[21] *Annual Report*, 1994, pp. 14-15.

[22] *1995 Pre-Assembly Report*, p. 157.

[23] *Annual Report*, 2000, Board of Pensions of the Evangelical Lutheran Church in America, p. 6.

[24] *1999 Reports and Records: Minutes*, Sixth Churchwide Assembly of the Evangelical Lutheran Church in America, Denver, Colo., August 16-22, 1999, p. 599.

As of January 1, 1999, nearly 9,500 active and retired plan members (and 15,000 family members) were in managed-care programs of Blue Cross and Blue Shield or Aetna. At that point, nearly 11,000 plan members, plus their families, were still covered through the board's standard benefits program.[25]

Initially, the program of Blue Cross and Blue Shield was open to members in Iowa, Minnesota, North Dakota, and Wisconsin, except for metropolitan areas still served at that time by Aetna U.S. Healthcare. Beginning January 1, 2000, members in the POS program in Pennsylvania and the metropolitan Chicago area were given the choice of either their current POS arrangement or PPO coverage through Blue Cross and Blue Shield. Difficulty with the availability of Aetna POS providers in some areas prompted many members to move to the PPO coverage of Blue Cross and Blue Shield.

By 2000, only about 15 percent of the members and their dependents remained in the standard benefits program. The others were in either PPO and POS arrangements.

The dawn of the new century saw more rapid shifts from the POS pattern to PPO benefits under the ELCA Medical and Dental Benefits Plan. Managed care spread to members in 45 states.[26] The expansion of PPO benefits saved $4 million in 2001 over the previous arrangements of indemnity coverage or the POS pattern.[27]

On January 1, 2008, the relationship with Aetna ended. Members previously under the Aetna plan were shifted to the PPO coverage of Blue Cross and Blue Shield.

Cost management for pharmacy benefit

A new "Prescription Drug Program" was introduced January 1, 1993, to reduce pharmacy costs under the medical plan. Selected to administer the program initially was Express Pharmacy Services (EPS), a subsidiary of the J.C. Penney Company. Members could purchase maintenance medication through a mail-order pharmacy system at substantial savings.

---

[25] "Report of the Board of Pensions," 1999 Pre-Assembly Report, Sixth Churchwide Assembly of the Evangelical Lutheran Church in America, Denver, Colo., August 16-22, 1999, p. 131.

[26] "Report of the Board of Pensions," 2001 Pre-Assembly Report, Seventh Churchwide Assembly of the Evangelical Lutheran Church in America, Indianapolis, Ind., August 8-14, 2001, p. 136.

[27] 2001 Pre-Assembly Report, p. 135.

Reimbursement for those who purchased drugs at a retail pharmacy was 50 percent. The program initially permitted members to purchase both short-term and maintenance medication at a local pharmacy.[28] Savings through the program during the first year amounted to $2.9 million, an amount two-thirds larger than originally anticipated.[29] In addition, members themselves saved $1.9 million in lower out-of-pocket costs.[30] At the start, the co-payment for brand name drugs was $12; for generic, $5.

In the decade between 1982 and 1992, the average cost of prescription drugs in the United States jumped 152 percent, nearly three times higher than the general inflation rate for that period.[31] The upward trend continued. For instance, in the late 1990s and early 2000s, pharmacy costs grew about 20 percent a year. The mail-order pharmacy system proved essential for obtaining savings amid enormous increases in the level of usage and cost of drug benefits.

All long-term (greater than a month) pharmacy benefits were shifted on July 1, 2000, to Eckerd/EPS. A "third-tier" for non-preferred drugs was added that required a higher co-payment. At that time, the retail co-payment for generic drugs was $5 for a one-month supply and the mail order co-payment for a three-month generic supply was $10. For preferred drugs, the rates were $12 (one-month retail) and $24 (three-months mail order) or for non-preferred, $25 and $50 respectively. Given escalating costs, the co-payment rates had to be adjusted upward in succeeding years.

In 2002, the ELCA Board of Pensions joined eight other denominations that combined their purchasing power in negotiating a more cost-effective prescription drug contract with Express Scripts, Inc. Savings for ELCA congregations and other employers under the new contract was projected at $3.2 million in the first year.[32] The three-tier benefit system continued for the co-payments (generic, preferred, and non-preferred drugs).

As a cost-control measure, changes were made in the mental-health, chemical-dependency, and substance-abuse programs. Under the revised pattern, effective January 1, 1994, inpatient mental-health treatment and all chemical or substance abuse treatment (both inpatient and outpatient) were

[28] 1993 *Reports and Records*, Vol. 1, Part 2, Third Churchwide Assembly of the Evangelical Lutheran Church in America, Kansas City, Mo., August 25–September 1, 1993, p. 244.

[29] 1995 *Pre-Assembly Report*, p. 157.

[30] *Annual Report*, 1994, p. 16.

[31] *Annual Report*, 1994, p. 15.

[32] *Annual Report*, 2001, Board of Pensions of the Evangelical Lutheran Church in America.

made subject to network-based managed care through Value Behavioral Health. Except in emergency situations, members were required to contact an 800 number for authorization prior to inpatient hospital admission for mental-health treatment or any treatment for chemical dependency or substance abuse. The task of the contact person was to refer the member to the appropriate network facility or provider for treatment. If treatment commenced without pre-authorization, no benefit would be paid.

Outpatient mental-health treatment was not subject to the requirement of network-based managed care. So members could determine when treatment should be sought and from whom. About $2.5 million was saved annually as a result of these changes, the equivalent at that time of $150 per member.[33]

Value Behavioral Health was part of a merger that created an entity known as ValueOptions, effective January 1, 2001.[34] At that point, ValueOptions began administering for the board all mental-health and chemical-dependency benefits, as well as certain "wellness" services. Added at the same time were benefits for marital counseling and career guidance. ValueOptions handled pre-certification for inpatient and outpatient service, processing of claims, application of negotiated rates, and customer service. Those tasks shifted at the beginning of 2006 to CIGNA Behavioral Health.

Through an Employee Assistance Program (EAP), which was inaugurated in 2006, members had access by telephone 24 hours a day, seven days a week, to a counselor to talk about such matters as stress, relationships, family issues, or personal problems. Referrals also could be made for face-to-face counseling, legal consultations, or financial questions.

Delta Dental PPO became the vendor for the dental benefits on January 1, 2001. An initial annual savings of $900,000 a year was anticipated through the use of a single vendor for dental benefits.

To adjudicate and manage disability claims, Broadspire, a risk-management services company, was employed in 2004.[35]

As part of a Flexible Benefits Plan, which was inaugurated on January 1, 2008, members could make voluntary, pretax, salary deductions as contributions to spending accounts. The plan was designed in accord

---

[33] *1993 Reports and Records*, Vol. 1, Part 2, p. 245.

[34] "ValueOptions" as one word was the formal name of the entity.

[35] *Annual Report*, 2003, Board of Pensions of the Evangelical Lutheran Church in America, p. 3.

with Section 125 of the Internal Revenue Service Code as a tax benefit for members.[36] Through a health-care flexible spending account, members could be reimbursed with their pretax dollars for eligible health-care, pharmacy, and dental expenses. In addition, through a dependent care flexible spending account, participants could be reimbursed with their pretax dollars for eligible day-care expenses for the care of children or other eligible dependents, to enable participants to work outside the home.[37]

Rising expenses

After a few years of modest increases in medical costs, expenses began rising again at an alarming rate. Urgent attempts were undertaken to maintain a health-care plan that could be priced as competitively as possible for pastors, other church workers, and their families.

Part of the challenge in controlling costs involved the average age of plan participants—49 at the start of the twenty-first century, 10 years older than the U.S. average for the general working population. Rates remained based on a percentage of salary, however, to avoid age-related pricing and potential complications of the call process.[38]

About 43 percent of all medical and pharmacy claims for the ELCA health plan in 2005 resulted from potentially avoidable conditions. The cost of those claims amounted to $41 million. Seven percent of the persons covered that year under the ELCA's medical and dental benefits plan had claims in excess of $10,000 each. In total, those members accounted in 2005 for 56 percent of the total medical and pharmacy claims. Those percentages for ELCA plan members were larger than for most U.S. employers.

Statistics for 2005 identified a subset of "catastrophic situations" in the ELCA health plan for 188 lives covered that amounted to more than $22 million. Among those catastrophic claims in terms of amounts were 35 situations of cardiovascular needs for $3.4 million; 27 for cancer treatment, $2.7 million; six from injuries, $700,000; six related to chronic arthritis, $400,000; three for back conditions, $200,000; and three for high-risk pregnancies, $300,000. In reviewing those claims, Watson Wyatt, consultants for the Board of Pensions, estimated that about 37 percent of

---

[36] Action Number PN07.08.42, *Minutes*, Board of Trustees of the Board of Pensions of the ELCA, August 2-4, 2007, pp. 21-22.

[37] *Annual Report*, 2008, Board of Pensions of the Evangelical Lutheran Church in America, p. 19.

[38] *2001 Pre-Assembly Report*, p. 136.

the "catastrophic situations" potentially could have been avoided through improved health-related behaviors.[39]

In search of "wellness"

The theme of "wellness" shaped the endeavors of the Board of Pensions throughout the first decade of the twenty-first century. Convinced that healthy leaders are crucial for the ongoing life of a vibrant church, steps were taken to underscore the importance of healthy behaviors.

In partnership with what was then known as the Division for Ministry in the ELCA's churchwide organization, the Board of Pensions undertook extensive efforts to promote "wellness" among pastors. Funded through a grant from the Board of Pensions was a position of director for ministerial health and wellness in the Division for Ministry, beginning in 2001.[40] A medical doctor, Gwen Wagstrom Halaas, was named to the position.[41] As a resource for underscoring crucial steps toward wellness, she wrote *The Right Road: Life Choices for Clergy.*[42] In a review of claims data, Dr. Halaas identified four primary problems generating significant costs: (1) stress and stress-related illnesses; (2) excess weight and lack of physical activity; (3) lack of proper nutrition and elevated cholesterol; and (4) high blood pressure and heart disease.

After she resigned from the wellness position in 2003, staff members in the ELCA's churchwide office in Chicago and the office of the Board of Pensions in Minneapolis continued to highlight the concern.

The urgent need for changes in behavior was underscored in the Mayo Clinic's "Health Risk Assessment" survey of plan members in 2004. Of the people who took the online test, 65 percent reported being overweight. The same percentage indicated a lack of exercise, while 55 percent ate too much dietary fat and not enough fruits and vegetables. Added to the health plan to address these concerns were coverages of expanded preventive services as well as treatment to foster smoking cessation and weight loss.[43]

---

[39] John G. Kapanke, "Report of the President," *Agenda*, Board of Trustees of the Board of Pensions of the ELCA, August 3-5, 2006, pp. 6-8.

[40] This division was renamed the Vocation and Education program unit in a reorganization that was approved by the 2005 Churchwide Assembly of the ELCA.

[41] Dr. Halaas was elected to a six-year term on the board of trustees of the Board of Pensions by the 1997 Churchwide Assembly of the ELCA.

[42] The book was published in 2004 by Augsburg Fortress, Publishers.

[43] *Annual Report*, 2004, Board of Pensions of the Evangelical Lutheran Church in America, pp. 2-3.

The wellness effort—with the theme "Healthy leaders enhance lives" —encouraged members to participate annually in a online health-risk assessment through the Mayo Clinic. Some 4,500 participated in the first year the assessment was available.[44] That number grew to more than 11,000 in 2008, accounting for about 60 percent of those eligible for the survey. The results each year pointed to serious concerns. For instance, in 2008, the assessment showed "at risk" indications for those covered by the health plan for a variety of reasons, including: 76 percent, poor nutritional habits; 67 percent, overweight; 60 percent, poor emotional health; 57 percent, high blood pressure; 50 percent, lack of exercise; and 23 percent, high cholesterol.[45]

Starting in 2008, a two percent reduction in premiums within the respective synods was offered if a synod achieved 75 percent or greater participation in the health-risk assessment by all adults covered under the health plan within the synod. Congregations in five of the ELCA's 65 synods and four of the eight ELCA seminaries earned the discount in 2008 by achieving the 75 percent or greater participation in the survey.[46] In 2009, congregations in six synods and seven ELCA seminaries reached the 75 percent or greater participation level.[47] The discount opportunity was revised for 2010, lowering the required level of participation to 65 percent, but narrowing the window to earn the discount to four months (January through April). Those achieving a 65 percent participation rate by April 30 received the two percent discount for the entire year.

---

[44] "Report of the Board of Pensions," 2005 Pre-Assembly Report, Section III, Ninth Churchwide Assembly of the Evangelical Lutheran Church in America, Orlando, Fla., August 8-14, 2005, p. 96.

[45] Kami Lund, "Nutrition, Weight, Emotional Health Among Health Risks for ELCA Leaders," News Release 08-208-KL, Communication Services Unit, Evangelical Lutheran Church in America, December 22, 2008, p. 1.

[46] In 2008, the five synods and their percentage of survey participation of plan members were: West Virginia–Western Maryland Synod, 82.8 percent; Northwest Synod of Wisconsin, 80.4 percent; Southeastern Minnesota Synod, 80.1 percent; South Dakota Synod, 78.2 percent; and Montana Synod, 77 percent. The four seminaries were: Trinity, in Columbus, Ohio, 86.9 percent; Wartburg, in Dubuque, Iowa, 81.4 percent; Lutheran, in Gettysburg, Pa., 80.5 percent; and Luther, in St. Paul, Minn., 80.2 percent. One hundred percent of the plan members of the ELCA Board of Pensions participated in the survey, as did 76.9 percent of those in ELCA's churchwide units based in Chicago.

[47] The synods obtaining the discount in 2009 were: Montana Synod, 78.6 percent; Northern Great Lakes Synod, 78.9 percent; Northwest Synod of Wisconsin, 82.2 percent; South Dakota Synod, 81.6 percent; Southwestern Minnesota Synod, 80.1 percent; and Southeastern Minnesota Synod, 82.2 percent. The ELCA's churchwide units based in Chicago and the ELCA Board of Pensions also achieved the 75 percent or greater level of survey participation.

Individuals received $100 in "personal wellness dollars" for completing the assessment and an additional $200 for completing health improvement activities outlined on an "EmbodyHealth" Web site. As a result, participants gained $1.9 million to offset their medical deductible costs.

The relationship with Mayo Clinic Health Management Resources that was started in 2003 provided a monthly newsletter, *Mayo Clinic HealthQuest*, for members. A Web site also was established, www.elcaforwellness.org, to provide information and encourage healthier behaviors.[48]

Through the Inter-Lutheran Coordinating Committee for Ministerial Health and Wellness of the ELCA and The Lutheran Church–Missouri Synod, the importance of ministerial wellness was emphasized in both church bodies. A "wholeness wheel" was developed as a graphic reminder of various dimensions of wellness. The circular image—used on bookmarks, posters, brochures, and other material—urged members to pursue a spiritually balanced life. Attention was drawn to the dimensions of spiritual well-being. Definitions were offered of various aspects of wholeness, including (1) intellectual,[49] (2) vocational,[50] (3) social and interpersonal,[51] (4) emotional,[52] (5) physical,[53] and (6) financial well-being.[54]

---

[48] *Annual Report*, 2003, Board of Pensions of the Evangelical Lutheran Church in America, p. 2.

[49] A brochure prepared by the Inter-Lutheran Coordinating Committee for Ministerial Health and Wellness highlighted intellectual well-being in this way: "Using our minds keeps them alert and active. Stay curious, ask questions, seek answers. Explore new responsibilities, experience new things, and keep an open mind. And remember, knowing when and how to let your mind rest is as important as keeping it active."

[50] "We all have a calling—a vocation—to follow Christ's example, living a life of meaning, purpose, and service to our neighbor. Our vocations are our life's work and passions—our everyday roles through which God calls us to help make this world a better place. Those who are well vocationally are faithful stewards of their talents and abilities, and find opportunities to build and use them."

[51] "We are created by God to be social beings, living in community and instructed to help and love each other. Make time to build and maintain social well-being through interaction, play, and forgiveness. Take time to nurture your relationships with family, friends, congregation, and co-workers."

[52] "Being emotionally well means feeling the full range of human emotions and expressing them appropriately. Self-awareness is the first step. Recognizing and honoring our own feelings and those of others—stress, contentment, anger, love, sadness, joy, resentment—will help you live life abundantly."

[53] "While we are not all born perfectly healthy or able to live life without injury or illness, we can live well with tending and nurturing. Honor your body as a gift from God. Feed it healthy foods, keep it hydrated, build your physical endurance through regular exercise and respect your body's need for rest."

[54] "In all aspects of well-being, we are called to be stewards. Good financial stewards make decisions based on their values . . . evident in the way they save, spend, and share. This understanding of stewardship embraces resilience, sustainability, and generosity."

The inter-Lutheran committee also published a pamphlet, "A Letter of Peace and Good Health," written by the Rev. James P. Wind. The letter outlined succinctly the biblical foundations for a Christian's concern for health and wholeness. It offered to readers a starting point for reflection on issues of health faced by individuals and society.

High price of "risk factors"

Concern persisted regarding the health of ELCA clergy. Mr. Kapanke sought in October 2006 the support of members of the ELCA Conference of Bishops to promote wellness awareness among pastors, those on the official lay rosters, and their families. He told the Conference of Bishops, "We firmly believe that healthy leaders enhance lives, and if we do not have healthy leaders . . . , we are not going to have effective leaders."

Mr. Kapanke translated the bleak picture of the health statistics into financial terms for the Conference of Bishops. He said that, in 2003, about nine percent of total income in congregations was devoted to synodical and churchwide mission support, while four percent was used for health premiums. If health-care costs continued in the coming years to increase by 10 percent a year, the total amount needed for health premiums in 2013 would be eight percent and the percentage available for mission support could dwindle to five percent.[55]

By 2008, the ELCA health plan shifted from being a "traditional disease model" to a model that emphasized wellness. The message was emphasized repeatedly, "Live well. Healthy leaders enhance lives."[56] This emphasis on healthy leaders was consistent with the commitments made in the "Social Statement on Caring for Health—Our Shared Endeavor." That statement was adopted by the August 2003 ELCA Churchwide Assembly. Declared the statement:

> Each of us has responsibility to be a good steward of his or her own health out of thankfulness for the gift of life and in order to serve God and the neighbor. This means taking effective steps to promote health and prevent illness and disease (for example, eating well, getting adequate exercise and sleep, avoiding use of tobacco and abuse of drugs, limiting alcohol, and using car seat

---

[55] John G. Kapanke, "Report on Clergy Wellness," Conference of Bishops of the Evangelical Lutheran Church in America, October 9, 2006.

[56] *Annual Report*, 2006, Board of Pensions of the Evangelical Lutheran Church in America, p. 1.

restraints). It means balancing responsibility for health with other responsibilities. It also means seeking care as needed. . . .[57]

New rate structure

A new rate structure for the ELCA's Medical and Dental Benefits Plan was put into place in 2001. The rates were adjusted to reflect differences in the cost of health care in various geographic areas. Rates were set synod-by-synod in accord with local costs.[58] As a result, congregations and employers in higher-cost areas for medical and dental care paid more for coverage than those in lower-cost markets.[59] Some congregations and employers, therefore, experienced significant increases in premiums while others remained steady or decreased in the first year of the new rates. With this change, the Board of Pensions began basing the minimum and maximum charges on cost factors in local areas, seeking to ensure that the total contributions of each synod were in line with the cost of coverage within the given area.[60]

System-wide cost-sharing for medical and dental coverage had been embraced prior to the formation of the ELCA. Theoretically, congregations of greater means throughout the ELCA were to subsidize the health-care costs of those with lesser means. What actually was happening, however, was this: Congregations located in areas with lower medical costs were subsidizing those in areas of higher medical costs. As a result, even though rates were based on salaries paid, congregations paying higher salaries were not necessarily subsidizing those paying lower salaries, as the original concept had suggested. Thus, the shift to synodically based rates resulted in more effective implementation of actual cost-sharing for the health care of members.[61]

A health-care advocacy line was established in the years 1999-2001 to assist plan members and their families. Then, in 2006, a 24-hour "NurseLine®" was added to the program.[62] Through this service, registered nurses helped

---

[57] CA03.05.13, "Social Statement on Caring for Health—Our Shared Endeavor," *2003 Reports and Records: Minutes,* Eighth Churchwide Assembly of the Evangelical Lutheran Church in America, Milwaukee, Wis., August 11-17, 2003, p. 173.

[58] *Annual Report,* 2000, p. 5.

[59] *2001 Pre-Assembly Report,* p. 134.

[60] Action Number PN99.11.65, *Minutes,* Board of Trustees of the Board of Pensions of the ELCA, November 5-7, 1999, p. 20.

[61] *Minutes,* Board of Trustees of the Board of Pensions of the ELCA, November 6-8, 1998, p. 6.

[62] Minutes, Board of Trustees of the Board of Pensions of the ELCA, November 3-5, 2006, p. 5.

individuals evaluate their symptoms to decide between self-care, a visit to a physician, or emergency room treatment. Assistance also was offered to identify possible side effects and interactions of medications. Guidance was available too for managing chronic conditions. This "disease management program" was implemented to assist those living with chronic diabetes, heart disease, certain cancers, low-back pain, and fibromyalgia.[63]

The movement in the health plan from a "disease" model to a "wellness" model required no small effort. Thus, there could be no easing of efforts to motivate members to healthier patterns of behavior. The costs of "disease" versus "wellness" could be enormous. Indeed, the Board of Pensions warned in 2007 that if rising costs were left unchecked, health-care costs could grow to nearly 37 percent of the average defined compensation—from an average cost per member of $9,100 in 2005 to $26,000 in 2015. Meanwhile, if the annual health-care cost trends could be reduced by two percent, that effort could translate into a savings per plan member of $4,300 or a combined total of $150 million for ELCA congregations and other sponsors by 2015.[64]

By the time the plan moved past the middle of the first decade of the new century, the Board of Pensions had shifted from a transaction-based organization to one that was more relationship-based. In this shift, all health claims were outsourced and managed-care networks expanded. The board's collaboration with other denominations in the prescription drug program saved in four-years $12 million for ELCA congregations and other sponsors.[65]

Long-term care

Some synodical assemblies, in the late 1990s, urged the Board of Pensions to offer long-term care insurance under the medical and dental benefits plan. Acknowledging that nursing-home care potentially represented a major financial threat to retired pastors and other church workers, the ELCA Board of Pensions agreed to study the matter.[66] (Likely

---

[63] "Report of the Board of Pensions," 2007 Pre-Assembly Report, Section III, Part 2, Tenth Churchwide Assembly of the Evangelical Lutheran Church in America, Chicago, Ill., August 6-11, 2007, p. 33.

[64] 2007 Pre-Assembly Report, Tenth Churchwide Assembly of the Evangelical Lutheran Church in America, Chicago, Ill., August 6-11, 2007, pp. 34-35.

[65] Minutes, Board of Trustees of the Board of Pensions of the ELCA, August 3-5, 2005, p. 5.

[66] Action Number CA99.06.47, 1999 Reports and Records: Minutes, Sixth Churchwide Assembly of the Evangelical Lutheran Church in America, Denver, Colo., August 16-22, 1999, pp. 597-598.

unknown to the supporters of those resolutions was the fact that the proposal revisited discussion from the 1970s in the Lutheran Church in America.) After that study, a long-term care insurance program was not suggested, in view of the range available from various vendors.

Meanwhile, "financial coaches" of the Board of Pensions sought to help members in retirement planning, pointing to the importance of preparing for various needs. This meant determining core-living expenses such as housing, food, and health coverage, as well as potential concerns for long-term care.[67]

Retiree health-benefit coverage

A challenge with enormous financial implications involved a subsidy obligation inherited from predecessor churches for retiree health-benefit coverage. At one time, the cost of medical-supplement insurance for retired clergy and other retired church workers was paid by the ALC and LCA through allocations in their annual budgets. A phase-out schedule was adopted in each church body—in the ALC in 1982 and the LCA in 1986—to provide a cap on the eventual obligation that was rising sharply. Persons retiring after those dates had to pay an increasing percentage of the cost of coverage.

Under the predecessor ALC formula, the subsidy was to reach zero for those born after 1957. In the predecessor LCA formula, zero was to be reached for those born after 1962. Prior to formation of the ELCA, the AELC did not offer medical coverage for retirees. With changes put into effect in 1991, former AELC members became eligible for subsidized coverage when they purchased the ELCA Supplement to Medicare Benefits.

The ALC subsidized both member and spouse coverage, but limited any subsidies to those over age 65. By contrast, the LCA subsidized both pre- and post-65 coverage for plan members only. Retired LCA participants were responsible for the cost of spouse coverage.

For the formation of the ELCA, one complicating factor in handling the retiree medical subsidy obligation was the difference in funding practices between the ALC and LCA. The ALC, through a major appeal in the early 1980s for support of seminaries, had included a $7 million allocation to "pre-fund" the retiree subsidy. The LCA operated on a "pay-as-you-go" pattern.

The disparity in funding generated some intense feelings in the years of planning for the ELCA. A motion even was presented to the ALC's

---

[67] *Minutes*, Board of Trustees of the Board of Pensions of the ELCA, November 3-5, 2006, p. 9.

Church Council in 1985 that suggested a delay in the planned union of the ALC, LCA, and AELC until the funding matter could be resolved. ALC Presiding Bishop David W. Preus, however, asked that no action be taken on the motion. "We are in negotiations," he said. "I don't think we should throw in threats."[68]

In the pre-merger agreements, the decision was made that six percent of the contributions received from former LCA congregations in the ELCA would be allocated for the retiree medical subsidy of former LCA plan members. Philosophically, that decision reflected convictions of the previous half century—namely, that pension and benefits were to be treated as an expense of the congregations and other employing entities, not as a matter of benevolence or mission support. The basic problem with the decision was that the pattern of six percent from specific congregations fundamentally did not work.

The Church Council of the Evangelical Lutheran Church in America also expressed concern that the funding plan perpetuated the distinction among congregations based on predecessor church body affiliation. As a result, in November 1989, the council asked that the ELCA's Board of Pensions and various members of the churchwide staff develop other funding options.[69]

At its April 21-23, 1990, meeting, the ELCA's Church Council adopted changes in the post-retirement medical benefits coverage to: (1) subsidize through the churchwide budget post-retirement health benefits into the future, in spite of escalating costs and limited resources; (2) eliminate predecessor church distinctions in the subsidy; (3) avoid significant changes for persons closest to retirement; and (4) match future costs with existing funding.

Major changes for retirees

A new uniform formula for the subsidy of post-retirement medical benefits replaced the separate schedules that had been in place in predecessor plans.[70] Changes that became effective January 1, 1991, included:

---

[68] "To Pre-Pay or Not to Pre-Pay? Pension Boards Differ on Funding Practices for Future Benefits," News Release of the Lutheran Church in America, August 16, 1985, p. 2.

[69] Action Number CC89.11.158, *Minutes*, Church Council of the Evangelical Lutheran Church in America, November 18, 1989, p. 20.

[70] "Report of the Board of Pensions," *1991 Reports and Records*, Vol. 1, Second Churchwide Assembly of the Evangelical Lutheran Church in America, Orlando, Fla., August 28–September 4, 1991, p. 691.

(1) a cap on the Medicare Part B premium reimbursement under the LCA continuation plan at $40 per month;

(2) acceleration of indexing of the deductible amount, co-payments, and the maximum benefit limitations under all of the ELCA-operated retiree medical plans;

(3) implementation for most future retirees with predecessor service of a less generous subsidy formula that was called the "175 percent formula"; and

(4) allocation of necessary additional amounts in the annual budget of the ELCA churchwide organization to fund post-retirement subsidies, beginning with $5.8 million in fiscal year 1990. Actuarial projections at the time suggested that such an annual amount would fund fully the remaining obligation in about 20 years.[71]

Effective January 1, 1991, all eligible members retiring on or after that day were covered under the ELCA Medical and Dental Benefits Plan, rather than a predecessor plan for retirees.[72]

Prior to changes in the subsidy plan in 1991, a study commissioned by the Board of Pensions and conducted by consultants from Towers Perrin reported that, as of January 1, 1990, $63 million was held in trust for the former ALC's projected obligation of $72.4 million, but no funds were reserved for the former LCA's obligation of $94.2 million. Moreover, the obligation for LCA retirees had nearly doubled in the three years since December 31, 1987, when a figure of $49.4 million was projected.[73]

The "175 percent formula"

The percent of the subsidy for Medicare supplement coverage for those entitled to such a benefit was determined by what became known as "the 175 percent formula." Under the formula, the last two digits of the individual's birth year were multiplied by two. Then added to that number was the member's year of ordination. The combined total was subtracted from 175, resulting in the percentage of subsidy for the member.

---

[71] "Report to the Budget and Finance Committee," Minutes, Church Council of the Evangelical Lutheran Church in America, April 21-23, 1990, Exhibit L, Part 2.

[72] Action Number CC90.04.16, Minutes, Church Council of the Evangelical Lutheran Church in America, April 21-23, 1990, p. 28.

[73] Towers Perrin, "Analysis of Retiree Medical Benefit Obligations," Board of Pensions of the ELCA, February 1989, pp. 14 and 17.

For example, if a pastor was born in 1936 and ordained in 1961, he[74] would be entitled to a subsidy of 42 percent on his supplemental medical premiums (two times 36 equals 72; 72 plus 61 equals 133; 175 minus 133 equals 42). Or, for a pastor born in 1933 and ordained in 1958, the subsidy would cover 51 percent of the premiums. By contrast, a pastor born in 1941 and ordained in 1967 would receive a 26 percent subsidy. And a pastor born in 1949 and ordained in 1974 would be entitled to a subsidy of three percent. A subsidy based on one-half the member's percentage was added for a living spouse. For the surviving spouse, the subsidy was continued at three-fourths of the rate to which the pastor was entitled during retirement years.[75]

With the 1991 changes, any subsidy for those pre-age 65 was eliminated. In general, the formula meant that the more years a member served under the ALC or LCA plans, the higher the level of subsidy. For those who were eligible to retire on December 31, 1987, the previous tables applied, not the new formula.

Eliminated by a common phase-out schedule were the prior church body distinctions. Moreover, the cost for administering the retiree medical subsidy was reduced by the formula.

The changes led to a substantial reduction in the funding requirements for former LCA retirees, decreasing the ELCA's obligation from a 1989 projected, long-term obligation of $167 million to $120 million. The assumed level of savings in the subsidy, however, did not last long. Substantial increases in medical costs in the late 1990s, driven especially by sharply escalating pharmacy costs, raised the annual obligation for funding and extended the funding period well into the twenty-first century.

By 2000, the ALC pre-funding had grown to $117 million. Meanwhile, the balance in the fund for LCA and AELC funding stood at $17 million. The combined total of $134 million existed for projected obligations at that time of $258 million, a funded ratio of just over 52 percent.[76] The downturn in the market immediately following the turn of the century decreased the funds available. At the same time, projections made in 2002

---

[74] This pronoun is used here because women were not ordained in The American Lutheran Church and Lutheran Church in America until late in 1970.

[75] John G. Kapanke, Memorandum to Former Members of Predecessor Church Health Benefit Plans, "Post-Retirement Health Benefits Coverage," June 11, 1990, pp. 2-3. See also *Minutes*, Church Council, April 21-23, 1990, Exhibit L, Part 2, pp. 1-20.

[76] Attachment 1, "Report to the Budget and Finance Committee," April 2001.

suggested dramatic increases in the annual subsidies, peaking at more than $30 million in the year 2015 alone.[77]

The unfunded obligation was ballooning to some $300 million. In the face of that huge challenge, a study group was formed. The group recommended an increase in funding from both the churchwide budget and the contribution rate set by the Board of Pensions. In addition, for retirees not yet age 65 and those under 65 who were on leave from call, the contribution rate for the health plan was raised in a graduated way.

Anticipated in November 2002 was the need for funding from the ELCA's churchwide annual budget to increase from $5.7 million to $6.7 million within a three-year span. Further, the Board of Pensions agreed to collect a retiree-support contribution of up to 0.9 percent of the defined compensation of active members to help fund the growing obligation.[78] The separate contribution by congregations and other employers to cover the administrative costs of the pension plan was eliminated. Expenses for administration were to be paid, instead, from investment earnings and direct charges to the benefit trusts. That allowed about $1.6 million per year to be redirected to fund retiree medical subsidies.[79]

To slow the growth in the needed subsidy, an increase in the pharmacy co-payments for retirees was implemented. At the same time, some savings were achieved on pharmacy costs through an ecumenical purchasing coalition of about a score of participating church bodies. Initial savings amounted to 17 percent of previous costs.

Through the post-retirement medical subsidy, $17.2 million was provided in 2008 to eligible retired members with service in any of the three predecessor church bodies of the ELCA.[80]

Medicare reimbursement

The retiree medical plans of the predecessor churches were consolidated in the mid-1990s into a new ELCA retiree medical plan. The new plan coordinated more effectively with Medicare coverage, offered benefits that

---

[77] Report of the Ad Hoc Work Group on Post-Retirement Medical Benefits, October 24, 2002, p. 2.

[78] Action Number PN02.11.57, *Minutes*, Board of Trustees of the Board of Pensions of the ELCA, November 1-3, 2002, pp. 20-21.

[79] Report of Ad Hoc Work Group, October 24, 2002, p. 3.

[80] *Annual Report*, 2008, p. 19.

were easier to understand, and eliminated the differences in coverage that had been based on predecessor church affiliation.[81]

These steps were taken to save a substantial amount of money and, thereby, slow the rate of increases in premium costs for the ELCA's medical and dental benefits plan.[82]

At the start of the new century, the ELCA's supplement to Medicare for retirees reimbursed three-fourths of the Part A expenses and 60 percent of the Part B expenses not paid by Medicare. The benefits through the ELCA Medicare primary health coverage were administered by Marsh Affinity Group Services.

The picture for the ELCA retiree supplement changed significantly with the adoption of the Medicare Modernization Act of 2003 that provided drug coverage. A "retiree drug subsidy" became available to the Board of Pensions, beginning in 2006, thereby enabling retirees to gain the benefits of Medicare Part D without becoming a part of that program. The subsidy to the Board of Pensions through Medicare reduced significantly the projected obligation of the ELCA for the subsidy of retiree medical supplement premiums under the ELCA program.[83]

The Medicare drug subsidy initially amounted to about $5.5 million a year, resulting in a reduction in the supplement premium for members and a savings in the subsidy line item in the ELCA's churchwide budget. Revised actuarial projections on the long-term obligation permitted a further reduction in the ELCA's allocation of $2.8 million in 2007 and $2.5 million for 2008—some $4 million below the level that had been anticipated for the latter years of the first decade in the twenty-first century.[84]

Coverage for seminarians

The original ELCA Seminarian Medical Plan and Seminarian Survivor-Benefits Plan, which had been created for individuals and their dependents during their years of theological study, ran into drastic financial difficulty by 1991. Meeting with the Executive Committee of the Church Council on August 31, 1991, President Kapanke of the Board of Pensions reported

---

[81] *Annual Report*, 1996, Board of Pensions of the Evangelical Lutheran Church in America, p. 4.

[82] Memorandum for the Board of Trustees of the Board of Pensions of the ELCA, May 2000.

[83] "Actuarial Report of the ELCA Retiree Medical Plan as of January 1, 2007," Board of Pensions of the ELCA, April 4, 2007, p. 4.

[84] "Aide-Mémoire for Administration and Staff on Funding the Subsidy Related to Retiree Benefits," September 18, 2007, signed by the Secretary of the Evangelical Lutheran Church in America and the President of the Board of Pensions of the ELCA.

both (1) the short-term need to cover the cash-flow problems in the Seminarian Medical Plan and (2) the long-term need to eliminate patient coverage for emotional, chemical, and substance abuse. In 1990, expense reimbursements had exceeded revenues by $385,000; by that point, the plan had an overall deficit of $515,000. Nine large claims during 1990 and 1991 had amounted in themselves to $500,000.

Rates of the Seminarian Medical Plan for the 1991-1992 September-through-August period had to be increased 35 percent, Mr. Kapanke said. Of the 1,641 who were listed as "first professional degree" students at the eight ELCA seminaries, 783 participated at that time in the Seminarian Medical Plan. The average age of the participants was 34. Enrollment in the plan was mandatory for students enrolled in six credit hours or at least two courses per term unless they had other group coverage through an employer or a spouse's employer.[85]

The comparatively small base for the plan meant that any large claim had monumental impact on the program's viability. Amendments were adopted to increase the individual and family deductibles, but that step did not solve the deficit problem. Presidents of the ELCA's eight seminaries saw the need for an alternative program.[86]

The Church Council in November 1991 authorized its Executive Committee to review forthcoming proposals from the seminary presidents and the Board of Pensions on the seminarian health plan and to take immediate action when it was deemed necessary in regard to the plan.[87] President Kapanke urged that a "cap" of $50,000 per seminarian be placed on the lifetime reimbursement level in the plan, effective March 1, 1992. The committee also was told that about $1 million would be needed by August 31, 1992, to close out the plan.[88]

When the Executive Committee of the Church Council met in February 1992, the necessary course was evident. So the committee voted:

---

[85] *Minutes*, Board of Trustees of the Board of Pensions of the ELCA, October 4-6, 1991, pp. 21-22.

[86] *Minutes*, Executive Committee of the Church Council of the Evangelical Lutheran Church in America, August 31, 1991, p. 2.

[87] Action Number CC91.11.143, *Minutes*, Church Council of the Evangelical Lutheran Church in America, November 8-11, 1991, p. 46.

[88] *Minutes*, Executive Committee of the Church Council of the Evangelical Lutheran Church in America, January 15, 1992, p. 2.

To approve the termination of the [ELCA-sponsored] Seminarian Health Plan as of August 31, 1992, subject to payment of claims incurred prior to this date; and

To consent to an additional loan of up to $350,000 (in addition to the $350,000 authorized earlier [in August 1991]) to pay claims that become payable through the ELCA Seminarian Medical and Survivor Benefits Program through the August 31, 1992, termination of the plan, including claims runoff, from the funds for the ELCA continuation of the LCA Ministerial Health Benefits Plan, which loans shall pay seven percent interest per annum (the interest rate used for funding purposes under the ELCA Continuation of the LCA Ministerial Health Benefits Plan) with priority given to the repayment of such loans over the repayment of the loan from the ELCA Board of Pensions's Undesignated Fund [in the amount of $400,000].[89]

In April 1992, the Church Council approved steps to "address transitional issues resulting from the termination" of the seminarian health plan as of August 31, 1992.[90] The final loss from the plan was not as great as originally estimated because of lower than projected actual claims.[91]

To avoid "adverse selection" of only those with catastrophic needs being covered, mandatory enrollment for all seminarians was established under a revised plan. Effective September 1, 1992, the Commercial Travelers Mutual Insurance Company of Utica, N.Y., provided the coverage. To allow for seamless transition from the seminarian health plan into the regular ELCA Medical and Dental Benefits Plan upon their entry onto the roster of ordained ministers, amendments were adopted for the ELCA plan that provided month-for-month credit toward the pre-existing condition rule in place at that time for dependents who had been covered by the Commercial Travelers dependent plan as well as for those who had been

---

[89] Action Number EC/CC92.02.04, *Minutes*, Executive Committee of the Church Council of the Evangelical Lutheran Church in America, February 13-14, 1992, p. 5. The Seminarian Survivor Benefits Program had provided to a member's designated beneficiary, in the event of the member's death, a declining lump sum ranging from $25,000 under age 26 to $10,000 at age 55 or older.

[90] Action Number CC92.04.14, *Minutes*, Church Council of the Evangelical Lutheran Church in America, April 4-5, 1992, p. 57.

[91] *Minutes*, Board of Trustees of the Board of Pensions of the ELCA, October 16-18, 1992, p. 11.

covered by employer-provided group medical coverage prior to enrollment in the ELCA plan.[92]

Evolving experience

In the ELCA Medical and Dental Benefits Plan for pastors, church workers, and their dependents, some signs emerged in 2007 that emphasis on "wellness" was yielding positive results. Analysis of claims revealed "a small but statistically significant decline in potentially avoidable medical and prescription drug claims."[93] Furthermore, members were taking steps to reduce costs through consultation with the ELCA's "NurseLine®" as well as cost-effective use of generic prescription drugs and Express Scripts home delivery service.[94]

Little comfort could be found for members of the ELCA Pension and Other Benefits Program in the fact that the challenge of escalating costs of health care was shared by all entities that provide such coverage throughout the United States. Clearly, more adjustments would be required. Yet, the emphasis of the first decade of the twenty-first century on "wellness" already was proving to be a crucial step for the years ahead.

---

[92] Action Number PN93.07.36, *Minutes*, Board of Trustees of the Board of Pensions of the ELCA, July 16-18, 1993, p. 13.

[93] *Annual Report*, 2007, Board of Pensions of the Evangelical Lutheran Church in America, p. 3.

[94] *Annual Report*, 2007, pp. 2-3.

CHAPTER 4

Solutions Elusive
for Some Problems

Even a modest level of income in retirement for a pastor or church worker requires significant pension funds. The challenge of meeting minimum levels of pension payments faced predecessor church plans from their start. The same was true for the framers of the retirement plan of the Evangelical Lutheran Church in America (ELCA). Their solution was this: Continue the minimum pensions that had been granted in the predecessor American Lutheran Church and Lutheran Church in America. (No similar program existed in the Association of Evangelical Lutheran Churches.)

The planners imagined a phase-out of such pension grants. For the longer term, they reasoned, replacement income through pension and Social Security benefits would be the highest, in terms of the overall percentage, for those persons whose career compensation had been relatively low. In those instances, retirement income could equal or even exceed 100 percent of final compensation. Recognized, however, was the harsh reality that a "lifetime deficiency in compensation levels cannot be corrected suddenly through a pension plan in one's retirement years."[1]

The concern for persons with low pensions persisted in the ELCA. An analysis prepared in 2003 concluded that "the issue of pension equity would be best addressed by ensuring [that] compensation for rostered leaders at least meets minimum synod compensation guidelines. Additional efforts would be best spent on . . . [strategies] to meet the needs of those who served at low compensation and now have low pensions, and those currently serving at low salaries."[2]

---

[1] "Proposed Pension and Other Benefits Program," *Report and Recommendations of the Commission for a New Lutheran Church*, August 1986, p. 174.

[2] "Pension Equity Report," *Minutes*, Appendix VI.C., Section 3A, Board of Trustees of the Board of Pensions of the ELCA, February 28–March 2, 2003, p. 16.

Concern over low compensation

The problem of inadequate pensions for lower salaried members prompted extensive discussion over the years. Approved by various synodical assemblies in the ELCA were resolutions and memorials that called for changes to address the problem. Some of those resolutions even advocated equalized salaries for pastors.

The 1989 Churchwide Assembly received 12 memorials from synodical assemblies on equity in clergy salaries and "equalization of benefits" for pensions. Two additional memorials on the subject came to the 1991 Churchwide Assembly. An extensive report was prepared, declaring:

> . . . one of the principal issues the Evangelical Lutheran Church in America must face is the issue of undercompensation. It is a dual issue and, therefore, a complex issue.
>
> On the one hand, it must be recognized that a sizeable number of ELCA clergy are undercompensated relative to all ELCA clergy. Several distinct groups show a greater tendency to be undercompensated. These include, but are not necessarily limited to, (1) pastors who serve in rural areas, often serving small congregations and often serving two or even three congregations (even when a pastor serves more than one congregation, total compensation shows a strong tendency to be well below average), and (2) pastors who serve in impoverished central cities (congregations in these areas are often larger than rural congregations, but the incomes of the members tend to be quite low, resulting in small budgets and low compensation for the pastor). The question here, then, is whether the disparities that exist are significant enough to warrant a policy response from the Evangelical Lutheran Church in America.
>
> Second, the evidence is strong that ELCA clergy as a whole are undercompensated relative to other professionals with similar amounts and types of education and experience. . . .
>
> Our current system presupposes high levels of congregational and pastoral freedom. It conforms to the polity of the Evangelical Lutheran Church in America. From the perspective of the Lutheran two kingdoms theory, our current system invites a realistic discussion about compensation while affirming Christ's command to love one's neighbor. The abuses of freedom by pastors and congregations do not offset these advantages.

The idea of equalized salary has a strong appeal to some. If all were paid equally, personal advancement would matter less and mobility would be enhanced in this church. However, such a goal is difficult to achieve, and the disadvantages of salary equalization are many. In actual practice, salary equalization may not be as equitable as it appears conceptually.[3]

The nature of the ELCA pension plan was outlined in the compensation study, noting that "the money-purchase type of plan" was adopted by the ELCA for several reasons, including the fact that such a plan "is always fully funded." The ELCA's plan provides (1) protection of participants, (2) some investment control by them, and (3) a variety of retirement options for them. The individual's eventual pension benefit "is based on the amount of contributions to the plan plus investment earnings credited to the individual's account," the study explained. "The participant," however, "bears the investment risk, both before and during retirement."[4]

"The real issue"

The study found that the average clergy salary in the ELCA in 1990 was $31,000, slightly less than the average salary for professors at four-year private colleges. Notable geographical disparity existed for compensation. Clergy salaries in some synods were significantly lower than in other synods.[5] So the assembly urged congregations to follow synodical guidelines on compensation. Synods were asked to adopt or refine their compensation guidelines using data on local costs of living and local comparative compensation information, such as other professions with similar education experience and length of service.[6]

Concern over inadequate compensation persisted. So did advocacy by some for equalized pensions. Unrecognized, it seemed, was the fact that the plan could not be retroactively altered in terms of benefits to plan members. Furthermore, a plan based on the contributions that are a percent of salary meant that eventual benefits would be related to the level of one's salary in an active career.

---

[3] "Equalized Compensation and/or Pension Report," 1991 Reports and Records, Vol. 1, Part 2, Second Churchwide Assembly of the Evangelical Lutheran Church in America, Orlando, Fla., August 28–September 4, 1991, pp. 1261-1262. The entire report was provided to voting members of the 1991 Churchwide Assembly on pp. 1256-1285.

[4] "Equalized Compensation . . . ," 1991, p. 1265.

[5] "Equalized Compensation . . . ," 1991, p. 1266.

[6] Action Number CA91.07.109, 1991 Reports and Records, Vol. 2, pp. 720-722.

The perspective of the board of trustees of the Board of Pensions and also of the Church Council—as reflected in their formal actions—was that the plan was not defective in its design. Rather, the real issue was low compensation for many plan members.

Special Needs Retirement Fund

The 1993 Churchwide Assembly, in seeking to address the needs of those with very limited resources, voted:

> To establish in consultation with the ELCA Board of Pensions a special fund to provide both for additional pension contributions for pastors in situations of low compensation, and for pensioners who are receiving at or near the minimum pensions. This will be a churchwide program to encourage support throughout the Evangelical Lutheran Church in America. . . .[7]

What emerged from that action was a truly noteworthy effort—the "Special Needs Retirement Fund." In a sense, the fund resembled the efforts of Lutherans in the eighteenth, nineteenth, and early twentieth centuries to provide grants to destitute clergy and their survivors.

Of the 10,500 retirees in the plan in 1993, 1,300 persons were receiving minimum pensions of $350 per month for pastors and $233 for surviving spouses, dollar amounts similar to what existed in some of the predecessor plans in the 1950s.[8] Further, by 1998, there were 2,926 retirees and survivors over age 80, just under half of whom received less than $300 a month in pension payments.[9]

Extensive efforts were undertaken to seek resources for the Special Needs Retirement Fund. In meetings with synodical bishops, representatives of the Board of Pensions highlighted the fund, but also expressed concern regarding retired members living on low pensions and non-retired members receiving low compensation. In April 1999, the ELCA's Church Council allocated $500,000 to the endowment fund for the Special Needs Retirement Fund, bringing the total endowment at that point to $1 million.[10] Regular gifts—including a check-off system for contributions from retirees receiving

---

[7] Action Number CA93.08.100, *1993 Reports and Records: Minutes*, Third Churchwide Assembly of the Evangelical Lutheran Church in America, Kansas City, Mo., August 25–September 1, 1993, p. 579.

[8] *1993 Reports and Records: Minutes*, p. 577.

[9] John G. Kapanke, "Employee Information Session," Board of Pensions of the Evangelical Lutheran Church in America, November 19-20, 1998, p. 7.

[10] Action Number CC99.04.23, *Minutes*, Church Council of the Evangelical Lutheran Church in America, April 10-12, 1999, p. 45.

benefits and voluntary payroll deductions by ELCA churchwide staff—yielded additional resources.[11] The fund reached $2 million by 2003. At that point, 550 retirees and their surviving spouses were contributing some $185,000 per year.[12] By July 31, 2008, the balance had grown to $6.1 million.

The fund provided a supplement for those whose total income from all sources was less than $1,100 per month for an individual or $1,350 per month for a couple. Even so, because of the limited amounts in the fund, only about 57 persons in 2007 and 53 in 2008 were benefitting from it. Most of them were widows whose husbands served in the days when pastors were paid very little and pension contributions often were uncertain. The range of monthly payments in 2008 was between $17 and $1,028.

Disbursements from the fund amounted to: *2007*, $116,499; *2006*, $270,753; *2005*, $266,232; *2004*, $305,354; *2003*, $170,481; *2002*, $164,538; and *2001*, $282,429.[13]

Possible model begun in one synod

An innovative effort was undertaken by the ELCA's Eastern North Dakota Synod to address, for the long-term, the issue of low compensation resulting in low pensions. To do so, the Eastern North Dakota Synod Endowment Fund was established with a goal of $5 million. Beginning in 2001, if a pastor had received the previous year less than $33,000 in defined compensation, the synod made-up the shortfall for a pension contribution of 10 percent of that figure. The following year, for those pastors who had a defined compensation in the bottom third within the synod (that is, with less than $37,000), a supplemental pension contribution was made to reach the level of 10 percent of that figure. Market slumps limited progress, but those who had a defined compensation in 2003 of less than $38,000 were granted a pension-contribution supplement. The ultimate goal in the synod is to increase the dollar amount in supplemental pension contributions so that all full-time pastors in the synod will have pension contributions of 10 percent of the average salary of ELCA clergy in any given year.[14]

---

[11] "Report of the Board of Pensions," 1999 *Pre-Assembly Report*, Sixth Churchwide Assembly of the Evangelical Lutheran Church in America, Denver, Colo., August 16-22, 1999, p. 131.

[12] "Pension Equity Report," *Minutes*, Appendix VI.C., Section 3A, Board of Trustees of the Board of Pensions of the ELCA, February 28BMarch 2, 2003, p. 16.

[13] *Minutes*, "Disbursement Report," Special Needs Retirement Fund Managing Committee, August 27, 2008.

[14] "Pension Equity Report," pp. 20-21.

"Realistically" helping second-career members

Given the type of pension programs of the predecessor churches and the ELCA, the retirement plan could not address directly the full needs of "second-career" pastors. Reports indicated that many of them, for a variety of reasons, did not have significant retirement accumulations from prior employment. The ELCA plan was designed to provide a pension based on the total years of ordained or lay rostered service. Therefore, the plan could not ensure the adequacy of retirement accumulations for those with shorter terms of participation than 35 to 40 years. As expressed in the "core pension strategy report" in 2000, the primary responsibility of the Board of Pensions "to second-career members is to provide them with the tools to build their ELCA retirement income and to inform and educate them on a timely basis. This involves helping them to assess their prospects realistically and assisting them to develop a plan for maximizing their retirement income."[15]

Controversial coverage

The complexities of medical care and definitions of coverage were evident over the years in various ways. One of the most sensitive manifestations of that occurred in the mid-1990s. In May 1995, the board of trustees proposed an amendment to the ELCA Medical and Dental Benefits Plan to limit coverage of induced abortions to three situations: (1) where the mother's life was threatened; (2) where the pregnancy resulted from rape or incest; or (3) where the embryo or fetus had lethal abnormalities incompatible with life.[16] That amendment was submitted for consideration by the ELCA's Church Council. Before the amendment came to the council, however, a nine-member work group was appointed by then Bishop Herbert W. Chilstrom. The work group was to discuss how the "Social Statement on Abortion" was to be interpreted in relation to the church's health plan.[17] That social statement had been adopted by the

---

[15] "Core Pension Strategy," Appendix XI.C, Section 3A, *Agenda*, Board of Trustees of the Board of Pensions of the ELCA, November 3-5, 2000, p. 3.

[16] Action Number P95.05.19, *Minutes*, Board of Trustees of the Board of Pensions of the ELCA, May 12, 1995, p. 5.

[17] *Minutes*, Board of Trustees of the Board of Pensions of the ELCA, August 3-4, 1995, p. 6. The nine-member work group included trustees Sandra G. Gustavson and Carolyn S. Nestingen from the Board of Pensions, the Rev. Karen L. Bloomquist, director for studies, and the Rev. James M. Childs, board member from the Division for Church in Society, the Rev. Donald M. Hallberg and Ms. Deborah S. Yandala from the Church Council, Bishop Charles H. Maahs from the Central States Synod representing the Conference of Bishops, with the Rev. Lowell G. Almen, ELCA secretary, and Ms. Lita Brusick Johnson, executive assistant to the bishop, serving as co-conveners at the request of Bishop Herbert W. Chilstrom.

1991 ELCA Churchwide Assembly as guidance for moral discernment on the issue.[18]

Staff and trustees of the Board of Pensions had thought the amendment would make the health plan more consistent with the terms of the social statement. The churchwide unit responsible for interpretation of the social statement—then known as the Division for Church in Society—disagreed and sought to emphasize the importance of individual moral discernment on such an issue.

The work group studied the social statement and reviewed various issues, including medical confidentiality. In its report to the Church Council, the work group said:

> We appreciate the good faith effort of the Board of Pensions in suggesting amendments that attempt to bring the medical plan administration into closer conformity with this church's "Social Statement on Abortion." We find some basis in the "Social Statement on Abortion" for the suggested amendments. We recommend, however, that the Church Council consider what we believe is an alternative more consistent with a comprehensive understanding of the implications of the "Social Statement on Abortion." Such an understanding would include a recognition that "abortion ought to be an option only of last resort" because of the basic moral presumption to preserve and protect life as well as an awareness of the complex difficulties involved in moral decision-making. On this basis, the alternative that we recommend is to continue the current language and administrative practice of the ELCA's medical plan and to provide for the education of ELCA plan participants and all members of the ELCA through a communication that reflects the full range of concerns in the "Social Statement on Abortion," not only for specific abortion decisions but also for the creation of a general ethos of responsibility. . . .[19]

The ELCA's Church Council voted to concur with the work group's recommendation, "acknowledging especially that abortion ought to be an option only of last resort because of the basic moral presumption of

---

[18] Action Number CA91.06.38, *Reports and Records: Minutes*, 1991, p. 553.

[19] *Minutes*, Church Council of the Evangelical Lutheran Church in America, November 17-20, 1995, Exhibit J, Part 3d, p. 6.

preserving and protecting life. . . ." The council also underscored "the complex difficulties involved in moral decision-making" and asked for development of a document "to assist ELCA medical plan members and all members of this church in moral deliberation. . . ."[20]

Prior to the council's meeting, the Conference of Bishops endorsed the work group's recommendation. In so doing, the Conference of Bishops declared, however, that the report was to be understood as offering no support for anyone who would promote "abortion on demand or last trimester abortions."[21]

Upon recommendation by the board of trustees of the Board of Pensions, an amendment to the medical plan was adopted in April 1997 that specifically excluded late-term abortions, except when the life of the mother was threatened or when the fetus had lethal abnormalities indicating death as imminent.[22] "Late term," in the administration of the plan, was understood as a pregnancy beyond 20 weeks.

The ELCA's 1991 "Social Statement on Abortion" recognized the complexity of specific situations and said, "We recognize that conscientious decisions need to be made in relation to difficult circumstances that vary greatly. What is determined to be a morally responsible decision in one situation may not be in another."[23] The statement declared, "Abortion ought to be an option only of last resort,"[24] and added, "Because of the Christian presumption to preserve and protect life, this church, in most instances, encourages women with unintended pregnancies to continue the pregnancy."[25]

Interpreting the decision of the Church Council on this topic was an ongoing challenge. An abundance of letters and e-mails were received in the following years in which individuals charged that the ELCA health plan supported "abortion on demand." Clearly, that was neither the intent nor substance of the council's decision. To help plan members and others

[20] Action Number CC95.11.79, *Minutes*, Church Council of the Evangelical Lutheran Church in America, November 17-20, 1995, pp. 19-20.

[21] *Minutes*, Church Council of the Evangelical Lutheran Church in America, November 17-20, 1995, p. 19.

[22] Action Number CC97.04.31, *Minutes*, Church Council of the Evangelical Lutheran Church in America, April 6, 1997, p. 97.

[23] *Reports and Records*, 1991, p. 558.

[24] *Reports and Records*, 1991, p. 556.

[25] *Reports and Records*, 1991, p. 557.

understand the importance of moral deliberations on abortion as well as other medical questions, a brochure was developed and distributed to plan members. The brochure reminded readers:

> Lutherans do not have ethical "canon law" to direct us in moral decision-making. Such responsibility rests with each individual. Guided by God's Spirit, instructed by the witness of Scripture, and informed by the deliberations and conversations of the community of faith, Lutherans make decisions in daily life.[26]

Challenge of technology

An ongoing challenge for the operation of the Board of Pensions revolved around issues of technology. Changes and refinements in the ELCA Pension and Other Benefits Program over the years depended on adequate information technology to support such adjustments. Staff and trustees of the Board of Pensions learned at various times that, in any grand plan for development, technology may prove to be an effective means or an expensive culprit.

The original Pension and Benefits System (PBS) was viewed in the mid-1990s as cumbersome, outdated, and inadequate for the board's rapidly expanding services. A new Pension Administration System (PAS) was intended to support the pension and investment changes. That PAS dream, however, evolved into "a very challenging project."[27] The objective was to implement a system that would enable the Board of Pensions to meet, in cost-effective ways, "its information-processing needs and deliver competitive benefits and services to members and sponsoring organizations and support the goals of the Customer Service Strategy."[28]

The project proved to be significantly larger than originally estimated. Once scheduled to be operational in early 1997, repeated delays took place. By mid-1997, the project was running more than 50 percent over the original budget estimate of $4.4 million. Due to "Year 2000" (Y2K) issues, the trustees were told that PAS had to be completed within 18 months. Otherwise, other steps would need to be taken to (1) modify the then existing Pension Benefits System to meet "Y-2-K" requirements or (2) purchase an alternative system, if one were available.[29]

---

[26] "Abortion and the Church Medical Plan," a brochure distributed to members of the ELCA's Medical and Dental Benefits Plan, 1996, p. 3.

[27] *Minutes*, Board of Trustees of the Board of Pensions of the ELCA, May 29-30, 1997, p. 5.

[28] *Minutes*, Board of Trustees of the Board of Pensions of the ELCA, November 8-9, 1997, p. 9.

[29] *Minutes*, Board of Pensions, May 29-30, 1997, p. 5.

A subcommittee of the trustees was appointed in May 1997, including Emma Porter as chair, Willis Else, and John Roberts.[30] The subcommittee decided to proceed with an analysis of the existing Pension Benefits System to determine what work would be needed to make PBS "Year 2000" compliant.[31]

Both PriceWaterhouse and Actoras Consulting Group were retained by the Board of Pensions to study problems with the project. PriceWaterhouse identified the steps that would be needed to make the existing PBS system compliant for year 2000. (When 2000 arrived, no problems were experienced by the Board of Pensions on "Y2K" matters.)

The Actoras Consulting Group found PAS to be "a very high risk project." The project needed immediate corrective action if it was to be completed successfully, the trustees were told.[32] Based on its initial findings, Actoras was asked to proceed with a technical review of PAS technology or seek an alternative solution.[33] At that point, the estimated cost of the whole project was $8 million, including $5 million for contractors and $3 million for internal staffing.[34]

The project proved ill-fated. It was shut down in December 1997 because of unacceptable overruns in costs and the likely failure of the new system to achieve its goals.[35] Frustratingly, that was not the end of problems with information technology.

Another ill-fated software project involved Spherion Pacific Workforce, a firm that had been engaged in 2001 to design, develop, and make operational a new software system to serve the needs of the Board of Pensions. The new Enrollment and Eligibility System (EES), which was intended to replace the PBS system, was to be functioning by September 30, 2002, with a maximum expenditure of $3.7 million. After considerable cost overruns and still no functioning system, the Board of Pensions terminated the Spherion contract in April 2003.[36] The Board of Pensions sued Spherion

---

[30] *Minutes*, Board of Pensions, May 29-30, 1997, p. 2.

[31] "Consultant Reports and PAS Alternatives," Memorandum from John G. Kapanke to Board of Trustees, October 30, 1997, p. 1.

[32] *Minutes*, Board of Trustees of the Board of Pensions of the ELCA, July 31–August 1, 1997, p. 3.

[33] *Minutes*, Board of Pensions, July 31–August 1, 1997, p. 4.

[34] *Minutes*, Board of Pensions, November 8-9, 1997, p. 10.

[35] "Report of the Board of Pensions," *1999 Pre-Assembly Report*, p. 132.

[36] About $8 million had been spent on the project, which was a year behind schedule, with no end in sight.

for recovery of the money expended on the project. A settlement was reached in the matter in May 2006, and the lawsuit was dropped.

Meanwhile, the "architecture" for an EES program was simplified and redesigned for less complexity in operating and maintaining the system. Responsibility for development of the new program was assigned to staff of the Board of Pensions, assisted by some contract help and the guidance of a consultant. The new EES program was put into full operation in 2004.

Impact of Tax Reform Act of 1986

Early in the operation of the ELCA's Board of Pensions, the implications of the U.S. Tax Reform Act of 1986 had to be addressed. Although passed into law in 1986, its provisions did not go into effect until 1989. Prior to that time, no coverage rules or non-discrimination rules existed for tax-sheltered annuities. The non-discrimination rules ensured that participation and contributions would not unduly favor higher-compensated employees in any employer-provided retirement plans. The 1986 Tax Reform Act continued to offer an exception for church plans that covered congregations or qualified church-controlled organizations, such as day-care facilities or elementary schools operated by congregations to serve primarily church members. That exception, however, did not extend to other church-related organizations, such as social ministry organizations or Lutheran hospitals serving the general public. They had been excluded by the 1984 Deficit Reduction Act.[37] Two years later, the 1986 act clarified the rules, stipulating that employees of such church-affiliated institutions had to be in a separate plan.

As a result of those changes in federal law, institutional plans were created by the ELCA Board of Pensions for social ministry organizations. The ELCA Master Institutional Retirement Plan (MIRP) and the ELCA Master Institutional Savings Plan (MISP) were available to The Evangelical Lutheran Good Samaritan Society and 31 other ELCA institutions from 1988 into 2002. On July 1, 2002, MIRP and MISP were combined into one plan for 31 of those institutions, while a separate ELCA Retirement Plan for The Evangelical Lutheran Good Samaritan Society was established to serve the particular needs of that organization.[38]

---

[37] The Deficit Reduction Act of 1984 narrowed the definition of church plans and at that point excluded organizations that are not "qualified church-controlled organizations," meaning those that normally receive more than 25 percent of their support from the sum of governmental sources and fees or sales.

[38] *Minutes*, Board of Trustees of the Board of Pensions of the ELCA, March 1-3, 2002, pp. 26-27.

Both the institutional plan and the plan for the Good Samaritan Society offered the same investment funds as the ELCA plan. One key difference was that the Good Samaritan plan contained the option of a lump-sum withdrawal after retirement or separation from service.[39]

Active involvement in "Church Alliance"

While internal planning and administration were essential for operation of the Board of Pensions, continuing engagement in the Church Alliance was crucial in the external legislative and policy context. The Church Alliance, an ecumenical coalition of 38 Roman Catholic, Lutheran, Protestant, and Jewish groups, monitors federal legislation that may affect programs of church pensions and other benefits. Mr. John Kapanke of the ELCA Board of Pensions serves as chair of the steering committee of the Church Alliance and Mr. Robert Rydland, general counsel of the Board of Pensions, as the secretary and treasurer.

The Church Alliance advocates on behalf of church benefits programs. The alliance itself is a coalition of the leaders who oversee the pension, benefit, and health-care coverages of more than a million ordained ministers, lay church workers, and their dependents.

When the practice of granting ordained ministers a tax exclusion for their housing costs came under judicial attack and a possible legislative threat in 2002, the Church Alliance generated widespread ecumenical support for preserving the exclusion. The need for Congressional action had become evident in a U.S. federal case between the Internal Revenue Service and two West Coast petitioners, Richard D. and Elizabeth K. Warren. The federal "Clergy Housing Allowance Act" was approved by the U.S. Congress and subsequently was signed into law by President George W. Bush on May 20, 2002. The act clarified the portion that clergy may exclude from taxes for housing. Without that legislation, clergy of all denominations would have faced a substantial tax increase in addition to the continuing requirement that they must pay the "self-employed" rate for Social Security.[40]

The pattern of a federal tax exclusion of clergy housing expenses for ordained ministers who do not live in parsonages originated in the 1920s. Through various revisions in the U.S. tax code, the exclusion was defined and clarified. Perhaps history will show, however, that the most strategic

---

[39] *Minutes*, Board of Pensions, March 1-3, 2002, p. 27.

[40] *Annual Report*, 2002, Board of Pensions of the Evangelical Lutheran Church in America, p. 2.

legislative decision in relation to the tax exclusion for clergy housing expenses was the 2002 act of Congress.

In addition to the Church Alliance, engagement by the ELCA's Board of Pensions in ecumenical endeavor has included the Church Benefits Association (CBA), previously known as the Church Pensions Conference.[41] Each year since 1915, the CBA and its predecessor organizations sponsored an annual conference for church pension programs. The conference provides a forum for exploration of common challenges and attention to evolving developments affecting church pension programs. The conference includes seminars and workshops for key staff of church pension and benefit programs. In addition, the CBA compiles statistical information on various church pension plans and financial information about costs of benefits.[42]

Era of intense social activism

Some of the issues faced by the ELCA's Board of Pensions had their roots in the experience of the predecessor church bodies and also in the context of the times. For example, with the onset of intense social activism throughout many U.S. church bodies in the late 1960s and beyond, pension programs came under pressure related to investments. Clearly, from the perspective of subsequent history, many clergy and members seemed to fail to understand that the money invested through pension plans was not "the church's money." Those funds were to be held in trust for the clergy and other church workers who eventually were to receive their pension benefits. Moreover, boards of trustees had legal duties to exercise fiduciary responsibility guided by "prudent person" principles.

In various U.S. church bodies—not only among Lutherans—efforts emerged, especially in the 1980s and 1990s, to promote socially responsible investment practices. Proxy resolutions were promoted as a way of motivating or forcing change in the practices of publicly held corporations. Tensions, at times heated, developed between church activists and pension administrators. Gradually, understandings began to emerge that social responsibility committees in church bodies could provide advice to pension trustees but could not direct the decisions of those trustees on investment policies and practices.

---

[41] The group was known as the Interdenominational Secretaries' Conference prior to 1931 and from 1931 through 2000 as the Church Pensions Conference.

[42] "History and Background," Church Benefits Association (www.churchbenefitsassocation. org), pp. 1-2.

Both the administration and the governance of church pension plans represent a paradox. On the one hand, they are church-sponsored plans to be operated in accord with the church-approved documents. On the other hand, the trustees and administrators of the plans are legally bound to provide benefits to beneficiaries of the plans. So there is a functional interaction between the governance of the church body (in the case of the ELCA, the Churchwide Assembly and the Church Council) and the trustees of the pension programs who bear the fiduciary duty for the operation.[43] Trustees and administrators are obligated to seek the maximum retirement benefit for beneficiaries.

Topic dominated agendas

Apartheid in South Africa and the oppression of the people of Namibia by South African troops dominated the agendas of church conventions throughout the late 1970s and all of the 1980s (see Chapter 5). Caught in the "hurricanes" of those debates were the pension boards of the ALC and LCA, two of the ELCA's three predecessor church bodies.

Amid the debates on investment policies, options did emerge in various U.S. church bodies as alternative equity, bond, and balanced funds developed with particular criteria. Individual plan participants could opt to have contributions placed in funds with certain "screens" or social stipulations. Even plans for such "screened" funds were not adequate in the minds of some members. Thus, intense pressure was directed toward divestment of holdings in corporations with business interests in South Africa.

As of July 1, 1991, ELCA plan members were given the option of moving their accumulations to "South Africa Free" Funds. Those funds did not last long. Advocacy for them ended when Namibia gained its independence in 1990 and salutary changes began to emerge in South Africa. In the move to majority rule, Mr. Nelson Mandela was elected the first Black president of South Africa on April 27, 1994.[44] With the end to apartheid and the emergence of majority rule in South Africa, those funds were eliminated effective April 1, 1995.

---

[43] Trustees of the Board of Pensions of ELCA are elected to six-year, non-renewable terms by the voting members of the ELCA's Churchwide Assembly. The president of the Board of Pensions is elected to four-year, renewable terms by the board of trustees with the concurrence of the presiding bishop of the ELCA.

[44] Nelson Mandela was released from prison on February 11, 1990, after nearly 30 years of imprisonment for his opposition to apartheid.

Interestingly, the vocal pressure on divestment issues heard in ELCA assemblies actually was not shared by most clergy members of the ELCA pension plan, according to a survey on the investment screens. Kenneth W. Inskeep, a researcher in the ELCA's churchwide office, found that the "vast majority" of participants in the pension fund were "unwilling" to risk—by the "broad application" of investment screens—"their pension benefits in the cause of social justice." At the same time, however, he did find that some clergy favored screening all pension investments "to promote a more socially responsible society and a more just world," even at the risk of their eventual pension-retirement income.[45]

Various social purpose funds were developed and maintained for plan participants who wished to have the option of screened funds. The success of those funds offered an example of the ways in which the trustees and administrators of the Board of Pensions sought to serve conscientiously the needs of the ELCA.

---

[45] Kenneth W. Inskeep, "Views on Social Responsibility: The Investment of Pension Funds in the Evangelical Lutheran Church in America," *Review of Religious Research*, Vol. 33, No. 3, March 1992, p. 279.

CHAPTER 5

Divestment Debate
Dominates Early Years

In the escalating debate on divestment, roiling clouds of an impending storm loomed on the immediate horizon in late August 1989. As the first Churchwide Assembly of the Evangelical Lutheran Church in America was called to order in the Rosemont Center in suburban Chicago on August 23, 1989, many of the 1,037 voting members seemed focused exclusively on that single issue.

What resembled a circus atmosphere prevailed after individuals advocating immediate divestment leased space adjacent to the assembly's plenary hall. They greeted arriving voting members, passing out pamphlets and advocating for divestment from companies doing business in South Africa. Some voting members seemed confused, thinking that the divestment displays were part of the assembly's program. A false rumor even circulated that the space for divestment advocates was being funded by the churchwide budget.

In the previous biennium, 13 synodical assemblies in 1988 had adopted memorials on divestment, 10 of which were identical in urging that the "sense of the church be so communicated to the Board of Pensions that there be no question or doubt that the Evangelical Lutheran Church in America intends and insists that the board divest of all companies doing business in South Africa."[1]

In 1989, 41 synods approved memorials on the topic, 27 of which repeated the divestment action adopted at the constituting of the ELCA but they were even more expansive in their declarations. That May 2, 1987, resolution had declared the ELCA's "unqualified opposition to the apartheid system in South Africa, and the illegal occupation and oppression by South Africa of Namibia." At the same time, the promise was made to "work tirelessly to see

---

[1] *1989 Reports and Records: Minutes,* First Churchwide Assembly of the Evangelical Lutheran Church in America, Rosemont, Ill., August 23-30, 1989, p. 779.

that none of *our* ELCA pension funds will be invested in companies doing business in South Africa."[2] The resolution did not make clear the meaning of "our" in regard to pension funds. Did "our" refer to those voting who had pension accounts? Or did it suggest incorrectly that the funds belonged to the ELCA churchwide organization? The latter misunderstanding appeared to be a continuing issue in much of the debate on divestment.

The 1989 synodical memorials sought to define the meaning of the 1987 resolution as a commitment to "the intentional (not passive) and complete (not partial) divestment of all funds of the ELCA's Board of Pensions—new funds, pre-merger funds, consolidated funds and those managed by the board" involving "both direct and indirect investments in companies doing business in South Africa." Demanded was "complete divestment . . . before January 1, 1991."[3]

The memorials further asserted that if the Board of Pensions were to fail to complete divestment on that schedule, the Church Council was directed "to initiate changes immediately in the documents governing the Board of Pensions" that would be necessary "to require the Board [of Pensions] to implement resolutions of the Churchwide Assembly relating to investments."[4]

Policy statement on divestment

The printed report of the Memorials Committee to the 1989 assembly recounted the process of the previous two years in addressing the issue. Clearly, a long and somewhat complex "legislative" path on the issue of divestment had been trod in the biennium leading up to that first ELCA Churchwide Assembly.

The Church Council, in April 1988, had "transmitted as advice to the Board of Pensions" a social investment screen related to South African divestment. The screen had been proposed by the ELCA's churchwide Advisory Committee on the Church's Corporate Responsibility. At the same time, the council asked the Board of Pensions "to share its divestment strategy and projected time line for complete divestment . . ." at the council's July 1988 meeting.[5]

---

[2] Action Number ELCA 87.02.50, *Minutes*, Constituting Convention of the Evangelical Lutheran Church in America, Columbus, Ohio, April 30–May 3, 1987, p. 63. The italic type was added in this quotation for emphasis on the perspective expressed by it.

[3] *Reports and Records: Minutes*, 1989, p. 781.

[4] *Reports and Records: Minutes*, 1989, p. 781.

[5] Action Number CC88.04.41, *Minutes*, Church Council of the Evangelical Lutheran Church in America, April 9-11, 1988, p. 70.

In response to the Church Council's request, the board of trustees of the Board of Pensions adopted a policy statement on divestment. The statement, which was approved by the board of trustees on June 3, 1988, said:

> As part of the Evangelical Lutheran Church in America, the Board of Pensions continues to be sympathetic to the plight of the oppressed people of South Africa [and] Namibia. It joins Christians throughout the world in condemning, without reservation, the policies of apartheid that prevail in those nations. . . .

> The Board of Pensions of the ELCA . . . has expended a great effort in considering how it can respond, within the fiduciary responsibilities placed upon the Board [of Pensions] by Minnesota trust laws and the ELCA Bylaws, . . . to the will of the church as expressed, first in the constituting convention relative to divestment of U.S. companies with South Africa investments and, second, by the Church Council.[6]

> The Board [of Pensions] is responsible not only to the ELCA as a whole, but also . . . the Board [of Pensions] is responsible to the members of the Pension Plan and their beneficiaries. The Board [of Pensions] must constantly bear in mind that the trust assets it manages do not belong to the ELCA, but to the members of the Plan. Fiduciary responsibility means that the Board [of Pensions] is bound, not only by trust law, but also by the ELCA, to consider, in the first instance, the interests of the members and beneficiaries, and exercise its responsibilities in a prudent manner for the sole purpose of the financial well-being of the members and beneficiaries.

> Taking the above into consideration, the Board of Pensions has chosen the following steps:

> First, the Board of Pensions has directed that, whenever the conditions of risk and return are equal in the choice among stocks and bonds held by the Board [of Pensions] on behalf of plan members, or available for purchase, the holdings in companies with South Africa investments will be divested, and similarly, investments in these companies will not be made.[7]

---

[6] The reference here was to the resolution of advice transmitted by the Church Council on April 9, 1988 (see above).

[7] This was known as the "equivalency policy," which had been practiced previously for the pensions investments within The American Lutheran Church.

Second, in order to give the members of the pension plans maximum opportunity to direct their own accumulations to the existing Social Purpose Funds, which have no holdings in companies with direct investments in South Africa, the Board [of Pensions] seeks agreement from the Church Council to amend the Pension Plan so as to allow all non-retired members freely to respond to the South African divestment issue by transferring their accumulations among funds, and specifically to and from the Social Purpose Funds.

Third, the Board [of Pensions] seeks approval from the Church Council to establish a third Social Purpose Fund, a "balanced fund" that includes both stocks and bonds.

Fourth, although the Board of Pensions is prohibited from offering investment advice to members, it will fully inform all plan members regarding the nature and characteristics of the Social Purpose Funds so that members will know the issues involved in transferring their assets to, or from, Social Purpose Funds. . . .

Fifth, the Board of Pensions will continue to receive advice on proxy matters from the Corporate Social Responsibility Advisory Committee, and will respond cooperatively in shareholder actions to the extent that such actions are in the best interests of the plan members.

Sixth, the Board of Pensions is the manager of various funds that belong to other units of the Church and as such is amenable to direction from them as to the investment of these funds.

Seventh, the Board [of Pensions] will continue to seek constructive ways to deal with the issue of divestment in companies doing business in South Africa. . . .[8]

Response of Church Council

The Church Council responded to the board's policy statement on divestment in July 1988 and endorsed several elements of the board's statement, voting:

---

[8] *Minutes*, Exhibit I-1, Church Council of the Evangelical Lutheran Church in America, July 10-11, 1988, pp. 1-2. See also Action Number ES-PN88.06.36, *Executive Session Minutes*, Board of Trustees of the Board of Pensions of the ELCA, June 3, 1988, pp. 7-8.

1. To affirm:

> That, the resources managed by the Evangelical Lutheran Church in America are to be invested or expended in ways that enhance the mission of this church;[9]

> That, the Board of Pensions, as a churchwide unit of the Evangelical Lutheran Church in America, bears responsibility both to its members and beneficiaries and to the Evangelical Lutheran Church in America as a whole; and, in the light of the action of the ELCA constituting convention, that the Board of Pensions bears a clear responsibility to respond to the oppression of our brothers and sisters in South Africa and Namibia; and

> That, the Board of Pensions will fully reflect the action of the constituting convention that, "None of our ELCA pension funds . . . be invested in companies doing business in South Africa," within the context of its fiduciary responsibility.

2. To encourage the Board of Pensions to do all in its power to accomplish this goal as quickly as legally possible and to come to the November [1988] meeting of the Church Council with a plan that will result in the significant reduction of funds invested in South Africa in the near future.

3. To request that the Board of Pensions provide semi-annual reports to the Church Council that include separate listings of companies in which it has invested that directly or indirectly do business with South Africa.

4. To request that the Board of Pensions prepare for the November 1988 meeting of the Church Council:

> Amendments to the pension plan which would allow all non-retired members to transfer their accumulations among funds, and specifically to and from the Social Purpose Funds; and

> A description of a third Social Purpose Fund, which would be a "balanced fund" including both stocks and bonds.

5. To request that the Board of Pensions and the Commission for Church in Society explore ways to inform fully all plan members regarding the nature and characteristics of the Social Purpose Funds.

---

[9] This refers to funds in endowments of the ELCA churchwide organization.

6. To request that the Board of Pensions and the Commission for Church in Society explore jointly the feasability of petitioning the court of appropriate jurisdiction to seek an interpretation of the laws governing fiduciary responsibility as such laws relate to the divestment issue within the broad scope of the mission of the church; and that the Commission for Church in Society and the Board of Pensions report their findings to the Church Council.[10]

"Pressure-cooker" intensity

Recollections of the "pressure-cooker" intensity of the divestment discussion may have grown muted over the years. Perhaps a statement by the Rev. Herbert W. Chilstrom, the first bishop of the ELCA and chief executive officer of the churchwide organization, offers an example of the tone of the times. He addressed the Church Council at the July 10-11, 1988, meeting, saying:

> I have agonized with others over the question of divestment. There is some merit in the position of the late Alan Paton, a position which states that it is imprudent and prideful for American citizens to pretend to know what is best for South Africa.
>
> Yet, it is a fact of life that I am not as disconnected from South Africa as Mr. Paton and others think I am. It is my money—my pension funds—that are invested in companies doing business in a country that continued to practice apartheid and which persists in ignoring the mandates of the United Nations in its cruel treatment of the people of Namibia.
>
> The Board of Pensions, of course, has given me an alternative. I can transfer all of my accumulations to the social purpose funds. I appreciate this opportunity and have begun to do so. Others can do the same.
>
> But even when I have taken these steps, I find that there lingers with me a sense that it is not enough. I am part of a church. That church has acted repeatedly at its conventions and assemblies—both in predecessor churches and now in the ELCA—to request that we do more than take individual action. It has urged corporate action as well.

---

[10] Action Number CC88.07.83, *Minutes*, Church Council of the Evangelical Lutheran Church in America, July 10-11, 1988, pp. 31-32.

I am of the opinion that most members of the plan are re-alistic about what the Board of Pensions can do. We know that these movements of major amounts of investment funds cannot be done quickly and may never—because of the complexity of the international business community—be total. I believe we would be satisfied if the Board of Pensions took very deliberate steps in that direction, reducing its investments in South Africa whenever possible. Although there is not uniform agreement on how well it was done, I am of the opinion that the history of divestment in the former American Lutheran Church shows that it is possible to reduce significantly our investments in South Africa.

From its recent Policy Statement, the Board of Pensions appears to be reluctant to divest because of its fiduciary respon-sibility and because of the fact—clearly understood by all of us—that the monies in the fund belong to the members and not to the church. . . .

I would hope that the Board of Pensions would reconsider its Policy Statement from two perspectives: First, the Policy State-ment is framed in language that conveys a confrontive [sic] and . . . a combative tone. I have been assured that this was not the intention of the Board of Pensions. I believe a careful re-writing of the statement would resolve part of the difficulty.

But secondly, I would hope the Board of Pensions would go a step beyond this. What I would hope for would be a Policy Statement that more clearly and definitively outlines steps that will reflect a response to the repeated pleas . . . [for] a plan that will result in the significant reduction of funds invested in South Africa in the near future.

If the Board of Pensions finds it impossible to do so, then I would strongly urge the Church Council, in cooperation with the Board of Pensions, to initiate the process of seeking a court opinion regarding the investment of pensions funds.[11]

Three months later, Bishop Chilstrom met with the board of trustees of the Board of Pensions. In addressing the trustees, he acknowledged

---

[11] Minutes, Exhibit A, Addendum C, Church Council of the Evangelical Lutheran Church in America, July 10-11, 1988, pp. 1-2. The underlined emphasis on "my" is in the original text.

that divestment was a highly emotional topic. He added, however, that the original 1988 policy statement of the trustees did not meet the expectations of the Church Council, and he again encouraged revision of that statement.[12]

Creation of revised statement

During the October 6-8, 1988, meeting of the trustees, the policy statement of the previous June was revised to clarify the text, but the course of action identified in the June statement looking toward the creation of the "Social Purpose Balance Fund" was maintained. The revised statement read, in part:

> The Board of Pensions of the Evangelical Lutheran Church in America is an integral part of the church, with its mandate and ministry understood within the context of the church's total mission. The Board [of Pensions] is a separately incorporated Minnesota corporation, but as a component part of the ELCA shares in and is sensitive to the commitments of the whole church. Thus, the Board of Pensions is seriously engaged in an attempt to respond positively to the action . . . , mandating that the church "work tirelessly to see that none of our ELCA Pension Funds will be invested in companies doing business in South Africa" (ELCA 87.02.50).[13] The Board [of Pensions] joins Christians throughout the world in condemning, without reservation, the policies of apartheid that prevail in that part of the world.
>
> The Board [of Pensions] is aware of the need to be responsive to the mandate . . . , the moral imperatives inherent in the church's faith commitments, and its particular responsibility to provide economic security for pastors and lay workers of the church in retirement. . . . The Board [of Pensions] is also cognizant of its particular responsibility as a Minnesota corporation to manage the funds of plan members in a prudent manner in keeping with the trust laws of the state.
>
> The responsibilities and commitments which face the Board [of Pensions] are often in apparent tension and create difficulty

---

[12] *Minutes*, Board of Trustees of the Board of Pensions of the ELCA, October 6-8, 1988, p. 2.
[13] *Minutes*, Constituting Convention of the ELCA, p. 63.

for the Board [of Pensions] as it attempts to balance its commitments to the mandates of the church, its moral obligations, its responsibility to plan members and their beneficiaries and its fiduciary obligations. Accordingly, the Board [of Pensions] . . . establishes the following initial strategy:

1. In order to give all members of the pension plans freedom to direct their assets into the existing Social Purpose Funds, which have no holdings in companies with direct or indirect investments in South Africa, the Board [of Pensions] seeks agreement from the Church Council to amend the Pension Plan to allow all non-retired members to respond to the South African divestment issue by transferring their assets among funds, specifically to and from the Social Purpose Funds.

2. The Board [of Pensions] intends to establish a third Social Purpose Fund, a balanced fund, that includes both stocks and bonds.

3. Although the Board of Pensions is prohibited from offering investment advice it will fully inform all plan members regarding the nature and characteristics of the Social Purpose Funds so that members will know the issues involved in transferring their assets to, or from, Social Purpose Funds. Investment screens for the Social Purpose Funds will be regularly evaluated and new screens added as appropriate in consultation with the [ELCA] Advisory Committee on Corporate Social Responsibility.

4. The Board of Pensions will continue to receive advice on proxy matters concerning social issues from the Advisory Committee on the Church's Corporate Social Responsibility and, where appropriate, will participate in shareholder actions.

5. The Board of Pensions is the manager of various funds that belong to other units of the church and will continue to take direction from them as to the investment of these funds in ways which manifest the church's social concerns.

6. Whenever the conditions of risk and return are equivalent in the choice among securities held by the Board [of Pensions] on behalf of Plan members, or available for purchase, the

Board of Pensions has directed that the holdings in companies with South Africa investments will be divested, and similarly, investments in these companies will not be made.

7. The Board [of Pensions] will report semi-annually to the Church Council those securities it holds that appear on the IRRC[14] lists of companies that have direct or indirect investments in South Africa

Finally, having adopted these seven steps as an initial strategy, the Board of Pensions recognizes that they are not an end in themselves. Indeed, they are only a beginning in the arduous task that confronts us as a church in manifesting our solidarity with others throughout the world who oppose the evils of apartheid.[15]

In its revised policy, the trustees raised a warning flag:

In exploring additional steps, the Board of Pensions has requested and received opinions from three different law firms cautioning that divestment, with its resultant narrowing of investment choices, may actually breach fiduciary responsibility. Consequently, moving beyond the carefully constructed balance achieved in this revised policy statement would probably require the engaging of legal counsel and petitioning an appropriate jurisdiction to interpret fiduciary laws as it relates to establishing a divestment policy.[16]

The Church Council received the revised policy as information at its November 1988 meeting and expressed the hope that significant progress toward divestment would be achieved by the time of the council's next meeting in April 1989.[17] At the same time, the council learned that the Board of Pensions and the Commission for Church in Society recommended that the ELCA not seek a court interpretation of fiduciary responsibility within the context of a church organization.

Elements of debate

What was without debate during this period was the intense religious and moral objection to the practice of apartheid in South Africa. Substantive

---

[14] IRRC here refers to the Investor Responsibility Research Center, which was established in 1972 to provide information on corporate governance and social responsibility.

[15] Action Number PN88.10.94, *Minutes*, Board of Pensions, October 6-8, 1988, pp. 11-13.

[16] *Minutes*, Board of Pensions, October 6-8, 1988, p. 13.

[17] Action Number CC88.11.136, *Minutes*, Church Council of the Evangelical Lutheran Church in America, November 11-13, 1988, p. 101.

discussion transpired on effective methods to support justice there and seek the end to apartheid. Sometimes lost in the loud and dramatic debates on divestment, however, was awareness of the legal obligation that the church's pension plan had to be operated for the exclusive benefit of plan members.[18]

A divestment report was submitted to the Church Council in April 1989.[19] The council later conveyed an updated version of that report to the Churchwide Assembly for information.[20] That report indicated the Board of Pensions had reduced, in the investment portfolio, the number of companies with direct investment in South Africa from 40 to 25 (a decrease of 38 percent) in a 15-month period. This meant that the percentage of the portfolio of companies with direct investment in South Africa had declined from 9.9 percent to 5.2 percent during that period and the holdings had gone from $151.6 million to $84.9 million (a drop of 44 percent).[21]

At the same time, participation in the Social Purpose Funds had grown in the bond fund from 5.2 percent to 18.1 percent of plan members and in the equity fund from 4.1 percent to 17.3 percent.[22]

Underscored in the report was the particular responsibility of the Board of Pensions "to manage the funds of plan members in a prudent manner in keeping with the trust laws of the state" of Minnesota. Those funds "are held in trust for the exclusive benefit of the plan members," a reminder of the federal provision under which the plan operated.[23]

---

[18] The federal "exclusive benefit rule" applies to the ELCA pension plans because they are tax-deferred retirement income accounts for purposes of section 403(b)(9) of the Internal Revenue Code.

[19] Agenda Exhibit L, Part 4, Church Council of the Evangelical Lutheran Church in America, April 14-17, 1989.

[20] Action Number CC89.08.134, Minutes, Church Council of the Evangelical Lutheran Church in America, August 22, 1989, p. 12.

[21] Board of Pensions of the ELCA, Divestment Summary, August 1989, pp. 3-4. By the end of 1989, the percentage of the portfolio of companies with direct investment in South Africa was down to 3.1 percent and holdings had been reduced to $54.3 million (a decrease of 64 percent).

[22] Divestment Summary, August 1989, p. 5. At the end of 1989, 20.3 percent of plan members were participating in the Social Purpose Bond Fund and 20.2 percent in the Social Purpose Equity Fund.

[23] Divestment Summary, August 1989, p. 2.

Type of plan

To help broaden the understanding of assembly voting members and others, the 1989 *Divestment Summary* offered an explanation of the differences between "defined-benefit" plans and "defined-contribution" plans. Defined-benefit plans "provide a stated pension benefit upon retirement to the participant. In those plans, the employer, whether a state supported by taxpayers or a corporation with shareholders, is required to make up any deficiency that there may be in the funding of the stated benefit." By contrast, defined-contribution plans involve assets held in trust that belong to the plan members. "The investment risk in a defined-contribution plan is incurred by the plan member." Trustees serve as fiduciaries in the management of the pension assets.[24]

No major denomination's pension plan had "totally divested on a direct and/or indirect basis," the *Divestment Summary* noted. The Board of Pensions of the ELCA, however, had become a leader in divestment possibilities among church pension plans.[25]

The specific steps being taken by the Board of Pensions in response to the 1987 divestment declaration were:

1. Amendment of the pension plan to allow all non-retired members to transfer their assets among the funds, specifically to and from the Social Purpose Funds.

2. Creation of a third Social Purpose Fund as a balanced fund of both stocks and bonds, effective January 1, 1990.

3. Information for plan members regarding the nature and characteristics of Social Purpose Funds, along with regular evaluation of investment screens on those funds.

4. Consideration of advice on proxy matters concerning social issues from the Advisory Committee on the Church's Social Responsibility and, where deemed appropriate, participation in shareholder actions.

5. Management of endowments and other funds of the churchwide organization as directed to manifest this church's social concerns.

6. Divestment of holdings in companies with South Africa investments whenever "the conditions of risk and return are equivalent in the choice among securities held . . . on behalf of plan members."[26]

---

[24] *Divestment Summary*, August 1989, p. 2.

[25] *Divestment Summary*, August 1989, p. 6.

[26] This was a quotation of the "equivalency policy" that was practiced by the Board of Pensions for investments.

7. Semi-annual reporting to the Church Council of the list of companies held that have direct or indirect investments in South Africa.[27]

Legislative avalanche

At the same time that members of the Church Council and leaders of the Board of Pensions were struggling in the 1987-1989 biennium with issues surrounding divestment, synodical assemblies were debating the matter, often with great passion. As a result, a legislative avalanche descended upon the deliberative process of the 1989 Churchwide Assembly in the form of memorials (meaning resolutions of request and advocacy) on divestment.

As specified in the bylaws of the ELCA churchwide organization in regard to the Churchwide Assembly, a Memorials Committee was appointed to review all memorials from synods and prepare recommendations for action by the assembly. Following what proved to be contentious hearings at the assembly on the divestment issue, the Memorials Committee revised its original recommendation so that the proposed resolution read:

To affirm the July [1988] action of the Church Council stating:

That, the resources managed by the Evangelical Lutheran Church in America are to be invested or expended in ways that enhance the mission of this church;

That, the Board of Pensions, as a churchwide unit of the Evangelical Lutheran Church in America, bears responsibility both to its members and beneficiaries and to the Evangelical Lutheran Church in America as a whole; and, in the light of the action of the ELCA constituting convention, that the Board of Pensions bears a clear responsibility to respond to the oppression of our brothers and sisters in South Africa and Namibia; and

That, the Board of Pensions will fully reflect the action of the constituting convention that, "None of our ELCA pension funds . . . be invested in companies doing business in South Africa," within the context of its fiduciary responsibility.

---

[27] Board of Pensions of the ELCA, "Pensions Policy Statement," February 17, 1989, pp. 7-8.

To encourage members of the Evangelical Lutheran Church in America:

To investigate their own retirement and investment portfolios and consider action to divest of holdings in companies doing business with South Africa as a witness to their opposition to the system of apartheid;

To investigate the possibility of participating in the ELCA's Social Purpose Fund, if they [meaning ELCA members] are participants in the ELCA's pension plan; and

To give similar thought to these issues when considering purchases of goods from South Africa; and

To call upon the Board of Pensions:

To . . . work even more aggressively to divest of its holdings, and to refrain from purchase of new holdings, in companies that directly or indirectly do business with South Africa, doing all within its powers to accomplish the goal of full divestment as quickly as legally possible;

In cooperation with the Church Council, to consider seeking a court ruling, which will make divestment possible within the bounds of fiduciary responsibility and the "prudent person" requirement—inviting other church bodies with whom we are related in the National Council of the Churches of Christ in the U.S.A. and the Church Pensions Conference to join with us in this matter of mutual concern;

To report regularly to the Church Council, and to present a comprehensive report to the 1991 Churchwide Assembly regarding its accomplishment of the stated goal as well as rationale for exceptions, if any, of any remaining holdings in such aforementioned companies; and

To continue to use its proxy voting rights to urge companies to leave South Africa during the process of divestment.[28]

---

[28] *1989 Reports and Records: Minutes*, pp. 792-793.

Substitute motion

A substitute motion was made during the 1989 Churchwide Assembly by the Rev. David W. Olson, then bishop of the ELCA's Minneapolis Area Synod. He urged that his motion be embraced, thereby superseding the recommendation of the Memorials Committee. The substitute motion prevailed after one amendment was adopted. That amendment permitted exceptions "for humanitarian reasons. . . ."[29] The motion, as amended and adopted, read:

> WHEREAS, the constituting convention of the Evangelical Lutheran Church in America has expressed "our unqualified opposition to the apartheid system in South Africa," and has pledged "that we will work tirelessly to see that none of our ELCA pension funds will be invested in companies doing business in South Africa" (May 2, 1987); and
>
> WHEREAS, 44 synods[30] of the Evangelical Lutheran Church in America [in 1988 and 1989] have memorialized the [1989] Churchwide Assembly, calling for complete and full divestment within a specified time line from companies doing business in South Africa (*Reports and Records, Volume 2, Supplement*, pages M-83 through M-94); and
>
> WHEREAS, contrary to the clear intent of the resolution mandating intentional and complete divestment, the Board of Pensions has established a strategy of passive and partial divestment, which is neither a positive response to the action of the constituting convention, nor in keeping with the mandate of the constituting convention as the board claims in its policy statement (October 7, 1988); and
>
> WHEREAS, the ELCA constitution directs that "the functions of the Board of Pensions shall be enumerated in continuing resolutions by the Churchwide Assembly or the Church Council . . ."[31] (ELCA bylaw 16.51.37.); therefore, be it

---

[29] 1989 *Reports and Records: Minutes*, p. 795.

[30] This represented just over two-thirds of the ELCA's 65 synods. Seven of the synods adopted memorials on divestment in both 1988 and 1989.

[31] The resolution incorrectly quoted bylaw 16.51.37., which actually read in 1989: "The functions of the Board of Pensions shall be enumerated in continuing resolutions. Such continuing resolutions may be amended by a majority vote of the Churchwide Assembly or by a two-thirds vote of the Church Council. . . ."

RESOLVED:

1) That the 1989 Churchwide Assembly reaffirm the resolution of the constituting convention on southern Africa concerns, expressing "our unqualified opposition to the apartheid system in South Africa," and pledging "that we will work tirelessly to see that none of our ELCA Pension Funds will be invested in companies doing business in South Africa" (May 1987);

2) That the 1989 Churchwide Assembly state that this reaffirmation of the resolution means the intentional (not passive) and complete (not partial) divestment of all funds of the Board of Pensions—new funds, pre-merger funds, consolidated funds, and those managed by the board, and applies to both direct and indirect investments in companies doing business in South Africa; and

3) That the continuing resolutions applicable to the Board of Pensions be amended by the adoption of a new continuing resolution 16.51.C89., providing as follows:

> Notwithstanding the provisions of any other continuing resolutions, as of September 1, 1989, the board shall make no new investments of any funds in or with companies doing business in South Africa, whether directly or indirectly. Not later than September 1, 1990, the board shall have divested at least 50 percent of its investments in companies doing business in or with South Africa, whether directly or indirectly; and not later than September 1, 1991, the board shall have divested the balance of its investments in companies doing business in or with South Africa, whether directly or indirectly.
>
> Exception to these provisions may be granted for humanitarian reasons by two-thirds vote of the ELCA Church Council upon recommendation of the board of the Commission for Church in Society.

4) That the bishop of the Evangelical Lutheran Church in America inform the major corporations involved of this action, encouraging the withdrawal of their corporations and their financial resources from South Africa; and that each act of divestment be acknowledged with a letter to the corporation involved, said letter to be made public; [and]

5) That this assembly call upon the ELCA churchwide staff and boards, regions, synods, institutions, congregations, and in-

dividual members to join the efforts of the Evangelical Lutheran Church in America and other U.S. churches to explore all possible ways to continue to challenge the evil of racism in the United States [of America] and apartheid in South Africa.[32]

Exceeded authority of assembly

Clearly, the voting members of the 1989 Churchwide Assembly had exceeded their authority. Yet the vast majority seemed unaware of or indifferent to that concern. They were focused on divestment. Fiduciary duties, investment policies, and legal requirements were looked upon as foot-dragging rather than obligations.

In the intensity of the debate, the Rev. William H. Lazareth, then bishop of the ELCA's Metropolitan New York Synod, declared, "I am not going to listen to pagan lawyers who tell me how to be prudent as a baptized child of Jesus Christ."[33] In a calmer moment, Bishop Lazareth later said he did not mean "to suggest that all lawyers are pagan any more than all bishops are Christian" and he apologized to "any persons and their families offended" by his earlier comment.

Prior to the vote, Mr. John G. Kapanke, president of the ELCA's Board of Pensions, had cautioned voting members "that the time line as proposed"

---

[32] Action Number CA89.06.26, 1989 Reports and Records: Minutes, pp. 796-798.

[33] Transcript of debate at the 1989 Churchwide Assembly of the ELCA, Tape 20, Side 1, quoted in the appeal of the Board of Pensions to the Minnesota Court of Appeals in 1995, p. 15. The text of his statement offered an example of the tone of the debate. Said Bishop Lazareth: "I speak strongly in favor of the . . . substitute [motion] for four reasons as a pastor of the church. First, theologically: Apartheid is institutionalized racism. It is structured sin. It dehumanizes Black persons created in God's image, redeemed by Christ's blood. Second, economically: To support the South African regime is to subsidize sin. It is to support idolatry. It is to finance infidelity. It is to encourage unfaithful stewardship. Third . . . , legally: What is this high flouted fiduciary responsibility? Let me quote not from God, now, but from Caesar. This is the Minnesota statute under which one is to act prudently. How? With the care, skill, prudence and diligence, under the circumstances then prevailing, that a prudent man, excuse me, acting in a like capacity, and familiar with such matters, would use in the conduct of a careful enterprise of a like character with like aims. What kind of enterprise are we? What kind of aims do we have? Prudence is a Christian virtue. I am not going to listen to pagan lawyers who tell me how to be prudent as a baptized child of Jesus Christ. . . . Along with faith, hope, and love, these theological virtues are to govern: courage, temperance, justice, and prudence. We have a definition for prudence in the New Testament. Our Bible study has been guiding us in Acts. In our first Christian council at Jerusalem, the definition for Christians exercising prudence is, 'What seems good to the Holy Spirit and to us.' Therefore, I strongly support the substitute [motion]. It is to say that we will move forward with all deliberate speed in order to obey the 16th Article of the Augsburg Confession."

would "put the board [of trustees] in an almost impossible situation if the [pension] board is to divest within a prudent policy."[34] His warning went unheeded. Declared the Rev. Will L. Herzfeld of Oakland, Calif., former presiding bishop of the Association of Evangelical Lutheran Churches, one of the three predecessor church bodies of the ELCA, "The raising of legal problems, holding [over the church] the specter of [law]suits, being sued and those kinds of things . . . is, in the opinion of some of us, highly irregular."[35] Time would tell a different story.

True, the Churchwide Assembly is the ELCA's "highest legislative authority," but that authority is "limited by the provisions of the Articles of Incorporation, this constitution and bylaws, and the assembly's own resolutions."[36] The assembly itself did not have authority under the constitution or bylaws to direct investment policy for funds held in trust for pension plan members. Taken literally, the adopted continuing resolution appeared to assume that authority.

The continuing resolution, however, was just that—a continuing resolution, meaning that it was subservient to this church's constitution and bylaws. Under the bylaws, the Churchwide Assembly could "refer any amendments to the program initiated by the Churchwide Assembly to the Board of Pensions for recommendation before final action by the Church Council, assuring that no amendment shall abridge the rights of members with respect to their pension accumulations."[37]

As established in 1987, the Board of Pensions was to "invest the assets" of plan members "according to its best judgment" and operate "within the context of fiduciary responsibility."[38] Those duties could not be delegated by the board of trustees of the Board of Pensions either to the Church Council or the Churchwide Assembly.

When the 1989 assembly adjourned, laid at the feet of those responsible for the ongoing legislative processes of this church was the question: How was the action of the voting members to be understood since, under the bylaws, the new continuing resolution on divestment was out of order? The

---

[34] "ELCA Votes to Divest," News Release 89-C18, Commission for Communication, churchwide organization of the Evangelical Lutheran Church in America, p. 2.

[35] News Release 89-C18.

[36] Provision 13.11., Constitution, Bylaws, and Continuing Resolutions of the Evangelical Lutheran Church in America (1987 edition), p. 63.

[37] Bylaw 16.51.32.c., as numbered in the 1987 edition, Constitution, p. 100.

[38] Continuing resolution 16.51.C87.a. and b., as numbered in 1987 edition, Constitution, p. 101.

eventual solution was this: Read the assembly's resolution as the possible initiation of a change that would require a recommendation from the board of trustees of the Board of Pensions and then action by the Church Council.[39]

Surrounded by large audience

In the wake of that tumultuous Churchwide Assembly, the board of trustees of the Board of Pensions met October 12-14, 1989, and wrestled at length with the issue. They did so surrounded by an audience of people with competing convictions. Observers at that board meeting, in addition to representatives of the news media, were leaders of groups known as ELCA Members for Pension Responsibility, who opposed divestment, Pension Members for Justice, who favored it, and Lutherans for Religious and Political Freedom, who opposed it, as did the Justice for Pension Members, later renamed the Pension Defense Fund, led by the Rev. Thomas L. Basich, who would go on to file, beginning in 1991, a series of court actions against the Board of Pensions and the ELCA churchwide organization.

Recalling the experience of the 1989 Churchwide Assembly, the Rev. Jerald L. Wendt, then a trustee from Whitewater, Wis., said the process resembled a steamroller. "People talked about 'our' pension funds" as if they were "the funds of the church. That these funds belong to the members was completely lost." Ms. Elizabeth A. Storaasli, then a trustee from Duluth, Minn., argued that "we have no choice" but to practice the prudent-person rule.[40] "People are depending on us," she said.[41]

After lengthy discussion, the trustees adopted a resolution that emphasized:

---

[39] This is the plan-amendment process specified in bylaw 16.51.32.c. at that time.

[40] The "prudent" reference is to the fiduciary responsibility of trustees. Basically, the prudent-person rule means that a trustee in the investment of trust funds is to conduct himself or herself faithfully and exercise sound discretion. A trustee is to act in the manner of persons who show prudence, discretion, and intelligence in managing their responsibilities, caring for the permanent disposition of trust funds, considering the probable income as well as the probable safety of the capital to be invested. While grounded in common law, the "prudent person" legal standard is attributed to Massachusetts Judge Samuel Putnam, who wrote in 1830, "Those with responsibility to invest money for others should act with prudence, discretion, intelligence, and regard for the safety of capital as well as income."

[41] "Board Continues to Oppose Divestment," News Release 89-51-197, Commission for Communication, churchwide organization of the Evangelical Lutheran Church in America, October 18, 1989, p. 2.

Minnesota trust law and the documents governing the pension trust funds require us to abide by the prudent trustee rule in exercising our investment authority.

Contributions made on behalf of members are tax deferred under the provisions of Section 403(b)(9) of the federal tax law which requires that the pension trust funds must be established and maintained for the exclusive benefit of the members and their spouses and children.[42]

The trustees warned that any "exception to the prudent trustee and exclusive benefit rules as they are stated in the plan documents" would introduce "significant elements of risk," including the following:

It is highly likely that groups of members will commence a lawsuit to prevent the adoption and implementation of amendments to the plan documents to create an exception to the prudent trustee and exclusive benefit rules, that such lawsuit would be expensive to defend, and that the court is likely to rule that the plan documents cannot be amended to create such an exception.

There is a high risk that amendments to the plan documents to create an exception to the exclusive benefit rule would result in loss of the plan's 403(b)(9) status, which would cause members to lose deferral of income taxation on the contributions made on their behalf.

If the plan documents are amended and losses ultimately are incurred, both the members of the Church Council and we [as trustees of the Board of Pensions] could be personally liable for damages.[43]

Warning of possible "breach of faith"

The resolution of the trustees also expressed the conviction that "creating such an exception would be a breach of faith with our plan members." Recommending that the action of the 1989 Churchwide Assembly "not be implemented as proposed," the trustees declared:

As the Church Council deliberates its actions, the Board of Pensions, seeking to be responsive to the will of the Church, will:

---

[42] Action number PN89.10.112, *Minutes*, Board of Trustees of the Board of Pensions of the ELCA, October 12-14, 1989, p. 17.

[43] *Minutes*, Board of Pensions, October 12-14, 1989, p. 17

+Continue our current divestment policy, seeking to accomplish the goal of full divestment as quickly as legally possible, remaining open to additional avenues as they become known.

+Explore the development of an additional fund or funds which will have a single South African screen.

+Continue to provide regular progress reports to the Church Council and a full report to the 1991 Churchwide Assembly regarding accomplishment of these goals.

We offer to work with the Church Council in exploring ways to deal with impediments to accomplishing the goal of full divestment, and the implications of the Churchwide Assembly action.[44]

The resolution was adopted on a vote of 17 in favor and two opposed, with two other members absent.[45]

Serious words of caution

In preparation for the November 1989 meeting of the Church Council, President Kapanke of the Board of Pensions submitted a lengthy memorandum to the council on issues at hand. In many respects summarizing a collection of legal opinions that had been obtained by the Board of Pensions, he presented to the Church Council serious words of caution:

> *Minnesota Prudent Trustee Rule:* Minnesota law, which governs the pension plan, requires a trustee to observe the prudent trustee rule in the investment of trust assets unless the governing document provides otherwise. Consequently, the prudent trustee rule will apply to the ELCA pension plans unless it is expressly overridden. Amending the plan documents to override the prudent trustee rule could threaten the tax-deferred status of the pension plan and lead to litigation by Members [of the plan] asserting violation of their contract rights.
>
> *Exclusive Benefit Rule:* The federal "exclusive benefit rule" applies to the ELCA pension plans because they are tax-deferred retirement income accounts for purposes of section 403(b)(9)

---

[44] *Minutes*, Board of Pensions, October 12-14, 1989, pp. 17-18.

[45] *Minutes*, Board of Pensions, October 12-14, 1989, p. 18. Pr. Viviane Thomas-Breitfeld of Milwaukee, Wis., and Ms. Mary Nelson of Chicago voted against the resolution. Ms. Patricia Hasselmo of St. Paul, Minn., and Pr. Jerald L. Wendt of Whitewater, Wis., were not present at the time of the vote.

of the Internal Revenue Code. The exclusive benefit rule requires that plan assets be invested in accordance with the prudent trustee standard, and it cannot be overridden by the plan documents or state law. If the plan documents were amended to require the trustee to divest without regard to the prudent trustee rule, then it is likely that the plan's tax-deferred status would be revoked.

Individual Liability: If the plan fiduciaries divested in accordance with [continuing resolution] 16.51.C87.j.[46] regardless of the effect of divestment upon the value of plan assets, then the plan fiduciaries will be exposed to individual liability for losses to the portfolio. In determining whether and to what extent divestment may have caused damage to the plan portfolios, a court is likely to employ hindsight and compare the performance of the ELCA plan portfolios with the performance of similar defined contribution plans.

Breach of Faith: Plan Members, including predecessor ALC and LCA retirees and current ELCA members with vested accumulations, have relied on promises in pension plan documents and supporting materials relative to the management of the plan assets. Amendments to the plans to permit (or require) social investing, including divestment, would result in a breach of faith with Plan Members. If the predecessor ALC and LCA pension plans and the ELCA plans are amended to permit (or require) social investing, Plan Members must be offered the opportunity to withdraw their fund balances in lieu of being forced to continue participation in plans where the guidelines have been unilaterally changed.[47]

He predicted that if litigation were commenced against the board of trustees of the Board of Pensions and the ELCA churchwide organization,

---

[46] The actual number of the continuing resolution that was adopted by the 1989 Churchwide Assembly was 16.51.C89., not 16.51.C87.j., as stated in the 1989 memorandum of the Board of Pensions to the Church Council. There was some confusion even during the assembly when the continuing resolution was proposed as to its proper numbering for inclusion in the *Constitution, Bylaws, and Continuing Resolutions of the Evangelical Lutheran Church in America.*

[47] *Minutes*, Exhibit L, Part 3, "Memorandum to Members of the Church Council," John G. Kapanke, Church Council of the Evangelical Lutheran Church in America, November 18-19, 1989, pp. 1-2. See also *Minutes*, Church Council of the ELCA, November 18-19, 1989, pp. 32-33.

such litigation "would be wide ranging, expensive, emotionally devastating and, perhaps, inclusive."[48] His assessment in regard to litigation would come true in the years immediately ahead (see Chapter 6).

Mr. Kapanke was asked by a council member whether the only criterion for judging the moral status of an investment decision was maximizing the return on investment. He replied that the key matter is one of prudence, noting that—if taken literally and implemented immediately—the Churchwide Assembly's action would have eliminated 40 percent of the possible companies in which funds could be invested.[49]

Mr. John E. Harris of the law firm of Faegre and Benson in Minneapolis, legal counsel for the Board of Pensions, explained to the council that the term "social investments" applies to a pattern of investments being made for other than financial reasons. He emphasized that the assets of the pension fund do not belong either to the Board of Pensions or to the ELCA's churchwide organization, but to plan members. Therefore, a fiduciary must act prudently according to the law.[50]

Evidence of increased anxiety

Clearly, the intensity of the Churchwide Assembly had caused increased anxiety for both the pension trustees and council members. The tone of discussion in the November 1989 council meeting was sharp. Frustration on the part of some council members was evident over what seemed at the time to be "political ineptitude" and bumbling public relations on the part of the board.[51] For instance, shortly before the Churchwide Assembly, the Board of Pensions had sent to plan members a waiver document for signature for those moving assets into the social-purpose funds. The timing of that step was interpreted as a "scare tactic" on the eve of the assembly.

The question in the midst of what was seeming to become an increasingly complex mess of competing arguments was this: Where do we go from here? Escalating rhetoric was not helping. Reasoned exploration of options was needed.

To offer possibilities, an ad hoc work group on divestment was established at the November 1989 meeting of the Church Council. The

---

[48] *Minutes*, Exhibit L, Part 3, "Memorandum to Members of the Church Council," November 1989, p. 2.

[49] *Minutes*, Church Council, November 18-19, 1989, p. 36.

[50] *Minutes*, Church Council, November 18-19, 1989, p. 36.

[51] *Minutes*, Church Council, November 18-19, 1989, p. 36. See also Jean Caffey Lyles, "Council, Pension Unit Avoid Collision," *The Lutheran*, December 20, 1989, p. 24.

group was to prepare recommendations for the council's next meeting in April 1990. Appointed to the group by Ms. Christine H. Grumm as council chair were: the Rev. Herbert W. Chilstrom, then bishop of the ELCA; Ms. Grumm, then ELCA vice president; the Rev. David Olson and the Rev. Harold Weiss, then synodical bishops; the Rev. Paul Blom, the Rev. David Holm, Ms. Edith Lohr, and Mr. Athornia Steele, then members of the Church Council; Ms. Mildred Berg, then chair of the board of trustees of the Board of Pensions; Mr. John G. Kapanke, president of the Board of Pensions; Ms. Elizabeth A. Storaasli and Mr. Allan R. Nelson, then members of the board of trustees of the Board of Pensions; Ms. Lita B. Johnson and the Rev. Morris A. Sorenson Jr., then executive assistants to the bishop; Mr. David J. Hardy, then general counsel for the churchwide organization; and the Rev. Jerald L. Folk, Mr. Edward Crane, Mr. David A. Krueger, and Mr. Aurie Pennick of what was then called the Commission for Church in Society.[52]

The work group's report, according to the November 1989 enabling resolution, was to:

1.   Describe "possible options for implementing the divestment action" of the 1989 Churchwide Assembly; and

2.   Include "a listing of the advantages and disadvantages of each option for the church's commitment to justice in South Africa, as well as each option's legal and financial implications."

Further, the Church Council authorized "the bishop to initiate specific actions between meetings of the Church Council to test the legality of the objective of the Churchwide Assembly action on divestment or to ascertain the impact of changes in the plan document on the tax status of the plan." The council also expressed the expectation "that significant progress toward divestment" would be demonstrated by the Board of Pensions by the time of the council's April 1990 meeting.[53]

Recommendations of work group

With notebooks full of relevant memoranda and various documents, the work group met at the Lutheran Center in Chicago February 19-20, 1990. Emerging from that meeting was a series of recommendations:

---

[52] Action Number CC89.11.164, *Minutes*, Church Council of the Evangelical Lutheran Church in America, November 18-19, 1989, p. 37.

[53] Action Number CC89.11.164, *Minutes*, Church Council, November 18-19, 1989, p. 37.

1. The Board of Pensions would operate several funds:

    a. Social purpose funds (equity, bond, and balanced) that would continue to be "South Africa free" and would include several other screens.

    b. Alternative funds (the then current equity, bond, and balanced funds) that would be managed under the existing divestment policy that likely would not become fully "South Africa free."

2. Plan participants would be required to make one of the following investment choices for both their accumulated balances and current contributions:

    a. South Africa free funds or a combination of South Africa free funds and social purpose funds;

    b. Alternative funds or a combination of alternative funds and social purpose funds; or

    c. Social purpose funds.

3. In the event that an individual failed to make a choice, the South Africa free funds would be the default. Specifically, that person's new contribution would be placed in the South Africa free bond fund and the individual's accumulation also would be put into the South Africa free bond, equity, or balanced fund.

4. The record-keeping system of the Board of Pensions would be expanded with start-up costs estimated at $615,000. Acknowledged was the fact that the expanded computer capacity would be beneficial in allowing for greater flexibility of investment options. The cost for establishing and maintaining the funds would be covered by an increase of one-tenth to two-tenths of a percent over a multi-year period in the administrative fee charged to congregations and other employers. Average cost to congregations would be about $55.

5. Implementation of the plan would be completed by July 1, 1991.

6. The procedure to assign accumulations and contributions to the South Africa free funds would require prior IRS determination to address the issue of the "exclusive benefit rule."

7. Speculation was expressed that the risk of lawsuits "would be significantly reduced" by this approach compared to "full divestment," since individual choice would be exercised here.[54]

---

[54] Action Number CC90.04.15, *Minutes*, Church Council of the Evangelical Lutheran Church in America, April 21-23, 1990, pp. 24-27. The work group's full report was attached to the April 1990 minutes of the Church Council as Exhibit L, Part 6b.

The work group expressed the conviction that the proposed course of action:

1. Takes seriously the intent of the resolution passed by the Churchwide Assembly for more complete, faster, and more public divestment. . . .

2. Takes seriously the desirability of providing opportunity for personal choice.

3. Makes a clear witness by reflecting the corporate commitment of the Evangelical Lutheran Church in America to divestment. This option may be credible for the main body of divestment proponents since it incorporates an institutional commitment to divestment.

4. Builds upon the strengths of past efforts, including sponsorship of shareholder resolutions, which have placed the ELCA [churchwide organization] among the leaders in the religious community in actually implementing a broad divestment policy.

5. Preserves . . . [the] option [for plan participants] to invest in the Social Purpose Funds, should they wish to engage in this more extensive shaping of investment choices according to social purposes. . . .

6. Requires . . . commitment to communicate clearly and carefully with plan participants to avoid confusion among participants who are dealing with choices among nine different funds. Objectivity in the interpretation of the funds by the Board of Pensions is required, thus avoiding the appearance of discouraging investment in the ELCA South Africa Free Fund. Other ELCA entities that engage in educational efforts on this matter need to express the commitment of the Evangelical Lutheran Church in America to divestment and to prepare the South Africa Free Fund as normative, while avoiding the financial/legal liability that would result should they act as "investment advisors" to participants.[55]

Revision of 1989 assembly resolution

The resolution adopted by the council also directed that the problematic continuing resolution from the 1989 Churchwide Assembly be revised to

---

[55] *Minutes*, Church Council, April 21-23, 1990, pp. 26-27.

conform to the policy changes approved by the Church Council. To that end, the council's Legal and Constitutional Review Committee was asked to bring an amendment to the council's October 1990 meeting.[56]

Offered for future consideration by the Church Council was the possibility of seeking an amendment of the Minnesota pension law that would allow "non-ERISA funds to eliminate South Africa related companies from the prudent person standard."[57]

The work group's proposal had been tested with members of the Conference of Bishops in early March 1990. In a straw poll as advice to the Church Council, synodical bishops had affirmed the plan with one dissenting vote. As the members of the Church Council met in April, many seemed relieved that such an extensive and reasoned approach had emerged for their affirmation after relatively brief discussion in the meeting.

When the board of trustees of the Board of Pensions assembled on June 22, 1990, the steps followed in the divestment process to date were outlined, noting that:

1. Members were allowed to transfer existing balances to the Social Purpose Funds;

2. Clear information had been provided to participants regarding the nature of the Social Purpose Funds;

3. Additional South Africa free options had emerged with the creation of the Social Purpose Balanced Fund;

4. Work continued on proxy matters and shareholder resolutions on issues related to South Africa and other matters;

5. Investment directives of "non-pension" funds of other churchwide units were being followed; and

6. Securities had been divested when risks and returns were deemed equivalent.[58]

The plan for implementation of the "South Africa Free Funds" was presented in detail. The trustees requested on June 22, 1990, approval by the Church Council of plan amendments in order to put in place the new funds on July 1, 1991.[59]

---

[56] *Minutes*, Church Council, April 21-23, 1990, p. 27.

[57] *Minutes*, Church Council, April 21-23, 1990, p. 27.

[58] *Minutes*, Board of Trustees of the Board of Pensions of the ELCA, June 22, 1990, p. 4.

[59] *Minutes*, Trustees, June 22, 1990, pp. 5-23.

Adoption of the necessary plan changes had been delegated by the Church Council in April 1990 to its Executive Committee. When the Executive Committee of the Church Council met on August 2, 1990, the amendments to establish the South Africa Free Funds were affirmed.[60] Those amendments, as recommended by the board of trustees, included the option of transferability by members between the like funds being offered by the Board of Pensions.

The problematic continuing resolution that emerged from the 1989 Churchwide Assembly was eliminated when the Church Council met in October 1990. The council voted:

> To delete ELCA continuing resolution 16.51.C89. as no longer applicable in view of actions of the Board of Pensions and the Church Council (CC90.04.15)[61] in response to concerns and actions of the 1989 Churchwide Assembly on divestment.[62]

At the same meeting, the Church Council affirmed the "humanitarian exception" related to South Africa divestment. Specifically, the council voted "that companies [would] receive an exemption from this church's policy on divestment and [would] not be asked to cease doing business with companies . . . [in] South Africa when . . . they are in the pharmaceutical and medical equipment/technology sectors, where the equipment or technology would not otherwise be available in South Africa . . . and . . . they receive the highest rating under the principles applicable to the signatory companies (formerly the Sullivan principles). . . ." That action was forwarded as advice, not direction, to the Board of Pensions.[63]

Approval of South Africa Free Funds

Creation of the South Africa Free Funds received a satisfactory response in a letter ruling by Internal Revenue Service. That ruling was issued on the basis of facts in a 41-page request submitted to the IRS by the law firm of Faegre & Benson on behalf of the Board of Pensions.[64]

---

[60] Action Number EC90.08.10, *Minutes*, Executive Committee of the Church Council of the Evangelical Lutheran Church in America, p. 5. The full account of consideration of that matter was recorded on pages 2 through 5 of the minutes. The detailed amendments were included as *Minutes* Exhibit A, Part 3, and Exhibit A, Part 4.

[61] This action referred to the plan to establish the South Africa Free Funds.

[62] Action Number CC90.10.61, *Minutes*, Church Council of the Evangelical Lutheran Church in America, October 20-22, 1990, p. 44.

[63] Action Number CC90.10.77, *Minutes*, Church Council, October 20-22, 1990, p. 115.

[64] *Minutes*, Board of Trustees of the Board of Pensions of the ELCA, April 5-7, 1991, p. 8.

In preparation for the beginning of the new funds, trustees of the Board of Pensions approved revisions in the 1988 policy statement on divestment, which now read, in part, in April 1991:

> In order to give all Members of the Pension Plans freedom to direct their assets into funds which have no holdings in companies with direct or indirect investments in South Africa, the Board [of Pensions] and the Church Council agreed to amend the Pension Plan to establish three new South Africa Free Funds and to enable all non-retired Members to respond to the South Africa divestment issue by transferring their assets among Funds, specifically to and from the South Africa Free Funds and Social Purpose Funds which are also South Africa Free.
>
> In addition to the three new South Africa Free Funds, the Board [of Pensions] established a third Social Purpose Fund, a balanced fund, that includes both stocks and bonds.
>
> Although the Board of Pensions is prohibited from offering investment advice, it will fully inform all Plan Members regarding the nature and characteristics of the South Africa Free and Social Purpose Funds so that Members will know the issues involved in transferring their assets to, or from, South Africa Free and/or Social Purpose Funds. Investment screens for Social Purpose Funds will be regularly evaluated and new screens added as appropriate in consultation with the Advisory Committee on Corporate Social Responsibility. . . .
>
> Whenever the conditions of risk and return are equivalent in the choice among Alternative Fund securities held by the Board [of Pensions] on behalf of Plan Members, or available for purchase, the Board of Pensions has directed that the holdings in companies with South Africa investments will be divested, and similarly, investments in these companies will not be made. . . .[65]

To prepare for the new funds, a memorandum was sent to all plan members on June 28, 1991, on the "required election process" for the ELCA South Africa Free Funds. The six-month election period ran from July 1 through December 31, 1991. In bold print on the first page was the warning: "Failure to file the enclosed election form may result in a realignment of your pension fund investments." That reflected the decision for default to

---

[65] Action Number PN91.04.16, *Minutes*, Board of Pensions, April 5-7, 1991, p. 8.

the South Africa Free Funds.[66] Members were to select funds for both their existing accumulations and future contributions. A multi-page booklet was provided on investment options with descriptions of potential risks in allocation possibilities. Follow-up contacts were made by telephone to those who did not submit their choices.[67]

Did not last long

Within two years of their creation, steps were taken to terminate the South Africa Free Funds as no longer needed. Upon recommendation of the board of trustees of the Board of Pensions, the Church Council voted in December 1993 to inaugurate the end of those screened funds.[68]

As a result, after only four years, the South Africa Free Funds were eliminated on April 1, 1995. South Africa and the world changed far more quickly than most imagined possible at the beginning of the decade of the 1990s. At their termination, assets in South Africa Free equity, bond, and balanced funds of $130.7 million were transferred to Social Purpose Funds or unscreened funds. Plan members directed $3.7 million (or 2.9 percent) to the Social Purpose Funds and the remainder shifted into the unscreened funds.[69]

---

[66] John G. Kapanke, "Memorandum on ELCA South Africa Free Funds," June 28, 1991, pp. 1 and 4.

[67] *Minutes*, Church Council, April 21-23, 1990, p. 26.

[68] Action Number CC93.12.79, *Minutes*, Church Council of the Evangelical Lutheran Church in America, December 3-5, 1993, pp. 70-71.

[69] *Agenda*, Board of Trustees of the Board of Pensions of the ELCA, May 11-12, 1995, Appendix A-6a, p. 1.

CHAPTER 6

A Courtroom Drama
In Several Venues

The threat was not new. Demands and claims had been made with escalating intensity:

- Catastrophic-sounding allegations in articles in various publications.

- A privately published book intended as an exposé of a "shameless" pension scandal.

- Shouted declarations in repeated, harassing phone calls, day and night to the president of the Board of Pensions and others.

- Organized efforts to flood with phone calls the switchboard of the Board of Pensions, thereby blocking incoming calls from members.

- Meetings marked by unremitting belligerence.

- Picketers marching with bold signs on Marquette Avenue in downtown Minneapolis outside the office of the Board of Pensions of the ELCA: "ELCA Pension Board—This Jericho Wall Soon Will Fall"; "We Want Economic Justice for Pastors"; "Thou Shalt Not Steal"; "ELCA Guilty of Pension Fraud"; and "Bishops—Stop Using Our Pension Money to Promote Your Political Goals."

Then, one summer day in 1991, a lawsuit listing three counts was filed in Minnesota's Hennepin County District Court.

Plaintiffs: Thomas Basich, Matthew Basich, and Advent Lutheran Church, a Minnesota corporation; and Judith H. Boal.

Defendants: Board of Pensions of the Evangelical Lutheran Church in America, a Minnesota corporation; and the Evangelical Lutheran Church in America, a Minnesota corporation.

Claim: That the Board of Pensions was not investing in a prudent manner on behalf of plan participants and was "giving other considerations to the investing of funds in violation" of fiduciary responsibilities.[1]

Antagonism on divestment

The Revs. Thomas L. Basich and Matthew J. Basich, father and son respectively, were pastors of Advent Lutheran Church. The senior Basich had developed an intense antagonism to efforts in the ELCA on South Africa concerns. Attempts for divestment in corporations doing business in South Africa were objects of special scorn for him.

The elder Basich was ordained in 1953 in the Augustana Lutheran Church and became the founding pastor of Advent Lutheran Church in Roseville. Through successive mergers, he and the Advent congregation became members of the Lutheran Church in America and later the ELCA. He was born on July 28, 1926, so at the time of the filing of the 1991 lawsuit, he was five days short of his 65th birthday.

In various stages in his pastoral career, Pr. Thomas Basich had been a vocal, public advocate for a variety of humanitarian and social concerns. For example, he marched with the Rev. Martin Luther King Jr. at Selma and Montgomery, Alabama, in the 1960s and served as chair of the Governor's Human Rights Committee of the State of Minnesota. He engaged in political party activities on local and state levels. He also pursued environmental preservation efforts for a time. Then came the issue of opposition to apartheid in South Africa and proposals for divestment from corporations doing business in South Africa. Those divestment proposals lit within him antagonism that was manifested in the ELCA for several years before he formed his own church body.

Basich alleged that the "equivalency policy" on investments had harmed him and other plan members.[2] Although he did not claim specific damages, he sought the right to withdraw his funds. Under the plan at that time, such a withdrawal was not permitted. Early in the turmoil, however, he was informed that if he were to leave the ELCA and move to another Lutheran or other church body, those funds could be transferred to the

---

[1] Basich et al., Summons, State of Minnesota, County of Hennepin, Fourth Judicial District, July 23, 1991, p. 7.

[2] The board of trustees of the ELCA Board of Pensions had adopted in 1988 an "equivalency policy," whereby the Board of Pensions agreed to divest (and refrain from making new investments) in companies with South African holdings whenever the conditions of risk and return would be equal in other stocks and bonds held or available for purchase by the Board of Pensions on behalf of plan members (see Chapter 5).

pension plan of his new denomination. Eventually, that did happen, but not until a legal struggle of half a decade ended.

A five-year legal drama

In a quick overview, what transpired?

1. The plaintiffs filed the lawsuit on July 23, 1991, in Minnesota's Hennepin County against the Board of Pensions of the ELCA and the ELCA churchwide organization.[3]

2. Attorneys for the Board of Pensions and the ELCA churchwide organization sought a "summary judgment" to throw out the case.

3. Judge Ann D. Montgomery of Minnesota's Fourth Judicial District in Hennepin County granted the motion for summary judgment on February 11, 1992.

4. The plaintiffs argued in a filing that the court's summary judgment deprived them of their right to be heard.

5. Judge Montgomery denied on April 30, 1992, the plaintiffs' motion to vacate her original judgment.

6. The plaintiffs appealed Judge Montgomery's February 11, 1992, decision to the Minnesota Court of Appeals on May 18, 1992.

7. The Minnesota Court of Appeals, on December 8, 1992, affirmed Judge Montgomery's original decision.[4]

8. On September 27, 1993, Pr. Basich and initially 29 other plaintiffs filed a second suit against the Board of Pensions of the ELCA and the ELCA churchwide organization.[5]

9. The defendants filed a motion heard on December 16, 1993, by Judge Harry Seymour Crump, seeking "summary judgment" once again, arguing that the matter had been dismissed previously by the courts.

10. On February 7, 1994, Judge Crump declined to dismiss the "breach of contract" complaint of the plaintiffs, but ruled that the complaints related to the South Africa Free Funds were moot since steps had been initiated by the Board of Pensions in November 1993 to eliminate those funds.

---

[3] Minnesota Fourth Judicial District, Court File No. CT-91-015486.

[4] Minnesota Court of Appeals, Basich v. Board of Pensions, 493 N.W.2d 293.

[5] Minnesota Fourth Judicial District, Court File No. 93-16711.

11. A separate lawsuit was filed on May 16, 1994, by 18 plaintiffs, but the content was identical to the one initiated in 1993. That action was withdrawn on June 17, 1994, and the September 27, 1993, complaint was amended to include the additional plaintiffs.

12. The plaintiffs amended their complaint on June 17, 1994, increasing the number of plaintiffs to 49, 47 of whom were receiving a pension or had pension accounts, one of whom was a member of a congregation participating in the ELCA Pension and Other Benefits Program, and one of which was a congregation, namely Advent Lutheran Church in Roseville, Minn.

13. The "discovery" phase of the process began with requests for the production of numerous boxes of documents, preparation of lengthy interrogatories (questions of opposing parties for sworn answers), and filings of legal responses to the scores of questions addressed to plaintiffs and defendants.

14. Dozens of sworn depositions transpired.

15. At the close of the discovery phase, the defendants moved again for summary judgment. The key point was whether the court had jurisdiction over an internal religious dispute on church doctrine.

16. After a hearing on December 16, 1994, Judge Crump dismissed two of the plaintiffs' three revised counts. What remained was a claim for "breach of contract."

17. Following a hearing on April 3, 1995, Judge Crump again refused to dismiss the action. He did so in a written judgment signed on April 18, 1995. He also ordered that the trial proceed.

18. The defendants filed a notice of an "interlocutory appeal" on April 25, 1995, on the issue of the court's jurisdiction of a religious matter. An interlocutory appeal relates to particular types of issues that may be appealed to a higher court before litigation is completed and final judgment issued in a lower court.

19. The Minnesota Court of Appeals, on May 5, 1995, directed that memoranda on jurisdictional questions be prepared.

20. Judge Crump officially recorded on May 11, 1995, the judgment that he issued on April 18, making it part of the judicial record.

21. The Minnesota Court of Appeals denied on May 31, 1995, the motion of the plaintiffs to dismiss the appeal of the defendants.

22. Oral arguments were made in the "interlocutory appeal" of the defendants before the Minnesota Court of Appeals on October 10, 1995.

23. The Minnesota Court of Appeals dismissed on November 28, 1995, the second Basich lawsuit, finding that the ELCA's divestment strategy was motivated by the ELCA's conclusion that apartheid had to be rejected as a matter of faith and therefore the civil courts did not have jurisdiction to decide the issues. Further, the court held that the board's "equivalency policy" was a proper response to the ELCA's sincerely held religious belief.

24. The Minnesota Supreme Court denied the plaintiffs' petition for review of the matter on January 25, 1996.

25. The plaintiffs appealed to the U.S. Supreme Court on April 24, 1996.

26. The U.S. Supreme Court on October 7, 1996, refused to consider the claims of the plaintiffs.

Long ordeal

The long ordeal finally came to an end. In the meantime, free elections had taken place in South Africa and the existence of the South Africa Free Funds had ended on April 1, 1995. When Pr. Basich established his own Augustana Orthodox and Evangelical Lutheran Synod in March 1997 with its own pension plan, his pension funds were transferred to his new plan.

The five-year legal drama, however, had required enormous amounts of time and effort on the part of leaders and staff of the Board of Pensions. Legal costs had been substantial. Upholding crucial principles meant the stakes were high. Protecting the pension assets for all members of the plan demanded utmost dedication. At the same time, leaders and staff members had to attend to the ongoing operation of the pension and other benefits program. Clearly, that was a difficult time in the life of the ELCA's Board of Pensions.

Consider now in detail what transpired during this very long and, at times, intense courtroom saga.

In the first Basich et al. lawsuit in 1991, the plaintiffs alleged that the ELCA churchwide organization had "forced" the Board of Pensions to adopt and implement an imprudent policy regarding investments with ties to South Africa. Specifically, they charged that the Board of Pensions had violated the prudent person rule and breached its fiduciary duties when what were characterized as social and political concerns about apartheid in South Africa influenced investment decisions. The lawsuit sought immediate relief for all plan members and amendment of the plan to permit lump-sum withdrawals. The lawsuit said they were seeking "declaratory relief" on behalf of *all* participants in the plan.

Specifically, the plaintiffs asked that the court direct the Board of Pensions "to adopt a portability plan, the terms of which would allow any beneficiary to withdraw the funds credited to that beneficiary's account, plus interest or other accumulations."[6] In addition, the court was urged to order the separation the Board of Pensions from the ELCA churchwide organization and to preclude the use of any criteria other than prudence in investment policies.[7]

In answer to the allegations, the Board of Pensions indicated in a court filing that "pre-retirement withdrawals from . . . accounts (which plaintiffs incorrectly style as a 'portability plan') would be inconsistent with the fundamental purposes of the [Pension] Plan . . . and with the fiduciary obligations of the Board."[8]

On February 11, 1992, District Judge Ann D. Montgomery dismissed the Basich et al. claims, ruling that the plaintiffs did not have standing since the Board of Pensions, as a corporation, does not have "members" as understood in corporation law.[9] On April 30, 1992, the plaintiffs brought a motion to vacate the judgment dismissing their lawsuit. Judge Montgomery denied the motion and affirmed that the entire lawsuit had been dismissed. Her decision was appealed by the plaintiffs.

Accosted outside courtroom

Attorneys representing the ELCA Board of Pensions and the ELCA churchwide organization found themselves accosted outside the courtroom. In a letter to attorney Robert C. Bell, who represented the plaintiffs, Ms. Bonnie M. Fleming representing the Board of Pensions and Mr. Robert

---

[6] While the plaintiffs demanded "portability" in the ELCA's pension plan, the term "portability" technically referred to the right of a plan member to transfer pension entitlements that are vested with an employing organization from which the individual has terminated an employment relationship to a new employing organization with which the individual is commencing employment.

[7] Basich et al., p. 14.

[8] Filing dated August 20, 1991, p. 15.

[9] State of Minnesota, County of Hennepin, Fourth Judicial District, Court File No. 91-015486, p. 4.

H. Rydland on behalf of the ELCA churchwide organization wrote that they were bringing to Mr. Bell's attention "disturbing and inappropriate behavior involving your client." They recounted:

> Immediately following the court appearance before Judge Montgomery on April 30, and after your departure, we were verbally and physically assaulted by Pastor Thomas Basich. In spite of the fact that we repeatedly informed your client that we were unable to discuss the case with him, he verbally harassed us and physically prevented both of us from leaving the courthouse. When Lynn Basich, your co-counsel, was asked to intervene, she refused. In our many years as attorneys, we have never observed such abusive and intimidating behavior on the part of a litigant, let alone seen it condoned by counsel.[10]

In the same letter, Ms. Fleming and Mr. Rydland expressed objection to the repeated distribution by Pr. Basich of false statements related to the Board of Pensions and actions on divestment. A broadly distributed mailing by Pr. Basich earlier in April of 1992 offered examples, they said, of their concern about false statements.[11] They noted that the assertion of Pr. Basich claiming that the pension plans were over funded could not be true since the ELCA plan was a defined-contribution plan. In their letter to Mr. Bell, Ms. Fleming and Mr. Rydland said they were "asking that your client discontinue making untrue statements and engaging in improper behavior."[12]

After Judge Montgomery's ruling, Ms. Mildred M. Berg, then chair of the board of trustees of the Board of Pensions, and Mr. John G. Kapanke, president, decided to update pension-plan members on developments in the matter. In a memorandum dated May 8, 1992, they wrote:

> The Board of Pensions believes that the overall design of the pension plan is well suited to the needs of the plan members and their families. The purpose of the ELCA Pension and Other Benefits Program is to assist individuals serving the ELCA, and their families, in maintaining financial security in the event of illness, injury, retirement, or death. . . .[13]

---

[10] Bonnie M. Fleming and Robert H. Rydland, Letter to Robert C. Bell, August 21, 1992, p. 3.

[11] Thomas L. Basich, "Pension Defense Fund Report" (Roseville, Minn.: Advent Lutheran Church, April 1992).

[12] Basich, "Pension Defense Fund Report," pp. 1 and 3.

[13] Mildred M. Berg and John G. Kapanke, "Memorandum to Pension Plan Members," May 8, 1992, p. 1.

They recalled that Pr. Thomas Basich had distributed widely a document called the "Pension Defense Fund Report." The Board of Pensions did not attempt to answer the allegations made in the "Pension Defense Fund Report" while the Basich et al. lawsuit was pending. But the time had come, Ms. Berg and Mr. Kapanke wrote, that members needed to receive the facts in the matter. The memorandum proceeded to cite the Basich allegations and the board's response:

Allegation: The Trustees and staff of the Board of Pensions have violated their fiduciary duties.

Answer: The Trustees and staff of the Board of Pensions have adhered to Minnesota trust law and the terms of the pension plan documents and have administered and invested the assets of the pension plan in accordance with the prudent trustee rule.

Allegation: You are no longer "plan members" but "plan participants."

Answer: You are still plan members. "Plan members" and "plan participants" are synonymous. You are not voting members of the Board of Pensions because the Board [of Pensions] has no voting members. The Board of Pensions is governed by 21 Trustees elected by the Churchwide Assembly, of which six are plan members.

Allegation: The ELCA Church Council and the ELCA Commission for Church in Society (now the ELCA Division for Church in Society) determine, through the Advisory Committee on the Church's Corporate Social Responsibility, how pension assets will be invested.

Answer: The Trustees and staff of the Board of Pensions do not receive orders as to how pension plan funds are to be invested from the Advisory Committee on the Church's Corporate Social Responsibility or from the Church Council. The Trustees and staff of the Board [of Pensions] receive advice from the Advisory Committee and the Church Council concerning the implementation of investment screens for the Social Purpose Funds, the filing of shareholder resolutions and the casting of proxy ballots for corporate social responsibility. Any such action, however, is taken only if it is consistent with the Trustees' and Board's fiduciary obligations and duties. Neither the Church Council nor the Division for Church in Society . . . control . . . investment decisions.

Allegation: All of the funds in the Pension Plàn are subject to investment screens.

Answer: Of the investment funds available as part of the pension plan, only the Social Purpose Funds and the South Africa Free Funds are subject to investment screens. The Alternative Funds and the predecessor ALC and LCA Funds are not subject to any screens.

Allegation: All of the funds in the Pension Plan are subject to a "South Africa screen."

Answer: All of the funds which are part of the pension plan are subject to a Policy Statement which provides that whenever conditions of risk and return are equivalent in the choices of securities, the pension plan's holdings in companies with South Africa investments will be divested or not made. This is not a South Africa free screen. This type of direction is recognized by the United States Department of Labor and by the Employee Retirement Income Security Act (ERISA) as being acceptable for fiduciaries. Under this policy statement, at some times the number of investments in companies with ties to South Africa . . . [has] increased and at other times it has decreased. The pension plan continues to have holdings in companies doing business in South Africa.[14]

The memorandum emphasized that plan members and their beneficiaries remained the first concern of the Board of Pensions. Concluded Ms. Berg and Mr. Kapanke, "We hope this letter has been helpful to you, the plan member, in understanding and knowing the facts surrounding the lawsuit."[15]

On December 8, 1992, the Minnesota Court of Appeals affirmed Judge Montgomery's February 1992 decision.[16] In a letter to pension plan members at that time, Ms. Berg as chair of the trustees and Mr. Kapanke

---

[14] Berg and Kapanke, "Memorandum," pp. 1-2. Capitalization and underlining in this quotation are shown as presented in the original memorandum.

[15] Berg and Kapanke, "Memorandum," p. 3.

[16] "Basich v. Board of Pensions," 493 North West Reporter 2d 293 (Minnesota Court of Appeals, 1992).

as president expressed hope that the court's decision would bring "to an end this unwarranted litigation which, though successfully defended, has created substantial expenses in terms of time and money."[17]

Unfortunately, that was not the end of this courtroom odyssey.

Apocalyptic-sounding letter

Just prior to filing the initial lawsuit, the Rev. Thomas Basich had written an apocalyptic-sounding letter to "friends of the Pension Defense Fund and other interested persons." It was dated July 19, 1991, and in it he made a series of allegations, among them:

1. "Our ELCA pension plan is controlled by the ELCA Church Council which has right of 'final action' over pension policy."

2. "Our ELCA pension plan is a _political_ pension plan whose political goals are set by a handful of bureaucrats at ELCA headquarters."

3. "By politicizing our pension plan, and in other ways, the Church Council and the pension trustees have altered and compromised the original purpose of our pension plan and thus breached their contract with us."

4. "The ELCA Church Council and the Board of Pensions will try to crush us. We are a threat to their non-competitive, non-regulated, no-exit monopoly. They resent the fact that the once-voiceless, once-powerless plan members are taking action now to defend their own vital interests."

The memorandum also carried a fund appeal: "At Advent Lutheran Church, we have diverted benevolence money to the Pension Defense Fund because we believe that this lawsuit is also a type of benevolence since its aim is to benefit all plan members. Your congregation may wish to consider the same thing."[18]

Somewhat later in 1991, Pr. Basich published and distributed a book, *Pension Gate: The Hi-Jacking [sic] of the Pension Fund of the Evangelical Lutheran Church in America*. The cover blurb read: "Here is the truth about the hijacking of the ELCA pension fund for political purposes. The scandal of shameless use and abuse of your pension dollars."

---

[17] "Court Upholds Dismissal of ELCA Pension Lawsuit," *The Lutheran*, February 1993, p. 34.

[18] Letter by the Rev. Thomas L. Basich, senior pastor of Advent Lutheran Church, Roseville, Minn., July 19, 1991.

In the preface, Pr. Basich wrote: "I have spent most of my pastoral career nourishing, defending, and teaching. But now, once again, I must bite and fight," thereby echoing a statement by Martin Luther. Further, Pr. Basich declared, "The Church Council of the Evangelical Lutheran Church in America (ELCA) and the ELCA Board of Pensions are brazenly exploiting the 42,000 members of the ELCA pension plan."[19]

His charges included allegations that the Church Council had "usurped" the "fiduciary role of the pension trustees" and was "systematically" imposing "blacklists (euphemistically called 'screens') upon the Board of Pensions" of "companies in which the pension trustees are forbidden to invest."[20] He also asserted that the pension accumulations of members had been "permanently expropriated."[21]

Before the courtroom drama began to unfold, Pr. Basich had voiced emphatic opposition to calls for divestment. Just days prior to having the opportunity on October 12, 1989, to address the board of trustees of the Board of Pensions, he sent a letter—dated October 7, 1989—reporting that the Congregation Council of Advent Lutheran Church had approved a resolution on September 7 which

> . . . opposes the Chicago directive regarding divestment, supports the Board of Pensions in its present resistence to the Chicago directive, and serves notice to the Board of Pensions and to the ELCA that, by itself or in concert with other congregations and individuals, it will take whatever legal steps are necessary to prevent the Chicago directive from being implemented, and that such steps may include instituting a lawsuit against the Board and ELCA Church for the purpose of withdrawing all of our funds from the Pension Fund.[22]

The basis for the lawsuit, he said, was the introduction of "political criteria into investment decisions" that he charged "is illegal and represents a breach of contract with Pension Plan members and congregations."[23]

---

[19] Thomas L. Basich, *Pension Gate* (St. Paul: Prince Publishing Co., 1991), p. 1.

[20] Basich, *Pension Gate*, p. 1

[21] Basich, *Pension Gate*, p. 2.

[22] Thomas L. Basich, Letter to President John G. Kapanke of the Board of Pensions, October 7, 1989, p. 1.

[23] Basich, Letter, October 7, 1989, p. 1.

"To thank and commend you . . . "

In his statement to trustees on October 12, 1989, he said that "my main reason for coming here today is to thank and commend you, the trustees and the members of the staff, who have faithfully obeyed" the law that requires those exercising fiduciary responsibility to discharge their duties solely in the interest of plan participants and beneficiaries.[24] He spoke in the wake of the August 1989 Churchwide Assembly of the ELCA that called for immediate divestment in companies doing business in South Africa. Said Pr. Basich to the trustees: "Divestment is a bad idea being employed on behalf of a good cause—the good cause being the eradication of apartheid in South Africa."[25] He declared, however, that:

> Social engineering is certainly not the function of the Board of Pensions. And the pension fund is not a bank from which those with schemes for solving social problems can draw funds.
>
> There is a major battle going on in the ELCA between those who want to use the ELCA and its assets as a political weapon in our society, and those of us who think it is wrong for the Church and its assets to be captive to anyone's political agenda.
>
> If the ELCA ever falters, it will be chiefly because the leadership didn't understand the difference between being a Church and being a political organization. . . .
>
> Frankly, I fear that there is a movement under way first to take control of the Board of Pensions and its assets and later to place the Board [of Pensions] under the direct supervision of the Church Council of the ELCA. . . .
>
> Luther said "no" to councils which erred. May God give *you* the strength to say "No!"[26]

Pr. Basich later characterized that statement as "one of my more eloquent speeches." He added, "I thought it was an excellent speech. . . . Ranks right up there with the Gettysburg Address or just below."[27]

---

[24] Thomas L. Basich, "A Statement to the ELCA Board of Pensions," Minneapolis, Minn., October 12, 1989, p. 1.

[25] Basich, "Statement," October 12, 1989, p. 2.

[26] Basich, "Statement," October 12, 1989, pp. 3-4.

[27] Deposition of the Rev. Thomas L. Basich, Minnesota Fourth Judicial District, Court File No. 93-16711, March 22, 1995, pp. 161-163.

A second time

Pastor Basich spoke a second time to a meeting of the board of trustees of the Board of Pensions, this time on April 6, 1991. The previous day he had made a similar statement to the Benefits Committee of the board. He charged that the trustees had failed "to abide strictly" to the original mission of the Board of Pensions by "allowing your investment enterprise to be dragged into the highly controversial arena of politics and social change."[28]

> We are convinced that the right of portability should be extended to all plan members. . . . We are making this demand
>
> because the original mission of the pension plan has been subverted, and
>
> because the contract under which we became plan participants has been breached, and
>
> because the policies of the Board of Pensions are now under the control of the ELCA Church Council, who claim the right of "final action," and
>
> because reform of the Board of Pensions is impossible under present conditions (those present conditions include the silence or complicity of the bishops and the appeasement policy of the pension trustees), and
>
> because we anticipate continuation of and expansion of socio-political investing and divesting operations with deleterious consequences, and
>
> because we have lost confidence in the pension trustees' willingness and ability to protect our vital interests.[29]

If his demand for withdrawal was not accepted, he declared that he would file a lawsuit. He added, "Of course we will win any lawsuit."

> Your cause is unjust. Heaven itself is against you. And you have no case. . . . You have a choice between peace and war. May God guide you to choose peace and not war.[30]

---

[28] Thomas L. Basich, "A Statement to the ELCA Board of Pensions," Minneapolis, Minn., April 5 and 6, 1991, p. 1.

[29] Basich, "Statement," April 5 and 6, 1991, p. 5.

[30] Basich, "Statement," April 5 and 6, 1991, pp. 9 and 11.

This 1991 presentation he looked upon as "another one of those magnificent speeches I gave . . . to the Benefits Committee . . . and the trustees of the Board of Pensions. . . ."[31]

After hearing Pr. Basich, the members of the board of trustees of the Board of Pensions adopted a resolution, indicating they had considered the written requests from March 19, 1991, of Pr. Thomas L. Basich and his son, Pr. Matthew J. Basich, in which they had "demanded" the right to transfer all of their ELCA pension accumulations to an investment vehicle of their choice. In the resolution, the board "concluded that the present provisions of the ELCA Regular Pension Plan do not permit such transfers under their particular circumstances." The board also declined to recommend plan amendments to permit the transfers.[32]

Demand of the Church Council

Subsequent to his presentations to the trustees, Pr. Basich demanded from the Church Council the right of withdrawal of his pension funds. He sought to make a presentation to the Church Council at its April 13-15, 1991, meeting. As he recounted in *Pension Gate*:

> Our request to speak was denied in a letter from Lowell G. Alme [sic], Secretary of the ELCA, in which he said, "The council does not have authority to act on your request regarding your pension accumulations."
>
> *Baloney Deluxe!* Don't you remember, Lowell, the Church Council has the right of "final action" over pension matters?[33]

A stream of letters, news releases, articles, and telephone calls followed. In a mailing on February 13, 1993, Pr. Thomas Basich urged members of the Pension Defense Fund to "keep phoning" then ELCA Bishop Herbert W. Chilstrom and President John Kapanke of the Board of Pensions.

> Please recruit fellow parishioners, friends, and relatives to join in the Protest Phone-In. . . . The success of this Protest Phone-In depends on numbers and duration, that is, the num-

---

[31] Deposition of the Rev. Thomas L. Basich, Minnesota Fourth Judicial District, Court File No. 93-16711, March 23, 1995, p. 314.

[32] John G. Kapanke, Memorandum to the Church Council of the Evangelical Lutheran Church in America, May 14, 1991, p. 1. The memorandum was prepared as requested by the board of trustees of the Board of Pensions at the board's meeting in Minneapolis, Minn., April 5-7, 1991.

[33] Basich, *Pension Gate*, p. 58.

ber of phone calls we make and the length of time we keep at it. . . . The purpose of this Phone-In is to pressure these people into returning our money. Our opponents and their lawyers are hard boiled and tough. They are immune to appeals to morality, conscience, or even legality. . . .[34]

Notes from a telephone call to Bishop Chilstrom on February 23, 1993, by one identifying himself as Pr. Matthew Basich offer an example of the tone of the "Phone-In" campaign. Recalled Bishop Chilstrom: "He started off by saying that John Kapanke and I have told lies to the church and that we are stealing the money of the members. He wanted me to know that this is a personal issue with him—that 'you [Chilstrom] are a threat to me and to my family. We have been watching how you've been behaving. The truth will come out. I can't control what the consequence of the truth will be. We will never give up.'"[35]

Again, in 1993

The second Basich et al. lawsuit was filed two years after the first one—this time on September 27, 1993—against the same defendants, namely, the Board of Pensions of the ELCA and the ELCA churchwide organization. Initially, Pr. Basich and 29 other plaintiffs were listed in the second suit.[36] Claimed in that second lawsuit was breach of contract. Alleged, too, was that any political and social investing would violate fiduciary duties. Sought was "an injunction enjoining and restraining [the] defendants from continuing to make investment decisions based on political and social criteria rather than solely in the interest of . . . beneficiaries."[37] Requested was a court-ordered change in the pension plan to allow the plaintiffs to withdraw their funds.

Two of the claims were dismissed on February 7, 1994, upon the motion of the defendants. Judge Harry Seymour Crump in Minnesota's Fourth Judicial District in Hennepin County threw out the plaintiffs' claims related to the South Africa Free Funds. He did so because steps already were under way to eliminate those funds. But he declined to dismiss the

---

[34] Thomas L. Basich, "Our Friends in 40 States" (Roseville, Minn.: Pension Defense Fund, February 11, 1993), p. 2.

[35] Herbert W. Chilstrom, "Conversation with Matthew Basich, 4 p.m.," Memorandum to the File (February 23, 1993), p. 1.

[36] Minnesota Fourth Judicial District, Court File No. 93-16711, filed September 27, 1993.

[37] Minnesota Fourth Judicial District, Court File No. 93-16711, p. 13.

"breach of contract" complaint. In essence, the plaintiffs alleged that the Board of Pensions had promised to invest their pension funds according to the prudent-person rule and the legal standards of ERISA, thereby creating a "contract" between each individual plaintiff and the Board of Pensions. Further, the plaintiffs asserted that the ELCA churchwide organization exercised "control" over the Board of Pensions and forced the board to make investment decisions based on social or political factors rather than sound investment principles. Because of such an alleged breach of the board's "contract" with plan members, the plaintiffs argued that the members should be entitled to withdraw their entire pension accumulations.

In the course of the litigation, the ELCA Board of Pensions reported that most of the funds, including the social purpose funds, had outperformed appropriate benchmarks over the previous five-year period. Disputing that report, a representative for the plaintiffs had prepared illustrations that claimed to show what could have been earned by the plaintiffs in alternative investments.

For an article, *The Wall Street Journal* asked Mr. Alan Glickstein, an actuary at Kwasha Lipton and an expert in the type of retirement plan of the ELCA, to review the illustrations offered by the plaintiffs. He called the illustrations "unrealistic," adding, "It's a shame people are getting upset about this."[38]

Following the "discovery" phase in the 1995 litigation, the defendants moved again for summary judgment, i.e., dismissal of the claim for breach of contract. They argued that the court lacked jurisdiction over the subject matter because the lawsuit concerned an internal religious dispute about church doctrine. Resolution of the dispute by a civil court, they said, would violate the First Amendment of the U.S. Constitution as well as the Freedom of Religion Clause of the Constitution in the State of Minnesota. That motion was denied by Judge Crump, who again refused in an order signed on April 18, 1995, to dismiss the action. He ordered that the trial proceed.

An "interlocutory appeal" was filed immediately with the Minnesota Court of Appeals by the Board of Pensions of the ELCA and the ELCA churchwide organization on the question of jurisdiction.

In greater detail

On that question of jurisdiction, the Minnesota Court of Appeals issued a ruling on November 28, 1995. The decision provides a summary

---

[38] "Reality Checks on Funds Help Calm Doubters," *The Wall Street Journal*, December 8, 1995, p. C25. Kwasha Lipton was a benefits consulting firm in Fort Lee, N.J.

of the journey through the courts in this matter. Judge P. J. Kalitowski, in the written opinion, recalled that the plaintiffs had filed claims "for breach of contract and breach of fiduciary duty" against the Board of Pensions of the ELCA and the ELCA's churchwide organization.[39] Both the ELCA's churchwide organization and the Board of Pensions had moved for a summary judgment of dismissal on the grounds that the First Amendment of the U.S. Constitution and the Freedom of Conscience Clause of the Minnesota Constitution precluded court jurisdiction in the matter. Said the Court of Appeals (capitalization shown as rendered in the original):

> The Pastors participate in defined contribution pension accounts, contributed to by their congregations and administered by the Board of Pensions. The Pastors allege that the Board of Pensions has mismanaged funds by investing and divesting pursuant to social concerns rather than solely in the economic best interests of the plan participants.
>
> The ELCA and the Board of Pensions are organized as Minnesota nonprofit corporations. The ELCA is comprised of 65 Synods governing 11,000 congregations. Each Synod elects representatives to the Churchwide Assembly, the highest legislative authority in the ELCA. When the Churchwide Assembly is not in session, the ELCA is governed by the Church Council. The Board of Pensions was established by the ELCA in 1988 to provide retirement income and benefits to Lutheran pastors and lay church employees. The ELCA Constitution provides that the Board of Pensions is to manage and operate the pension fund with the "design and policy adopted by the Churchwide Assembly." The Board of Pension's [sic] Articles of Incorporation provide that the Board is
>
>> organized and shall be operated exclusively for religious purposes and exclusively for the benefit of and to assist in carrying out the purposes of the ELCA.
>
> The ELCA Churchwide Assembly and Council have final authority and control over policies implemented by the Board of Pensions.
>
> In 1977 the Lutheran World Federation Assembly declared that apartheid was so contrary to the Lutheran understanding

---

[39] Court of Appeals of Minnesota, November 28, 1995, Nos. C8-95-882 and CX-95-883, 540 *North Western Reporter*, 2d Series, p. 84.

of believers in Christ that it must be rejected as a matter of faith itself. The ELCA expressed its opposition to apartheid by passing a resolution to "see that none of our ELCA pension funds will be invested in companies doing business in South Africa." The Board of Pensions responded in 1988 by adopting the "equivalency policy," whereby the Board of Pensions agreed to divest (and refrain from making new investments) in companies with South African holdings whenever the conditions of risk and return were equal between stocks and bonds held by the Board. The equivalency policy governed investment decisions until its repeal in 1993.

A dissenting group of Lutherans led by respondent Reverend Thomas Basich disagreed with the Churchwide Assembly's divestment policy. Basich and others published articles opposing the ELCA's decision to use its assets as a political weapon and condemning the Board of Pensions for "acquiescing" to the Churchwide Assembly's pressure on the issue of apartheid. Basich requested that he and others be allowed to withdraw their pension funds. The Board of Pensions denied this request. In response, Basich and others filed a derivative action suit against the Board of Pensions. This court held the Pastors did not have standing to bring a derivative suit. *Basich v. Board of Pensions of the Evangelical Lutheran Church in Am.*, 493 N.W.2d 293, 296 (Minn. App. 1992). The Pastors then filed this action for individual relief on the grounds of breach of contract and breach of fiduciary duty.

ISSUES

1. Does the First Amendment of the United States Constitution prevent the district court from exercising jurisdiction over this dispute?

2. Does the Freedom of Conscience Clause of the Minnesota Constitution prevent the district court from exercising jurisdiction over this dispute?

. . .

The Pastors argue that a review of this case will not require the court to entangle itself in issues of Lutheran doctrine. We disagree. . . . While the Board of Pensions is required to prudently invest its holdings, the ELCA created the Board to *both* provide for pastors' retirement needs *and* assist the ELCA in accomplishing doctrinal goals. The ELCA enacted the equivalency policy in an effort to further its social and doctrinal goals of opposing apartheid. Accordingly, any review of the Board of Pensions' divestment and equivalency policies would entangle the court in reviewing church doctrine and policy.

In addition, the district court would be required to examine church doctrine and organization to determine whether a breach of contract occurred in this case. The plan document is the primary "contract" between the parties. It provides that the Board of Pensions shall discharge its duties with the care that a prudent person would use in the conduct of an enterprise of like character with like aims. Thus, the district court would be required to examine the ELCA's "aims" before it could determine the breach of contract issue. Such inquiry into church motives is forbidden by the Establishment Clause of the United States Constitution.

The Pastors also contend that this case can be resolved on neutral principles of contract and trust law. We disagree. The flaw in this contention is illustrated by the Pastors' admission that the ELCA could properly prohibit investments by the Board of Pensions in morally obnoxious commercial activity such as prostitution or pornography. There are no neutral principles of law that would enable a district court to distinguish between investments that Lutheran doctrine would find to be morally acceptable and those that it should find to be morally unacceptable. We conclude that the Establishment Clause of the First Amendment deprives the district court of subject matter jurisdiction in this dispute because review of this issue would require the district court to look beyond neutral principles of contract and trust law and entangle itself in issues of church doctrine. . . .

An analysis of the four elements of the Freedom of Conscience Clause test leads us to conclude that allowing the district court's review of this matter would violate the Freedom of Conscience Clause [of the Minnesota Constitution]. First, there is no question that the ELCA acted pursuant to a sincerely held religious belief by enacting the equivalency policy. The Lutheran

World Federation declared that apartheid must be rejected as a matter of Lutheran faith itself. Similarly, the Constituting Convention of the ELCA passed a resolution stating that divestment was the appropriate response to the "sin of apartheid."

Second, review of this case would burden the exercise of the ELCA's religious beliefs. If the civil courts were allowed to rescind pension plan contracts every time a group of dissenting participants disagreed with the Board of Pensions' social or moral investment strategies, the ELCA's ability to express its faith through social and moral investment would be substantially compromised. Additionally . . . , to review this case, the district court would be required to question the ELCA's basis for a decision that it contends was founded in Lutheran doctrine. Judicial inquiry into issues of church doctrine is itself a substantial burden. . . . Accordingly, a review of this case would burden the ELCA's exercise of religious beliefs.

Third, the government does not have a compelling interest in reviewing this case. The Pastors argue that there is an important government interest in providing a forum for review of this matter. We disagree. The forum best suited to review the Pastors' grievance is the Churchwide Assembly. . . . As the highest legislative authority in the ELCA, the Churchwide Assembly's determination on this issue is final. The civil courts need not hear this case to ensure public "peace and safety. . . ."

We conclude that a review of this case would substantially burden the ELCA's exercise of religion. Therefore, the Freedom of Conscience Clause of the Minnesota Constitution deprives the district court of subject matter jurisdiction in this dispute.

DECISION

The district court erred in denying appellants' motion for summary judgment on the grounds that the court did not have subject matter jurisdiction. The district court's decision is reversed and this matter is dismissed pursuant to the Establishment Clause of the First Amendment and the Freedom of Conscience Clause of the Minnesota Constitution.[40]

---

[40] Court of Appeals of Minnesota, November 28, 1995, Nos. C8-95-882 and CX-95-883, 540 *North Western Reporter*, 2d Series, pp. 84-88.

Another step in the legal drama

The plaintiffs then took the matter to the Minnesota Supreme Court, which denied on January 25, 1996, the petition for review of the matter.[41] They undertook yet another step on April 24, 1996. They appealed to the U.S. Supreme Court to overturn the decision of the Minnesota Court of Appeals. In their petition for judicial review ("writ of certiorari") of the decision of the appeals court, they argued that the lawsuit was not about religious doctrine. Rather, the entire litigation, they said, focused on the pension assets belonging to the individual participants in the plan and not to the ELCA. Further, they declared that the ELCA "owes direct fiduciary duties to all participants in the plan."[42]

The U.S. Supreme Court refused on October 7, 1996, to consider the claims of Pr. Thomas L. Basich and the other plaintiffs. Read the court record:

> No. 95-1796. Thomas L. Basich, et al., Petitioners v. Board of Pensions, Evangelical Lutheran Church in America, et al. Petition for writ of certiorari to the Court of Appeals of Minnesota denied.[43]

The U.S. Supreme Court left in place the decision of the Minnesota Court of Appeals supporting the ELCA churchwide organization and the Board of Pensions of the ELCA on the basis of both the U.S. and Minnesota constitutions. The journey through the courts had ended.

Even years later

But there was more to the story. On March 13, 1997, Pr. Thomas Basich and others received a certificate of incorporation from the State of Minnesota for the Augustana Orthodox and Evangelical Lutheran Synod. Advent Lutheran Church voted on April 30, 1997, to withdraw from the ELCA and join the newly created synod.[44] Later, the elder Pr. Basich claimed that some "co-conspirators inside Advent were planning

---

[41] Supreme Court of the State of Minnesota (St. Paul, Minn.: C8-95-882 and CX-95-883).

[42] Petitioners' Reply Brief, "Petition for Writ of Certiorari to the Minnesota Court of Appeals," Supreme Court of the United States (File No. 95-1796, October 1996 term), pp. 2-4.

[43] United States Supreme Court, Monday, October 7, 1996, No. 95-1796, p. 10.

[44] Irregularities in the conduct of that meeting were outlined by the Rev. Mark S. Hanson, then bishop of the ELCA's Saint Paul Area Synod, in a letter of censure to Advent Lutheran Church of Roseville, Minn., dated May 2, 1997, pp. 3-4.

to overthrow the two pastors of Advent (Thomas Basich and Matthew Basich) and take control of Advent's pulpit and [the congregation's] very valuable property. . . . The internal co-conspirators, unmasked, confused, and demoralized, fled, never to return. . . . The angel of the Lord swept them all away with a flick of his little finger."[45]

After the pension plan of that new Augustana Orthodox and Evangelical Lutheran Synod was established in July 1997, the pension assets of Pr. Thomas Basich were transferred in August 1997 to the new plan, with Charles Schwab serving as custodian of the funds.

There was still more: Pr. Thomas Basich wrote then ELCA Presiding Bishop H. George Anderson on October 6, 2001. That was the final month of Bishop Anderson's term. In that letter, Pr. Basich included a copy of a 21-page document that he said was intended for distribution by him to members of the Pension Defense Fund. The title of the document: "The Evangelical Lutheran Church in America and Its Board of Pensions Should Repent and Make Amends."

Nearly six years had passed at that point since the Minnesota Court of Appeals had dismissed his case. Five years had elapsed since the U.S. Supreme Court had refused to hear the matter. More than four years had unfolded since he had formed his own church body and ceased to be an ordained minister of the ELCA. He had observed his 75th birthday and was still writing about his lawsuits.

At the beginning of the controversy, Pr. Thomas Basich declared that he would be persistent. Clearly, he kept his promise.

---

[45] Thomas L. Basich, *The Evangelical Lutheran Church in America and Its Board of Pensions Should Repent and Make Amends* (St. Paul, Minn.: Pension Defense Fund, October 2001), pp. 21-22.

CHAPTER 7

Key Leaders Shape Strong Foundation: "This Has To Be Done"

Emerson wrote, "There is properly no history; only biography."[1] The observation is an insightful and accurate one. History often is shaped chiefly by individuals and their actions.

Many people over the past two and a half centuries performed significant roles in the unfolding history of Lutheran pension and benefit programs. That certainly has been true for the Board of Pensions of the Evangelical Lutheran Church in America and the programs of the ELCA's predecessor church bodies.

Accounts of Lutheran pension programs could be filled with the biographies of various trustees and leaders. Consider a few of them who had special, lasting impact. (A complete listing of the trustees who have served, to date, in overseeing the ELCA's Board of Pensions is provided in Appendix One.)

As first chair

Ms. Mildred Berg was the first person elected by the trustees of the ELCA Board of Pensions. She was chosen as chair at the inaugural meeting of the trustees that was held June 29–July 1, 1987. Simultaneous meetings of the various boards and committees of the newly formed ELCA churchwide organization took place on three days at the Hyatt Regency Hotel in Rosemont, Ill., near O'Hare Airport in Chicago.

Ms. Berg served as chair for six years through 1993, when her term ended. She was interviewed in West Palm Beach, Fla., on Friday, February 3, 2006. She died unexpectedly at the age of 83 the following Monday, February 6.[2]

---

[1] Ralph Waldo Emerson, *Essays: First Series*, 1841.

[2] Quotations of observations by Ms. Mildred Berg on her role as the first chair of the board of trustees of the Board of Pensions are from the oral history interview conducted by Mr. John G. Kapanke, president of the Board of Pensions, and the Rev. Lowell G. Almen, then secretary of the ELCA, on February 3, 2006, in West Palm Beach, Fla.

Ms. Berg came to her role as chair with an extensive background in business and management. She worked in a New York bank for 40 years, half of that time as a bank officer. For a number of years, she was corporate secretary of the bank. She retired as a senior vice president and looked forward in retirement to serving the church in various ways. In the freedom of retirement, she devoted generous time to her work as chair not only in trustee meetings but also beyond those meetings in contacts on behalf of the Board of Pensions with key leaders of the ELCA's churchwide ministries and the ELCA's Church Council.

She served in a firm, but fair, way in guiding the trustees through their early decisions for the establishment and operation of the ELCA's Board of Pensions. Among those initial decisions was the election of the president of the Board of Pensions.

Ms. Berg had been a member of the Recruitment and Interview Committee of the ELCA's churchwide Transition Team, the committee appointed to determine the nominees for the position of president. The interview committee, she recalled, had established three primary criteria for the president: (1) understanding and knowledge of the investments of the pension program; (2) experience in organization and management; and (3) ability to work with a governing board. Recalling the selection of Mr. John Kapanke as the first president, she observed, "Obviously, it was the right decision."

In her work as chair, Ms. Berg believed that it was important to get the board "to operate as a complete whole." Trustees came from three different church bodies—The American Lutheran Church (ALC), Lutheran Church in America (LCA), and, by far the smallest, Association of Evangelical Lutheran Churches (AELC). "The LCA and ALC had different concepts to a certain extent in the operation of the pension system," she recalled. At the same time, representatives of the smallest of the three merging bodies came with "agendas [and] some fixed ideas" that apparently had been shaped by that group's withdrawal in 1976 from The Lutheran Church–Missouri Synod. Yet, through ongoing effort in the initial years, greater cohesiveness among the trustees and a steady focus on the program of the ELCA's Board of Pensions emerged.

After the election of the president, the second major decision for the new board of trustees was the location of the office in Minneapolis. The space that had served the LCA's Board of Pensions was available. Likewise, the space that had served as the ALC's national office at 422 South Fifth

Street was vacant. The Publishing House of the ELCA (Augsburg Fortress, Publishers) occupied only the lower part of that building. Other locations in downtown Minneapolis were considered too. Eventually, the space that had been used by the LCA Board of Pensions was selected as more adequate than the other possibilities, Ms. Berg recalled. In addition, the data information system was in operation there.

As the years passed, the trustees developed increased abilities to work together as a group:

> We [had] members on the board who really understood how to move an issue down the table. That was important, as it is in any church group. Particularly in the board of trustees of the Board of Pensions, we needed the people who had the expertise and the abilities to understand the issue involved. They understood the mission, the call, and the charge of the church. Those were . . . important points. And that is what I always stressed. That's what came true and has come true over the years.[3]

Decision on the first president

Shortly before 6 P.M. (Central Daylight Time) on Tuesday, June 30, 1987, Mr. Kapanke was elected by a two-thirds vote as the first president of the ELCA's Board of Pensions. Earlier that afternoon, the trustees had interviewed the two nominees whose names had been submitted by the churchwide Transition Team. Mr. Kapanke began immediately his first four-year term. With re-elections, he led the Board of Pensions in the ensuing decades through turbulent times and crucial developments.

Mr. Kapanke, who was 43 at the time of his election, came to the position of president and chief executive officer after nearly a decade and a half of service with the LCA's Board of Pensions. He had worked in the LCA pension program from 1973 through 1987, eventually becoming senior vice president for investments. Prior to his service with the LCA's board, he was a financial analyst for what was then known as Aid Association for Lutherans in Appleton, Wis., now Thrivent Financial for Lutherans. He was a 1969 graduate of the University of Wisconsin at La Crosse with a degree in business administration. During his studies, he was the recipient of *The Wall Street Journal* Student Achievement Award and graduated with honors.

Upon election as president, his focus had to shift immediately from his previous responsibilities to getting the ELCA's Pension and Other

---

[3] Berg oral history, p. 7.

Benefits Program and systems ready for full implementation on January 1, 1988. That was no simple task. "We had to preserve this quirk for [one predecessor plan] . . . and . . . something else from [another predecessor] plan." If the new program could have started with "a clean slate, it would have been so much better," he observed. Planners sought to preserve the best in each of the predecessor plans.[4]

He recalled that "we had a fairly positive meshing of our staffs" from the ALC and LCA pension and benefits programs. "[W]e just had a huge task of making sure that we were up and running [on January 1, 1988] that people . . . got together and they worked together pretty well."[5]

Predecessor allegiances, however, did show themselves in trustee meetings. Those allegiances presented a challenge in the early days "where some of the divisions of the merger became apparent . . . during board discussions."

> I always will be . . . thankful for the leadership of Mildred Berg who . . . was instrumental in holding that board together during times [in which] some of the old issues and arguments were still being debated. She . . . was a very strong leader, but she had a wonderful sense of being able to keep her eye on the big picture and make sure that wasn't derailed through some petty problems at the trustee level.[6]

Looking back on the first two decades of the operation of the ELCA's Board of Pensions, Mr. Kapanke identified various difficult issues. "[T]here is no question the whole divestment issue was the biggest challenge," he observed. That was an issue prior to the formation of the ELCA and continued even to 1996 when the U.S. Supreme Court declined to hear a lawsuit that had been filed against the Board of Pensions and the ELCA on that matter (see Chapter 6).

Reflecting on the development of pension plans in predecessor churches, Mr. Kapanke praised the visionary leaders who moved to defined-contribution plans that gave individuals responsibility in managing their assets and benefits, but also provided protection to the sponsoring church

---

[4] John G. Kapanke, "Transcript of an Oral History Interview," conducted by the Rev. Lowell G. Almen in the office of the Board of Pensions in Minneapolis, January 23, 2008, p. 4.

[5] Kapanke oral history, January 23, 2008, p. 5.

[6] Kapanke oral history, January 23, 2008, p. 6.

bodies. Churches led the way in such plans long before the 401(k) plans came into existence, he noted.[7]

In the early years, staff of the Board of Pensions faced the need to undertake a "major overhaul of both the health plan and the pension plan" as well as add new fund options. Rates for the ELCA's Medical and Dental Benefits Plan needed major adjustments, given the rapid growth in the cost of health care in the late 1980s and early 1990s. Operation of the plans of predecessor churches and the ELCA needed to be streamlined to reduce costs and increase efficiency.[8]

"Corporate" and "church" culture

An ongoing challenge over the years related to the style of operation of the Board of Pensions. "[W]e had a blend of a business, a corporate culture, along with the church culture. And it could not be 'either/or,' but had to be both," Mr. Kapanke emphasized. "[W]e are a unit of the church that operates a very significant business, and it is a very delicate business. . . . [O]ne piece . . . in our culture [within the Board of Pensions] is the understanding of those whom we serve and how we serve them. . . . We always have said one of our core competencies is this customer intimacy . . . , and that continues" amid the changes of the passing years.[9]

He led in efforts for advocacy on behalf of plan members, and sought to serve their best interests. In addressing a group of retirees in 1999, he employed the image of a small sailboat in heavy winds and choppy water. Competitors, like sharks, may be seeking customers. Yet congregations and plan members need "life rafts" of services through the Board of Pensions to meet safely their needs. The image he used reflected the turbulence experienced amid fluctuating markets, escalating health costs, and other uncertainties. Yet the Board of Pensions sought over the years to provide a dependable harbor of programs and services to fit the needs of plan members.

In various settings, Mr. Kapanke urged greater awareness of the importance of health and wellness. Analysis of claims highlighted key issues leading to health problems among members. For example, weight and lack of physical exercise were reported, with about two-thirds of ELCA clergy overweight or obese. High blood pressure, heart disease, cholesterol, poor

---

[7] Kapanke oral history, January 23, 2008, p. 13.

[8] Kapanke oral history, January 23, 2008, p. 9.

[9] Kapanke oral history, January 23, 2008, p. 15.

nutritional habits, difficulty handling stress, and instances of depression were matters of concern too. He was not afraid to underscore the long-term consequences of such problems both as a threat to individuals who gave inadequate attention to wellness and in terms of the overall cost of the medical plan.

As he looked ahead, Mr. Kapanke underscored the importance of enhanced service to members as well as the need for growth and financial viability in the operation. Improved use of technology also was seen by him as important.[10]

When asked what he hoped would be seen as the chief legacy of service as president from the perspective of 25 to 50 years in the future, Mr. Kapanke suggested two things: (1) the commitment of the Board of Pensions to the work and well-being of the people of the Evangelical Lutheran Church in America; and (2) his effective leadership of the Board of Pensions as a unit of the ELCA's churchwide ministries. Keeping in mind the vision statement, "Helping people lead healthy lives and achieve financial security," he expressed the hope that people will say that the Board of Pensions "under my leadership really strived to help people achieve financial security" and demonstrated "a genuine interest" in the health and wholeness of members.[11]

Mr. Kapanke said he hopes that when people view his era of leadership, they will see that the Board of Pensions "really cared about people, cared about the people we served . . . , understood the ministry of this church, and helped support that ministry through benefit programs" established by this church.[12]

Experienced church leader

Another key leader in the initial years of the ELCA's Board of Pensions was the Rev. Reuben T. Swanson. He served from 1978 to 1987 as secretary of the Lutheran Church in America, and prior to that was bishop of the LCA's Nebraska Synod from 1964 to 1978.[13] As a trustee of the Board of Pensions elected upon the constituting of the ELCA, Pr. Swanson

---

[10] Transcript of interview with Mr. John G. Kapanke by the Rev. Lowell G. Almen, October 21, 2008, pp. 2-3.

[11] Kapanke interview, October 21, 2008, p. 4.

[12] Kapanke interview, October 21, 2008, p. 4.

[13] During the years that he served the Nebraska Synod, the title of the office was "president." In 1980, the LCA changed the title to "bishop," the term by which the office of oversight is known today in the ELCA.

combined his knowledge of the needs of pastors and other church workers with his keen understanding of wise investment practices and effective administration for pensions and other benefits. He worked closely with Ms. Berg in her role as chair in helping to guide the trustees through various contentious issues. He served as vice chair of the board of trustees and chair of the Investment Committee until his term ended in 1993.

Pr. Swanson remembered well the years of the Great Depression. As a child and teenager, he saw what his father faced at that time. His parents were farmers near Bertrand, Neb. His father also was a bank director who, with others, sought to keep the local bank afloat in the 1930s.

Pr. Swanson served in the Pacific Theater in the U.S. Navy during World War II. He returned from military service to complete his bachelor of arts degree at Augustana College and his theology studies at Augustana Lutheran Seminary, both in Rock Island, Ill. He was ordained on June 17, 1951, and served congregations in West Hempstead, N.Y., and Omaha, Neb., before being elected to his synodical responsibilities. He died at the age of 86 on October 3, 2008. Throughout his long service, he kept foremost in his mind the care of the whole church as well as its pastors and members.

Characterizing the initial development of the ELCA's Board of Pensions, Pr. Swanson said that he harbored a "vivid recollection" of "a coming together of people from different backgrounds" who were "working with a commitment to form a good organization that would provide governance and leadership in the pension program." At the same time, he saw that "the most challenging issue, and frustrating to a certain extent, [was] helping people understand that, in fulfilling our fiduciary responsibility [as trustees], the board [members] had to be very, very careful."[14]

In the planning for the ELCA's Board of Pensions, past differences clouded at times a vision for the future. Pr. Swanson said "that the disagreements and the tensions . . . were the result of an unwillingness to see anything different from the practice" that individuals had known in their particular church body. Some refused to accept the fact "that there might be a benefit" from another church body.[15]

He regretted that the pension plans of the predecessor church bodies and that of the ELCA did not have a way to provide greater equality in the pensions of retirees. He recalled that the Augustana Lutheran Church,

[14] Reuben T. Swanson, "Transcript of an Oral History Interview," conducted by the Rev. Lowell G. Almen and Mr. John G. Kapanke, Omaha, Neb., May 5, 2006, p. 2.

[15] Swanson oral history, pp. 14-15.

which merged into the LCA in 1962, had a partially socialized pension program. That is, the portion contributed by each congregation for pension purposes was divided equally among all the Augustana pastors. By contrast, the amount that each pastor submitted for pension purposes was reserved for the benefit of that individual pastor. In planning for the ELCA pension program, "I would have wished that somehow we could have . . . equalize[d] the benefits in retirement" for church workers.[16] He acknowledged the complexity of such an effort, but recalled with appreciation his roots in the Augustana Lutheran Church and the cohesive care for all pastors reflected through the sharing of pension contributions from congregations.

Leaders for predecessor programs

Other leaders also were crucial in contributing to the solid foundation that existed for the ELCA's Board of Pensions. That foundation emerged through the experiences of the ALC and LCA pension and other benefit programs.

Mr. L. Edwin Wang was named executive secretary of the LCA's Board of Pensions upon its formation in 1962.[17] The title later was changed to president, and he continued in that capacity until he retired in the spring of 1987. His service with the LCA board was interrupted only briefly when he took a leave of absence in 1967 to serve as acting insurance commissioner for the state of Minnesota. He did so as a favor for a friend, Mr. Harold LeVander, then Minnesota's governor.

Mr. Wang died at Missoula, Mont., on January 28, 2009, at the age of 89. His mission in life, he believed, was to provide pension and health insurance support for Lutheran pastors and church employees. Pastors then could care for the spiritual needs of those whom they served because they could know that their pension needs and health-care benefits were in good hands.[18]

Reflecting on his years of service in church pension plans, Mr. Wang expressed concern that "our antecedent churches got started too late with too small pension contributions."

---

[16] Swanson oral history, p. 9.

[17] In 1962, the Lutheran Church in America was constituted through a merger of the Augustana Lutheran Church, with Swedish immigrant roots, the American Evangelical Lutheran Church, with Danish roots, the Finnish Evangelical Lutheran Church (Suomi Synod), and the United Lutheran Church in America, which was heavily concentrated in the East, with strong early immigrant German roots. The ULCA was the largest of the four merging church bodies.

[18] "Edwin Wang dies at 89," Missoulian.com news online, February 6, 2009.

I must say it was very sad to see the plight of pensioned ministers when I came on the job with the antecedent Augustana [Lutheran] Church in 1956. By the time of our previous merger [to form the LCA], 1963, the benefit levels were so low it was sad. It makes one cringe to think that retirement and survivor pensioners were forced to live on such tiny monthly incomes from the church plans.

On the other hand, I do recognize it is easy now for us, when the plans are at this stage, to criticize what congregations did earlier. We need to remember that when pensions were commenced in the antecedent United Lutheran Church in America (ULCA) and Augustana Lutheran Church, it took courage on the part of lay persons to speak up and say, "This has to be done." It is easy now for us to say the contribution rate in the ULCA should have been four-eight [four percent from the member and eight percent from the congregation] when it started. Or, in Augustana, it should have been four-eight [percent], instead of on a much smaller basis—the equivalent of three [percent] for the member and, on a congregation per capita basis, a really tiny amount. The pension plans might not have been started if they had not commenced on a small basis. . . .

[M]uch credit has to be given for what was done. It may not be what should have been done as we look in retrospect, but we must be grateful for that start.[19]

Perhaps the most intense focus of an October 22, 1986, interview with Mr. Wang was the result of timing. Clearly, the issue of investment policy loomed large for him. He recalled that heated debates took place in the late 1970s and throughout the 1980s over the exercise of corporate social responsibility.[20] "The South Africa situation . . . caused a great tension, not only for us but for others in the church."[21]

---

[19] L. Edwin Wang, "Transcript of Oral History Interview," October 22, 1986, pp. 28-29. The interview, which was conducted by Franklin L. Jensen in Minneapolis, was one of a series in an oral-history project of the Lutheran Council in the USA. Interviews were conducted with various leaders in The American Lutheran Church, the Association of Evangelical Lutheran Churches, and the Lutheran Church in America, the three church bodies that came together to form the Evangelical Lutheran Church in America. The ELCA was constituted on April 30, 1987, and became the successor corporation for the three predecessor churches, effective at 12:01 a.m. (Central Standard Time), on January 1, 1988.

[20] Wang oral history, p. 20.

[21] Wang oral history, p. 21.

Oppression of the Black majority by the White minority government in South Africa was the chief point of concern. Various resolutions had been approved by conventions in both the LCA and ALC that urged divestment from corporations doing business in South Africa. Proponents of such resolutions saw divestment as a strategy to bring favorable change for those oppressed.

From the tone of the debate, some clearly viewed the leadership of both the LCA and ALC pension programs as recalcitrant on the issue, even as the legal obligations of trustees to follow the prudent-person rule in investments were underscored. In the midst of the debates, Mr. Wang and others sought to lead with wisdom as well as commitment to those served through the LCA's pension and other benefits program. (For additional discussion of the LCA's "divestment battles," including observations of Mr. Wang on that issue, see Chapter 13.)

Lacking similar interview

A similar interview, unfortunately, was never conducted with the Rev. Henry Fritz Treptow, who served as executive secretary of the ALC Board of Pensions from July 1976 through December 1987. He had been assistant executive secretary of the Board of Pensions for a year prior to becoming executive secretary, the senior position in the unit.

Before he undertook leadership of the ALC's pension and other benefits program, he was assistant executive secretary of the ALC's Board of Trustees from 1971 to 1975. In the ALC, responsibility for investment management, including pension funds, resided with the Board of Trustees. Program and operational functions were carried out by the Board of Pensions.

Pr. Treptow retired in 1988 upon the formation of the ELCA and died on June 13, 2002, in Kerrville, Texas, at the age of 74. In eulogizing Pr. Treptow upon his death, a former chair of the ALC's pension board, Ms. Elizabeth Storaasli of Duluth, Minn., said the ALC's Board of Pensions under his direction became a place where "personal connections with people" were emphasized.[22]

Before he began his work with the ALC's Board of Trustees and Board of Pensions, he served as a parish pastor and a staff member of the ALC's American missions unit.

---

[22] "Treptow, Former Director of ALC Board of Pensions, Dies," News Service of the Evangelical Lutheran Church in America, June 20, 2002.

When he undertook his responsibilities in the ALC Board of Pensions, Pr. Treptow stepped into a circumstance that few would envy. He was succeeding a widely known leader in Lutheran church pension plans in the second half of the twentieth century.

His predecessor, the Rev. George Henri Berkheimer, served as executive secretary of the ALC's Board of Pensions from 1963 until he retired in 1976. Previously, Pr. Berkheimer had been executive secretary of the Board of Pensions of the United Lutheran Church in America from 1955 until the Lutheran Church in America began operation in 1963.

When Mr. Wang was chosen to be the executive secretary of the LCA's Board of Pensions, Pr. Berkheimer was selected as associate executive secretary of the new LCA Board of Pensions. Before he had accepted election to that post, however, he chose instead the call from The American Lutheran Church.

Prior to his pension responsibilities, Pr. Berkheimer was secretary and assistant to the president of the ULCA's Central Pennsylvania Synod from 1949 to 1955. He was, for a time, a parish pastor. During World War II, he was called to be a U.S. Army chaplain in the Pacific region from 1942 through 1945, when he was discharged with the rank of major. He died at the age of 76 on June 16, 1987.

Pr. Berkheimer succeeded Mr. Harlan N. Rye in the ALC's Board of Pensions. Mr. Rye retired at that time after serving the pension department of the former Evangelical Lutheran Church from 1954 through 1960 and then leading the ALC's Board of Pensions in its initial two years of operation.[23] In addition to Mr. Rye's retirement, the ALC faced in 1963 the loss of the board's chair, Judge Henry N. Graven of Green, Iowa, because the ALC had a compulsory retirement age of 70 for those elected to office. Judge Graven had led in the formation of the pension plan of the American Lutheran Church of 1930 and had "spent more than 40 years in the interests of retirement income for church workers."[24] Judge Graven died on February 1, 1970, and Mr. Rye on June 11, 1970.

---

[23] The American Lutheran Church was constituted in April 1960 and began operation in 1961. The ALC was formed through a merger of the Evangelical Lutheran Church, which had Norwegian immigrant roots, the American Lutheran Church of 1930, with German immigrant roots, and the United Evangelical Lutheran Church, with Danish roots. The Lutheran Free Church, which had Norwegian immigrant roots, joined the ALC, effective February 1, 1963.

[24] "ULCA Pension Expert Takes Post with ALC," news release of the National Lutheran Council, September 5, 1962 (number 62-106).

A model pension plan

Visionary leadership was shown by a significant cadre of laity in the first half of the twentieth century. Through their efforts in the late 1920s, the American Federation of Lutheran Brotherhoods developed a model pension plan for Lutheran churches. In the ensuing years, several churches adopted the plan, sometimes with some variations. A report on the topic at the federation's 1931 convention declared:

> A deeper and more sympathetic concern of the laity of the church about provisions for the clergy in disability or superannuation is cause for thanksgiving.

> The change in popular opinion, which began to look upon a definite provision for old age as a right resulting from service rather than as charity has not only relieved the embarrassment of the clergy, but, as well, cleared the way for placing the pension fund upon a proven actuarial basis, which will assure pensioners of a fixed income during life.

> The American Federation of Lutheran Brotherhoods records its satisfaction over the progress toward sound and permanent pension plans. . . .[25]

Perhaps the key figure in the creation of the model pension plan for Lutheran churches was Mr. George A. Huggins. He established in 1911 the actuarial firm of Huggins and Company in Philadelphia. He was an active member of the Episcopal Church, but he served as the actuarial advisor for several of the Lutheran churches from at least the mid-1920s to his death in 1959. His work with various denominations is documented as far back as 1904.[26] He became prominent as a key "architect of denominational pension programs."[27] Indeed, he was the ranking authority of his era on clergy pension plans.

---

[25] Third Biennial Convention of the American Federation of Lutheran Brotherhoods, Pittsburgh, Pa., November 10-11, 1931, p. 50.

[26] E. J. Moorhead, "Historical Background," 1938, Huggins Actuarial Services, Inc., Philadelphia, Pa., http://www.hugginsactuarial.com/history.html. In the early part of the twentieth century, Mr. George A. Huggins played a key role in developing the actuarial basis for the Ministerial Sustentation Fund of the Presbyterian Church, a pension plan with employers providing 80 percent of the funding and the clergy and lay employees the other 20 percent. His actuarial knowledge and advice also were crucial in helping to shape the model contributory pension plan that was put in place for various Lutheran churches by the middle of the twentieth century.

[27] R. Douglas Brackenridge and Lois A. Boyd, *Presbyterians and Pensions: The Roots and Growth of Pensions in the Presbyterian Church (U.S.A.)* (Atlanta: John Knox Press, 1988), p. 65.

Mr. Huggins was "the motivating force for the whole field of church pension plans," according to Mr. Michael Mudry, who is retired from what is now known as the Hay Huggins firm.[28] In his early career, he knew Mr. Huggins. Following in the footsteps of Mr. Huggins, Mr. Mudry served as an advisor to Lutheran pension plans in the second half of the twentieth century. While various pension and aid plans had existed since the 1700s, churches led the way in the twentieth century in creating actuarially based, funded pension plans.

The efforts of members of the American Federation of Lutheran Brotherhoods were crucial in moving churches to embrace actuarially sound, contributory pension plans. The association itself had its origins in the Lutheran Brotherhood of America, an umbrella organization for the men's societies initially in the United Lutheran Church in America and the Augustana Lutheran Church but later embracing similar groups in other Lutheran churches. The group's first convention was held in Chicago in 1919.

When the Norwegian Lutheran Church of America was constituted in 1917, two lifelong Lutherans—Mr. Jacob Preus, the insurance commissioner of the State of Minnesota, and Mr. Herman Ekern, a former insurance commissioner for the State of Wisconsin—urged formation of a not-for-profit mutual aid society for members of that church body. Launched, as a result, was the Lutheran Union. In its first year of operation, the Lutheran Union undertook negotiation with leaders of the Lutheran Brotherhood of America (LBA). As a result, the Lutheran Union became, in effect, the insurance auxiliary of LBA, although it remained a separate organization. Through that LBA relationship, the Lutheran Union ceased to be strictly a mutual aid society for members of one church, the Norwegian Lutheran Church of America. In fact, the scope of potential customers for insurance was expanded considerably in that relationship to include other Lutheran churches. Even the name of the Lutheran Union was changed to Lutheran Brotherhood, effective June 11, 1920.[29]

---

[28] This observation by Mr. Michael Mudry was made in an interview with the Rev. Lowell G. Almen in February 2009.

[29] In 2001, Lutheran Brotherhood of Minneapolis merged with Aid Association for Lutherans of Appleton, Wis., to form Thrivent Financial for Lutherans.

The American Federation of Lutheran Brotherhoods reached its zenith in the 1930s and 1940s.[30] During its active years, the federation played a significant role in supporting religious centers for soldiers and sailors and undergirding scouting programs in Lutheran congregations. Through the federation, assistance also was provided for such inter-Lutheran efforts as the National Lutheran Council,[31] the Commission for Soldiers' Welfare, the Lutheran Student Association of America, and the National Lutheran Committee on Scouting.

The most long-term legacy of members of the federation, however, was their support for actuarially sound and adequately funded pension plans for Lutheran pastors, other churches workers, and their families. Without the federation's inter-Lutheran efforts, even greater delays may have occurred before churches moved to embrace contributory pension plans.

The federation's promotion of a uniform pension plan for Lutheran churches in the 1920s, 1930s, and beyond changed the course of history by fostering pension plans for the well-being in retirement of pastors, other church workers, and their dependents.

Indeed, the galaxy of visionary leaders truly is large, even stretching back to the concern of the Rev. Henry Melchior Muhlenberg in colonial days in seeking support for elderly pastors. Through the dedication of numerous leaders, solid foundations were formed for the Board of Pensions of the Evangelical Lutheran Church in America.

---

[30] The original Lutheran Brotherhood Association dissolved in 1927 and reorganized as the American Federation of Lutheran Brotherhoods. In 1958, the federation was renamed the Lutheran Church Men of America. Lutheran Brotherhood, the fraternal benefit society, provided funds and office space for Lutheran Church Men of America. In the early 1960s, however, that support was withdrawn. Following the merger that created The American Lutheran Church in 1960 and the Lutheran Church in America in 1962, Lutheran Church Men of America reorganized in 1962 as the Council of Lutheran Church Men and functioned for a brief time before ending its operation following the formation of the Lutheran Council in the USA.

[31] The National Lutheran Council was succeeded by the Lutheran Council in the U.S.A. on January 1, 1967.

CHAPTER 8

Helping "The Worn Out Soldier of the Cross"

The saga of Lutheran pension and benefit plans in North America begins surprisingly early, reaching back even into the 1700s. Long before pension plans became a common benefit in banking and business and 150 years before the Social Security program emerged as U.S. public policy, Lutherans envisioned the need to care for pastors and their families. The dream of a fully functioning pension plan would remain just that, a dream, for many decades. Yet immediate steps were undertaken to provide for pastors and their survivors in desperate need.

The challenge of meeting that need would prove difficult. The story also would have complicating twists, among them the discovery of the self-serving financial entanglement of an early treasurer of the aid funds. That problem alone would not be resolved for more than a quarter century. Even more severe problems would emerge before an effective program was fully functioning to provide dependable retirement benefits for pastors and their survivors.

Two centuries of unfolding history

Now, from the perspective of more than two centuries of unfolding history, take a look at what happened in the beginning.

After the Rev. Henry Melchior Muhlenberg's arrival from Germany as a pastor in the Philadelphia area in 1742, he began appealing to his sponsors in Germany for the support of needy pastors, their widows, and orphans in colonial America. He received some assistance for that purpose, but those needs remained a deep concern.

At least as early as 1783, the first traces of a Lutheran pension and aid system in North America began to emerge. By formal action, support was provided for "sick and old preachers . . . as well as each widow of a regular preacher" in the Ministerium of Pennsylvania and Adjacent States, the earliest Lutheran synod organized in North America. Funds for those grants in aid came from proceeds of a type of endowment, "the Streit legacy," which had been received from Germany. In at least one year, the interest earned on the principle of the legacy—$400—was lost when that interest payment was confiscated by the British during the War for Independence.[1]

The minutes of the Ministerium's annual meetings contain numerous references to grants in aid, especially for widows. For example, in 1786, the Ministerium voted:

> *Resolved*, That the interest [on the Streit legacy] shall be applied as follows:
>
> (1) For tuition for six academical students, according to the appointment of the Fathers in Halle.[2]
>
> (2) For the regular preachers present at the annual Synodical Meeting.
>
> (3) For old and sick preachers who cannot attend.
>
> (4) For the widows of regular preachers.
>
> (5) These also shall have their share who satisfactorily and in writing excuse their absence from the annual Synodical Meeting.[3]

Grants to widows of clergy

Greater clarity was sought from Germany on the intended purposes of the Streit legacy.[4] Several years elapsed, however, before documentation was obtained on the legacy's purpose, as expressed in a will that was signed in Halle, Germany, on October 15, 1753. Proceeds from the legacy had been intended for the building of churches for Lutheran congregations in Pennsylvania. Therefore, subsequent grants to widows of clergy were

---

[1] "Proceedings of the Thirty-Sixth Convention of the Ministerium of Pennsylvania," York, Pa., 1783, *Documentary History of the Evangelical Lutheran Ministerium of Pennsylvania and Adjacent States* (Philadelphia: Board of Publication of the General Council of the Evangelical Lutheran Church, 1898), p. 191. Hereafter, unless otherwise cited, all references to the proceedings of the Ministerium of Pennsylvania are from this volume.

[2] This is a reference to the Halle institute in Germany, an early sponsor of the work of German pastors in Pennsylvania and elsewhere.

[3] "Proceedings of the Thirty-Ninth Convention of the Ministerium of Pennsylvania," Philadelphia, Pa., 1786, *Documentary History*, p. 209.

[4] "Proceedings of the Thirty-Sixth Convention of the Ministerium of Pennsylvania," York, Pa., 1783, *Documentary History*, p. 191.

provided chiefly from the synodical treasury and not out of income from the legacy fund.[5]

In 1807, for example, the Ministerium decided to "pay each of the widows of the preachers, namely, Widows Kurtz, Weinland, Krug, Ernst, Schaum, Ludke[6] [sic] and Jung, the sum of five dollars from the Synodical Treasury."[7] Similar references occur in the following years:

> Upon approval of the Synod the following sums from the treasury were granted for the support of the preachers' widows, whose names follow, viz.: To the Widow Kurtz, $15.00; to the Widow Jung, $15,00; to the Widow Krug, $15.00; to the Widow Lütke, $15.00; to the Widow Weinland, $15.00.[8]

> That $10 from the Synodical Treasury be given each preacher's widow this year. . . ."[9]

> Resolved . . ., a petition from Mr. Stock to the Synod, for assistance in his great poverty, that $20 be sent him from the Synodical Treasury. Thereupon $15 were granted each of the poor preachers' widows, Jung, Kurtz, Krug, Lüdgen, Weinland and Fogt. . . .[10]

> That the poor preachers' widows, Kurtz, Krug, Lüdgen, Weynland[11] and Streit, be granted $20 each this year.[12]

> That to our five poor preachers' widows twenty dollars each be allowed out of the Synodical Treasury for this year. . . .

---

[5] Separately published minutes: "Proceedings of the Eighty-First Convention of the Ministerium of Pennsylvania," Lancaster, Pa., 1829, p. 18; and "Proceedings of Eighty-Fifth Convention of the Ministerium of Pennsylvania," Berks County, Pa., 1832, pp. 10-13.

[6] The reference apparently is to the widow of the Rev. Anton Ulrich Lütge, although the name is spelled in various ways in the minutes.

[7] "Proceedings of the Sixtieth Convention of the Ministerium of Pennsylvania," Lancaster, Pa., 1807, *Documentary History*, p. 381.

[8] "Proceedings of the Sixty-First Convention of the Ministerium of Pennsylvania," Lebanon, Pa., 1808, *Documentary History*, pp. 388-389.

[9] "Proceedings of the Sixty-Third Convention of the Ministerium of Pennsylvania," Harrisburg, Pa., 1810, *Documentary History*, p. 421.

[10] "Proceedings of the Sixty-Fourth Convention of the Ministerium of Pennsylvania," Philadelphia, Pa., 1811, *Documentary History*, pp. 428-429.

[11] As was the case with the varied spellings in reference to the widow of Pr. Lütge, similar variations in spelling occurred in reference to the widow of Pr. Friedrich Weinland.

[12] "Proceedings of the Sixty-Fifth Convention of the Ministerium of Pennsylvania," Carlisle, Pa., 1812, *Documentary History*, p. 441.

Besides this, nine dollars of the legacy, which is divided in the Ministerium, were granted to each widow.[13]

Resolved, that out of the Synodical Treasury there be sent to each of the poor preachers' widows $12, to aged Pastor Butler, $20; to Pastor Stock, $10; and to Pastor Scriba, $15. The congregation at Lancaster sent a contribution of $10 for the support of poor preachers and preachers' widows.[14]

Resolved, That $12 from the Synodical Treasury be sent to each needy preacher's widow.[15]

Resolved, That $12 be sent to each needy preacher's widow out of the Synodical Treasury.[16]

Resolved, That each of our preachers' widows shall receive fifteen dollars this year.[17]

Resolved, To send each needy preacher's widow fifteen dollars from the Synodical Treasury this year.[18]

As reflected periodically in the minutes of the Ministerium of Pennsylvania, some steps toward a pension for elderly pastors occurred prior to the Ministerium's becoming one of the district synods of the General Synod.[19]

First "umbrella body"

The pattern of grants in aid by the Ministerium of Pennsylvania foreshadowed the assistance program that emerged in the succeeding decades through the General Synod. A key figure in that effort was the

---

[13] "Proceedings of the Sixty-Fifth Convention of the Ministerium of Pennsylvania," Reading, Pa., 1813, *Documentary History*, p. 458.

[14] "Proceedings of the Sixty-Ninth Convention of the Ministerium of Pennsylvania," Philadelphia, Pa., 1816, *Documentary History*, p. 492.

[15] "Proceedings of the Seventieth Convention of the Ministerium of Pennsylvania," Yorktown, Pa., 1817, *Documentary History*, p. 503.

[16] "Proceedings of the Seventy-First Convention of the Ministerium of Pennsylvania," Harrisburg, Pa., 1818, *Documentary History*, p. 517.

[17] "Proceedings of the Seventy-Third Convention of the Ministerium of Pennsylvania," Lancaster, Pa., 1820, *Documentary History*, p. 560.

[18] "Proceedings of the Seventy-Fourth Convention of the Ministerium of Pennsylvania," Chambersburg, Pa., 1821, *Documentary History*, p. 582.

[19] Harry Hodges, "Twenty Years of Pension History," *The Lutheran*, magazine of the United Lutheran Church in America, November 23, 1938, p. 7.

Rev. Dr. Samuel S. Schmucker, one of the giants in North American Lutheran history. He was a leader in the formation of the General Synod, which was the first "umbrella body" for various regional synods. He and his colleagues sought to "adapt Lutheranism to American soil by divesting it of its distinctive traits and making it conform to the average American type of religion," historian Abdel Ross Wentz observed.[20] They were committed to Lutherans becoming fully "at home" in the young republic of the United States of America.

Dr. Schmucker was keenly aware of the need to provide pastors for the rapidly expanding population of immigrants. At the direction of the General Synod, he founded in 1826 the Lutheran Theological Seminary at Gettysburg, Pa., the oldest continuously operating Lutheran seminary in North America.[21] Subsequently, in 1832, he led in the formation of what was first known as Pennsylvania College, later renamed Gettysburg College.

The General Synod was established in 1820, 72 years after the formation of the Ministerium of Pennsylvania in August 1748. The Ministerium was the first organized certifying body for the ordination of Lutheran pastors. Subsequently, other regional synods were created in keeping with the pattern of that first synod. To group the synods together for some common purposes, the General Synod came into being.[22]

Dr. Schmucker's name appears prominently throughout Lutheran records in the first half of the nineteenth century, including in the minutes of the General Synod's convention in 1831. There we find this reference:

> On a motion of Rev. Prof. Schmucker, it was
>
> *Resolved*, That one half of the profits of those works to be published with the sanction of the General Synod, after having been approved by the "Book Committee," shall be paid into the treasury of the General Synod, to constitute a *fund for the relief of superannuated ministers* belonging to the Synods in connexion [sic] with this Body, and their *widows and orphans*.

---

[20] Abdel Ross Wentz, *The Lutheran Church in American History* (Philadelphia: United Lutheran Publication House, 1933), p. 198.

[21] Hartwick Seminary in New York was the first one formed by Lutherans but had limited impact. It ceased operation as a seminary prior to World War II.

[22] The General Synod was constituted at Hagerstown, Md., October 22-24, 1820, with the adoption of its first constitution. The General Synod met biennially, beginning in 1821. In its initial years, special attention was given to the need to establish a seminary.

Resolved, That a committee of three be appointed to draft a constitution for the enlargement, management and appropriation of the fund for the relief of superannuated ministers, their widows and orphans, and that said committee report at the next meeting of this Body.[23]

Plan in detail in 1837

That same resolution was cited in the minutes of the seventh biennial session of the General Synod in 1833[24] and again in the eighth biennial session in 1835.[25] A detailed plan was submitted to the General Synod in 1837, which read:

1st. There shall be appointed by the General Synod three lay members and two clergymen, who shall act as Trustees. . . .

2d. Said Trustees shall receive into their hands the funds remaining in the Treasury at this time, from the sale of Hymn Books and Catechisms, after the current expenses and other appropriations of this Synod are defrayed.

3d. It shall be the duty of said Trustees to appropriate from such surplus funds $50 towards the necessities of any disabled or superannuated minister connected with this Synod, or to the widow and children of such ministers, who in their judgment may require and merit the same.

4th. Whatever sums shall remain in the hands of the Trustees aforesaid, on the 1st day of August next, unappropriated in the manner defined in the third resolution, shall be by them placed out at interest on bond and secured by mortgage upon unincumbered [sic] real estate worth at least double the amount.

5th. All accumulations from the sale of Hymn Books and Catechisms, hereafter, over and above current expenses, shall be appropriated to the objects herein defined, and the same ratio of distribution shall be continued, until circumstances require a change.

---

[23] *Proceedings*, Sixth Session of the General Synod, Frederick, Md., October 31–November 2, 1831 (Philadelphia: Lutheran Publication Society), p. 11. In the quotation above, italic type is shown as in the original. For the sake of simplicity, the publisher is not hereafter cited for the proceedings of the General Synod.

[24] *Proceedings*, Seventh Session of the General Synod, Baltimore, Md., October 26-30, 1833, p. 6.

[25] *Proceedings*, Eighth Session of the General Synod, York, Pa., June 20-24, 1835, Appendix A.

6th. Any minister, or pastoral district, which does not use the Hymn Book of the General Synod, who shall pay, or have paid in, in his name, an annual contribution to this fund of not less than $5, or the sum of $50 in one payment, shall be entitled to receive his division of the interest accumulated, annually on the lst Monday in November, commencing on that day in the year 1838; and this provision shall apply to his widow or orphans under age.

7th. If ministers so contributing do not demand such dividend of interest, in two months after the said first Monday of November, in each and every year, their right to the dividend of said year shall be considered forfeited, and the portion of interest accruing to them shall be added to the accumulation fund as their donation.

8th. The surplus funds from the sale of Hymn Books and Catechisms, and the amount received in the manner provided in resolution 6th, shall constitute one fund, which shall be disbursed, according to previous resolutions.

9th. The Trustees hereby appointed shall report at the next meeting of this Synod whether in their opinion any alterations are necessary in the foregoing regulations; and at that time, and all subsequent meetings of the Synod, a statement of the amount of funds in their possession, and how invested, together with the accumulation of interest, to whom they have distributed the same, and the state of the funds generally. And shall add all necessary suggestions connected with their duties.[26]

The report was signed by three persons—Mr. P. W. Engs, Mr. Jacob Kausler, and Mr. Ernest L. Hazelius. Each section was considered, according to the minutes, and then the entire resolution was adopted. Subsequently trustees were appointed and listed as Mr. C. A. Morris, Dr. David Gilbert, Mr. Isaac Baugher, the Rev. B. Kurtz, and Prof. Schmucker.[27]

"Lutheran Pastors' Fund"

At the Tenth Convention of the General Synod in 1839, the resolution of the 1837 convention was replaced by a new constitution

---

[26] *Proceedings*, Ninth Convention of the General Synod, Hagerstown, Md., May 27-31, 1837, p. 23.

[27] *Proceedings*, General Synod, 1837, p. 24.

for the "Lutheran Pastors' Fund." Elected as trustees of the fund in 1839 were the Rev. Dr. B. Kurtz, the Rev. Dr. S. S. Schmucker, the Rev. A. H. Lochman, the Rev. J. G. Morris, Mr. C. A. Morris, Mr. Frederick Smith, and Dr. David Gilbert.[28]

The decisions of the General Synod in the context of the time were courageous ones. The panic of 1837 in the markets led to the country's first economic depression. Among the 850 banks in operation in 1837, 343 closed and 62 partially failed before the U.S. economy regained stability by 1843. In spite of the challenges of those years, the General Synod persisted in seeking to develop the "Lutheran Pastors' Fund."[29]

The Ministerium's grants of 1783 and following to aged pastors and widows and the General Synod's "Lutheran Pastors' Fund" were not the earliest effort among churches in North America to address such needs. The "Fund for Pious Uses" in the Presbyterian Church was inaugurated in 1717. Later, in 1759, the "Corporation for Relief of Poor and Distressed Presbyterian Ministers and of the Poor and Distressed Widows and Children of Presbyterian Ministers" was chartered.[30] Provisions of the "Lutheran Pastors' Fund" resembled elements of the Presbyterian program. That also was true in regard to requirements of the "Corporation for the Relief of the Widows and Children of the Clergymen in the Communion of the Church of England in America," which was chartered in 1769 in the colony of Pennsylvania.[31] Given the location in the Philadelphia

---

[28] *Proceedings*, Tenth Convention of the General Synod, Chambersburg, Pa., June 1-5, 1839, p. 19.

[29] From a financial perspective, 1837 was not an opportune time for the General Synod to inaugurate such a fund. A major banking crisis gripped the country in the Panic of 1837, leading to an economic depression. Banks restricted credit and called in loans. Depositors rushed to banks and sought to withdraw their funds. The panic followed several years of rampant land speculation and widespread economic exuberance during the administration of President Andrew Jackson. Some economic policies of the Jackson era are believed to have sowed the seeds of the banking crisis that hit in the early days of the administration of his successor, President Martin Van Buren. A severe economic downturn followed the panic with the failure of nearly half the existing banks and, for that time, record high unemployment.

[30] R. Douglas Brackenridge and Lois A. Boyd, *Presbyterians and Pensions: The Roots and Growth of Pensions in the Presbyterian Church (U.S.A.)* (Atlanta: John Knox Press, 1988), pp. 9-18.

[31] Harold C. Martin, *"Outlasting Marble and Brass": The History of the Church Pension Fund* (New York: Church Publishing, 1986), p. 22. To create resources for the fund, the 1871 General Convention of The Episcopal Church assigned to the trustees the copyright, licensing power, and royalties from that church's new hymnal. Later, in 1892, proceeds were added from publication of the *Book of Common Prayer*.

area of certain Lutheran, Presbyterian, and Anglican leaders in these efforts, it is possible that they were acquainted with one another and shared information on these efforts. The minutes of the General Synod, however, do not provide any confirmation of that possibility. Yet to be developed in the various churches was a program for long-term pension care of retired pastors and support for clergy with disabilities and their dependents.

Amazingly comprehensive

Within the General Synod, the adopted "Articles of Association for the Establishment of the Lutheran Pastors' Fund" are amazingly comprehensive, given their historical context within the relatively new nation.[32] The articles contained fascinating principles and safeguards. They addressed the means of support for the program, the scope of the benefits, and the investment practices that were to be followed by the officers and trustees.

The means of support for the plan included proceeds from the sale of hymn books and catechisms as well as individual donations, payments by participating ministers, and revenue from various publications (Article 4). The possibility of other deposits by pastors also existed (Article 7) as well as contributions by congregations for their pastors (Article 9).

The method for the payment of benefits was specified (Articles 15 and 16). Procedures for benefits to surviving spouses and children were defined (Article 10). Special provision was made for the care of pastors with disabilities and for destitute widows or orphans of clergy (Article 17). Limitations were stated related to situations of remarriage (Articles 18, 19, and 20). Circumstances of clergy misconduct also were addressed (Article 23).

Investment policies and the requirement of prudent practices in that regard were explicitly stated (Articles 12 and 13). Operation of the fund was managed through appointed trustees who were clearly accountable to the General Synod (Articles 2, 3, 14, 24, and 25).

The "Articles of Association for the Establishment of the Lutheran Pastors' Fund" read:[33]

---

[32] Only 50 years had passed since George Washington became in 1789 the first president of the United States of America. In 1839, Martin Van Buren was midway through his only term as the eighth U.S. president.

[33] Spelling, punctuation, abbreviations, and italic type are reproduced as in the published text of the proceedings.

Article I. The means of collection by the following regulations shall be designated and kept as the *Lutheran Pastors' Fund.*

Art. II. The business of this Association shall be managed and controlled by the General Synod, through a Board of seven Trustees, viz.: four ministers and three laymen, to be biennially appointed by the Synod; and four of the Trustees shall constitute a quorum for the transaction of business.

Art. III. The Board of Trustees shall elect from among themselves a President, Secretary, and Treasurer, whose duties shall be as hereafter stated:

a. The President shall call meetings of the Trustees whenever he thinks proper; he shall approve all claims, and sign all orders on the Treasury, before money is disbursed, and see in general that the affairs of the Association are well cared for.

b. The Secretary shall keep regular minutes of the proceedings of the Trustees and all other transactions, and shall produce those minutes at the meetings of the Synod.

c. The duties of the Treasurer shall be as defined in Article 15.[34]

Art. IV. The Fund, whence relief is to be derived, shall be created in the following manner:

a. By the annual payment into the hands of the Treasurer of all the profits accruing from the sale of the General Synod's Hymn Book and Catechisms, after the current expenses and other appropriations of this Synod shall have been defrayed.

b. By voluntary donations, subscriptions, legacies, &c.[35]

c. By the annual payment of a specified sum in order to entitle any minister to membership and to a subsequent interest in the Fund.

d. The Trustees may also, if they think proper, devise other suitable means to increase the Funds, such as the publication

---

[34] The duties actually are listed in Article 14.

[35] This sign, "&c.," is in the original text and also appears in Articles IV.b, XII, XIV, and XVII.

of valuable books, the appointment of agents to solicit donations, &c.

Art. V. Every minister of the Evangelical Lutheran Church in the United States, not over 25 years of age, who is a member of good standing of any of the Synods belonging to the General Synod, may secure an interest in this fund by paying into the Treasury any sum annually, during life, not under Ten Dollars.

Art. VI. Any minister as above, who is over 25 years of age, may become a member of this Association by paying to the Treasurer a sum of money equal to the amount of his annual rate considered as an annuity in arrears for a term of years equal to one-half the excess of his age over 25 years, with interest.

Art. VII. Each member may deposit a sum of money in the hands of the Trustees, the annual interest of which at 6 per cent, shall be equal to the annual rate which he has chosen, which sum shall be funded by the Trustees, and returned to his family after the death of the contributor, if required by his representatives, within six months from that time.

Art. VIII. If any contributor [were to] die in arrears to the fund, the amount must be made up from the annuity due him, before his family shall be entitled to receive it, unless the Trustees should think proper, from peculiar circumstances to do otherwise; and if such contributor neglect, while living (being able)[36] to pay his contributions for two years, his previous payments shall be forfeited to the permanent fund, due notice being first given to the recipient.

Art. IX. Congregations may contribute for the benefit of their Pastors agreeable to the above Articles, or by paying a sum for life-membership, to be agreed upon by the Trustees; and the Pastors, their widows, and orphans, shall enjoy all the benefits of the Association, as if contributed by themselves. Should any Congregation change its Pastor, however, and call one more advanced in life, such Congregation shall pay a sum of money additional, equal in amount to the annual rate considered as an annuity in arrears for a term of years equal to one-half of the difference of their ages, with interest.

---

[36] The parenthetical insertion is in the original text.

Art. X. At the decease [sic] of any minister of the Association, whose circumstances may require it, so soon as written notice is given of the same, from a source satisfactory to the Officers, it shall be their duty to forward immediately, to the widow or children, out of the Treasury, One Dollar for each member of the Association—the same to be repaid by the members at the time of making their next annual contribution.

Art. XI. Ministers having contributed to the fund, may at any time, upon six months' notice being given, relinquish their interest therein, and shall be allowed to withdraw two-thirds of the amount (not embracing interest) actually paid by them respectively.

Art. XII. All receipts of money, whether from the sale of Hymn Books and Catechisms, from the annual payment of subscribers, collections in churches, donations by individuals, legacies, &c. or other sources, shall be safely invested and allowed to accumulate, until the fund shall amount to *ten thousand dollars*; after which, the payments made by ministers, donations, collections, legacies, &c. when so especially directed by the donor, shall be considered income. All other donations, collections in churches, legacies, &c. to be considered principal, and the interest only used as income.

Art. XIII. The Fund shall be administered by the Board of Trustees according to these Terms, and such other instructions as may hereafter be prescribed by the General Synod. Said Board shall invest, from time to time, all moneys contributed to the principal of the fund in such manner as shall appear to them most safe and profitable. No money, however, belonging to this fund, shall be loaned upon individual responsibility, unless secured by bond and mortgage on real estate of double the amount of the sum so loaned.

Art. XIV. The Treasurer's duty shall be to collect the income and to make all payments. He shall report minutely and fully to the General Synod, at each of its meetings—stating the amount of funds on hand and due, how invested, the accumulation of interest, how much disbursed, to whom, and for what purposes, &c., making his report as detailed and satisfactory as the General Synod may require. His accounts to be audited by a committee appointed by said Synod. He shall give security for the faithful discharge of his trust, &c. If deemed proper, the Board may allow him a reasonable compensation for his services.

Art. XV. In disbursing the income of the fund, when a minister is the applicant, he shall be required to produce a certificate from the Synod to which he belongs, or other satisfactory evidence, declaring that by reason of sickness, old age, or other providential cause, he is incapable of ministerial services—where a widow is the applicant, like satisfactory evidence of the death of her husband, and the date thereof, shall be required—and in the case of children, both whose parents have deceased, like evidence of the death of their parents, and of their own age, shall be required.

Art. XVI. The payments to annuitants shall be made half-yearly—on the first Monday of May and November after the application is approved. The Treasurer's books, or authentic vouchers, shall furnish the evidence of payment of subscriptions. Annuitants shall be admitted to the benefit of the fund by a vote of the Trustees of the fund, or of a committee specially appointed for that purpose.

Art. XVII. It shall also be the duty of the Trustees to make annual appropriations to such disabled ministers, and destitute widows, and orphans of ministers, who are now receiving aid out of the general fund; the amount to be determined by the income derived from sources heretofore in existence, such as books, &c. published by the General Synod. Any minister, widow, or orphans *not* now in the fund, who may desire aid hereafter, and who are not entitled to the benefits secured by annual contributions, shall receive such annual appropriations—the amount to be determined by the state of the funds derived from general sources.

Art. XVIII. Annuities shall not be transferable.

Art. XIX. A widow of a minister, contracting marriage, forfeits her claim to the annuity; but, in such case, the children under sixteen years of age, shall be entitled to their annuities, as though both parents had deceased—and it shall be disposed of for their benefit as the Trustees may direct.

Art. XX. Every contributor, at his second and every subsequent marriage, shall, if required by the Trustees, pay according to their judgment an additional sum for each such marriage.[37]

Art. XXI. The first annual payment shall be made to the Treasurer in the month of July, 1839, and thereafter in July of each year. Those residing at a distance may transmit their contributions by mail. If not paid within 3 months from the first day of July in each year, 20 per cent will be added in consideration of the delay.

Art. XXII. Such annuities as are not applied for within one year from the time they are due, shall revert back to the permanent fund—due notice having been given to the annuitants.

Art. XXIII. Any clergyman who shall be deprived of his "good standing" in the Synod to which he is attached, by reason of mal-conduct, shall be stricken from the list of members, and shall cease to enjoy the benefits of this fund; but the Trustees may extend it to his widow and children after his decease.

Art. XXIV. The Trustees shall have the power to make such by-laws as are necessary for their Government, provided they are not contrary to the foregoing rules.

Art. XXV. This Plan shall not be altered except by a vote of two-thirds of the attending members of the General Synod; and, in all such cases, the alterations or amendments contemplated must be proposed by the Board of Trustees, and public notice be given at least three months before the meeting of the Synod. If any three members of the Association unite in requesting the Board to propose an alteration, it shall be the duty of the Board to do so.[38]

Treasurer David Gilbert reported to the 1841 convention of the General Synod that the Lutheran Pastors' Fund had a balance of $63.90,[39] and to the 1843 convention, a balance of $99.90.[40] (For perspective, those

---

[37] This provision existed in view of the mortality rate, including occurrences of death in childbirth. It did not relate to divorce.

[38] *Proceedings*, Tenth Convention of the General Synod, Chambersburg, Pa., Appendix B, June 1-5, 1839, pp. 27-31.

[39] *Proceedings*, Eleventh Convention of the General Synod, Baltimore, Md., May 8-13, 1841, p. 29.

[40] *Proceedings*, Twelfth Convention of the General Synod, Baltimore, Md., May 21-25, 1843, p. 11.

amounts in 2008 dollars approximately would be equivalent to $1,300 and $2,200, respectively.) In 1845, the balance was reported at $135.90.[41] By May 16, 1848, the Lutheran Pastors' Fund had grown to $1,184.28.[42] Most of the increase had been obtained through the sale of books.[43] The following biennium showed modest growth in income to $1,320.47 in 1850.[44]

Point of controversy

In spite of the fund's gradual growth, the 1850 convention directed that the Lutheran Pastors' Fund be divided among the member synods in proportion to the number of pastors in each synod. The stated purpose of the action was to "stimulate the efforts of the district Synods" for the support of such funds.[45]

The proposed disbursement of the fund in 1850 appears to have created significant controversy. At the subsequent convention in 1853, Treasurer Gilbert indicated the fund had a balance of $1,545.90.[46] In a report dated May 21, 1853, he also claimed that his report reflected all of "the moneys received and distributed *since the establishment* of the fund, in order to facilitate the division provided for by the action of the last General Synod."[47] He added:

> I regret to say that the Synods entitled to a share in the distribution have not complied with the [1850] resolution requiring them to send the number of ministers belonging to each Synod to the Treasurer. . . . Part of the funds are secured by a mortgage, for which the money cannot be realized immediately. Let the distribution be made, however, and orders given to each Synod for the amount it is entitled to, and satisfactory arrangements will be made.[48]

[41] *Proceedings*, Thirteenth Convention of the General Synod, Philadelphia, Pa., May 16-22, 1845, p. 32.

[42] *Proceedings*, Fourteenth Convention of the General Synod, New York, N.Y., May 13-18, 1848, p. 7.

[43] *Proceedings*, General Synod, 1848, p. 8.

[44] *Proceedings*, Fifteenth Convention of the General Synod, Charleston, S.C., April 27–May 3, 1850, p. 16.

[45] *Proceedings*, General Synod, 1850, p. 17.

[46] *Proceedings*, Sixteenth Convention of the General Synod, Winchester, Va., May 21-26, 1853, p. 22.

[47] *Proceedings*, General Synod, 1853, p. 23. Italics in original.

[48] *Proceedings*, General Synod, 1853, p. 23.

What happened? Dr. Gilbert was removed at that point as treasurer. The proposed distribution of the fund was challenged by a three-member committee in a report dated May 26, 1853. Mr. P. W. Engs, Mr. M. M. Yeakle, and Mr. C. A. Morris questioned the wisdom of the 1850 proposed division of the fund and wondered whether such a step could be taken "with propriety and justice."[49] In essence, the committee argued that the convention of 1850 exceeded its authority in directing a course of action that could not legally be followed. Disbursing the fund among the member synods would be "utterly impracticable" and would not be in keeping with the way in which the funds had been originally gathered.[50] Instead, "our dear Lutheran church" should remain committed to providing "the necessities of her worn out ministers and their families."

> What then is to be done? This fund has been created for a most noble and Christian purpose, no less than aiding *the worn out soldier of the cross*, and those dependent upon him, in old age, in sickness or in want. The solemn obligation is upon *us* that it shall be devoted to this purpose, and this only. Let us then keep it within the enclosure already provided, and dispense it according to the original intent. No great good could result from its division if it even were right to make it.
>
> We have now a nucleus, around which we have but to exercise a fostering care, and it will gather and gather and gather by proper financial management, under a system based and improved upon that on which we set out, until there may be added to the characteristic features of our dear Lutheran church, one that may enable us to say, when inquiry is made, what she is doing: That, among other things, she provides for the old age, and the sickness and the necessities of her worn out ministers and their families.[51]

The "course taken at the last Synodical meeting" showed that too many individuals had "lost sight" of the need for care of the clergy, according to the committee's 1853 report. Further, the committee alleged that, due to inadequate care of investments, the balance in the fund was "at least $1,000 less than it should have been." That clearly was a serious claim in view of the enormous value of $1,000 in 1853.[52]

---

[49] *Proceedings*, General Synod, 1853, p. 25.

[50] *Proceedings*, General Synod, 1853, p. 26.

[51] *Proceedings*, General Synod, 1853, p. 26. Italic emphasis was added to highlight the vivid expression of the time.

[52] That amount would be equivalent to about $25,000 in 2007.

The amount in the fund was reported by the committee of three at $2,416.78,[53] including special allocations of $870.88 by the Lutheran Book Concern in Baltimore, although those allocations remained under the ownership of the Book Concern.

The original articles of 1839 for the Lutheran Pastors' Fund were still in force, the report emphasized. Therefore, the committee recommended the following resolution, which was adopted:

> Resolved, That this Synod will continue to keep the Pastors' Fund under their [sic] own supervision, in according their [sic] original purpose.

> Resolved, That five Trustees of the Pastors' Fund, consisting of two clergymen and three laymen, be now appointed to take its management into their charge.

> Resolved, That a Treasurer be selected from the Trustees, by their own number, and that he be authorized to receive the assets of the fund from his predecessor.

> Resolved, That the articles of organization be referred to a committee to report such alterations as they may deem proper at the next meeting of the General Synod.[54]

Questions on handling of funds

Elected as trustees in 1853 were Mr. P. W. Engs, Mr. A. Ockershausen, Mr. M. M. Yeakle, the Rev. J. L. Schoch, and the Rev. Dr. W. D. Strobel. Mr. Engs and Mr. Yeakle were two of the three members of the committee that submitted the forthright report on the state of the fund to the synod. Sixteen years earlier, Mr. Engs also had served as a member of the committee that originally provided to the synod in 1837 a detailed proposal for the fund.

A loan of $1,245.90 had not appeared in the record until after Dr. Gilbert ceased to be treasurer of the Lutheran Pastors' Fund. After the 1853 reorganization of the fund, Dr. Gilbert's property at the southwest corner of Front and Mifflin Streets in Philadelphia was listed, effective May 21, 1856, as collateral for the loan. At the same time, the $300 loan for property in Gettysburg, Pa., remained unpaid.

---

[53] Proceedings, General Synod, 1853, p. 27. In its critique, the committee indicated that a $300 loan from 1839 to the previous treasurer, Dr. David Gilbert, had not been paid. The loan itself may have violated Article XIII of the 1839 governing articles of the fund.

[54] Proceedings, General Synod, 1853, p. 27.

Dr. Gilbert was directed in 1853 to turn over the fund's assets to the successor treasurer, Mr. Engs. In minutes of the 1855 General Synod, however, Mr. Engs reported: "Reference to the report of the proceedings of the last General Synod [1853] will show that there was due from Dr. Gilbert, treasurer to . . . [that] date, $1,545.90. This has not yet passed into my hands in the form of cash, but is represented by two notes of the former treasurer, one for $300, secured by mortgage, and the other for $1,245.90. . . . It will be seen by my account that the *interest* on Dr. Gilbert's indebtedness has been regularly paid."[55]

In 1855, the fund was gaining greater interest (six percent) on the Gilbert loan than the four percent being paid on the remainder of the fund by the Philadelphia Savings Fund Society.[56] The amount of the Gilbert loan for the Philadelphia property was later restated as $1,200 in a mortgage dated October 1, 1857.[57]

With renewed commitment to the fund by the General Synod in 1853, the convention declared:

> *Resolved*, that it be recommended to all the ministers in connection with the General Synod to take collections in their congregations, annually, for the increase of the Pastors' Fund.[58]

The cloud over the Lutheran Pastors' Fund did not dissipate quickly. Interest on Dr. Gilbert's indebtedness was paid regularly, however, as was interest on the allocation of $870.88 from the Lutheran Book Concern. As a result, interest income of $202.24 was reported by Treasurer Engs for the 1853-1855 biennium.[59] He continued:

> . . . [T]he expectation of the Synod will be far from being realized in this report, but a glance will enable members to perceive, that without the control of the funds *represented* as belonging to the "Pastors' Fund," the prospect of large accumulation could not be realized. None can be more disappointed in this matter

---

[55] *Proceedings*, Seventeenth Convention of the General Synod, Dayton, Ohio, June 14-21, 1855, p. 19.

[56] *Proceedings*, Nineteenth Convention of the General Synod, Pittsburgh, Pa., May 19-26, 1859, pp. 19-20.

[57] *Proceedings*, General Synod, 1859, p. 24.

[58] *Proceedings*, General Synod, 1853, p. 27. At that time, 20 district synods were part of the General Synod.

[59] *Proceedings*, General Synod, 1855, p. 19.

than I am, deprived by circumstances of the great satisfaction of laying a foundation for much future good.[60]

The 1855 minutes indicate that Mr. Engs's report was approved and the following trustees were named to serve until the next meeting of the General Synod: Mr. Daniel K. Gwin, Mr. William Anspach, Mr. J. P. Lehman, the Rev. E. W. Hutter, and the Rev. Benjamin Keller, all of Philadelphia.[61] The convention also voted:

> Resolved, That the [District] Synods, in connection with the General Synod, be requested to transfer any funds which may be in their possession, for the use of disabled pastors or the widows of deceased clergymen or their orphans, to the Treasurer of this Society.

> Resolved, That those having the more immediate control of the "Pastors' Fund" be instructed to communicate to our several Synods the constitution of the [Lutheran Pastors' Fund] association, as well as its financial condition.[62]

Named as successor trustees by the 1857 meeting of the General Synod were: Mr. W. M. Heyl, Mr. Lewis L. Houpt, and Mr. Isaac Sulger. Re-elected were the Rev. E. W. Hutter and the Rev. Benjamin Keller.[63] Subsequently, Pr. Keller was named president, Mr. Sulger, secretary, and Mr. Houpt, treasurer.

That 1857 convention also voted that the trustees of the Lutheran Pastors' Fund "be directed to have the fund safely secured" and to report on the matter at the next meeting of the General Synod. Further, the resolution declared:

> Resolved, That this Synod again urge upon the several District Synods connected with it to take the most active measures to increase the means for the support of superannuated ministers.

> Resolved, That whilst each District Synod seek to supply the wants of the superannuated ministers, widows, and orphans among themselves, whenever any funds remain unappropriated, those Synods be requested to transmit their surplus funds to the

---

[60] Proceedings, General Synod, 1855, p. 20. Italic emphasis in original.

[61] Proceedings, General Synod, 1855, pp. 20-21.

[62] Proceedings, General Synod, 1855, p. 20.

[63] Proceedings, Eighteenth Convention of the General Synod, Reading, Pa., May 14-20, 1857, p. 15.

Treasurer of the General Fund; and the Treasurer, together with the Trustees of this fund, be an Executive Committee to consider and decide all appropriations for relief from any portion of the church; also, that the Treasury be at all times accessible to all proper applicants whenever there are funds unappropriated; and further, that former rules and resolutions, not in accordance with this resolution, be and are hereby, rescinded.[64]

Harsh report

The report on the Lutheran Pastors' Fund submitted to the 1859 meeting of the General Synod was a harsh one. The trustees indicated that they had sought "to discover, if possible," why the Lutheran Pastors' Fund, "although twenty years and upwards have transpired since its organization, had so signally[65] failed in its object, and . . . [had] been almost abandoned by its founders and neglected by the church."[66]

The history of the fund was traced in the narrative of the report to its origin in 1831, but the report acknowledged that nothing seemed to have been done on the matter until 1837 "when the importance and necessity of making some provision for superannuated ministers and their families was again urged upon [the] General Synod."[67] The constitution for the fund from 1839 required "for the enjoyment and reception of its benefits . . . a stated annual contribution from its members, in order to entitle them or their families (in case of sickness and death) to be beneficiaries of its bounty."[68]

The requirement that the fund reach $10,000 before the payment of any benefits, according to the report, postponed the operation and usefulness of the fund for an indefinite period. This stipulation had been stated in Article XII of the 1839 "Articles of Association for the Establishment of the Lutheran Pastors' Fund." Said the trustees in addressing the 1859 meeting of the General Synod:

> In view of this apparent difficulty and embarrassment, the Trustees addressed a circular to the several District Synods, in connection with [the] General Synod, propounding certain questions and soliciting an expression of opinion upon the subject,

---

[64] *Proceedings*, General Synod 1857, p. 16.

[65] In this instance, the intended meaning here of "signally" is "conspicuously" or "obviously."

[66] *Proceedings*, General Synod, 1859, p. 21.

[67] *Proceedings*, General Synod, 1859, p. 20.

[68] *Proceedings*, General Synod, 1859, p. 20.

with a view to understand what were the wants and wishes of the church in reference to this Fund, and to reconstitute the Society, if practicable, upon a new basis, so that its moneys may the more steadily accumulate, and the income be accessible to all the destitute and worthy, who come within its provisions.[69]

The survey revealed that at least two district synods had established their own funds, one in the state of New York and another in Maryland. Their charters precluded their becoming auxiliaries of the Lutheran Pastors' Fund in the General Synod.

Extensive efforts were reported in seeking greater contributions to the fund. In addition, the trustees reported appropriating $50 for the benefit "of the widow of the Rev. E. R. Ginney, late of Urbana, Ohio."[70] The remaining balance in the Lutheran Pastors' Fund was $2,109.05 in 1859, according to Mr. Houpt as treasurer.[71]

Further, the trustees recommended approval of a revised constitution "in the hope that its adoption may stimulate the several District Synods to united and vigorous action in this behalf, and enable the Trustees to command the contributions of the Lutheran church, with a view to a more steady increase of the Pastors' Fund, greater efficiency and usefulness in its management, and the addition of a wise and liberal policy for the distribution of the means and accumulations constituting it, according to the original design and intent of its founders and patrons."[72]

Named as trustees were: the Rev. Benjamin Keller and Mr. Isaac Sulger, re-elected for six-year terms; the Rev. E. W. Hutter and Mr. Lewis L. Houpt, re-elected for four-year terms; Mr. W. M. Heyl, re-elected for a two-year term; and the Rev. J. A. Seiss, elected for a two-year term.[73]

Quest for incorporation

The trustees also were instructed by resolution "to procure, at an early period, an act of incorporation"[74] in keeping with the revised constitution, which read:

---

[69] *Proceedings*, General Synod, 1859, p. 20.

[70] *Proceedings*, General Synod, 1859, p. 21.

[71] *Proceedings*, General Synod, 1859, p. 24.

[72] *Proceedings*, General Synod, 1859, p. 21. Notice of the proposed new constitution had been published in the *Observer and Missionary*, one of the predecessor publications of *The Lutheran* of the ELCA.

[73] *Proceedings*, General Synod, 1859, p. 25.

[74] *Proceedings*, General Synod, 1859, p. 25.

WHEREAS, the Constitution of the General Synod's Pastors' Fund is so exceedingly complicated and its requirements such as can but in a few cases be complied with, and

WHEREAS, it is very desirable that the whole plan of operation should be changed and that each District Synod should establish, in connection with (and auxilliary [sic] to) the Pastors' Fund of the General Synod, a Pastors' Fund within its own limits, in accordance with the spirit of the Gospel of Christ, therefore, the present Trustees would beg leave to lay before the General Synod at its present Convention, the following Constitution as a plan of Union for combining the charitable operations of the District Synods in connection with the General Synod of the Ev. Luth. Church in the United States.

ARTICLE 1. The present fund for superannuated ministers, their widows or orphans, shall be known as the Pastors' Fund of the General Synod of the Lutheran Church in the United States.

ART. 2. The present Synod shall, at its present convention, elect six Trustees, namely: three clergymen and three laymen, all of whom shall be in good standing in the Luth. Church, residing at some point, where they can be conveniently assembled, who shall serve in [the] manner following, to wit: The first two shall serve until the next meeting of the General Synod. The next two shall serve until the next succeeding meeting of Synod, after which time, each Trustee shall serve a term of six years, two to be elected at every Session of Synod. Any Trustee may be removed by a vote of Synod.

ART. 3. The Trustees shall have power to elect their own officers, namely: President, Secretary and Treasurer, fill vacancies that may occur between the Sessions of Synod, and also to make their own By-Laws, which shall not conflict with their constitutions.

ART. 4. Said Trustees shall receive into their hands the Funds remaining in the Treasury at this time and they shall endeavor by all proper and lawful means, to increase these funds by bequests, donations from individuals, and contributions or collections from congregations belonging to such District Synods, in which no Pastors' Fund exists.

Art. 5. All congregations, within the bounds of such District Synods in which no Pastors' Fund exists, are earnestly solicited to take up annual collections, at or about the time when the Harvest Thanksgiving sermon is preached, and forward the amount, be it much or little, to the Treasurer of the Parent or General Fund.

Art. 6. The different District Synods, in connection with the General Synod, which have not already done so, are respectfully and earnestly requested to organize Synodical Pastors' Fund Societies, auxilliary [sic] to the Parent Society, and to forward to the Secretary of the Board of Trustees an *annual* statement of their operations.

Art. 7. Each District Synodical Society may make its own constitution and by-laws and carry on its operations, as it shall find expedient, provided the same shall not in any way militate against the constitution, by-laws and operations of the Parent Society.

Art. 8. While each District Synod seeks to supply the wants of the superannuated or disabled ministers, its widows and orphans within its bounds, whenever any Funds remain unappropriated at the end of each Synodical year, these Synods are respectfully requested to transmit their surplus funds to the Treasurer of the Parent or General Fund, and the Trustees of the General or Parent Fund shall consider and decide all applications for relief from any portion of the Church in connection with the General Synod, such applications being accompanied by proper and credible testimonials.

Art. 9. The Board of Trustees of the Pastors' Fund shall transmit to the several District Synods the constitution of this association with a statement of its financial condition.

Art. 10. This constitution may be altered or amended at any of the sessions of the General Synod by a majority of two-thirds of all the members present.[75]

Incorporation of the Pastors' Fund proved difficult. Application to the Court of Common Pleas of Philadelphia for incorporation was refused

---

[75] *Proceedings*, General Synod, 1859, pp. 22-23. Spelling, capitalization, and abbreviations reproduced as shown in the minutes.

because the Pastors' Fund Society was not deemed a "Local Society" in that it was "a creature of the General Synod" and "included within its province the entire Church in the United States." The trustees were directed to appeal to the legislature of the Commonwealth of Pennsylvania.[76] Many years would pass before the issue was resolved.

A gathering storm of division

As the 1859 meeting of the General Synod adjourned, a storm was descending upon the nation that would divide not only the union but also the General Synod itself. Beyond the North-South split in the country, a division within the General Synod soon would occur. The fractures would complicate enormously the efforts to provide a pension benefit for Lutheran pastors and their families.

The district synods of the General Synod in the 1850s were the: (1) Synod of Maryland; (2) Synod of West Pennsylvania; (3) Synod of South Carolina; (4) Synod of North Carolina; (5) Hartwick Synod; (6) Ministerium of New York; (7) Synod of Virginia; (8) Allegheny Synod of Pennsylvania; (9) Synod of East Pennsylvania; (10) Miami Synod; (11) Wittenberg Synod; (12) East Ohio Synod; (13) Synod of Illinois; (14) Synod of Western Virginia; (15) Olive Branch Synod of Indiana; (16) Ministerium of Pennsylvania; (17) Synod of Northern Illinois; (18) Pittsburgh Synod; (19) Synod of Texas; (20) English Synod of Ohio; (21) Synod of Kentucky; (22) Central Synod of Pennsylvania; (23) Synod of Northern Indiana; (24) Synod of Southern Illinois; (25) Synod of Iowa; and (26) Melanchthon Synod.[77] As participants departed from the 1859 meeting, clouds of turmoil and division were creeping over the horizon for the General Synod of the Evangelical Lutheran Church in the United States.

When Abraham Lincoln was inaugurated as the 16th U.S. president in March 1861, seven states already had seceded from the union. Five more would soon join them in secession. Then, on April 12, 1861, the first shot of the Civil War was fired on Fort Sumter in the Charleston, S.C., harbor.

A formal break in the General Synod did not happen immediately, but steps were taken at a meeting in Salisbury, N.C., on May 15, 1862, to appoint a drafting committee to prepare a constitution and the rules for constituting a

---

[76] *Proceedings*, Twenty-First Convention of the General Synod, York, Pa., May 5-12, 1864, p. 21.

[77] *Proceedings*, General Synod, 1859, pp. 3-7.

separate synod. The constituting convention of the General Synod in the South met in Concord, N.C., on May 20, 1863, only six weeks before the Battle of Gettysburg. The "General Synod of the Evangelical Lutheran Church in the Confederates States of America" was established. The Rev. John Bachman (1790-1874) of Charleston, S.C., was elected its first president.[78]

The General Synod had been scheduled to meet in Lancaster, Pa., at the end of May 1861, but the meeting was postponed in the hope of averting the threatened rupture. After a permanent Confederate government was organized in February 1862 and the North-South battles became more frequent and bloody, the General Synod decided to meet in Lancaster in May 1862. Five synods had withdrawn—North Carolina, South Carolina, Virginia, Western Virginia, and Georgia.[79]

At the General Synod's 1862 meeting, Mr. Houpt's report as treasurer for the Pastors' Fund showed a balance of $2,108.38, the equivalent of about $44,000 in 2008 dollars. Included were continuing interest payments by Dr. Gilbert on his outstanding loan of $1,500 on two properties and contributions of $336.89 from the East Pennsylvania Synod and $50 from the Synod of Virginia.[80] Interestingly, the reports also revealed disbursements in the following manner:

1859, Nov. 26, Amount appropriated to	Mrs. G.	$100.00
1859, Nov. 26,	Rev. A. R.	$100.00
1860, Oct. 3,	Mrs. M.	$ 50.00
1860, Nov. 27	Rev. A.R.	$100.00
1860, Dec. 6	Mrs. G.	$ 50.00
1861, May 14	Mrs. P.	$ 50.00
1861, Sept. 30	Rev. A.R.	$100.00
1861, Oct. 14	Rev. D.M.'s children	$100.00
1861, Oct. 21	Mrs. M.	$ 50.00
1861, Dec. 17	Mrs. G.	$ 50.00 [81]

---

[78] E. Clifford Nelson (ed.), *The Lutherans in North America* (Philadelphia: Fortress Press, 1980), p. 245. The synod's name was altered in 1866 to "The Evangelical Lutheran General Synod, South" and in 1886 to "The United Synod, South," p. 247.

[79] Nelson, pp. 242-243.

[80] *Proceedings*, Twentieth Convention of the General Synod, Lancaster, Pa., May 1-7, 1862, pp. 27-28. The date of the contribution from the Synod of Virginia was November 10, 1860, prior to the break with the General Synod.

[81] *Proceedings*, General Synod, 1862, p. 28.

Converted to 2008 dollars, a $100 grant in 1861 would amount to about $2,300—by today's standards, a small amount on which to live for a year.

The minutes indicate that the report of the trustees on the Pastors' Fund "was received and, with some modifications, ordered to be incorporated in the proceedings of Synod."[82] The report said, in part:

> We . . . urge that . . . District Synods appropriate an annual amount towards this object, so that the Pastors' Fund may steadily increase and become of some importance to the Church; that the interest alone may be sufficient to answer all applications for immediate relief made to the Trustees from all parts of the Church.
>
> . . . [T]his Fund is so established as to be of benefit to all proper applicants, and the hope is entertained that the same may be steadily increased, so that a dispensation of its benefits, judiciously managed and appointed, may bring relief to the disabled and superannuated ministers, their widows and children of our Church, who are the special objects for whom the Pastors' Fund was established.[83]

Re-elected to a six-year term as a trustee was Mr. W. M. Heyl. Newly elected, also to a six-year term, was the Rev. G. F. Krotel.[84]

Finally, on March 14, 1863, one of the loans to the original treasurer, Dr. Gilbert—which dated from March 10, 1839, in the amount of $300—was paid in full from proceeds of the sale property in Gettysburg, Pa. The second loan of $1,200 to Dr. Gilbert remained unpaid at that time. A dozen years would pass before the matter was resolved and then, apparently, not easily.

When Mr. Houpt reported to the 1864 meeting of the General Synod, he indicated that contributions to the Lutheran Pastors' Fund had been received from various district synods, as follows:

1862	September 12	Synod of Illinois	$7.00
	October 10	East Pennsylvania Synod	$ 48.72
1863	May 4	Pennsylvania Synod	$200.00
	June 8	West Pennsylvania Synod	$ 23.00
	October 17	East Pennsylvania Synod	$ 22.50
	October 31	Synod of Illinois	$ 0
	November 23	Synod of Northern Indiana	$ 39.50

---

[82] *Proceedings*, General Synod, 1862, p. 26.

[83] *Proceedings*, General Synod, 1862, p. 27.

[84] *Proceedings*, General Synod, 1862, p. 28.

Other income included interest paid by Dr. Gilbert as well as interest from the Philadelphia Savings Fund Society and on U.S. bonds. Disbursement to widows and pastors were reported for the period of 1862 through February 1864 as $1,316.[85]

At the subsequent meeting of the General Synod in May 1866 at Fort Wayne, Ind., Mr. Houpt reported additional contributions, including $25 from an individual as well as $27 from the Synod of Illinois, $44.50 from the Synod of Northern Illinois, $13.75 from the English Synod of Ohio, and $57.75 from the Wittenberg Synod of Ohio. Grants to individuals amounted to $550 for the biennium.[86]

A second fracture

Another lag in the development of the Pastors' Fund transpired in the midst of a second fracture in the membership of the General Synod. The withdrawal of the Ministerium of Pennsylvania from the General Synod to form a different general body proved to be a serious disruption. The point of contention erupted at the meeting of the General Synod at York, Pa., in 1864. At issue was the application by the Franckean Synod for admission to the General Synod. The Franckean Synod had never accepted the Augsburg Confession but instead had its own declaration of faith. After extended debate, the Franckean Synod was admitted on the condition that it declare adoption of the Augsburg Confession. Representatives of the Ministerium of Pennsylvania presented a paper specifying their objections and declaring their intention to withdraw from sessions of the General Synod.

Doctrinal tensions were evident in the debate. Apparent, too, was a conflict of strong personalities. When the conservative candidate of the Ministerium, the Rev. Charles Porterfield Krauth, was not chosen in 1864 to succeed Dr. Schmucker as president of Gettysburg Seminary, the Ministerium proceeded in July 1864 to establish a seminary at Philadelphia with Dr. Krauth as professor of systematic theology. Thus, the Lutheran Theological Seminary at Philadelphia was born.

The formal schism came when the General Synod met at Fort Wayne, Ind., May 17-24, 1866. The credentials of the representatives of the Ministerium were not accepted because the Ministerium was said to be in a "state of practical withdrawal from the governing functions of the

---

[85] *Proceedings*, General Synod, 1864, pp. 21-22.

[86] *Proceedings*, Twenty-Second Convention of the General Synod, Fort Wayne, Ind., May 17-24, 1866, p. 31.

General Synod." Parliamentary maneuvering continued but, in the end, the break was complete.[87]

Subsequently, the Ministerium issued a call to Lutheran synods acknowledging the Unaltered Augsburg Confession to become part of a new general body "on a truly Lutheran basis." The constituting meeting was held at Reading, Pa., in December 1866. Almost a year later, the first regular convention of the "General Council of the Evangelical Lutheran Church of North America" convened at Fort Wayne in November 1867. Eleven synods participated. They were: the Ministerium of Pennsylvania, the Ministerium of New York, the English Synod of Ohio, the Pittsburgh Synod, the Wisconsin Synod,[88] the English District Synod of Ohio, the Michigan Synod, the Augustana Synod, the Minnesota Synod, the Canada Synod, and the Illinois Synod.[89]

Initially, the General Council was four-fifths the size of the depleted General Synod. Very soon, the younger body was the larger of the two. Locally, debates resulted in fractures in various synods. For instance, a minority in the Illinois Synod wanted to remain in the General Synod. They seceded from the Illinois Synod in its move to the General Council and formed the Central Illinois Synod to remain in the General Synod.

The disruptions left the General Synod in the post-Civil War period a remnant of the large and growing body of 1860. As a result, the struggle to develop an effective pension and benefits program became even more complicated. The district synods that remained in the General Synod, however, were more inclined to cooperative endeavors than many of those in the General Council. So the efforts to maintain a fund with adequate resources continued.

In the aftermath of the divisions, the question of who was entitled to be a trustee of the Pastors' Fund loomed large. When the General Synod met in May 1868 in Harrisburg, Pa., the Rev. E. W. Hutter, as a trustee of the Pastors' Fund, reported that Mr. Houpt had declined to serve as treasurer and had submitted to him the fund's assets—$700 in U.S. bonds at six percent interest, $1,200 in Dr. Gilbert's mortgage, and $99.17 in cash.[90] Reported in

---

[87] Abdel Ross Wentz, *A Basic History of Lutheranism in America* (Philadelphia: Muhlenberg Press, 1955), pp. 148-152.

[88] This synod is not to be confused with the church body now known as the Wisconsin Evangelical Lutheran Synod.

[89] Wentz, p. 153.

[90] *Proceedings*, Twenty-Fourth Convention of the General Synod, Washington, D.C., May 13-20, 1869, p. 18.

the proceedings was this observation: "Owing to the peculiar composition of the Board of Trustees [of the Pastors' Fund]—one-half of its number having been appointed from churches which soon after dissolved their connection with the General Synod—no formal organization of the Board, nor indeed any meeting, had taken place during this interval of two years [from 1866 to 1868]."[91] The person who had been the fund's president, the Rev. Dr. G. F. Krotel, declined to serve any longer. Further, the withdrawal of the Ministerium of Pennsylvania from the General Synod meant that several members of the board from that synod likely had no legal right to continue serving as trustees of the Pastors' Fund.[92]

Named trustees of the fund in 1868 were: the Rev. E. W. Hutter, the Rev. L. E. Albert, the Rev. F. W. Conrad, Mr. Martin Buehler, Mr. A. G. Stein, and Mr. F. V. Beisel.[93] They were re-elected in 1869.[94] Pr. Hutter was designated treasurer of the fund.

Gilbert loan finally paid

During the subsequent biennium, the controversial Gilbert loan of $1,200 finally was paid. As noted in Pr. Hutter's 1871 report as treasurer, "The Gilbert mortgage has happily been realized, with interest, but only after much wearisome labor, and the employment of an attorney."[95] He warned, in view of limited income and necessary disbursements, "there is danger that the fund will soon be exhausted. . . ."[96] The fund's balance in 1871 was still only $1,626.82.[97] Two years later, not much had changed. Assets of the Pastors' Fund Society were listed on June 11, 1873, as $1,634.69. Payments to two pastors and three widows amounted for the biennium to $636.[98]

Near the end of the 1873-1875 biennium, Pr. Albert succeeded Pr. Hutter as treasurer of the Pastors' Fund Society of the General Synod. Two legacies, one for $3,650 and the other for $950, had increased

---

[91] *Proceedings*, Twenty-Third Convention of the General Synod, Harrisburg, Pa., May 7-14, 1868, p. 32.

[92] *Proceedings*, General Synod, 1869, p. 18.

[93] *Proceedings*, General Synod, 1868, p. 32.

[94] *Proceedings*, General Synod, 1869, p. 19.

[95] *Proceedings*, Twenty-Fifth Convention of the General Synod, Dayton, Ohio, June 8-15, 1871, p. 17.

[96] *Proceedings*, General Synod, 1871, p. 17.

[97] *Proceedings*, General Synod, 1871, p. 16. The amount in current dollars would be less than $40,000.

[98] *Proceedings*, Twenty-Sixth Convention of the General Synod, Canton, Ohio, June 11-20, 1873, p. 38.

substantially the fund's holdings.[99] Payments of $759.75 were made to one pastor and four widows on assets of $6,192.54. Once again, the trustees "were instructed to secure an act of incorporation for the [Pastors' Fund] Society."[100]

When the General Synod assembled at Carthage, Ill, on May 31, 1877, Pr. Albert as treasurer of the Pastors' Fund Society reported some additional synods had contributed but assets had increased only minimally, reaching $6,420.11. Disbursements of $650 had been made to two pastors and five widows.[101]

The financial picture would grow bleaker as the need for payments to beneficiaries of the fund increased. Pr. Albert's report as treasurer to the General Synod in 1879 showed a balance of $220.75,[102] and in 1881, $163.25.[103] Increased contributions from district synods offset expenditures in the following biennium, leaving a balance in 1883 of $410.59.[104] At the same meeting, a resolution was adopted that urged greater support of the fund. The resolution raised the issue of possible apportionment:

> WHEREAS, the support of indigent and disabled ministers is an object which should commend itself more heartily to our churches and ministers; and
>
> WHEREAS, in many of our Synods collections for the Pastors' Fund are altogether omitted; therefore,
>
> Resolved, that we recommend to the District Synods the opening of a column in their Parochial Reports, for such collections, and if feasible, the apportionment of a certain amount to the contributed.[105]

[99] Proceedings, Twenty-Seventh Convention of the General Synod, Baltimore, Md., May 26–June 3, 1875, pp. 51-52.

[100] Proceedings, General Synod, 1875, p. 52.

[101] Proceedings, Twenty-Eighth Convention of the General Synod, Carthage, Ill., May 30–June 6, 1877, pp. 8-9.

[102] Proceedings, Twenty-Ninth Convention of the General Synod, Wooster, Ohio, June 11-18, 1879, p. 7.

[103] Proceedings, Thirtieth Convention of the General Synod, Altoona, Pa., June 8-14, 1881, p. 8.

[104] Proceedings, Thirty-First Convention of the General Synod, Springfield, Ohio, May 16-22, 1883, p. 9.

[105] Proceedings, General Synod, 1883, p. 58.

"Just debt due the faithful minister"

While income increased in the biennium, so did disbursements, leaving a cash balance for the fund in 1885 of only $242.48.[106] When Pr. Albert reported in 1887 a cash balance of $597.34,[107] Mr. J. W. Rice, as a voting representative at that year's meeting of the General Synod, presented a resolution that read:

> Believing that the time has arrived in our history as a Church, when we should by some concerted effort, and the fostering of care of a Board, make more adequate provision for our aged and disabled ministers; therefore be it
>
> *Resolved* 1, That a fund shall be established to be known as "the Ministerial Annuity Fund," contributions to which shall be urged and collected in a manner similar to the other benevolence of the Church, and the custody and distribution of which shall be confided to a Board, to be appointed or elected by the General Synod.
>
> *Resolved* 2, That any moneys now in the treasury of what has been known as the "Pastors' Fund" of the General Synod, shall, together with any invested securities, the result of legacies made to the same, be transferred to this Board.
>
> *Resolved* 3, That we urge upon the churches represented in the General Synod, the claims which this cause has upon them and impressing, so far as possible, the fact that this is *not a charity*, but a just debt due to the faithful minister of the church, disqualified by age or sickness for the active work of the ministry.
>
> *Resolved* 4, That a Committee of five be appointed by the President, who shall prepare a plan for the organization of this Board, and the details of its working; the Committee to report at 10 o'clock a.m. Monday.[108]

The resolution was significant in pointing to an understanding of such a program as fulfilling "a just debt due to the faithful minister" and suggesting

---

[106] *Proceedings*, Thirty-Second Convention of the General Synod, Harrisburg, Pa., May 27–June 2, 1885, p. 12.

[107] *Proceedings*, Thirty-Third Convention of the General Synod, Omaha, Neb., June 1-13, 1887, p. 25.

[108] *Proceedings*, General Synod, 1887, p. 23. Italic type and capitalization are reproduced as in the printed minutes.

a more formal organization of the program under a board. The resolution was referred "to a special committee for report two years hence."[109]

Corporate charter gained in 1889

The long-standing issue of incorporation for the fund moved to resolution with the record showing an expense of $55.30 for the charter of incorporation in May 1889. That was no small step. Thirty years had passed since incorporation first had been requested by official action of the General Synod. The level of invested funds remained the same as in the previous biennium, at $6,600 with a cash balance of $510.66.[110]

The report of the committee that examined prospects for establishing a Ministerial Annuity Fund was tabled because of "the grave questions involved."[111] The minutes do not record what those questions may have been.

The 1887 resolution that had been submitted by Mr. Rice received further attention in 1891 when the General Synod voted:

> Believing that the time has not only arrived, but has long since passed, when the claims of the aged and infirm of the ministry should be pressed more vigorously upon the attention of the Church; therefore be it
>
> *Resolved,* That a committee of five be appointed to present a plan at this convention of the General Synod to transfer care of this interest to a Board co-ordinate[d] with the other Boards of the Church, and submit the same to the Pastors' Fund Society.[112]

Further, the 1891 meeting adopted a second resolution on the matter that sought for the next biennial meeting a recommendation on the Ministerial Annuity Fund proposal:

> *Resolved,* That the report of the committee on the Ministerial Annuity Fund be referred to the Pastors' Fund Committee, to take into consideration the changing of the Constitution of the Pastors' Fund Society, so as to constitute a Board with nine

---

[109] *Proceedings,* General Synod, 1887, p. 25.

[110] *Proceedings,* Thirty-Fourth Convention of the General Synod, Allegheny, Pa., June 12-21, 1889, p. 23.

[111] *Proceedings,* General Synod, 1889, p. 58.

[112] *Proceedings,* Thirty-Fifth Convention of the General Synod, Lebanon, Pa., May 20-29, 1891, p. 22. Treasurer Albert continued to report investments at $6,600. The cash balance in the fund was listed as $1,027.92.

directors, and also the adding of such features from the aforesaid report as may contribute to the greater efficiency of the Society; the whole to be laid before the General Synod at its next biennial meeting for action.[113]

A more formal operational pattern

Proposed changes for the fund were adopted by the General Synod in 1893. A system of apportionment was embraced as a way of sustaining the Pastors' Fund Society. The level initially was set at five cents per member of each congregation.

Greater interest was evident in the fund. Further, the improved financial status of the Pastors' Fund was welcome news for those who gathered for that 1893 meeting of the General Synod. Investments had increased to $7,600 and income for the biennium had reached $13,471.32, according to Pr. Albert, who continued to serve as treasurer of the fund.[114]

Noting that the fund was now incorporated, the fund committee argued that any "changes in its charter should not be made unless absolutely necessary." If the 1891 idea of the Ministerial Annuity Fund were to be pursued, changes in the charter would be required. Therefore, the committee argued for maintaining the existing terms for the fund.

In view of the complexity of charter changes, the General Synod determined that the present fund would be continued and its constitution would remain unchanged. The fund's board of trustees, however, was granted authority to employ a secretary, a step signaling a more formal operational pattern for the fund.[115]

---

[113] *Proceedings*, General Synod, 1891, p. 45.

[114] *Proceedings*, Thirty-Sixth Convention of the General Synod, Canton, Ohio, May 24–June 1, 1893, p. 33.

[115] *Proceedings*, General Synod, 1893, p. 34. The committee's resolution, as adopted, read: "That in view of the present prosperity of the Pastors' Fund, and the increased interest that is taken in it, together with the fact that it is an incorporated body, and that changes in its charter should not be made unless absolutely necessary, and also that many of the features in the Ministerial Annuity Fund could not probably be adopted without an amendment of its charter, and would not in the opinion of the Committee tend to the greater efficiency of the Society; therefore, the Committee would respectfully report, 1. That in its judgment, the Constitution of the Pastors' Fund Society should remain unchanged. 2. That the Board of Trustees be empowered to employ a paid Secretary, as soon as in the judgment of said Board it shall be deemed advisable or necessary to do so, at a salary to be fixed by the Board. 3. That the Board formulate a series of By-Laws for its government, and report them for approval at the next meeting of the General Synod."

To sustain the Pastors' Fund Society, the pattern of apportionments was maintained. In fact, the decision was made in 1895 to increase the apportionment from five to ten cents per capita. By that time, investments had grown to $11,100 and income for the biennium amounted to $14,501.41.[116]

As a way of meeting the ten cents per-member goal, the 1897 meeting of the General Synod asked that a special day be observed in member congregations as "Pastors' Fund Day" with an offering received for the fund.

Treasurer Albert reported in 1897 that investments had grown to $13,300 and income for the biennium amounted to $18,479.69. Current recipients of the fund numbered 65, of whom 30 were widows.[117] By 1899, the number of recipients had increased to 68, of whom 32 were widows; likewise the level of investments grew to $18,150.[118]

At the turn of the century, 86 individuals were recipients of the fund, of whom 42 were widows.[119] By 1903, the number grew to 93, of whom 46 were widows.[120] At the 1903 meeting, the apportionment was fixed at seven cents per member.[121] Assets in the form of mortgages, a temporary loan, some stock in one company, and cash amounted to $20,177.82 in 1905. Contributions from individuals and synods amounted to $30,554.91, but expenditures were $28,927.09, so the program of aid was largely operated on a "pay-as-you-go" basis.[122]

Both income and assets decreased slightly in the following biennium, but the number of regular recipients in 1907 also had decreased to 87, of whom 45 were widows.[123]

---

[116] *Proceedings*, Thirty-Seventh Convention of the General Synod, Hagerstown, Md., June 5-13, 1895, p. 26.

[117] *Proceedings*, Thirty-Eighth Convention of the General Synod, Mansfield, Ohio, June 9-17, 1897, pp. 25-27.

[118] *Proceedings*, Thirty-Ninth Convention of the General Synod, York, Pa., May 24–June 1, 1899, pp. 32-33.

[119] *Proceedings*, Fortieth Convention of the General Synod, Des Moines, Iowa, May 29–June 6, 1901, p. 25.

[120] *Proceedings*, Forty-First Convention of the General Synod, Baltimore, Md., June 3-11, 1903, p. 31.

[121] *Proceedings*, General Synod, 1903, p. 31.

[122] *Proceedings*, Forty-Second Convention of the General Synod, Pittsburgh, Pa., June 14-21, 1905, p. 35.

[123] *Proceedings*, Forty-Third Convention of the General Synod, Sunbury, Pa., May 22-30, 1907, pp. 28-29.

A significant change occurred at the 1909 meeting. The Rev. Luther E. Albert, who had served as the fund's treasurer for 34 years, died on March 6, 1909. The Rev. J. Eugene Dietterich succeeded him and reported that synods were meeting only about two-thirds of their apportioned responsibility ($22,686.43 versus what was then the apportionment rate of seven cents per member, which would have amounted to $31,993.36).[124]

Total assets of the fund rose to $30,452.29 by 1911, with one-third of that in a permanent endowment. Per-member contributions of $24,519.39 continued to lag behind the apportionment of $32,343.97 to member synods. The report noted for the biennium that 13 "pastor-beneficiaries were translated to the Father's house to rest from their labors and enjoy the fullness of the home everlasting." Receiving regular assistance were 32 pastors and 71 widows.[125]

At the 1911 meeting, Treasurer Dietterich underscored the urgent needs of the fund. He wrote:

> Many, after years of service to the Church, must spend their last years amid want and suffering, while memories of the past make it only harder to endure; and they can scarcely repress the feeling that the Church to which they have given their conse-crated and faithful endeavor is ungrateful and unappreciative. Such a condition does not encourage young men to enter the ministry; it does not make it easy for our pastors to serve weak points, where the salary affords only a scant living; it does not add to a sense of respect on the part of the world toward the Church; nor does it glorify God. God will provide; but when those through whom He provides forget or withhold, He is robbed and His people suffer.[126]

On behalf of the trustees, he urged that the per-member apportionment rate once again be raised to 10 cents. He also suggested that pastors bring concerns for support of the fund to the congregations they served. At the same time, he exhorted men's and women's organizations in congregations to take up this cause.[127]

---

[124] *Proceedings*, Forty-Fourth Convention of the General Synod, Richmond, Ind., June 2-10, 1909, pp. 30-31.

[125] *Proceedings*, Forty-Fifth Convention of the General Synod, Washington, D.C., June 7-14, 1911, pp. 32-35.

[126] *Proceedings*, General Synod, 1911, p. 36.

[127] *Proceedings*, General Synod, 1911, p. 37.

Steps toward a retirement annuity

The feasibility of establishing a "Lutheran Pastors' Sustentation Fund" was examined. A report on that possibility had been requested by the 1909 meeting of the General Synod. Suggested was a type of fraternal insurance and annuity program for participating clergy who would pay annual premiums that would "insure an income in the case of disability or at the age of seventy years." Benefits also could be provided to their widows or minor orphans.[128]

The proposal called for operation of the Sustentation Fund separate from the Pastors' Fund Society. The distinction was this: "The former provides a plan for ministers to protect themselves and prevent indigence at old age or disability, by paying a definite sum annually during their years of active service. The latter aims to relieve superannuated ministers, their widows and children, who are without means of support."[129]

Envisioned through the Sustentation Fund was an annuity of $500 at age 70 for those who had served at least thirty years. For those with a shorter term of service, the annuity at 70 would be a minimum of $100, with an additional $10 for each year in pastoral ministry over five years, but the total would not exceed $500. In the event of the participating pastor's death, the surviving widow would receive three-fifths of what would be due to the pastor, depending on his duration of service. In the case of the widow's death, the annuity would be divided equally for the minor children until the age of majority.

The premium was to be split, with the pastor paying 20 percent and the congregation 80 percent. The annual rate was to be $85.65 at 21 years of age, to $468.46 at the upper age limit for joining of 60 years. Payment of the premium would cease upon reaching age 70 or being disabled.

The plan was not deemed feasible at that time, especially in view of the urgency for greater support by congregations of the Pastors' Fund to provide grants to indigent pastors, their widows, and dependent children.[130]

By 1913, district synods were meeting a greater percentage of their apportionment ($32,459.46, slightly more than $7,000 short of the per-member allocation of $39,809). The permanent endowment stood at $12,136.63 in cash and bonds. Forty-three pastors and 80 widows of

---

[128] *Proceedings*, General Synod, 1911, p. 38.

[129] *Proceedings*, General Synod, 1911, p. 38.

[130] *Proceedings*, General Synod, 1911, pp. 38-39.

pastors had received assistance in the biennium from the fund. Regular income and receipt of some legacies had increased the cash on hand from $3,944.66 in 1911 to $10,131.72 in 1913. The per-member apportionment was continued at 10 cents.[131]

A significant milestone occurred on January 1, 1914, when the Rev. G. M. Diffenderfer of Carlisle, Pa., was called as the general secretary of the Pastors' Fund Society. With an annual salary of $2,500, he embarked on surveying needs and raising funds for both the general fund and the permanent endowment. In the biennium, district synods contributed $40,166.79 of their per capita apportionment of $47,526. Receiving assistance from the fund were 127, including 41 clergy and 86 widows of pastors, in the amount of $21,650.[132]

Greater diversification in the holdings of the permanent endowment was shown by 1915. Among the holdings were bonds of Commonwealth Power, Railway and Light Co., Charleston Consolidated Railway, Gas and Electric Co., Pacific Telephone and Telegraph, and Tennessee Power Co.[133]

On the threshold of change

The ecclesiastical landscape was about to change. That was evident when the General Synod met June 20-27, 1917, in Chicago. Six weeks before that meeting, a resolution had been received from the Committee of the General Council on Ministerial Pensions. The resolution asked that, if the proposed merger to form the United Lutheran Church in America were approved, cooperative efforts be undertaken for a uniform pension plan. In response, the participants voted to increase the membership of the board for the Lutheran Pastors' Fund to work on establishing a pension plan.[134]

Benefitting from the Lutheran Pastors' Fund in the 1915-1917 biennium were 44 pastors and 88 widows of clergy. Participating synods contributed $43,156 (about $590,000 in 2008 dollars) of the per-capita apportionment of $49,698.[135]

---

[131] *Proceedings*, Forty-Sixth Convention of the General Synod, Atchison, Kan., May 14-21, 1913, pp. 83-87.

[132] *Proceedings*, Forty-Seventh Convention of the General Synod, Akron, Ohio, May 26–June 2, 1915, pp. 75-80.

[133] *Proceedings*, General Synod, 1915, p. 85.

[134] *Proceedings*, Forty-Eighth Convention of the General Synod, Chicago, Ill., June 20-27, 1917, p. 101.

[135] *Proceedings*, General Synod, 1917, pp. 98-99.

In his 1917 report, General Secretary Diffenderfer called attention to a "recent decision of the Supreme Court of Wisconsin passing upon litigation affecting an annuity of $25,000 for the Methodist Church," which said, "The certificate issued by the Pastors' Fund of the Lutheran Church of the General Synod is the only legally incontestable bond of the twelve forms submitted to us, and we would advise your [Methodist] Board to prepare a similar form." He added that the General Synod's form

> ... avoids fees in settling your estate and guarantees you a safe income from your money thus placed into our hands. Ministers who save very small annual amounts would do well to invest it in this Fund, rather than to be induced by extraordinary offers of a high rate of income, to squander and dissipate their meagre [sic] and hard-earned savings.[136]

Pr. Diffenderfer also reported that representatives of several churches met in June 1916 in Atlantic City, including Northern Baptist, Christian (Disciples), Congregational, Episcopal, Methodist South, Methodist Episcopal, Presbyterian General Assembly, Presbyterian U.S.A., and Lutherans represented by the Augustana Lutheran Church and the General Synod.[137] Their concern was an effort to secure $60 million for Ministers' Relief and Pensions.

In 1917, the Episcopal Church became the first U.S. church body to embrace a reserve pension plan with contributions and defined benefits related to salary levels and years of service.[138] The Church Pension Fund of the Episcopal Church contained some ingredients of what eventually would become a model contributory pension plan for Lutheran churches and others. In the meantime, however, many church bodies in the early decades of the twentieth century continued to try to develop pension endowments to provide a defined annual stipend for retirees.

---

[136] *Proceedings*, General Synod, 1917, p. 98.

[137] Several churches, beginning in 1915, met annually in the Church Pensions Conference, which later was renamed the Church Benefits Association (see Chapter 4).

[138] "Clergy To Get Pensions," *The New York Times*, February 7, 1916; see also Brackenridge and Boyd, *Presbyterians and Pensions*, p. 70. The reserve pension plan of The Episcopal Church was chartered in 1914 and became operational on March 1, 1917. The Episcopal Church's clergy fund is a defined-benefit plan, with individual benefits calculated on the basis of years of credited service and highest average compensation. The pension amount is not determined by the total of the money contributed on the person's behalf or the performance of investments during the person's working life. The pension contribution rate for parishes and other employing entities is 18 percent of the individual's salary, including any housing allowance.

Seeking increased resources for the Lutheran Pastors' Fund, Pr. Diffenderfer proposed a one-year goal of $1 million for the General Synod, half of which would be used to inaugurate a guaranteed pension plan at retirement and half for the care of the aged and those with disabilities.[139] Clearly, the time was not right for consideration of such an ambitious goal by the General Synod.

In spite of the broad attention being given to pension concerns, the General Synod determined in 1917 that a resolution calling for development of a regular pension plan could not receive a favorable consideration until the "entire system" could be "placed upon a sound financial basis."[140] The resolution originally had been submitted in 1913 by the Maryland Synod. The story of funded pension plans would unfold in far greater detail in the subsequent decades for various churches.

A key historic moment

The recessed forty-eighth convention of the General Synod reconvened almost a year and a half after that meeting began in Chicago. The venue of the reconvened convention was New York. To conclude its work, the General Synod met November 12-14 and again on November 18, 1918. Representatives gathered for the merger of the General Synod, the General Council, and the United Synod South to form the United Lutheran Church in America (ULCA).

In one of the key historic moments for U.S. Lutherans, a new chapter was about to unfold. That unfolding story, however, would prove in some respects even more complex than the General Synod's efforts throughout the previous nine decades for the relief of "superannuated ministers, their widows, and orphans."

---

[139] *Proceedings*, General Synod, 1917, pp. 96-97.

[140] *Proceedings*, General Synod, 1917, pp. 100-101.

CHAPTER 9

When Compassion
Had a Name

From the beginning of the Augustana Lutheran Church in 1860,[1] support of clergy and their families in special need had a face and a name. Five years into the life of that immigrant Swedish church body, the Rev. J. P. C. Boreen became the first Augustana pastor to die in active service. His death meant that the Augustana Lutheran Church had to consider how to provide support for the survivors of Pr. Boreen, whose small salary had not allowed for any savings.[2]

Searching for solutions, a special committee recommended in 1867 the creation of a synodical aid fund for widows of pastors. Under the plan, each pastor was to contribute one percent of his salary to the fund. Congregations were to make voluntary gifts to the degree possible for them.[3] Two years later, in 1869, aged and disabled pastors were added as beneficiaries of the program.[4] Aid was to be disbursed on the basis of need.

Precarious in early years

Thus, the Augustana Lutheran Church, from its earliest days, did attempt to assist needy pastors and their families. Like the aid fund of the General Synod, however, the Augustana endeavor was a precarious one. As the Rev. Dr. G. Everett Arden, a Lutheran church historian, acknowledged in his overview of Augustana's heritage, interest and support were so limited that Augustana voted in 1875 "to wash its hands of the whole business, and turn

---

[1] The Augustana Lutheran Church had various official names throughout its existence. "Augustana" was the consistent element in the name.

[2] *Protokoll*, Augustana Synod meeting at Princeton, Ill., June 9-14, 1865, pp. 5 and 13; cited by G. Everett Arden, "Marshalling the Resources: Reorganization of the Pension and Aid Fund," *Augustana Heritage: A History of the Augustana Lutheran Church* (Rock Island, Ill.: Augustana Book Concern, 1963), p. 218.

[3] *Protokoll*, Augustana Synod meeting at Berlin, Ill., June 13-18, 1867, p. 12.

[4] *Protokoll*, Augustana Synod meeting at Moline, Ill., June 16-23, 1869, p. 41.

the responsibility of caring for needy pastors' families over to the several conferences."[5] A change of heart emerged three years later when the synod again assumed the obligations of the aid program.[6] Recounts Dr. Arden:

> Though several attempts were made to place the pension and aid on a sound footing, it was not until 1892 that a thorough overhauling of the entire project was finally undertaken. At the convention at Lindsborg, Kansas, 1892, new rules for the administration of this agency were adopted which provided that each pastor was to contribute one fourth of one percent of his salary annually. Each congregation was to receive an annual offering for the fund. At the death of any pastor, all other pastors were to contribute one fourth of one percent of their salaries and each congregation was to receive a special offering. The new rules stipulated that each pastor must fulfill his obligation to the fund, if he or his survivors were to benefit. The benefits were to be $5.00 per week to disabled pastors, $2.50 per week to pastors' widows, and $1.00 per week for the support of each minor child under sixteen years of age. No family was to receive more than $7.50 per week. If a widow remarried, she was to receive no more aid. And aid was to be given only where real need existed.[7]

Six years later, in 1898, the contribution rate was changed. Each pastor was to contribute annually $5 (about $125 in 2008 dollars), and at the death of any pastor, all other pastors were to contribute $1.50 each as a death benefit to the widow.[8] At that point, the fund shifted from being only a relief fund and began to evolve into a type of pension fund.[9]

Move beyond aid to pension

As the twentieth century dawned, attempts were undertaken to strengthen the fund. The Augustana Ministerial Aid Fund was incorporated

---

[5] *Protokoll*, Augustana Synod meeting at Baja in Goodhue County, Minnesota, June 19-29, 1875, p. 32.

[6] *Protokoll*, Augustana Synod meeting at Princeton, Ill., June 17-24, 1878, p. 38.

[7] *Augustana-Synodens Referat*, Augustana Synod meeting at Lindsborg, Kan., May 31–June 7, 1892, pp. 75ff.; see also A.D. Mattson, "Pension and Aid," *Polity of the Augustana Lutheran Church* (Rock Island, Ill.: Augustana Book Concern, 1952), pp. 92-93.

[8] *Augustana-Synodens Referat*, Augustana Synod meeting at Galesburg, Ill., June 2-9, 1898, p. 81.

[9] Titus A. Conrad, "The Augustana Pension and Aid Fund," *After Seventy-Five Years* (Rock Island, Ill.: Augustana Book Concern, 1935), p. 177.

in 1900 in the state of Iowa as an agency of the church body.[10] Its purposes were defined in the Articles of Incorporation in this way:

> 1. To aid sick and superannuated ministers of the Augustana Synod and professors in the Institutions of learning belonging to said Synod or its Conferences.

> 2. To aid surviving families of such ministers and professors.[11]

The rules for the operation of the fund, which originally were prepared in 1898, were revised in 1910 to specify that each congregation was to pay one cent per communicant member on the death of any member of the fund. This amount later was adjusted to two cents per communicant member. To this point, the aid had been distributed on the basis of need, making the fund largely a charitable matter. Now the fund was becoming in practice both a pension plan as well as an aid fund.[12]

The rules and bylaws of the fund had been translated into English by 1913.[13] The purpose of what was still named the Ministerial Aid Fund was to provide "support of sick, disabled and aged ministers and regular professors within the Augustana Synod . . . and for their families."[14] Eligible for membership in the Ministerial Aid Fund were all pastors and regular professors of the synod. As protections against what generally came to be known as "adverse selection," the rules specified that "no minister or professor, who neglects to become a member of the Fund while in his younger years and in good health, shall become a member when he becomes sickly, aged or unable to pursue his calling."[15]

After authorization in 1914, an executive secretary was called. The Rev. S. A. Lindholm began work in May 1915, thereby setting in motion increased organizational and operational attention to the pension and aid fund.[16] Through an amendment of the bylaws, the name of the fund

---

[10] *Augustana-Synodens Referat*, Augustana Synod meeting at Burlington, Iowa, June 15-19, 1900, p. 63.

[11] Article IV, *Referat*, 1900, p. 64.

[12] Mattson, pp. 93-94.

[13] *Augustana-Synodens Referat*, Augustana Synod meeting in Chicago, June 11-17, 1913, p. 133.

[14] Article I, *Referat*, 1913, pp. 133-134.

[15] Article VIII, *Referat*, 1913, p. 135.

[16] *Augustana-Synodens Referat*, Augustana Synod meeting in Minneapolis, Minn., June 9-16, 1915, p. 144; Mattson, p. 95.

officially was changed in 1915 to the Ministerial Pension and Aid Fund of the Evangelical Lutheran Augustana Synod of North America.[17]

Fund appeal

Seeking greater fiscal stability for the fund, the synod's 1915 Minneapolis convention voted:

> That the Synod adopt as its goal for the next five years an ingathering for the Pension and Aid Fund, and that a committee of laymen be elected to supervise this ingathering; that the several conferences of the Augustana Synod be instructed to elect one layman for every two thousand communicant members as a member of the layman's committee to raise $500,000 for the Ministerial Pension and Aid Fund, and that the committee be authorized to elect ten members at large.[18]

Nearly seven years passed before the goal was achieved, but $500,000 was delivered by 1922 to the board of the Pension and Aid Fund.

At the 1915 convention when the fund appeal originally was approved, revised regulations were adopted reducing the age at which a pastor could receive pension benefits from 70 to 65 years.[19] A 1921 revision specified the level of benefits at $400 per year for each pensioner. Widows were to receive $200 per year, and $25 per year was granted for each child under 16 years of age.[20] Implementation of that benefit schedule, however, was deferred until 1925, when the accumulated funds were sufficient to meet the obligation.[21]

Amendments to the Articles of Incorporation were approved by the board on February 24, 1921. The corporation was therein identified as The Augustana Pension and Aid Fund, which was to be "owned, maintained, and controlled by the Evangelical Lutheran Augustana Synod of North America."[22] Its purpose was "the support of disabled and aged ministers, permanent professors, lay missionaries, and their families. . . ."[23] The

---

[17] *Referat*, 1915, p. 151.

[18] *Referat*, 1915, p. 150.

[19] *Referat*, 1915, p. 151.

[20] *Augustana-Synodens Referat*, Augustana Synod meeting in Chicago, June 8-13, 1921, p. 140.

[21] Mattson, p. 94.

[22] Article I, Section 1, "Amended and Substituted Articles of Incorporation of the Augustana Pension and Aid Fund," *Referat*, 1921, p. 131.

[23] Articles of Incorporation, Article 1, Section 2, *Referat*, 1921, p. 131.

principal office was identified as Des Moines, Iowa. That would continue to be the case until the mid-1950s when the pension operation joined the other Augustana church offices in Minneapolis.

In the 1921 amendments of the articles, more extensive attention was given to the management of assets, a change perhaps emerging from the fund-raising effort that, by then, was nearing its $500,000 goal. Revised Article VI specified:

> Section 1. In order to carry out the purposes of this corporation, it shall have power to receive money, personal property, real estate, either by sale, gift, donations, bequests or devise, or by assessment of its own members or admission fee and annual fee, also endowment contributions and contributions from congregations, individuals and other sources.
>
> Section 2. The Board of Directors shall judiciously invest all money which shall come into their hands as such in first mortgage loans on farm real estate and no loan shall exceed fifty per cent of the appraised value of the property managed.[24]

The revised articles specified a new process for their future amendment. Any such amendments would not be approved directly by the board but would be recommended by the board to the annual meeting of the synod. They would require at least a two-thirds vote for adoption.[25]

Duty to belong

The 1921 bylaws declared that pastors and permanent professors of the synod "shall be duty bound to affiliate with the Augustana Pension and Aid Fund."[26] Delinquency was addressed in this way:

> Should a member fail to pay his annual dues or any assessments within thirty days after becoming due or fail to pay the endowment contribution . . . , he shall forfeit all rights and benefits as [a] member of the Augustana Pension and Aid Fund.
>
> If such lapsed member desires to become reinstated, he shall be required to present a reputable doctor's certificate of good health and to pay all lapsed annual dues, assessments and contributions.[27]

---

[24] Article VI, Sections 1 and 2, *Referat*, 1921, p. 133.

[25] Article X, Section 1, *Referat*, 1921, p. 134.

[26] Bylaw Article VI, *Referat*, 1921, p. 138.

[27] Bylaw Article IX, Sections 1 and 2, *Referat*, 1921, p. 139.

By 1924, the assets of the fund were approaching $1 million, standing at $944,754.27. The synod asked that "pastors and congregations be earnestly requested loyally and liberally to support this important cause" and that conference presidents make certain "that all pastors and others eligible to membership in the pension fund join the fund."[28]

At that point, a "group insurance plan" was requested.[29] After investigation, however, the insurance proposal was deemed in 1925 neither feasible nor wise:

> Your committee has investigated the matter of group insurance on ministers of the Augustana Synod, ranging in age from 26 to 89 years. It would cost about $24.00 per thousand capita per year on a $1,000.00 policy, or a total of about $18,000.00 for [a] $773,000.00 blanket policy, which would be paid at the death of the insured or the death of each pastor, this being only a nominal amount, and in our opinion not any better than the present method of handling the question of insurance or protection of each pastor. . . .
>
> There seems to be an utter lack of responsibility and good will, as well as cooperation by about 20 percent of our pastors towards a pension system. . . .
>
> We feel that the educational work must go on until we can get 100 percent cooperation by all of our pastors and their congregations. Only then can we discuss group insurance of a larger amount than herein mentioned. . . .[30]

The board was instructed by the 1925 meeting of the synod to "negotiate settlements with all delinquent congregations" on their per-communicant assessment. Further, the adopted resolution declared:

> That the Synod deplores the indifference and inexcusable neglect of duty and responsibility to God and His servants on the part of many congregations to neglect or refuse, year after

---

28 *Minutes*, Sixty-Fifth Annual Convention of the Augustana Lutheran Church, DeKalb, Ill., June 12-17, 1924 (Rock Island, Ill.: Augustana Book Concern, 1924), p. 163. The publisher of the minutes of the Augustana Lutheran Church was the Augustana Book Concern of Rock Island, Ill. Citation of the publisher of the minutes is not repeated in subsequent footnotes.

29 *Minutes*, 1924, p. 163.

30 *Minutes*, Sixty-Sixth Annual Convention of the Augustana Lutheran Church, Minneapolis, Minn., June 11-16, 1925, pp. 128-129.

year, to meet their just and common obligations towards the pension fund, both with regard to the two-cent fees as well as their pledges to the laymen's pension fund.[31]

By contrast, the next meeting of the synod in 1926 affirmed:

> That we gratefully acknowledge the manifold blessings of God shown by the splendid help given many in need; by interest in the fund manifested in general; by the willingness of most of our congregations and members of the fund to pay promptly the stipulated dues and essesments [sic]; and also by the steady growth of this fund, now having reached the one million mark.

> That, realizing the increasing demands upon this fund and the absolute necessity of keeping the endowment funds intact, we urge upon all delinquent churches and members to promptly fulfill their obligations.[32]

Investment in farm loans

Interestingly, during and immediately following World War I, farm loans were the primary arena of the fund's investments. The post-war period of deflation in the farm economy adversely affected the fund's investments, but the fund continued to grow through contributions.[33] Apparently, farm loans had become an issue of controversy and, therefore, the matter was addressed in the fund's 1926 annual report.[34] The dispute may have accounted for the 19-page audited financial statement published that year in the synod's convention report.

By 1926, a total of $19,433.33 was being expended for the pensions of 50 clergy members, while 117 widows were receiving $21,349.54 and 38 minor children, $947.02. The report indicated, "When we compare with other Lutheran bodies, we are paying a higher pension than any of them. The highest pension paid by any other Lutheran synod is $320.00 while we are paying $400.00."[35]

---

[31] Minutes, 1925, p. 137.

[32] Minutes, Sixty-Seventh Annual Convention of the Augustana Lutheran Church, Philadelphia, Pa., June 8-13, 1926, pp. 138-139.

[33] Minutes, 1926, p. 118.

[34] Minutes, 1926, p. 118. The report charged that "some unscrupulous persons have even spread false reports relative to the condition of the Fund."

[35] Minutes, 1926, pp. 117-118.

Although income remained sufficient to meet the fund's pension and aid obligations, the issue of property holdings continued to cause concern in 1927. "Everything is done to care for the lands which have come into our possession through foreclosures, now twenty-seven in number," the annual report said. "It seems advisable not to dispose of these properties until times have improved."[36] Clearly, that did not happen very soon.

Change in leadership

After serving for sixteen and a half years as general secretary and treasurer of the Augustana Pension and Aid Fund, Pr. Lindholm resigned effective October 7, 1927. He was succeeded immediately by the Rev. Titus A. Conrad, whose salary was set at $2,500 per year, the same as his predecessor. Through per-member congregation assessments and donations, the fund had assets by this time of $1,090,671.86. Yet the issue of holding foreclosed farms remained a concern. The board, in the annual report, expressed the belief "that as soon as agriculture comes into its own these farms can be disposed of without any substantial loss to the Fund."[37]

In 1928, the decision was made to move the payment of pensions to a quarterly schedule from the semi-annual pattern that previously had been practiced.[38]

Assets by 1929 amounted to $1,147,742.44. Additional farm loan delinquencies, however, were reported as a result of "continued and unprecedented depression in farm values. . . ."[39] Yet hope was expressed that the fund would continue to grow in spite of the investment difficulties from farm loans:

> The sickle of time has reaped a large harvest among our clergymen. Some have been cut down at the noon day and others at the golden sunset of their lives. The assistance which this fund has been able to disburse to the bereaved has been most timely and has been gratefully received. The regret of the board has been that the relief could not be more generous. It is hoped that in the no [sic] distant future this fund may be doubled or even tripled.[40]

---

[36] *Minutes*, Sixty-Eighth Annual Convention of the Augustana Lutheran Church, Omaha, Neb., June 16-21, 1927, p. 117.

[37] *Minutes*, Sixty-Ninth Annual Convention of the Augustana Lutheran Church, Des Moines, Iowa, June 8-13, 1928, pp. 136-139.

[38] *Minutes*, 1928, p. 141.

[39] *Minutes*, Seventieth Annual Convention of the Augustana Lutheran Church, Rockford, Ill., June 7-12, 1929, p. 162.

[40] *Minutes*, 1929, p. 163.

The Augustana fund had begun as a way of meeting special needs and later evolved into a pension fund. The aid or relief element of the fund remained, however, "to extend a helping hand to those of our pastors, professors and missionaries and their families who on account of sickness and trials are in actual need." Eligible for special grants were persons in "extraordinary distress," regardless of whether they were members of the fund. The relief aspect of the fund was supported by donations, including the steady contributions of Mr. D. A. Hillstrom of Corry, Pa., who sent $50 a month to that fund. In addition, an allocation of $72,000 from the synod's budget was requested in 1930 for grants in aid.[41]

As the economic catastrophes of the Great Depression multiplied, so did the foreclosures. The report of the Augustana Pension and Aid Fund in 1931 portrayed the situation in this way:

> This past year has been one of the most trying in the history of the Pension Fund, as most of the assets have been invested in farm loans and as the unprecedented depression has made it impossible in many instances for the farmers to meet their obligations. For several years we have been in hopes that land values had reached the bottom, but because of the light crops during this past year and also because the prices of farm products were cut almost in two, the land values are lower now than they have been for twenty-five years. . . .
>
> The farms that the Fund has had to take over through foreclosure have also caused the Board a great deal of concern, primarily because most of them are located in districts where there has been almost total crop failures for several years. Consequently, the people have moved away making it almost impossible to secure good tenants. The work in connection with the proper attention to the farms as well as to the loans, together with the correspondence and other matters that need careful attention, has placed too heavy a burden on the Secretary-Treasurer,[42] and for this reason it will be necessary to engage a farm manager and perhaps in the near future someone who will take care of the whole investment problem.[43]

---

[41] *Minutes*, Seventy-First Annual Convention of the Augustana Lutheran Church, Rock Island, Ill., June 6-11, 1930, p. 172.

[42] The report noted that costs were kept low for the secretary-treasurer's extensive travel to oversee land matters because many railroads at the time gave clergy free passes.

[43] *Minutes*, Seventy-Second Annual Convention of the Augustana Lutheran Church, Jamestown, N.Y., June 11-16, 1931, p. 166.

Unexpected bounty in Oklahoma

No one could have imagined at the time how the picture would change for some of the land that happened to be located in Oklahoma. There were complications that first had to be addressed regarding that land. In order to comply with Oklahoma law as a land owner, the Augustana Pension and Aid Fund had to form the Augustana Annuity Trust, with three trustees, to manage the properties in that state.[44] The foreclosed land had represented a burden. Eventually, however, gas and oil deposits were discovered on some of the properties. Substantial income was gained over the years from the oil and gas royalties. As a result, all of the money initially invested was recovered. Even when some of the land was sold following World War II, the trust retained half or more of the mineral rights.[45]

The first ray of hope appeared as early as 1932 when an oil lease was granted by the Augustana Annuity Trust on 160 acres in Okfuskee County, Okla.[46] In subsequent years, other leases were negotiated, but drilling for oil was delayed because of an oversupply of oil and the country's economic conditions at that time.[47] By 1937, however, oil leases on land in eight Oklahoma counties were yielding income that year for the pension fund in the amount of $29,006.[48] The discovery of oil was fortunate for income as well as constructive use of the land, because substantial tracts of land had "been made worthless by erosion." The Dust Bowl of the 1930s was real and costly.[49]

---

[44] Article 22, Section 2, of the constitution of Oklahoma precluded any corporation from buying, acquiring, trading or dealing "in real estate for any purpose except such as may be located in such [incorporated] towns and cities, and further except as such shall be necessary for proper carrying on of business for which it was chartered or licensed."

[45] *Report*, Eighty-Seventh Annual Convention of the Augustana Lutheran Church, Duluth, Minn., June 11-16, 1946, p. 212. See also Robert H. Rydland, "Memorandum on Augustana Annuity Trust," October 25, 1994, p. 1.

[46] *Minutes*, Seventy-Third Annual Convention of the Augustana Lutheran Church, Fargo, N.D., June 9-14, 1932, p. 174.

[47] *Minutes*, Seventy-Fourth Annual Convention of the Augustana Lutheran Church, Chicago, June 14-18, 1933, p. 151.

[48] *Report*, Seventy-Eighth Annual Convention of the Augustana Lutheran Church, Omaha, Neb., June 15-20, 1937, p. 188. The name of the record of Augustana's annual convention was changed in 1937 from *Minutes* to *Report*.

[49] *Report*, Eighty-First Annual Convention of the Augustana Lutheran Church, Rock Island, Ill., June 4-9, 1940, p. 173.

Major revision under way

In preparation for major changes in the operation of the pension plan, Augustana pastors, teachers, and missionaries had been surveyed. Discovered was a demographic challenge. The average age of Augustana pastors was 52 in 1931, and an older subset of 300 Augustana pastors had an average age of 68. Some salary disparity was noted too. The average salary with a parsonage was $2,040 and without, $2,400.[50] There were 171 pastors with an annual salary of $2,070, 22 at $2,185, 122 at $2,300, 20 at $2,400, 18 at $2,500, 12 at $2,600, 10 at $2,700, 41 at $2,760, 14 at $2,875, 15 at $3,000, 10 at $3,105, and 31 at $3,450. Three earned a salary of $4,000 and had a parsonage.[51]

Until 1900, little attention had been paid to pensions. The concentration had been on aid to those with desperate needs. From 1865 to 1898, only $5,453.95 was distributed. By contrast, with a shift of attention to ongoing pensions, $742,744 was provided in pension and aid in the first three decades of the twentieth century.[52]

Amid the extreme economic struggles of the Great Depression, Augustana and various other church bodies were taking a careful look at their pension plans. Revisions were envisioned, including a shift from notions of charity to understanding a pastor's pension as "simply deferred salary."[53] The revised plan was intended to provide pastors with

> ... the assurance that when they have given their life and all to the church, the church will see to it that they and their dependents will be provided for, not only as long as they are able to work, but as long as they live, and they must be made to feel that when they no longer, because of disability or old age, are able to serve, they shall not be looked upon as objects of charity but as pensioners, that is, as having earned what the church is granting them in pension.[54]

In 1931, the assets of the Augustana Pension and Aid Fund stood at $1,218,985. The balance actually had increased $57,000 from the previous

---

[50] Equivalent to about $31,000 in 2007. According to the National Education Association, the average annual salary for teachers in 1931 was $1,440. At the same time, the average annual salary of accountants was $2,250. Incidently, Babe Ruth's salary in 1931 was $80,000 and President Hoover's, $75,000.

[51] *Minutes*, 1931, p. 167.

[52] *Minutes*, 1931, p. 167.

[53] *Minutes*, 1931, p. 169.

[54] *Minutes*, 1931, p. 169

year. Proposed bylaw amendments pointed toward a broader mix of assets beyond loans on farm land to include municipal, public utility, and railroad bonds.[55] The 1931 convention asked that the fund limit new investments to 40 percent in any one class of securities.[56] The experience of having put so many "eggs" in the "one basket" of farm loans was prompting calls for diversification for future investments. By 1943, much of the real estate once owned by the fund had been sold, with the money being invested instead in governmental and industrial bonds.[57]

The revised pension plan—submitted in 1931 for study throughout the synod—followed a model proposed by an Inter-Lutheran Joint Pension Committee for consideration by the various Lutheran church bodies.[58] The plan was designed

> . . . to provide age retirement annuities approximating one-half of the average salary during service for a period of 35 years, but the actual annuity payments will vary for longer or shorter periods of service, and somewhat according to the various salary bases of the members.[59]

Under the proposed plan, the contribution rate for pastors in the Augustana Synod was set at two and one-half percent of salary. "Salary" was understood to include, for those in parsonages, the equivalent of an additional 15 percent of the fixed-salary amount. Congregations and other salary-paying entities were to contribute eight percent of the member's salary. Prior to retirement, members were permitted to contribute additional amounts.[60]

Upon reaching age 65, the member could begin to draw a pension. The amount of the pastor's monthly pension was based on the amount of the member's own contributions and a portion of the contributions by the congregations that the pastor served throughout his active ministry. Actuarial tables were used in establishing the size of the annuity and thereby the monthly pension. The surviving spouse was to receive one-half

---

[55] *Minutes*, 1931, pp. 169 and 171.

[56] *Minutes*, 1931, p. 188.

[57] *Report*, Eighty-Fourth Annual Convention of the Augustana Lutheran Church, Minneapolis, Minn., June 2-6, 1943, p. 206.

[58] *Minutes*, 1931, p. 199.

[59] *Minutes*, 1931, p. 199.

[60] *Minutes*, 1931, p. 197.

the amount of the annuity payment upon the death of the pastor.[61] The minimum for a widow was set at $200, which could be supplemented by $50 for each child under 18 years of age.[62]

For disability, the amount of the annuity was set at about 40 percent of the individual's average salary during the preceding years of service, but it was not to exceed $500. Upon the death of a member, the widow was to receive a death benefit of $1,000. Both the disability payments and the death benefit were funded through the pool of contributions from congregations and other church employers.[63]

An interest crediting system was to be used by the board in the revised pension plan to determine the annual earnings on investments for the member accounts.[64] Each member's contribution was to be held in trust, but the contributions of the congregation or other employing entity were not credited directly to the individual's account, as reflected in the regulations on withdrawal benefits:

> In the event of the termination of ministerial relationship with the Synod, the member's accumulations may remain to be applied towards providing annuity benefits as outlined in the plan but without further claim against the Fund for benefits provided out of the Church's funds, except in the event that such member enters the ministerial service of a Synod with a reciprocal Lutheran pension relationship, in which case all accumulations to his credit out of the church's funds shall remain to be applied towards providing annuity benefits as outlined in the plan.[65]

The revised pension plan that first had been requested in 1929[66] clearly had prompted widespread discussion following the synod's 1931 meeting. As reported in 1932, the plan had "not met unanimous acceptance." That was "quite evident from the way some pointed pens have hurled their

---

[61] *Minutes*, 1931, pp. 194-195.

[62] *Minutes*, 1931, p. 199.

[63] *Minutes*, 1931, p. 194.

[64] *Minutes*, 1931, p. 197.

[65] *Minutes*, 1931, p. 196.

[66] *Minutes*, 1929, Item 8, p. 182.

criticisms at both the board and the plan."[67] While discussion continued on the new plan, the board was asked to formulate a possible plan that "would equalize the benefits and provide for a more equitable distribution of the cost."[68]

In response to that request, revisions in the contribution rates were proposed and adopted. The member rate was set at three and one-half percent of salary. The rate for the congregation contributions was changed from the proposed seven and one-half percent of the member's salary to 50 cents per communicant member.[69]

Urgency of change

The urgency of shifting to a new plan was underscored by the growing financial obligations in the existing plan. Reported in 1933 was the expanding pattern of distribution, given the growing number of members entitled to benefits. The pension and relief amounts paid were: 1865-1898, $5,453.95; 1899-1904, $6,218.68; 1905-1909, $18,950.90; 1910-1914, $50,276.27; 1915-1919, $85,842.94; 1920-1924, $170,487.20; 1925-1929, $294,739.27; and 1930-1932, $182,343.86. There were 760 members in the plan in 1933, plus spouses and dependents.[70]

The ratio of assets of the fund to annual payments of pensions was troubling, shifting from 22-to-one in 1922, to 19-to-one in 1927, to 16-to-one in 1932.[71] Payments were reduced by 12.5 percent in 1932 because one-half of a quarterly installment to pensioners could not be paid.[72] The challenge of meeting pension obligations continued into succeeding years.[73]

Income for the fund had declined from $133,657.88 in 1930 to $98,722.35 in 1933, largely as a result of a substantial reduction of more than 50 percent in the allocation from the synodical budget. Contributions by members also had declined by nearly one-third.[74]

---

[67] *Minutes*, 1932, p. 175.

[69] *Minutes*, 1933, pp. 174-175. See also item 2, *Report*, 1937, p. 171.

[70] *Minutes*, 1933, p. 165.

[71] *Minutes*, Seventy-Fifth Annual Convention of the Augustana Lutheran Church, Minn., June 7-12, 1934, p. 130.

[72] *Minutes*, 1934, p. 129.

[73] *Minutes*, 1934, p. 145.

[74] *Minutes*, 1934, pp. 128-129.

Plan delayed

Consideration of the new pension plan was tabled in 1933, an action that drew a word of warning:

> To postpone consideration is an easy way out of any difficult situation, but it brings no permanent solution. The future of the Pension Fund is of real concern to every member and the problem which was pressing should be fully considered.[75]

The original fund that began in 1867 had reached the point where income from contributions and returns on investments were not sufficient to pay the pension, aid, and other obligations of the fund. Given that reality, the synod moved in 1934 to consideration and adoption of the new pension plan. It was scheduled to go into effect on January 1, 1937,[76] in the form that had been proposed in 1933.[77] The 1936 meeting, however, delayed its implementation until January 1, 1938.[78]

Amendments to the plan itself were made in 1936,[79] 1937,[80] 1938,[81] 1942,[82] 1945,[83] 1947,[84] and 1948.[85] Throughout the decade of the 1950s,

---

[75] *Minutes*, 1934, p. 130.

[76] *Minutes*, 1934, p. 145.

[77] See *Minutes*, 1933, pp. 172-180, for the full text of the bylaw governing the new reserve pension plan of the Augustana Synod.

[78] *Minutes*, Seventy-Seventh Annual Convention of the Augustana Lutheran Church, St. Peter, Minn., June 11-16, 1936, p. 177.

[79] *Minutes*, 1936, pp. 164-165. The language in certain articles was defined in greater detail.

[80] *Report*, 1937, p. 186. Technical corrections were made in references to certain dates.

[81] *Report*, Seventy-Ninth Annual Convention of the Augustana Lutheran Church, Brooklyn, N.Y., June 21-26, 1938, pp. 180-181. Provision was made for optional membership by non-tenured professors and teachers in academic institutions of the church.

[82] *Report*, Eighty-Third Annual Convention of the Augustana Lutheran Church, Jamestown, N.Y., June 9-14, 1942, pp. 178-181. The amendments addressed in greater detail provisions for the retirement annuity.

[83] *Report*, Eighty-Sixth Annual Convention of the Augustana Lutheran Church, Moline, Ill., June 6-10, 1945, pp. 247-254. More extensive definitions and greater details on the rate schedule were included in the bylaws of the fund.

[84] *Report*, Eighty-Eighth Annual Convention of the Augustana Lutheran Church, Kansas City, Mo., June 10-15, 1947, p. 232.

[85] *Report*, Eighty-Ninth Annual Convention of the Augustana Lutheran Church, Rock Island, Ill., June 7-13, 1948, p. 165. The congregation contribution rate was increased by 50 cents per communicant member.

various technical amendments were adopted in 1952,[86] 1953,[87] 1954,[88] 1955,[89] 1957,[90] 1958,[91] 1960,[92] and 1961.[93]

For member accounts, the interest crediting rate from 1938 through 1958 was three percent. Favorable investment experience enabled the board to increase the crediting rate, beginning on January 1, 1959, to three and one-half percent.[94]

The issue of participation in the plan continued to be a concern. As a result, when the synod met at Rock Island, Ill., in 1935, a forthright resolution was adopted that read:

> The Synod notes with sorrow that many pastors have withdrawn from the pension fund. It realizes the dangers both to the pastors and the pension fund if this condition is permitted to prevail. To avert this danger the Synod again affirms its decision that *all eligible pastors shall belong to the pension fund, and declares that any pastor who willfully disregards this decision has violated his ordination vows.*[95]

The exhortation appears to have yielded results. In 1936 and 1937, 88 lapsed members of the plan were reinstated, representing about 10 percent of Augustana's clergy.[96]

---

[86] *Report*, Ninety-Third Annual Convention of the Augustana Lutheran Church, Des Moines, Iowa, June 10-15, 1952, pp. 261-263 and 273.

[87] *Report*, Ninety-Fourth Annual Convention of the Augustana Lutheran Church, Chicago, June 9-14, 1953, p. 126.

[88] *Report*, Ninety-Fifth Annual Convention of the Augustana Lutheran Church, Los Angeles, June 14-20, 1954, pp. 183-185.

[89] *Report*, Ninety-Sixth Annual Convention of the Augustana Lutheran Church, St. Paul, Minn., June 13-19, 1955, pp. 185-189.

[90] *Report*, Ninety-Eighth Annual Convention of the Augustana Lutheran Church, Omaha, Neb., June 17-23, 1957, pp. 172-173.

[91] *Report*, Ninety-Ninth Annual Convention of the Augustana Lutheran Church, Jamestown, N.Y., June 16-22, 1958, pp. 195-198 and 200.

[92] *Report*, One Hundred and First Annual Convention of the Augustana Lutheran Church, Rock Island, Ill., June 6-12, 1960, pp. 226-227 and 229.

[93] *Report*, One Hundred and Second Annual Convention of the Augustana Lutheran Church, Seattle, Wash., June 12-18, 1961, pp. 204-205.

[94] *Report*, 1960, p. 223.

[95] *Minutes*, Seventy-Sixth Annual Convention of the Augustana Lutheran Church, Rock Island, Ill., June 5-10, 1935, p. 145. Italic type was added for emphasis in this quotation.

[96] *Report*, 1938, p. 165.

As the fund prepared to move toward anticipated implementation of the new pension plan, a change of leadership occurred. Pr. Conrad completed eight years of strenuous service as executive secretary-treasurer of the fund, serving from October 7, 1927, through his resignation on June 18, 1935. He was succeeded by the Rev. O. T. Engquist on November 26, 1935. Prior to undertaking his new position, Pr. Engquist had been president of the fund and chair of the board.[97] He would continue to serve even beyond his planned retirement in 1955 until July 1956 when Mr. L. Edwin Wang succeeded him as executive secretary and treasurer of the fund. Mr. Wang came to the position from years of experience in management at Standard Insurance Company in Oakland, Calif.[98] Later, when the Augustana plan was merged into the Lutheran Church in America's Board of Pensions, Mr. Wang become the head of the LCA's Board of Pensions in 1962 and served until his retirement in the spring of 1987.

Aware of pension concerns

The report of the Augustana Pension and Aid Fund in 1937 began with a quotation from the Rev. M. F. Amelung, who was described as well-informed "on insurance in general" and who had devoted several months to studying the pension plans of various churches, including the Augustana Synod. Wrote Pr. Amelung in *Rethinking Church Pension Plans*:

> The American people seemingly overnight have become pension minded. Pensions for aged persons are intelligently discussed by millions of people now interested in the subject. . . . Is the church to be the leader in doing social justice to its employees or will it lose its social leadership?[99]

Clearly, the Augustana Synod was ready in 1939 to express satisfaction with the beginning days of the new plan. In so doing, the synod praised "the favorable results of the first-year period of operation of the new pension plan" and underscored the hope there would be "still greater cooperation on the part of churches and pastors who, to date, have not responded in a satisfactory manner."[100]

---

[97] *Minutes*, 1936, p. 163.

[98] *Record*, Ninety-Eighth Annual Convention of the Augustana Lutheran Church, Omaha, Neb., June 17-23, 1957, p. 166.

[99] *Report*, 1937, p. 168.

[100] *Report*, Eightieth Annual Convention of the Augustana Lutheran Church, Lindsborg, Kan., June 14-18, 1939, p. 220.

Following the model of the United Lutheran Church in America, the bylaws of the Augustana Pension and Aid Fund were amended in 1947 to create a Lay Pension Plan.[101] Participation proved to be very limited.[102] During this period, the synod declined to broaden the program to include health benefits and expanded group life insurance coverage for clergy and lay members.[103]

Concern for participation continued and efforts to gain participation succeeded. By the post-war period, only 99 of Augustana's 1,175 clergy were failing to participate. Beyond member and congregations contributions, however, additional funds were needed to sustain the plan. So a special appeal with a goal of $500,000 was authorized in 1948.[104] By 1954, nearly $460,000 had been received.

In the early 1950s, annual disbursements by the fund were 33 percent for current benefits, 64 percent for future benefits, and three percent for operating costs. Sixty percent of the fund's investments were in bonds.[105]

The combined assets in the fund reached $1.4 million by the close of the difficult decade of the 1930s. Annual benefits paid totaled $100,075.24.[106] Ten years later, combined assets had grown to $4 million and benefits paid as of December 31, 1950, were $148,897.[107] Assets in 1960 amounted to $10.1 million, and annual benefits paid stood at $460,375. Sources of income were the equivalent of 43 cents per dollar from congregations, 32 cents from investments, 23 cents from members, and two cents as other income.[108]

Social Security opened for clergy

When coverage under Social Security became a possibility for ordained ministers, the Augustana Lutheran Church in 1955 urged participation and called the attention of pastors "to the necessity of making the requisite filings immediately, but in no event later than April 15, 1957, after which

---

[101] *Report*, 1947, p. 217.

[102] *Report*, Ninety-Second Annual Convention of the Augustana Lutheran Church, Galesburg, Ill, June 12-17, 1951, p. 273.

[103] *Report*, 1947, p. 217.

[104] *Report*, 1948, pp. 227 and 242.

[105] *Report*, 1954, p. 173.

[106] *Report*, Eighty-Second Annual Convention of the Augustana Lutheran Church, Minneapolis, Minn., June 10-15, 1941, p. 180.

[107] *Report*, 1951, p. 272.

[108] *Report*, 1961, pp. 196-198 and 203.

date they forfeit for all time their right to participate in Social Security."[109] The synod underscored that encouragement in 1956:

> We urge all pastors to participate in both the Augustana Pension and Aid Fund and the Federal Social Security program so as to provide for themselves a more adequate and effective retirement program. . . .
>
> We remind congregations of the recommendation by the Church that they reimburse pastors for one-half of their Social Security contributions.[110]

The clergy death-benefit element of the fund was adjusted in 1956 and became a type of declining term-insurance policy. The benefit for those age 45 and under was $6,000, decreasing to $1,000 for plan members age 66 and older.[111]

Shift from Iowa to Minnesota

Reflecting awareness of the growth of the fund and the responsibility of trustees, the Articles of Incorporation in Iowa of the Augustana Pension and Aid Fund were amended in 1943 to highlight the fiduciary duty of the trustees to operate in a prudent manner.[112]

The interdependence of the fund with the ongoing life of the Augustana Lutheran Church and its congregations was reflected in discussion within the board as well as annual meetings of the synod. Emerging from those discussions was the decision to shift the site of the fund's office from Des Moines, Iowa, to Minneapolis and the state of incorporation from Iowa to Minnesota. A charter was granted in Minnesota on November 4, 1955, to the Augustana Pension and Aid Fund of Minnesota.[113] In that same year, Mr. Bernhard LeVander of Minneapolis became counsel for the fund, a role that he would continue on behalf of the pension program of the Lutheran Church in America.

---

[109] *Report*, 1955, p. 184.

[110] *Report*, Ninety-Seventh Annual Convention of the Augustana Lutheran Church, Moorhead, Minn., June 11-17, 1956, p. 177. The enrollment deadline later was extended by the U.S. government to April 15, 1959.

[111] *Report*, 1957, p. 167.

[112] *Report*, Eighty-Second Annual Convention of the Augustana Lutheran Church, Minneapolis, Minn., June 2-6, 1943, pp. 209-210 and 225.

[113] *Report*, 1956, p. 167.

In the autumn of 1958, executives and board members of the pension funds of the Augustana Lutheran Church, American Evangelical Lutheran Church, Finnish Lutheran Church, and United Lutheran Church in America met in Chicago. They gathered to make recommendations to the Joint Commission on Lutheran Unity. That commission was planning for the formation of the Lutheran Church in America. Emerging from the Chicago meeting was a proposal that the LCA's new plan resemble that of the United Lutheran Church in America, a plan that was seen as typical of church pension funds in general.[114]

Amid preparation for the LCA, Mr. Wang, as executive secretary of the Augustana Pension and Aid Fund, reviewed the fund's history:

> Augustana's concern for the welfare of its pastors and their families was well established over ninety years ago when it became the first Lutheran body in the United States to establish a Ministerial Contributory Pension Plan.[115] The Church's continuing concern has been evidenced over the years by a number of increases in the contribution rate which have enabled the Fund to increase benefits on several occasions. Although by comparison Augustana's contribution in total for pensions (congregations and employing organizations only, none is received from the Church) is still somewhat smaller than that which is set aside for this purpose by other major Lutheran bodies, it is nevertheless a considerable sum. . . .
>
> The benefit formula used by the Augustana Pension and Aid Fund is the money-purchase plan. Contributions from congregations and employing organizations (divided equally among qualified plan members), plus contributions from plan members and interest credits, are combined at death, disability, or retirement to provide a pension for the member or his beneficiaries. . . .[116]

An even more extensive historical overview was provided to the synod's meeting in 1962. Noted in looking ahead was the fact that, in addition to the pension and death-benefit elements of the Augustana Pension and Aid

---

[114] *Report*, One Hundredth Annual Convention of the Augustana Lutheran Church, Hartford, Conn., June 15-21, 1959, p. 189.

[115] The aid fund of the General Synod—which was first proposed in 1831, nearly 30 years before the formation of the Augustana Lutheran Church—was primarily a fund for charity until pension elements were made a part of it later in the nineteenth century.

[116] *Report*, 1960, pp. 224-225.

Fund, the new LCA plan would include comprehensive medical insurance coverage.

As a momentous step into the future, the "Agreement of Consolidation" was approved in 1962 for the Augustana Pension and Aid Fund of Minnesota and the Board of Pensions of the United Lutheran Church in America, which had been incorporated in Pennsylvania in 1920. The successor corporation, known as the Board of Pensions of the Lutheran Church in America, was chartered in the state of Minnesota.[117]

The LCA Board of Pensions became fully operational effective January 1, 1963. At that moment, the 95-year history of the Augustana Pension and Aid Fund ended, leaving behind a significant record of dedication and compassion for the care of pastors and their families.

---

[117] *Report*, One Hundred and Third Annual Convention of the Augustana Lutheran Church, Detroit, Mich., June 25-27, 1962, pp. 179-180 and 184-185.

CHAPTER 10

Deferred Decisions
Carried a Huge Price

When the United Lutheran Church in America (ULCA) was formed in 1918, only one of its three predecessor church bodies had a retirement fund for pastors.[1] With meager but real beginnings dating from 1831, the General Synod had created a fund "for superannuated ministers" and "their widows and orphans." Throughout most of the General Synod's existence, that fund was operated as a charity, rather than a regular pension program. Grants in aid were made for those in extreme need.

Late in its life, the General Council, which had been formed in 1867, began considering a "Ministers' Pension Fund," to be operated either by the council itself or by the member synods. Identified as "the most effective plan thus far in operation" was the fund of the Augustana Synod, then a member synod of the General Council, although Augustana functioned largely as a separate church body.[2] A Committee on Ministerial Pensions was appointed to develop a proposal for the General Council.[3] In view of merger plans well under way, the committee recommended in 1917 that the General Council "wait for the carrying out of a plan for Ministerial Pensions until the United Lutheran Church can take up and develop the matter."[4] The recommendation was adopted. Thus, the next step for a pension and aid plan took place after the General Council dissolved into the new church body.

---

[1] The United Lutheran Church in America brought together the General Synod, the General Council, and the United Synod South.

[2] Theodore E. Schmauk, "Report of the President," *Minutes*, Thirty-Fifth Biennial Convention of the General Council of the Evangelical Lutheran Church in North America, Rock Island, Ill., September 9-14, 1915 (Philadelphia: General Council Publication Board), p. 24. The Augustana Synod withdrew from the General Council shortly before the merger that formed the United Lutheran Church in America.

[3] *Minutes*, General Council, 1915, p. 31.

[4] *Minutes*, Thirty-Sixth Biennial Convention of the General Council, Philadelphia, Pa., October 24-29, 1917, p. 81.

Ministerial Relief in ULCA

At the constituting of the ULCA, a Board of Ministerial Relief was created. Through that board, retired pastors received a $300 annual grant. For survivors, $200 was given annually to widows of clergy "so long as they remain widows." An additional annual allowance of $50 was made for each child under age 16. These were paid in monthly installments.[5]

Recognized quickly was the problem of financing even that modest program from the church's budget. Therefore, the 1920 ULCA convention in Washington, D.C., approved the creation of an endowment fund with an initial goal of $2 million, later raised to $4 million.

The early days of the ULCA's Board of Ministerial Relief were not quiet ones. After considerable debate that revealed sharply differing perspectives on the board's purpose, the board's name was expanded in 1924 to the Board of Ministerial Pensions and Relief. The change was made to reflect the board's expanded scope. Yet two decades would pass before a fully functioning contributory pension plan would be in place for the ULCA.[6]

A limited amount of money was inherited by the ULCA's pension and relief board, including about $100,000 from the General Synod and funds from 12 individual synods ranging from $100 to $20,000, for a combined total from those synods of $80,000.[7] To provide benefits by 1922 to 648 persons, funding from the church's budget was needed but would not be sufficient to cover the growing obligation. Envisioned was an endowment fund that would permit a higher annual payment and provide a more solid financial foundation for the program of pension grants.

Other churches already had far exceeded per capita the ULCA's endowment goal of $4 million. The Augustana Lutheran Church—with only 291,000 members, in contrast to the 1.1 million members in the ULCA—had an endowment fund in 1924 of $1 million. Perhaps not surprisingly, some larger church bodies had accumulated far greater assets.

---

[5] *Minutes*, Second Biennial Convention of the United Lutheran Church in America, Washington, D.C., October 19-27, 1920, p. 423. The ULCA's minutes were published by the United Lutheran Publishing House in Philadelphia; a publisher for the ULCA's minutes is not hereafter cited in the footnotes.

[6] E. Theodore Bachmann, *The United Lutheran Church in America, 1918-1962* (Minneapolis: Fortress Press, 1997), pp. 342-343.

[7] *Minutes*, ULCA, 1920, p. 422.

For example, the Methodists had reached by the early 1920s $16 million, the Episcopal Church, $14 million, and the Presbyterians, $7 million.[8]

The ULCA's initial plan provided an equalized pension at a defined level, as determined by the resources available and the decisions of the board. By contrast, in the contributory plans of some church bodies, funding came from a certain percentage of the pastor's salary as submitted by the pastor, the congregation, or both. The amount of the eventual pension was determined by the level of the pastor's compensation. The goal in those plans at that time was to offer one-half of the pastor's average salary after 35 years of active service.[9]

Seeking an endowment

The endowment campaign for the ULCA's defined-benefit plan attained pledges for $4.2 million by August 1, 1928, with $820,000 of that amount already paid.[10] The pledges were to be paid by April 1, 1930, but only 67 percent or $2.8 million was received by July 1 of that year. The impact of the Great Depression was evident.[11] Two years later, slightly more than three-fourths of the pledges had been paid, in the amount of $3.2 million.[12] Little more would be received in subsequent years. The goal of receiving all of the pledged amounts never was achieved. The board's report to the 1932 ULCA biennial convention observed:

> Thousands of our people are without employment.
>
> Many of our churches had their funds in neighborhood banks which closed their doors. In many instances, money which should have been forwarded to the Board of Pensions was deposited in these banks.[13]

Controversy also haunted this appeal. As the money was received, Mr. Peter P. Hagan of Philadelphia was authorized by the pension board

---

8 *Minutes*, Third Biennial Convention of the United Lutheran Church in America, Buffalo, N.Y., October 17-25, 1922, p. 405.

9 *Minutes*, Fifth Biennial Convention of the United Lutheran Church in America, Richmond, Va., October 19-27, 1926, p. 321.

10 *Minutes*, Sixth Biennial Convention of the United Lutheran Church in America, Erie, Pa., October 9-17, 1928, p. 494.

11 *Minutes*, Seventh Biennial Convention of the United Lutheran Church in America, Milwaukee, Wis., October 7-14, 1930, p. 557.

12 *Minutes*, Eighth Biennial Convention of the United Lutheran Church in America, Philadelphia, Pa., October 12-19, 1932, p. 176.

13 *Minutes*, UCLA, 1932, p. 177.

to invest the appeal's proceeds in what were described as guaranteed mortgages. He did so with the Oak Lane Trust Company of Philadelphia. At that time, Mr. Hagan was treasurer of the pension board, a member of the board's Executive Committee, and also a member of the board's Finance Committee. He simultaneously was a stockholder and director of the Oak Lane Trust Company. Then, when that company merged with three other banks[14] on October 6, 1928, to form the new Bank of Philadelphia and Trust Company, he became a stockholder, director, and member of the Executive Committee of the new bank. He *did* disclose this fact to the ULCA's convention in Erie, Pa., in October 1928.

In the economic turmoil of the time, the Bank of Philadelphia was taken over for liquidation in July 1930 by the Bankers Trust Company, also of Philadelphia. The financial statement revealed the bank's total mortgages amounted to $2,650,000, of which the ULCA pension board held $2,400,000 in about 340 separate mortgages. In other words, the pension board, guided by Mr. Hagan, had been "the principal outlet for mortgages negotiated for sale by the Bank of Philadelphia and Trust Company and by its predecessor, the Oak Lane Trust Company."[15] In the bank records, the ULCA pension board's mortgages were shown as "The Hagan Fund." As a result of numerous foreclosures, the pension board ended up owning about $1.2 million in real estate.[16]

Mortgages were not the only issue. When the Pennsylvania banking department closed the Bankers Trust Company on December 22, 1930, the pension board lost about $85,000, $54,000 of which had been deposited on November 26, 1930, less than a month before the bank was shut down permanently.[17] That large deposit was made even in the midst of a heavy "run on the bank" by other depositors.

The ULCA's 1932 convention in Philadelphia demanded an investigation. The investment practices of the Board of Ministerial Pensions and Relief were to be examined. That decision followed a contentious

---

[14] The three other banks were the Broad Street National Bank, National Bank of North Philadelphia, and Queen Lane National Bank.

[15] "Report of the Sub-Committee of the Investment Commission Appointed to Investigate the Affairs of the Pension Board," *Executive Board Minutes*, United Lutheran Church in America, April 27, 1933, p. 62.

[16] "Confidential Documentation of Findings in an Investigation of the Work and Finances of the Board of Ministerial Pensions and Relief," United Lutheran Church in America, March 31, 1933, pp. 20 and 10.

[17] "Report of the Sub-Committee . . . ," *Minutes*, ULCA, April 27, 1933, p. 64.

evening hearing at the 1932 convention, which at points resembled a courtroom trial. At issue were the real estate investments of the board.

The hearing—which was conducted in Suite 202 of the Benjamin Franklin Hotel in Philadelphia on October 15, 1932—included members of the pension board and representatives of the investigation commission. After extensive questioning of the key figures in the matter, the Honorable Elwood N. Rabenold, a judge from New York who was a member of the ULCA, declared that "my very soul is outraged . . . that the money that was here entrusted . . . [to the board] should have been so badly and so ill-advisedly devoted" to real estate investments by officials of the Board of Ministerial Pensions and Relief. His statement, he said, was "not challenging their sincerity. It is not challenging their integrity. It is not challenging their good faith. It is challenging their capacity and the degree of sound business judgment" they exercised. He called for "guarantees of meticulous regard for the sanctity of these fiduciary funds [so] that nobody can again even raise a voice."[18]

The Rev. F. H. Knubel responded in what must have sounded like sharp criticism of the board's work by the president of that church body. He said:

> Mr. Rabenold, you haven't been the only man who has thought that the work of this Board [of Ministerial Pensions and Relief] was not conducted well. I have thought so for many years. Then there are men in this room to whom I had talked about this very thing—men in positions of influence. There are three or four men here who can tell you how seriously I have been working with them for four years in the effort, not merely that this board shall manage its work better, but that all the boards of the church shall manage their work better.[19]

Following an extensive review in the month after that hearing, an investigative subcommittee reported to the ULCA's Executive Board, declaring:

> It is evident that the bank took advantage of the lax manner in which the Board [of Ministerial Pensions and Relief] conducted its affairs and used funds of the Board to finance building operations, to liquidate its real estate and in other improper

---

[18] Transcript of Hearing, October 15, 1932, Minutes, ULCA, pp. 135-137.

[19] Transcript of Hearing, October 15, 1932, Minutes, ULCA, pp. 137-138.

ways, including the application of $500,000 for the erection of its bank building.

However well intentioned, your Committee believes that the methods employed by the Pension Board and by its treasurer were in many respects inexcusably faulty. . . . Delegating this whole matter to a community bank which was a profiting party in the making of these loans, with little or no check by a committee of the Board of the properties offered as security[,] was an error which lies at the root of the difficulty.[20]

Upon receiving the report of the investigation subcommittee, the ULCA's Executive Board adopted a resolution that read in part:

We keenly regret that a Board of the Church was not alert to its great responsibilities and was found to be neglectful to a sad degree. We appeal to the members of all Boards that this necessary chastisement of one Board be accepted as a solemn warning to each individual to recognize that he has been given a trust which he must vigorously carry out under the clear eyes of his own conscience, of the Church, and of God.[21]

At the request of the Executive Board, a legal committee examined issues of potential liability on the part of the former treasurer, Mr. Hagan, and concluded that the members of the pension board and the ULCA had notice of his banking relationship as a stockholder and director. The committee reported that "there is no finding that he acted fraudulently or that he profited personally from any transaction except indirectly, if at all, as a stockholder of the bank." Said the legal committee:

We are, therefore, unable to find the necessary foundation for legal liability of the officers and directors of the Pension Board for any losses on the securities purchased by them.[22]

Hope for an increase in pension grant

The results of the ULCA's 1928 fund appeal were to have enabled the annual pension grant for retired clergy to increase from $300 to $400, an amount slightly less than $5,000 in 2008 dollars. The amount for widows was to shift from $200 to $300 a year with dependent children under 16

---

[20] "Report of the Sub-Committee . . . ," *Minutes*, ULCA, April 27, 1933, p. 62.

[21] "Report of the Sub-Committee . . . ," *Minutes*, ULCA, April 27, 1933, p. 67.

[22] "Report of Legal Committee," *Executive Board Minutes*, United Lutheran Church in America, January 11, 1934, p. 106.

receiving $100 a year.[23] That was not possible, however, under the financial constraints of the time. Retired and disabled clergy still got only $300 a year or 83 cents a day, widows $200 a year or 55 cents a day, and dependent children $50 a year or 13 cents a day.[24] The needs were significant, as illustrated by this request from an elderly pastor:

> I am 80 years of age and have served as a minister in the Church for 55 years. My congregation tells me to move on; that I am too old to serve them acceptably longer.

> My salary has never exceeded $800 [a year], so that I have been unable to save money for my old age. I have a son in the West with whom I can make my home, but neither he nor I has transportation money.

> I am not asking for a pension, but am asking for transportation money that I may go home to my son to die.[25]

A specific response to this pastor's request is unknown. His plight, however, was emblematic. The existing program was inadequate. Thus, as was the case in several other Lutheran church bodies in the 1930s, the ULCA began to consider moving to a contributory pension system to replace the 1918 defined-benefit plan.[26]

A promise due: "deferred salary"

The challenge of interpreting for pastors and people in the pew the nature of a pension plan loomed large. Thus, a bold statement appeared in 1936:

> This Board [of Ministerial Pensions and Relief] declares that it is not one of the benevolent boards of the Church. *Pensions are not benevolence; they are . . . deferred salary.* The Standard Dictionary says: "A pension is an allowance paid to an individual or those who represent him for some past service or some meritorious work done by him."

> The idea of a pension for a retired minister, his widow and dependent children is not to make a gift in order that they can

---

[23] *Minutes*, ULCA, 1932, pp. 180-181.

[24] *Minutes*, Ninth Biennial Convention of the United Lutheran Church in America, Savannah, Ga., October 17-24, 1934, p. 384.

[25] Harry Hodges, "Not Just Statistics, *The Lutheran* magazine, December 4, 1946 (Philadelphia, Pa.: Board of Publication of the United Lutheran Church in America), p. 19.

[26] *Minutes*, ULCA, 1934, p. 384.

have easier lives. Rather it is to pay the promised part due him from the Church in obligation to him for putting in his life for a mere "support." The retired minister is the Church's graduated leader, not its pauper dependent. These men have been faithful to all tasks assigned to them and have earned the appreciation of the Church.[27]

Recognizing that the endowment fund and a budget allocation would not be sufficient to meet growing demands, the board submitted to the 1936 ULCA biennial convention a new pension plan. The proposal called for a contribution by each participating pastor of two and one-half percent of salary and eight percent from the congregation being served. The plan followed the model under consideration at the time by several Lutheran churches.[28] The proposal was considered again in 1938 with a change in the contribution rate to five percent of salary by the pastor and five percent by the congregation. After lengthy debate, the matter was referred, just as in 1936, to a study committee.[29] Then, on October 14, 1940, the ULCA biennial convention voted:

> . . . that the Board of Ministerial Pensions and Relief be instructed to put the Contributory Pension Plan into operation when 500 clergymen and their congregations and/or employing agencies shall have applied for admission.[30]

The ULCA was on its way to a new pension plan—or so it seemed at that moment. Within weeks of that decision, however, serious differences became evident on how to interpret the action of the 1940 Omaha convention. To help resolve the issue, the ULCA's Executive Board appointed a Legal Committee. After many months of deliberation, that committee reported in April 1942 that "we have made an exhaustive study of the entire pension situation, collaborating extensively with Mr. George A. Huggins, consulting actuary of the Pension Board, and with a special committee of that board with whom joint meetings were held." Defects in the Omaha resolution included a failure to identify the relationship between the existing plan

---

[27] *Minutes*, Tenth Biennial Convention of the United Lutheran Church in America, Columbus, Ohio, October 14-21, 1936, p. 327. Italic type added to underscore a principle rationale for what would become the ULCA's new contributory pension plan.

[28] *Minutes*, ULCA, 1936, pp. 332-333.

[29] *Minutes*, Eleventh Biennial Convention of the United Lutheran Church in America, Baltimore, Md., October 5-12, 1938, pp. 416 and 425.

[30] *Minutes*, Twelfth Biennial Convention of the United Lutheran Church in America, Omaha, Neb., October 9-16, 1940, p. 379.

and the new plan. Further, the committee said that the Omaha resolution called for improper disposal of the existing pension endowment fund. In addition, that resolution did not offer an adequate foundation for defining "the exact provisions" of a new plan. Therefore, the committee declared that "the only satisfactory way to proceed" would be "to present the whole pension matter afresh at the approaching Louisville Convention of the Church with a view to securing new actions. . . ."[31]

Specifically, the committee urged that the forthcoming convention rescind the actions of the Omaha convention and adopt instead a new constitution for a contributory pension plan in the ULCA.[32]

During those days of late October in 1942 in Louisville, debate occurred at various times throughout the convention until a decision was made to rescind "all actions on pension matters taken at the [1940] Omaha Convention." Subsequently, the following resolution was adopted:

> WHEREAS, the income under the pension plan of the Church is inadequate for the needs of retired pastors, their widows and children, and it is desired to enable those now in active service to supplement the same by means of a contributory pension system; now, therefore, be it resolved:
>
> (a) That the present pension system, by which income from endowment is combined with apportionment and other receipts to provide equal pensions for all, be continued.
>
> (b) That the United Lutheran Church in America hereby establishes a contributory pension plan and authorizes, empowers, and directs its Board of Ministerial Pensions and Relief to inaugurate the same when 500 clergymen and their congregations and/or employing agencies shall have applied for admission.[33]

In contrast to the Omaha proposal for a five percent of salary contribution rate for the pastor and five percent for the congregation, the 1942 plan set the rate at four percent for each. Initially, a graduated scale was

---

[31] *Minutes*, Thirteenth Biennial Convention of the United Lutheran Church in America, Louisville, Kentucky, October 14-21, 1942, pp. 87-89. The reference to Mr. George A. Huggins in the report offers an example of his broad impact on various Lutheran pension plans as well as other church pension plans in the first half of the twentieth century.

[32] *Minutes*, ULCA, 1942, p. 90.

[33] *Minutes*, ULCA, 1942, p. 607.

put into place. In the first year of operation, the congregation's contribution rate was to be two percent; the second year, three percent; and thereafter, four percent. For pastors, in the first year following ordination or the date of eligibility to become a member of the plan, the rate was two percent of the pastor's salary; in the second year, three percent; and thereafter, four percent per year.

For the congregation's amount, the pension plan specified that the "contributions shall be items of current expense and not of benevolence." Both the contribution of the congregation and the pastor were to "be credited to the individual account of the member and be increased by the interest credits thereon."[34]

> Interest credits shall be added annually to such amounts as may be credited to or accumulated for a member, out of the earnings on investment at a rate to be determined periodically by the Pension Board.[35]

This interest-crediting pattern continued in successor plans throughout most of the remainder of the twentieth century until changed in the mid-1990s for the ELCA's pension plan (see Chapter 1).

In place in other churches

Four years before the ULCA's contributory plan got under way, 682 of the 1,655 clergy in the American Lutheran Church were participating by 1941 in the ALC's contributory pension plan, while 826 of the 932 clergy in the Augustana Synod, 2,725 of the 5,400 clergy in The Lutheran Church–Missouri Synod, and 434 of the 1,409 in the Evangelical Lutheran Church also were participating in contributory pension plans.[36] Still more encouragement was needed to get ULCA clergy and congregations to support the change to a contributory plan.[37] Thus, Mr. Huggins explained the proposed plan in an article in *The Lutheran* magazine:

---

[34] *Minutes*, ULCA, 1942, p. 609.

[35] *Minutes*, ULCA, 1942, p. 610.

[36] Harry Hodges, "The Church Pensions Conference," *The Lutheran* magazine, December 17, 1941, p. 8.

[37] In a contributory or defined-contribution plan, the amount of an individual's eventual pension income depended on the total amount contributed by or for the individual and the investment experience for the growth of those funds during the individual's active service. This pattern differed from a defined-benefit plan in which the amount of an individual's pension income in retirement was determined by the board or organization that established the plan.

The objective of the reserve pension systems is to provide benefits according to pre-arranged plans and rules, to be financed out of reserve funds accumulated during the active years of service so as to make more sure the payment of the promised benefits when they fall due. Pension benefits payable out of currently raised income [as was the case at that time] may not always be payable in full out of available resources, especially as the tendency under adverse economic conditions is to have more pensioners on the roll with greater need for their pensions at a time when the current available income may be reduced. That is the reason for the trend to the reserve pension systems. . . .

The success of a group pension system . . . is . . . largely dependent upon the continued participation of practically the entire group of eligible persons. . . .[38]

Beginning of ULCA's contributory plan

The ULCA's contributory plan finally became operational on January 1, 1945,[39] but in its early stages debate swirled around greater equalization of pension benefits. On a vote of 180-103, the ULCA's 1944 convention in Minneapolis acted to:

. . . go on record that all congregation and board contributions to the Contributory Pension Plan be equalized among the beneficiaries after the cost of operation and that the Board of Ministerial Pensions and Relief be instructed to prepare an appropriate amendment to the Constitution and By-Laws of the Contributory Pension Plan and present it at the next regular convention. . . .[40]

The pension board opposed the idea, noting that The Lutheran Church–Missouri Synod had tried such a pattern and abandoned it because those with larger salaries would not participate in such a plan. At the same time, however, the American Lutheran Church had socialized its plan by one-half of one percent. "The opinion of their [the ALC] office is

---

[38] George A. Huggins, "The Churches and Pensions," *The Lutheran* magazine, December 8, 1942, pp. 6-7.

[39] *Minutes*, Fifteenth Biennial Convention of the United Lutheran Church in America, Cleveland, Ohio, October 5-12, 1946, p. 290.

[40] *Minutes*, Fourteenth Biennial Convention of the United Lutheran Church in America, Minneapolis, Minn., October 11-17, 1944, p. 424.

that the results do not justify the labor," reported the ULCA board. The Evangelical Lutheran Church also socialized one-sixth of the congregation's contribution. The Augustana Synod practiced socialization of the per-capita assessment of congregations. The actuary for the ULCA plan advised, "In a group where there is a wide variation in salaries, an equalization program is hardly worthwhile attempting."[41]

The ULCA pension board was not alone in its objections to the socialization proposal. Opposition also was voiced in synods. For example, the Ministerium of Pennsylvania and Adjacent States memorialized the ULCA's convention, declaring "that the pending socialization amendment has caused confusion" and prompted "many pastors and congregations to refrain from entering the plan."[42]

The proposed amendment in 1946 read, "The balance of all . . . congregation contributions shall be pooled and after the completion of each fiscal year shall be credited in equal amounts to the individual accounts of the members who in that year have remitted the full member contributions and whose congregations also have remitted their full payments for that year. . . ."[43] The plan for socialization was rejected.[44]

In spite of the contributory plan being in place, obligations under the previous plan continued for 1,162 beneficiaries, including 379 clergy, 23 disabled pastors, 639 widows, 114 children, and seven missionaries. Retired clergy in 1947 received $200 annually under the previous plan and their widows, $50.

The name of the board was simplified in 1946 from Board of Ministerial Pensions and Relief to Board of Pensions and Relief.[45] Later, in 1952, the name was revised again to Board of Pensions of the United Lutheran Church in America.[46]

---

[41] Minutes, ULCA, 1946, p. 273.

[42] Minutes of the Proceedings of the Annual Convention of the Evangelical Lutheran Ministerium of Pennsylvania and Adjacent States, Reading, Pa., May 14-15, 1945, p. 127.

[43] Minutes, ULCA, 1946, p. 274.

[44] Minutes, ULCA, 1946, p. 291.

[45] Minutes, ULCA, 1946, p. 160.

[46] Minutes, Eighteenth Biennial Convention of the United Lutheran Church in America, Seattle, Wash., October 8-15, 1952, p. 611.

Three-fourths participating

Participating in the new contributory plan were nearly three-fourths of the ULCA's active clergy. Under that new plan, 23 individuals already were receiving benefits by 1948.[47]

A lay contributory pension plan was proposed in 1946 for the ULCA's program.[48] The contribution rate in the lay plan was four percent of the employee's salary paid by the employee and four percent by the congregation or employing entity.[49]

A family protection benefit—specifically, a decreasing benefit term-insurance plan—was included in the ULCA's plan, beginning January 1, 1951. The annual rate for coverage was $36, providing a death-benefit payment of $3,000 up to age 60, with decreasing amounts after that.[50] From age 61 through 65, the amount was $2,000; 66 through 70, $1,000; and 71 and beyond, $500.[51] The coverage later was changed to an annual decreasing term policy with coverage for age 40 and under at $7,000, declining at $200 per year thereafter to $1,000 at age 70.[52]

The earlier non-contributory plan continued to grant benefits but was closed by 1953 to any new retiree claims. Through church offerings and an increase in the assessed rate for congregations under the contributory pension plan, the minimum benefit paid for members of the contributory plan was raised in 1954 to $900 a year for clergy and $450 for widows.[53] The increased benefit applied to those who had joined the contributory plan by November 1, 1947.[54] Clergy who were not part of the contributory plan continued to receive only $300 per year.[55]

---

[47] *Minutes*, Sixteenth Biennial Convention of the United Lutheran Church in America, Philadelphia, Pa., October 6-14, 1948, p. 719.

[48] *Minutes*, ULCA, 1946, pp. 93-99.

[49] *Minutes*, ULCA, 1946, pp. 94-95.

[50] *The Lutheran* magazine, January 17, 1951, p. 6.

[51] *Minutes*, Seventeenth Biennial Convention of the United Lutheran Church in America, Des Moines, Iowa, October 4-12, 1950, p. 985.

[52] *Minutes*, Twenty-First Biennial Convention of the United Lutheran Church in America, Dayton, Ohio, October 8-15, 1958, pp. 604-605.

[53] *The Lutheran* magazine, October 22, 1952, p. 9.

[54] *Minutes*, ULCA, 1952, p. 573.

[55] *The Lutheran* magazine, January 21, 1953, p. 11.

The minimum pension for members of the contributory plan was raised to $1,200 in 1958 and increased by $100 in each succeeding year to $1,500 in 1961.[56] Widows of pastors received half those amounts.[57]

To bridge the transition for middle-aged clergy entering the contributory plan, a supplementary plan was established in 1946 for pastors age 51 or over as of July 1, 1947. That benefit was created because they would not have enough years to build up a reserve in the contributory plan prior to retirement.[58]

In an overview of the operation of the ULCA's Board of Pensions, Albert P. Stauderman and Richard T. Sutcliffe, in an article in the ULCA's *Lutheran* magazine, wrote:

> With the United Lutheran Church evidencing a growing awareness of the need for improved pensions for its retired servants, the board can foresee the day, perhaps not too far off, when minimum pensions will be $1,200 a year. Not until after A.D. 2000 will all retired pastors be sufficiently protected under the Contributory Plan to make available for other use the amount now invested in Endowment Funds.
>
> Until then, the Board of Pensions will continue quietly and progressively along the course outlined in its charter ". . . the relief and support of ministers of the United Lutheran Church in America, their widows and children."[59]

Much would change in regard to pension and benefits before the year A.D. 2000, as projected in that mid-twentieth century article.

The onset of the Korean War resulted in the call-up of several reserve chaplains. Questions arose as to their continued participation in the ULCA's contributory plan, since the contribution of congregations on their behalf had ceased. The ULCA determined that the congregation portion for reserve chaplains who would not otherwise qualify for a government pension should be paid through the ULCA's national budget during the period of their active duty status. The contribution was based on an assumed

---

[56] *The Lutheran* magazine, October 22, 1958, p. 21. See also *Minutes*, ULCA, 1958, p. 598.

[57] *The Lutheran* magazine, October 29, 1958, p. 9.

[58] *The Lutheran* magazine, January 21, 1953, p. 14.

[59] Richard T. Sutcliffe and Albert P. Stauderman, "We Love Our Old Pastors," *The Lutheran* magazine, January 21, 1953, p. 15.

annual salary level of $3,000.[60] That was raised to an assumed level of $3,600 in 1960.[61]

Changes for Social Security

The prospect of coverage under Social Security for church workers resulted in adjustments to encourage participation.[62] The change initially applied to lay church workers who were covered in 1950 amendments to the Social Security Act. Under the revision for lay members of the plan, the employee's four percent contribution was decreased in relation to the amount paid in Social Security taxes.[63]

Clergy coverage under Social Security emerged in the mid-1950s. When the option opened, about 80 percent of active ULCA clergy joined the Social Security program.[64] The clergy rate for the contributory plan was set at four percent of the amount of the pastor's salary above the level of one-half of that salary for which Social Security contributions were required at that time.[65]

By 1960, the assets of the ULCA's Board of Pensions had reached $25.3 million, with an investment return rate for the previous year of nearly four percent.[66]

Noted in the 1960 report of the ULCA Board of Pensions was the death of Mr. George A. Huggins on December 30, 1959. He was the founder and senior member of the actuarial firm of Huggins and Company. Since the mid-1920s, he had been the key advisor for the pension programs of most Lutheran churches as well as those of several other denominations.[67] Without his vision and leadership, the life of most Lutheran clergy in the middle twentieth century would have been even more spartan than what was the case for many of them.

---

[60] *Minutes*, ULCA, 1952, pp. 263 and 831.

[61] *Minutes*, Twenty-Second Biennial Convention of the United Lutheran Church in America, Atlantic City, N.J., October 13-20, 1960, p. 269.

[62] Robert J. Myers, "Reply to Criticisms of Pension Proposals," *The Lutheran* magazine, August 22, 1956, pp. 16-18.

[63] *Minutes*, ULCA, 1952, pp. 142-143.

[64] *The Lutheran* magazine, January 22, 1958, p. 20.

[65] *Minutes*, Twentieth Biennial Convention of the United Lutheran Church in America, Harrisburg, Pa., October 10-17, 1956, p. 348.

[66] *The Lutheran* magazine, October 12, 1960, p. 24.

[67] *Minutes*, ULCA, 1960, p. 686. Mr. George A. Huggins provided guidance, even prior to the World War I era, to Presbyterians and others on pension matters. Following the war, he was a key architect of the model pension plan that eventually was adopted by several Lutheran church bodies.

American Evangelical Lutheran Church

The pension fund of the American Evangelical Lutheran Church (AELC) was supported by annual offerings of congregations and member dues.[68] Retired pastors were receiving $200 a year under the program. Assets, primarily in the form of mortgages, were less than $25,000 at the time.[69] Under revised rules in 1942, the annual amount was to increase to $400 for married retirees, paid on a quarterly basis.[70] Revenue permitted an increase to $700 per couple and $400 for individuals in 1949.[71] By the early 1950s, six couples and 20 individuals were receiving pension payments.[72] A new level was reached by the middle of that decade allowing a pension to couples of $1,000 per year and to individuals, $550.[73]

Debate persisted over several years after a clergy membership fee was introduced in 1940. The fee was based on a graduated schedule according to income.[74] Later set at a flat two percent rate, the dues initially were one-half percent for those with annual income up to $800, one percent for those $800 to $1200, and two percent for those over $1200.[75]

The idea of a contributory pension plan was introduced to the AELC in 1948. The existing AELC plan was similar to the earlier endowment plan that had operated in the ULCA. The Rev. A. E. Frost, then president of the AELC's pension fund, observed in 1948 that the ULCA's contributory pension plan:

---

[68] *Report*, Sixth-Fifth Annual Convention of the Danish Evangelical Lutheran Church in America, Dwight, Ill., June 16-21, 1942 (Cedar Falls, Iowa: Holst Printing Co.), p. 14. Actually, this church body's name was Danish Evangelical Lutheran Church in America until 1953 when it was renamed American Evangelical Lutheran Church (E. Clifford Nelson, ed., *The Lutherans in North America* (Philadelphia: Fortress Press, 1975), p. 271). For simplicity, its latter name is used in this narrative.

[69] *Report*, AELC, 1942, p. 72.

[70] *Report*, Sixth-Sixth Annual Convention of the Danish Evangelical Lutheran Church in America, Minneapolis, Minn., June 22-27, 1943 (Blair, Neb.: Lutheran Publishing House), p. 69.

[71] *Report*, Seventy-Second Annual Convention of the Danish Evangelical Lutheran Church in America, Greenville, Mich., June 21-26, 1949, p. 88.

[72] *Report*, Seventy-Fifth Annual Convention of the Danish Evangelical Lutheran Church in America, Omaha, Neb., August 12-17, 1952, p. 106.

[73] *Report*, Seventy-Eighth Annual Convention of the American Evangelical Lutheran Church, Kimballton, Iowa, August 9-14, 1955, p. 113.

[74] *Report*, AELC, 1949, p. 88.

[75] *Rules for Pension Endowment Fund and Pension Operating Fund of the Danish Evangelical Lutheran Church in America*, May 1948, p. 5.

. . . undoubtedly is very business-like and efficient. But I doubt very much if our pastors are ready to submit such monthly withholdings and if congregations would be willing to support such a program. Furthermore, this plan does not have the feature of mutual aid whereby all our pastors receive the same pensions regardless of their contribution or their income.[76]

By contrast, his successor a few years later, the Rev. Richard H. Sorensen, observed:

. . . I have thought for some time . . . that our AELC pension system is an ancient, financially unstable, very inadequate system that should have been replaced or supplemented a generation ago when most other Lutheran bodies were reviewing and improving their systems.[77]

With that perspective, he urged that a committee be appointed to bring a proposal to the AELC's 1957 annual convention. To support his recommendation, he noted:

a. Our [AELC] pension program does not provide accumulated reserves which assure the contributors or their heirs of definite returns in line with their annual contributions.

b. Our pension program does not provide death benefits or any funds for "special relief" in cases of dire need.

c. Our pension program does not provide any means for equalizing retirement income of present pensioners who were ineligible for Social Security with retirement income of future pensioners who are eligible to receive large Social Security benefits in addition to their church pension.

d. Our pension fund income in 1954 included about a 2% contribution ($2,380.12) from pastors on the basis of their salary; no contribution from individual congregations; earnings [of] $5,589.03 . . . from a $55,000 endowment fund; [and] 12% ($7,619.88) of the general synod budget. These sources are to be compared with present sources of income in other Lutheran church pension systems. Their sources generally include a 4%

[76] Report, Seventy-First Annual Convention of the Danish Evangelical Lutheran Church in America, Solvang, Calif., June 22-27, 1948, pp. 80-81.

[77] Report, Seventy-Ninth Annual Convention of the American Evangelical Lutheran Church, Muskegon, Mich., August 14-19, 1956, p. 116.

contribution from the pastor and an 8% contribution from the congregation based on the pastor's salary; endowment fund earnings comparable to ours; and from 4% to 12% of the general church budget.[78]

The following year, 1957, the study committee declined to recommend a "drastic revision" of the AELC's existing plan "in view of the merger talks" under way with other Lutheran church bodies. An increase in annual benefits was approved, however, to $1,000 for couples and $750 for individuals. The two percent contribution rate for active pastors was maintained.[79]

All active pastors were urged to study the pension plan of the merged church body—the Lutheran Church in America—to be operational on January 1, 1963. Said the chair of the AELC's pension fund, the Rev. Harald Ibsen, "Perhaps the contributory pension plan will be the most attractive to the majority of our ministers."[80]

As the operation of the AELC's plan drew to a close, 13 couples and 22 individuals were receiving benefits.

Finnish Evangelical Lutheran Church

The regulations for the pension plan of the Finnish Evangelical Lutheran Church, also known as the Suomi Synod, were printed in the Finnish language even in the 1950s. The plan, first approved in 1942, originally called for pastors to pay $2.50 a month into the plan and congregations 15 cents annually per contributing member.[81]

A revised plan was proposed in 1954 that called for congregations to pay six percent of the pastor's salary to the retirement fund and also submit $2 per contributing member to a reserve fund to pay existing obligations. The pastor's contribution was four percent of his annual salary. Under the revised plan, retirees received $300 a year and surviving widows half that amount.[82]

[78] *Report*, AELC, 1956, p. 116.

[79] *Report*, Eightieth Annual Convention of the American Evangelical Lutheran Church, Ringsted, Iowa, August 6-11, 1957, pp. 116-118

[80] *Report*, Eighty-Fourth Annual Convention of the American Evangelical Lutheran Church, Detroit, Mich., reconvened June 24-27, 1962, following the first part of the 84th annual convention held in Tyler, Minn., August 15-20, 1961, p. 89.

[81] *Yearbook*, Seventy-Third Annual Convention of the Finnish Evangelical Lutheran Church of America (also known as the Suomi Synod), Detroit, Mich., June 24-27, 1962 (Hancock, Mich.: Finnish Lutheran Book Concern), p. 121. The publisher of the Suomi Synod's *Yearbook* is hereafter not cited in the footnotes.

[82] *Yearbook*, Sixty-Fifth Annual Convention of the Finnish Evangelical Lutheran Church of America, Waukegan, Ill., June 20-23, 1954, p. 85.

As was the case in the Augustana Lutheran Church, all clergy of the Finnish Evangelical Lutheran Church were "required to become members of the pension plan on the day that they become members of the Ministerium of the Synod."[83]

Assets—which largely were invested in savings accounts and U.S. Savings Bonds—amounted in 1954 to just over $32,000.[84]

A significant change was proposed and approved in 1956 that called for "all eligible pastors" to elect coverage under the provisions of the Social Security program. Further, the church's recently established contributory pension plan was dissolved and the contributions refunded to pastors. Instead, a new non-contributory retirement and disability benefit fund was established on the basis of $1.25 assessment per contributing member of the congregations. A benefit of $50 per month was paid to retirees.[85] By 1958, 15 retired pastors, one pastor who was disabled, and 10 widows were drawing benefits.[86] That number grew to 31 by 1960.[87]

In retrospect, the decision of the Finnish Evangelical Lutheran Church in 1956 to shift from a contributory plan to a non-contributory system seems ill-timed. That move came just six years before a new church body was formed. Negotiations already were under way in 1956 in anticipation of the forthcoming merger. Other than encouragement for clergy participation in the Social Security program, the record indicates little rationale for the drastic change.

The decisions made—and even more significantly, the decisions deferred prior to the 1962 formation of the Lutheran Church in America—carried a huge price in terms of covering the costs of even modest minimum pensions for pastors and their spouses in the years to come.

---

[83] *Yearbook*, Suomi Synod, 1954, p. 86.

[84] *Yearbook*, Suomi Synod, 1954, p. 88.

[85] *Yearbook*, Sixty-Seventh Annual Convention of the Finnish Evangelical Lutheran Church of America (Suomi Synod), Ashtabula, Ohio, June 17-20, 1956, pp. 94 and 96.

[86] *Yearbook*, Sixty-Ninth Annual Convention of the Finnish Evangelical Lutheran Church of America (Suomi Synod), Detroit, Mich., June 22-25, 1958, p. 152.

[87] *Yearbook*, Seventy-Second Annual Convention of the Finnish Evangelical Lutheran Church of America (Suomi Synod), Fairport Harbor, Ohio, June 25-28, 1961, p. 120.

CHAPTER 11

Four Churches Struggle to Develop Pension Plans

One of the challenges in the Lutheran church mergers of the 1960s involved bringing together the pension operations of predecessor church bodies. Efforts had been made, beginning in the 1930s in several of those churches, to develop somewhat common pension patterns. Even so, differences remained that had to be resolved.

American Lutheran Church

After the American Lutheran Church (ALC) of 1930 was formed, adoption of a uniform pension plan that had been developed for Lutheran church bodies was postponed. Limited funds amid the struggles of the Great Depression made the step to a new plan seem impossible at that time.[1] From the merging synods, the ALC's Board of Aids received $499,654 from the Iowa Synod,[2] $64,442 from the Joint Synod of Ohio, and $8,631 from the Buffalo Synod. The Buffalo Synod had a defined-benefit pension system in place at the point of the merger that guaranteed $150 a year to eight beneficiaries.[3]

To delay having to meet retiree obligations, the ALC's Board of Aids urged that older pastors be retained in active service and that younger ones without call move into other arenas of work:

> In order to prevent elderly pastors with sound theological knowledge, who are physically and mentally able to have

---

[1] *Minutes*, Second Convention of the American Lutheran Church, Fond du Lac, Wis., October 14-20, 1932 (Columbus, Ohio: Wartburg Press), pp. 227 and 282. Wartburg Press of Columbus, Ohio—known until the mid-1940s as Lutheran Book Concern—published all the minutes of the ALC's conventions and therefore is not cited subsequently in the footnotes.

[2] The Texas Synod operated as a district of the Iowa Synod, but it was separately incorporated and therefore was part of the four-way merger that created the American Lutheran Church of 1930.

[3] *Minutes*, ALC, 1932, pp. 163-164.

charge of a congregation . . . , from becoming beneficiaries of our Board [of Aids], we kindly request all districts to retain the services of these experienced men as long as possible and to . . . recommend them eventually to congregations who have to call a new pastor.

We request . . . the respective District Executive Committees and District Boards of Appeal to advise a change of vocation to . . . [younger] pastors as soon as their inability to maintain themselves in a congregation becomes conclusively apparent.[4]

By the mid-1930s, the 225 beneficiaries of the ALC aid program were receiving about $17 per month ($204 a year). The aid program basically was being operated on a "pay-as-you-go" basis from the churchwide budget.[5]

Almost a decade after the ALC's formation, a Board of Pensions was established and incorporated in the state of Illinois. It began operation on January 1, 1939.

From the beginning of the ALC, the urgent need for an adequate pension program had been emphasized. Declared the Board of Aids at the 1932 ALC convention:

If we bear in mind that practically all European churches and many churches in America . . . are paying a pension to their retired pastors and pastors' widows irrespective of personal property; that the United States pays a rural mail carrier retired after only thirty years of service a pension of $100 a month; that cities pay their retired policemen a pension of $70 a month: we certainly must admit that the amount of support which our Church can give our needy retired pioneers after forty, fifty, or more years of hard service at small salaries is absolutely inadequate.[6]

Crucial role of Judge Graven

The key figure in the development of the ALC pension and benefits program was Judge Henry N. Graven of Greene, Iowa. He saw early the need for a church pension plan, even when few church bodies showed much interest in adopting such a plan. He persisted because he felt that

---

[4] *Minutes*, Third Convention of the American Lutheran Church, Waverly, Iowa, October 12-18, 1934, pp. 136 and 255.

[5] *Minutes*, Fourth Convention of the American Lutheran Church, San Antonio, Texas, October 9-15, 1936, p. 109.

[6] *Minutes*, ALC, 1932, pp. 164-165.

the church would be unfair if pastors, after many years of faithful service, would be dependent for their material needs upon charity or the limited largess of the church. He wanted pastors to live with a sense of dignity during their retirement years. So he kept pressing the ALC to implement a contributory pension plan. As a result, the ALC became one of the first U.S. Lutheran church bodies to adopt a formal "money-purchase" or contributory pension plan.

Judge Graven served as chair of the ALC's Board of Pensions from 1939 until the 1960 church merger. Following that merger that formed the "new" American Lutheran Church, he served for two years as chair of the "new" ALC Board of Pensions. So significant was Judge Graven's impact on the pension program in the ALC of 1930 and also in the ALC that was formed in 1960 that his death on February 1, 1970, was noted in the report of the Board of Pensions to the Fifth General Convention of The American Lutheran Church in October 1970. Tribute was paid to him for his wisdom and heroic efforts for an effective pension program for pastors and lay church workers.[7]

The initial contribution rate in the ALC plan was set at four percent of the member's salary, with the same percentage being submitted by the congregation or institutional employer. A portion of the congregation's contribution was credited to the member and another portion was used to pay benefits for those already retired and their beneficiaries. Members were eligible to draw retirement benefits beginning at age 65. Disability coverage was included in the program.[8]

By 1942, a majority of the ALC's pastors and church workers had become members of the contributory pension plan. An interest-crediting rate of three percent was used at the time for member accounts.[9] The crediting rate was set annually by the trustees on the basis of short-term and long-term returns on investments. The interest-crediting system moderated both the peaks and valleys of the market. Members were "protected" in that way from wide fluctuations in the rates of return on investment. In the later 1940s, the interest-crediting rate was reduced to 2.5 percent for several years and then raised to 2.75 percent before returning to the 3

---

[7] *Reports and Actions*, Fifth General Convention of The American Lutheran Church, San Antonio, Texas, October 21-27, 1970, pp. 679-680.

[8] *Minutes*, Sixth Convention of the American Lutheran Church, Detroit, Mich., October 11-17, 1940, pp. 172-177 and 359.

[9] *Minutes*, Seventh Convention of the American Lutheran Church, Mendota, Ill., October 9-15, 1942, p. 160.

percent level in 1952.[10] The rate was increased to 3.5 percent in 1957 and again in 1958[11] and 4 percent in 1959.[12]

The need for continued growth in plan membership was underscored by the ALC's Board of Pensions, especially in regard to newly ordained seminary graduates. Both increased participation and additional grants from the church's budget were sought to provide "minimum pensions" to care for "those pastors who have been receiving lower salaries and those whose membership in the [Pension] Fund because of their advanced age will be insufficient to pay them adequate pensions."[13]

To encourage participation, the ALC voted in 1942 that "any student who enters one of the seminaries of the Church will do so with the understanding that, upon call and ordination, he will become a member of the Pension Fund."[14]

At the five-year mark for the ALC's pension plan, the number of members had grown from 407 in 1939 to 1,157 in 1944.[15]

A "Good Samaritan Fund" was established "to assist pastors and other church workers who have been grievously stricken on life's highway." To inaugurate the fund that provided special grants for catastrophic situations, the ALC Women's Missionary Federation gave a $20,000 gift.[16] Additional gifts were provided for the fund in succeeding years by the federation.

With the dawning of the post-World War II era, 78 percent of the ALC's pastors were members of the pension fund. Total membership for clergy and church workers in 1946 was 1,427. By means of a subsidy, seminary graduates were encouraged to join. The subsidy covered 75 percent of their membership assessment in their first year of ordained service, 50 percent in the second year, and 25 percent in the third year.[17]

---

[10] *Minutes*, Fourteenth Convention of the American Lutheran Church, Blue Island, Ill., October 4-11, 1956, p. 303.

[11] *Minutes*, Fifteenth Convention of the American Lutheran Church, San Antonio, Texas, October 9-15, 1958, p. 333.

[12] *Minutes*, Sixteenth Convention of the American Lutheran Church, Minneapolis, Minn., April 19-21, 1960, p. 237.

[13] *Minutes*, ALC, 1942, pp. 151 and 157.

[14] *Minutes*, ALC, 1942, p. 279.

[15] *Minutes*, Eighth Convention of the American Lutheran Church, Sandusky, Ohio, October 9-14, 1944, p. 215.

[16] *Minutes*, ALC, 1944, p. 233.

[17] *Minutes*, Ninth Convention of the American Lutheran Church, Appleton, Wis., October 10-17, 1946, p. 193.

In the post-war context of the 1940s, the ALC acted to assist chaplains in "the transition back into civilian Church work." That assistance included pension payments while they were serving as military chaplains and an education allowance of up to $500, plus a $100 credit at Wartburg Press in Columbus, Ohio, for the purchase of books.[18]

The contribution rate structure was changed in 1948, increasing the congregation's contribution from what had been four percent to seven percent of the pastor's salary. At the same time, the amount allocated in the ALC's budget for minimum pension payments was raised to $132,000, thereby providing $50 a month for each of those receiving such payments.[19]

By 1950, 93.6 percent of the ALC pastors and church workers were enrolled in the pension plan. The total that year was 1,734. Assets had grown from nothing in 1939 to $3.2 million in 1950.[20] Two years later, the percentage of participation was 97.6, with assets in the plan of $4.6 million.[21] At the time of the 1960 merger, participation had reached 98.2 percent, with assets at $13,853,671.[22]

A "death-benefit" payment was added to the ALC's plan in 1952. With declining "term" coverage, beneficiaries of those 59 or younger at the time of death would receive a one-time payment equivalent to the pastor's annual salary, with a minimum of $1,000 and a maximum of $6,000. Between 60 and 64, the benefit payment would be the equivalent of nine months of salary (minimum, $750; maximum $4,500). For those 65 through 69, the benefit payment would amount to six months' salary (minimum, $500; maximum $3,000), and 70 or above, three months' salary (minimum $250; maximum $1,500).[23] Within the first year of this coverage, 16 payments were made ranging from $450 (equivalent of three months' salary) to $4,600 (one year's salary).[24]

---

[18] *Minutes*, ALC, 1946, p. 199.

[19] *Minutes*, Tenth Convention of the American Lutheran Church, Fremont, Ohio, October 7-14, 1948, p. 171.

[20] *Minutes*, Eleventh Convention of the American Lutheran Church, Columbus, Ohio, October 5-12, 1950, p. 252.

[21] *Minutes*, Twelfth Convention of the American Lutheran Church, Waverly, Iowa, October 9-16, 1952, p. 275.

[22] *Minutes*, ALC, 1960, p. 237.

[23] *Minutes*, ALC, 1952, p. 424.

[24] *Minutes*, Thirteenth Convention of the American Lutheran Church, Beatrice, Neb., September 30–October 7, 1954, p. 281.

When the Social Security Act was amended in 1954 to open the way for participation by clergy in the program, a survey indicated that about 73 percent of ALC pastors intended to do so.[25] A later survey reported 81 percent had joined the Social Security program.[26]

As early as 1950, conversations were being held by the pension executives of the ALC, the Evangelical Lutheran Church, and the United Evangelical Lutheran Church. Being examined were the implications of a church merger for the pension program.[27]

Effective January 1, 1961, operation of a new pension program became the responsibility of The American Lutheran Church, constituted in 1960 as a merged church body encompassing the ALC of 1930, the Evangelical Lutheran Church of 1917, and the United Evangelical Lutheran Church of 1896. In 1963, the Lutheran Free Church of 1897 became a part of the ALC.

Evangelical Lutheran Church

The Evangelical Lutheran Church (ELC) of 1917[28] established a pension fund upon its formation, but the resources for payment of any pensions were limited, although nearly a half-million dollars had been raised for an income-producing endowment.[29] The number of persons already qualifying for benefits put pressure on the fund from its beginning.

By the mid-1920s, nearly 200 plan members were receiving pension or survivor benefits at a rate of $320 a year for regular pensioners.[30] Contributions from congregations and gifts from "ladies' aid societies" as

---

[25] *Minutes*, ALC, 1956, p. 306.

[26] *Minutes*, ALC, 1958, p. 339.

[27] *Minutes*, ALC, 1950, pp. 256-257.

[28] The original name of this church body was the Norwegian Lutheran Church of America. The name was changed in 1946 to Evangelical Lutheran Church. For consistency in this narrative, Evangelical Lutheran Church is the name used in references to this church body. The Articles of Incorporation and the church's constitution were amended on the afternoon of June 14, 1946, for implementation of the new name.

[29] *Report*, "Report of the Board of Pensions Submitted to the District Conventions of the Norwegian Lutheran Church of America," 1924 (Minneapolis: Augsburg Publishing House), p. 247. Augsburg Publishing House of Minneapolis published all the annual reports and minutes of the Norwegian Lutheran Church of American (beginning 1946, the Evangelical Lutheran Church). Therefore, the publisher is not cited subsequently in the footnotes related to documents of the Evangelical Lutheran Church.

[30] *Report*, Third Extraordinary General Convention of the Norwegian Lutheran Church of America, St. Paul, Minn., June 9-14, 1925, p. 415.

well as individuals were needed to sustain the fund. Funds also were received from a percentage of the revenue exceeding expenses in the operation of the ELC's publishing house.[31]

The program, at its formation, promised a maximum annual annuity payment upon retirement or disability of a pastor in the amount of $500 and an equal amount upon a pastor's death to his widow and orphans. The problem of funding such benefits loomed large:

> The Church did . . . not realize what obligations it undertook when it started the fund on the present endowment plan. For an endowment pension plan means that a permanent fund must be collected, sufficiently large to produce interest enough to pay the annuities to an increasing number of pensioners. The fund started in 1917 with 80 pensioners taken over from the three uniting bodies. It has now 215 and, according to the actuary's projections of the present membership, the pension roll will continue to increase during the next 22 years until in 1948 there will be 600 pensioners, and if new members are taken in, there will be still more, for each new member will some day become a pensioner, or die and leave a widow as beneficiary.[32]

At that point, the estimated endowment needed to sustain the program was up to $4 million or seven times as large as the program's assets.[33] The 1932 convention authorized the pension board to assess congregations $70,000 in 1933 and $80,000 in 1934 to cover payments of current minimum commitments to pensioners. At the same time, the church's Board of Trustees was authorized to borrow up to $40,000 for that obligation.[34] Shrinking resources prompted decreases in payments from $431 per year in 1918 to $235 in 1932, $135 in 1933, and a low of $120 in 1934.[35] Income from the special assessment was very limited.[36] Even so,

[31] *Report*, NLCA, 1925, pp. 415 and 417.

[32] *Report*, Third General Triennial Convention of the Norwegian Lutheran Church of America, Minneapolis, Minn., June 2-9, 1926, p. 433.

[33] *Report*, NLCA, 1926, p. 433.

[34] *Report*, NLCA, 1932, p. 383.

[35] *Report*, Fifteenth General Convention of the Norwegian Lutheran Church of America, Minneapolis, Minn., June 9-14, 1942, p. 230.

[36] *Report*, Eleventh General Convention of the Norwegian Lutheran Church of America, Minneapolis, Minn., June 6-13, 1934 , p. 180.

the minimum pension was raised in 1942 to $250 a year.[37] That amount was doubled in 1953 to $500.[38]

To address the long-term problem of meeting pension obligations, the ELC Board of Pensions recommended in 1926 shifting to a contributory reserve plan to which pastors would submit two and one-half percent of their salary and the congregations would contribute seven and one-half percent, for a combined total of 10 percent annually.[39] When a revised plan was outlined in 1928, the contribution from each pastor remained, as previously proposed, at two and one-half percent, but the congregation's rate was raised to eight percent of salary. The issue was referred to the ELC's congregations for consideration.[40]

Various objections were addressed in the pension board's report to the ELC's 1929 district conventions. Said the board:

> The minister's pension should not be looked upon as a matter of charity . . . [meaning] benevolent gifts for which no value has been received. But in the minister's case, the Church has received full value; it has received his life service, and the pension is therefore deferred salary payments laid aside for him in the Pension Fund, until the day comes when his work and his usual salary cease and he has nothing else to live on than the pension.[41]

Cited as worthy examples were the pension plans operating in several church bodies, including The Episcopal Church as well as among Presbyterians, Congregationalists, Methodists, and Baptists.[42]

The ELC's 1930 general convention postponed consideration of the revised pension plan.[43] When the new plan finally was approved in 1932,

---

[37] *Report*, "Report of the Board of Pensions Submitted to the District Conventions of the Norwegian Lutheran Church of America," 1943, p. 169.

[38] *Report*, Twenty-First General Convention of the Evangelical Lutheran Church, Minneapolis, Minn., June 9-15, 1954, p. 350.

[39] *Report*, NLCA, 1926, pp. 433-434.

[40] *Report*, Eighth General Convention and First Biennial Convention of the Norwegian Lutheran Church of America, Minneapolis, Minn., May 31–June 7, 1928, pp. 359 and 363.

[41] *Report*, "Report of the Board of Pensions Submitted to the District Conventions of the Norwegian Lutheran Church of America," 1929, p. 372.

[42] *Report*, NLCA, 1929, p. 375.

[43] *Report*, Ninth General Convention of the Norwegian Lutheran Church of America, Minneapolis, Minn., May 21-28, 1930, pp. 485-486.

the contribution rate for each participating pastor was set at five percent of the individual's salary. The congregation's portion also was five percent of the pastor's salary.[44] The plan, after 35 or more years of service, was designed to provide, upon retirement at age 65, one-half of the pastor's average annual salary.[45] Although approved, implementation of the plan was delayed for nearly a decade. Finally, an amended plan was put into operation on February 1, 1941.[46]

By the time of its implementation, the new plan called for contributions, as a percentage of salary, of four percent by pastors and six percent by congregations.[47] Funds generated by two percent of the contributions from congregations were used to cover obligations for retirees under the endowment plan that had been established upon the ELC's formation in 1917.[48]

As with other church bodies, enrollment was a concern. By May 1942, little more than a year into the new plan, 65 percent of the ELC's pastors and 40 percent of the congregations were participating.[49] In the succeeding two years, half the ELC's congregations were contributing and 70 percent of the pastors were enrolled.[50]

During the World War II era, the average salary for ELC clergy was $1,973.[51] By 1947, the average had grown to $2,596, including a 15 percent calculation for the value of housing.[52]

Three-fourths of the pastors and 70 percent of the congregations were involved in the pension plan in 1946. The voters in the general convention

---

[44] *Report*, Tenth General Convention of the Norwegian Lutheran Church of America, Minneapolis, Minn., June 1-8, 1932, pp. 379-380 and 383.

[45] *Report*, "Report of the Board of Pensions Submitted to the District Conventions of the Norwegian Lutheran Church of America," 1935, p. 156.

[46] *Report*, "Report of the Board of Pensions Submitted to the District Conventions of the Norwegian Lutheran Church of America," 1941, p. 155.

[47] *Report*, Fourteenth General Convention of the Norwegian Lutheran Church of America, Minneapolis, Minn., June 5-12, 1940, p. 221.

[48] *Report*, NLCA, 1940, p. 226.

[49] *Report*, NLCA, 1942, p. 231.

[50] *Report*, Sixteenth General Convention of the Norwegian Lutheran Church of America, Minneapolis, Minn., May 30–June 4, 1944, p. 288.

[51] *Report*, Seventeenth General Convention of the Evangelical Lutheran Church, Minneapolis, Minn., June 11-18, 1946, p. 270.

[52] *Report*, Eighteenth General Convention of the Evangelical Lutheran Church, Minneapolis, Minn., June 8-13, 1948, p. 348.

resolved that "non-member congregations and pastors be strongly urged to enroll in the Pension Plan. . . ."[53] The exhortation yielded result. Eighty-three percent of the pastors were in the plan by 1949.[54]

To give greater stability to the pension plan's financial situation, a fund appeal was launched in 1950. That appeal reached $910,377 in 1954. With greater resources, the minimum pension for retirees was increased to $900 per year.[55]

Added to the program in 1954 was a death-benefit payment. That took place two years after the American Lutheran Church inaugurated such a benefit as part of its program.[56]

To encourage pastors to join the Social Security program, the ELC urged congregations in 1958 to pay to the pension plan the entire amount of both the pastor's and congregation's assessment. In effect, that action moved the ELC toward an employer-paid pension plan.[57]

By the time of the 1960 merger, 132 pastors and widows were still receiving benefits under the pre-1941 pension plan and 575 had pensions under the ELC's 1941 contributory program.[58]

United Evangelical Lutheran Church

The comparatively small Danish-immigrant church body, the United Evangelical Lutheran Church (UELC), also had a pension plan.[59] That plan, which was basically a minimum pension aid plan, was established on January 1, 1918.[60] By the middle of the next decade, there were 138

---

[53] *Report*, ELC, 1946, p. 271.

[54] *Report*, "Report of the Board of Pensions Submitted to the District Conventions of the Evangelical Lutheran Church," 1949, p. 333.

[55] *Report*, "Report of the Board of Pensions Submitted to the District Conventions of the Evangelical Lutheran Church," 1955, p. 319.

[56] *Report*, ELC, 1955, p. 319.

[57] *Report*, Twenty-Third General Convention of the Evangelical Lutheran Church, Minneapolis, Minn., June 17-24, 1958, p. 255.

[58] *Report*, Twenty-Fourth General Convention of the Evangelical Lutheran Church, Minneapolis, Minn., April 19-21, 1960, p. 263.

[59] The name of this church body originally was United Danish Evangelical Lutheran Church. In 1946, the word "Danish" was removed from the name. For consistency, the revised name is used in this narrative.

[60] *Report*, Thirty-Second Annual Convention of the United Danish Evangelical Lutheran Church, Racine, Wis., June 5-10, 1928 (Blair, Neb.: Danish Lutheran Publishing House), p. 85. All of the reports and minutes of the United Evangelical Lutheran Church were published by the Danish Lutheran Publishing House of Blair, Neb., known from the mid-1940s as the Lutheran Publishing House. The publisher is not cited in subsequent footnotes for the UELC's minutes.

members in the plan. Forty-five plan members were receiving a pension at a rate of $350 annually for pastors and $225 for widows. The primary source of funds came from offerings in congregations. Some money also was received through bequests. An endowment fund of $117,151.73 was managed primarily with investments in mortgages and U.S. bonds.[61]

In contrast to the higher retirement-age requirements of other Lutheran pension plans at the time, the UELC defined-benefit plan permitted the granting of a pension to pastors beginning at the age of 60.[62] That possibility placed added stress on the plan for funding, especially as the number of pensioners increased. To help ensure ongoing contributions to the plan, the board began urging required participation in the plan by pastors within five years of their ordinations.[63] That did not happen.

With the onset of the Great Depression, the UELC's plan lost some money in bank failures and farm-land loans that could not be repaid. Declining resources led to a reduction in the annual pension to $300 for pastors and $200 for widows.[64] The amount continued to decrease to $291 for pastors and $196 for widows in 1935.[65]

The repeated pleas of the pension board to establish membership requirements and a more consistent funding pattern went unheard year after year until 1936 when initial steps were taken to create a contributory pension plan with language similar to that being considered in other Lutheran churches. The proposed plan called for pastors to contribute four percent of salary, but they had the option of submitting one, two, three, or four percent. Obviously, the level chosen would affect that amount of pension eventually to be paid. Congregations were to contribute 50 cents per confirmed member. The congregation's contribution—as was the case in certain other churches—was to be understood as a "current expense" and not as benevolence. The pension to be paid to pastors initially was not to exceed $300 a year and to widows, $200 a year. Disability coverage was

---

[61] *Report*, Twenty-Ninth Annual Convention of the United Danish Evangelical Lutheran Church, Albert Lea, Minn., June 9-14, 1925, pp. 69-71.

[62] *Report*, Thirtieth Annual Convention of the United Danish Evangelical Lutheran Church, Waupaca, Wis., June 15-20, 1926, p. 74.

[63] *Report*, Thirty-First Annual Convention of the United Danish Evangelical Lutheran Church, Blair, Neb., June 7-12, 1927, pp. 89-90.

[64] *Report*, Thirty-Fifth Annual Convention of the United Danish Evangelical Lutheran Church, Blair, Neb., June 2-7, 1931, p. 62.

[65] *Report*, Fortieth Annual Convention of the United Danish Evangelical Lutheran Church, Blair, Neb., June 2-7, 1936, p. 65.

included in the plan.[66] The new plan, however, was not implemented; the defined-benefit system that had been inaugurated in 1918 continued.

By the end of World War II, income for the plan improved, permitting an increase to $345 in annual pensions for pastors and $230 for widows, as well as $57.50 for minor children.[67] Payments continued to grow, eventually reaching $900 annually for pastors and $540 for widows by 1959.[68]

As the decade of the 1940s was nearing its end, the UELC pension plan had 188 members, of whom 132 pastors were in active service while 25 pastors and three widows were drawing pensions.[69]

The possibility of an anticipated church merger underscored the need for adjustments in the UELC's pension plan. As the chair of the board, Mr. A. Hofgaard, reported to the convention in 1950:

> . . . I met with Pastor Chas. E. Johnson, executive secretary of the Board of Pensions of the Evangelical Lutheran Church, and with Judge Henry Graven, chairman of the Board of Pensions of the American Lutheran Church. We met in Minneapolis for the purpose of comparing our different pension plans and to get acquainted in view of a possible merger. These two larger bodies have similar pension plans, both on the percentage basis. The pastors pay 4% of their salary and the churches pay 6% or 7%.[70] If we are to merge with other Lutheran bodies, it would be a wise procedure to revise our pension plan as soon as possible to a percentage basis.[71]

Noted was the fact that the UELC did not have an annuity plan in operation, although such a plan once had been approved.[72] Instead, the

---

[66] *Report*, Forty-Third Annual Convention of the United Danish Evangelical Lutheran Church, Oakland, Calif., June 12-18, 1939, pp. 70-80.

[67] *Report*, Fiftieth Annual Convention of the United Evangelical Lutheran Church, Blair, Neb., June 18-23, 1946, p. 57.

[68] *Report*, Sixty-Third Annual Convention of the United Evangelical Lutheran Church, Sidney, Mont., June 18-23, 1959, p. 108.

[69] *Report*, Fifty-Third Annual Convention of the United Evangelical Lutheran Church, Blair, Neb., June 21-26, 1949, p. 107.

[70] Under the ALC plan, pastors paid four percent of their salary and congregations seven percent; in the ELC, the rate for pastors was four percent, but for congregations six percent.

[71] *Report*, Fifty-Fourth Annual Convention of the United Evangelical Lutheran Church, Hutchinson, Minn., June 13-18, 1950, p. 92.

[72] *Report*, UELC, 1950, p. 93.

annual offering of most UELC congregations at Thanksgiving was a key source of funds for paying pensions.[73]

Guiding the UELC in its shift to a contributory pension plan was Mr. George A. Huggins, an actuary from Philadelphia. He also served as a key advisor for several other Lutheran pension plans at the time.[74] With his wise encouragement, the new UELC plan emerged and received final approval in 1952. The new plan specified a contribution rate for pastors at four percent of salary and congregations at eight percent of the pastor's salary. Age for retirement was 65. The new plan, which also had both disability and death-benefit components, went into operation on January 1, 1954, under rules established by the 1953 convention.[75] An interest-crediting system was used for determining the annual growth of member accounts.[76]

Following the pattern of some other church bodies, the UELC permitted pastors who joined the Social Security program to reduce their contribution to the UELC's plan from four percent of salary to two percent.[77] Later, the UELC determined that the basic membership fee for pastors was to be $120 a year, the equivalent of four percent of what was considered the basic salary of $3,000.[78]

The pension amounts received by UELC pastors who retired after May 1, 1954, were determined under the contributory plan that became operational that year. For those who retired prior to that date, the church had a continuing, but unfunded, obligation that was carried forward into the merger that formed the ALC of 1960.[79]

Most of the early Lutheran plans, including the UELC's, had begun as mutual aid funds supported by the fees paid by active members and special offerings from congregations. Gradually, those aid funds moved toward efforts to establish endowment reserves, as was the case in the UELC.

---

[73] *Report*, UELC, 1949, p. 108.

[74] *Report*, Fifty-Fifth Annual Convention of the United Evangelical Lutheran Church, Westbrook, Maine, June 19-24, 1951, p. 79.

[75] *Report*, Fifty-Sixth Annual Convention of the United Evangelical Lutheran Church, Albert Lea, Minn., June 17-22, 1952, pp. 96-98.

[76] *Report*, Fifty-Seventh Annual Convention of the United Evangelical Lutheran Church, Atlantic, Iowa, June 16-21, 1953, pp. 95-99.

[77] *Report*, Fifty-Ninth Annual Convention of the United Evangelical Lutheran Church, Lynwood, Calif., June 21-26, 1955, p. 86.

[78] *Report*, Sixtieth Annual Convention of the United Evangelical Lutheran Church, Cedar Falls, Iowa, June 19-24, 1956, p. 116.

[79] *Report*, UELC, 1959, p. 108.

Funding from the churchwide budget also was needed to sustain the grants in aid as the number of retirees grew.

The move to a contributory plan was crucial to ensure fully funded retirement benefits. As Mr. Keith Knudsen, president of the UELC pension fund, observed in his concluding report:

> By the last half of the twenties and the early part of the thirties, it became evident that a reserve type of program was necessary if a member was to have the assurance that funds would be available to provide his benefits upon disability, retirement or death. . . .
>
> Changing from a pay as you go type plan to a reserve accumulation during years of active service proved to be an extremely difficult hurdle for conventions to overcome because [of] their thinking of pensions in terms of benevolence or grants in aid rather than something that was earned. . . .
>
> The successful reserve programs in existence today were established on the principle of 12% of salary contribution paid directly by the salary paying organization to the pension fund.[80]

He urged in his final report that pastors considering retirement in 1960 delay that decision until they learned the terms of the new pension plan in the ALC. They would not have long to wait.

Lutheran Free Church

Following the formation of the Lutheran Free Church (LFC) in 1897, initial discussion of clergy pensions did not occur until 1909. After that, a decade passed before that possibility became more than talk.[81] Limited resources and a lack of interest caused the delay.

The LFC's annual conference in 1914 did approve the formation of a Pension Society to provide pensions for pastors, missionaries, professors, and their dependents.[82] The rules for the program were approved in 1915 and the program was ready to begin operation, except for the need for

---

[80] *Report of the Sixty-Fourth Annual Convention*, United Evangelical Lutheran Church, Minneapolis, Minn., April 18-21, 1960, p. 82.

[81] *Beretning . . . .Den lutherske Frikirke*, Lutheran Free Church, Montevideo, Minn., June 9-15, 1909 (Minneapolis: Lutheran Free Church Publishing Co.). All of the annual reports of the Lutheran Free Church were published by the LFC's publishing company; therefore, the publisher is not cited in subsequent footnotes related to the LFC's annual reports.

[82] *Beretning . . . .Den lutherske Frikirke*, Brainerd, Minn., June 17-23, 1914.

participants.[83] A minimum number of 100 participants had been set and that figure was not reached until 1919. Six years later, in 1925, enough funds had been accumulated to offer small annual pensions of $200. That year, out of the fund's total resources of $30,000, 14 members received that modest pension. Even that sum had to be reduced because of limited funding.[84] Congregations gave meager financial support, and many newly ordained pastors did not join the program.[85]

The LFC Pension Board was incorporated in May 1929, but it limped along throughout the following decade. At the point of its incorporation, the board had an endowment fund of $35,599.48.[86] With only 80 active members and additional persons qualifying for pensions, the challenges facing the plan were enormous. Contributions in the amount of $3,414 the previous year had come from only 25 percent of the LFC's congregations. Exhortations were offered, but apparently little heard:

> There are many pastors . . . that have bread in abundance and that live in comparative luxury, when those on our pension roll receive such an insignificant pension. Must we not as a Church body acknowledge our slowness in recognizing this important activity?

> Surely it is a matter of justice—not simply charity—this the paying of an annuity to the old minister, professor, missionary, and their widows, who have spent their lives in faithful service. . . .[87]

The entrance fee for what was then called the Ministers' Pension Society was $200, plus the annual assessment of participants. If a pastor delayed joining the program, the fee increased. Debate persisted on the question of continuing the program:

> It would be nothing less than traitorous to our friends and co-workers who have been helped and who are being helped by this society if we should heed the occasional voice that has been raised that we should cease functioning as a mutual aid society

---

[83] *Beretning . . . .Den lutherske Frikirke*, Marinette, Wis., June 9-15, 1915, pp. 128-133.

[84] Clarence J. Carlsen, *The Years of Our Church* (Minneapolis: Lutheran Free Church Publishing Co., 1942), p. 193.

[85] Carlsen, p. 193.

[86] *Beretning . . . .Den lutherske Frikirke*, Thief River Falls, Minn., June 11-16, 1929, pp. 104-105.

[87] *Beretning . . . .Den lutherske Frikirke*, 1929, p. 105.

such as we are—at least until some other provision has been made for helping our needy co-workers. . . .

Our list of beneficiaries is growing longer each year. This means either one of two things: Either each beneficiary will receive less or our Board must receive more funds to disburse to those entitled under our rules to receive aid. . . . Here is one of the ties that can bind our hearts in Christian love.[88]

In 1936, perhaps in a form of instruction to foster greater understanding, the report of the pension society characterized its name as a "misnomer" because:

Strictly speaking our society is not a pension society. To qualify for that designation it would have to be organized on the basis whereby each member and each congregation in the Lutheran Free Church paid into the Society's Fund a percentage of the pastor's salary sufficient upon an actuarial basis to provide for the payment of pensions at the age of retirement or death. We are not organized in that manner. . . . We are really an aid society, giving assistance to superannuated pastors and to dependents of deceased or incapacitated pastors.[89]

By this time, the payment to retirees had decreased to only $52.50 annually from the society.[90]

Given the difficulties facing the society, the LFC was examining other models, according to the Rev. Leland B. Sateren in his 1938 report as president of the Pension Society:

In those church bodies where the pension system appears to work best it is the prevailing custom for the pastors to pay 5% of their annual salary, and the congregations pay in an equal amount for the purpose of building up a reserve fund. To cite an instance, if a pastor has an annual salary of $900.00, then he would be obliged to pay $45.00 as his share, the congregation an equal amount as its share annually. . . .

How does this compare with what is actually being done among us as far as the congregations are concerned. [Some that

---

[88] *Annual Report of the Lutheran Free Church*, Minneapolis, Minn., June 11-16, 1935, pp. 98-99.

[89] *Annual Report of the Lutheran Free Church*, Fargo, N.D., June 9-14, 1936, p. 89.

[90] *Annual Report*, June 9-14, 1936, p. 90.

on a new basis] . . . would pay $30.00 to $40.00 a year . . . are
now paying $5.00 to $10.00 to the Pension Society.[91]

A study committee appointed in 1937 submitted in 1939 a
recommendation that the Pension Society be liquidated. The reason for the
recommendation was "the fact that there is so little interest shown for the
Pension Society both among the lay people as well as among the pastors. .
. ." At that point the society had 44 active members and 46 pensioners.[92]
Instead of liquidation, the board recommended that the Pension Society be
reorganized into a Ministers' Aid Society. Its purpose would be to distribute
"aid to needy pastors" and their dependents.[93]

Termination of the Pension Society was approved in 1941 on the
condition that an alternative program would be proposed.[94]

The new Ministers' Aid Society was constituted in 1942 for LFC
pastors, missionaries, and professors. Each participant was to pay an annual
fee of $5 and each congregation was asked to receive an offering in the
Thanksgiving season for the fund. The society operated as a charity,
rather than a pension plan. Needy members could obtain assistance upon
recommendation of the president of the church body. A one-time payment
of $125 was provided as a death benefit to a pastor's immediate survivors.[95]
For the long term, however, the Ministers' Aid Society proved to be
inadequate. The actual needs could not be met by charity; clearly, a more
reliable system was needed.

Finally, in 1950, the LFC adopted a workable, contributory pension
plan. The plan followed the model previously instituted by the Evangelical
Lutheran Church. The initial contribution rate, as a percentage of salary,
was set at four percent to be paid by the pastor and seven percent contributed
by the congregation or employing agency. Of the latter percentage, three
percent was to be allocated to a contingent fund to support current
pensioners whose accumulations were not sufficient to meet the level of

---

[91] *Annual Report of the Lutheran Free Church*, Thief River Falls, Minn., June 7-12, 1938, p.
91.

[92] *Annual Report of the Lutheran Free Church*, LaCrosse, Wis., June 11-16, 1940, p. 109.
Incidently, the chair of the committee making this recommendation, the Rev. P. O.
Laurhammer, was at that time the pastor of the congregation in which I grew up, St.
Peter Lutheran Church of rural Park River, N.D.

[93] *Annual Report*, June 11-16, 1940, p. 111.

[94] *Annual Report of the Lutheran Free Church*, Morris, Minn., June 1941, p. 96.

[95] *Annual Report of the Lutheran Free Church*, Fargo, N.D., June 9-14, 1942, pp. 90-91, 95,
and 120.

annual payments by the LFC's new pension plan. A member could begin drawing benefits at age 68.[96] Eligible for participation in the plan were both clergy and lay employees of LFC congregations and institutions.[97]

The plan began operation on February 1, 1952. In the first three months of the new plan, one-third of the LFC's pastors and congregations joined. Current pensioners were receiving $300 a year through the new plan.[98] The previous Ministers' Aid Society was discontinued with the inauguration of the new plan.[99]

In 1955, a "death-benefit" payment was proposed as an addition to the plan. Under the declining-term coverage, beneficiaries of those 59 or younger at the time of death would receive a one-time payment of the equivalent of the pastor's annual salary, with a minimum of $1,000 and a maximum of $6,000. Between 60 and 64, the benefit payment would be the equivalent of nine months of salary (minimum, $750; maximum $4,500). For survivors of those 65 through 69 at the time of death, the amount would be six months salary (minimum, $500; maximum, $3,000) and 70 or above three months (minimum $250; maximum $1,600). The model followed what already was in place in the American Lutheran Church of 1930.[100] The death-benefit option, however, could not be implemented because of limited response.[101] The proposal later was rejected.[102] In 1959, a death benefit again was proposed on a declining scale: Under 60, $2,000; 60-64, $1,500; 65-69, $1,000; and 70 or above, $500.[103] That proposal was postponed.[104]

The possibility of retirement with benefits at age 65 was opened in 1956, and the congregation's contribution rate was raised from seven to eight percent of salary. The additional income was to be added to the contingent fund.[105]

---

[96] *Annual Report of the Lutheran Free Church*, Minneapolis, Minn., June 14-18, 1950, p. 111. The articles defining and governing the plan appear on pages 112-121.

[97] *Annual Report*, June 14-18, 1950, p. 114.

[98] *Annual Report of the Lutheran Free Church*, Fargo, N.D., June 11-15, 1952, pp. 107 and 109.

[99] *Annual Report*, June 9-14, 1942, p. 109.

[100] *Annual Report of the Lutheran Free Church*, Minneapolis, Minn., June 8-12, 1955, pp. 98 and 101.

[101] *Annual Report of the Lutheran Free Church*, Fargo, N.D., June 13-17, 1956, p. 92.

[102] *Annual Report of the Lutheran Free Church*, Minneapolis, Minn., June 12-16, 1957, p. 91.

[103] *Annual Report of the Lutheran Free Church*, Minot, N.D., June 10-14, 1959, p. 100.

[104] *Annual Report of the Lutheran Free Church*, Fargo, N.D., June 8-12, 1960, p. 121.

[105] *Annual Report*, June 13-17, 1956, p. 93.

Every congregation of the Lutheran Free Church should feel a moral responsibility to share in bringing some financial assistance to our aged, retired pastors and/or their widows. Pious preaching and sentiment without the cash to implement our good intentions do not pay grocery bills, etc. Anyone we speak with will acknowledge that our older pastors, missionaries and their wives have been shamefully underpaid during their working years. Now that they are old and retired we must show them that we will carry through and make their lot a little more tolerable.[106]

Limited participation in the LFC's pension program was a persistent concern.[107] That proved to be true throughout the entire life of the plan.[108]

The Lutheran Free Church became a part of The American Lutheran Church on February 1, 1963. At that point, the LFC's pension plan was folded into the already functioning ALC pension and other benefits program.

---

[106] Annual Report, June 13-17, 1956, pp. 91-92.

[107] Annual Report, June 8-12, 1955, p. 97.

[108] Annual Report, June 8-12, 1960, p. 121.

CHAPTER 12

Blending Four Plans Into Two for New ALC Pension Program

When The American Lutheran Church (ALC) began operation on January 1, 1961, the existing contributory, "money-purchase" pension plans of the predecessor churches were blended into the ALC's new program. One complicating factor was the difference in the duration of the predecessor plans, even though they were similar in their design.

The predecessor American Lutheran Church had inaugurated in 1939 the model defined-contribution plan (see Chapter 7 regarding development of that model for Lutheran churches). Two years later, the Evangelical Lutheran Church initiated largely the same plan. The Lutheran Free Church began a similar "money-purchase" pension plan in 1952, followed by the United Evangelical Lutheran Church in 1954.

At the time of the ALC's formation,[1] the predecessor Evangelical Lutheran Church had 2,242 ordained ministers and 1,174,494 baptized members in 2,672 congregations. The American Lutheran Church of 1930 had 2,237 ordained ministers and 1,059,195 baptized members in 2,086 congregation. The United Evangelical Lutheran Church had 225 ordained ministers and 73,091 baptized members in 181 congregations.[2] As of December 31, 1962, just prior to merging with the ALC, the Lutheran Free Church reported having 260 ordained ministers and 92,900 baptized members in 328 congregations.[3]

---

[1] The American Lutheran Church's constituting convention was held in Minneapolis, Minn., April 22-24, 1960.

[2] *1961 Yearbook of The American Lutheran Church*, p. 18, and *1962 Yearbook of The American Lutheran Church* (Minneapolis: Augsburg Publishing House, 1961), p. 206. All of the ALC's Yearbooks were published by Augsburg; therefore, in subsequent notes for ALC Yearbooks, the publisher is not cited.

[3] *1964 Yearbook of The American Lutheran Church*, p. 280.

Continuity in leadership

The ALC's Board of Pensions experienced substantial continuity of leadership during its 27 years of operation.[4] Mr. Harlan N. Rye was the board's first executive director, effective January 1, 1961. He previously had served the pension program of the Evangelical Lutheran Church, beginning in 1954. Prior to that time, he was a banker in Forest City, Iowa. Mr. Rye retired as the ALC board's executive director on January 31, 1963.[5]

The Rev. George H. Berkheimer succeeded Mr. Rye as executive director. He had served as executive secretary of the Board of Pensions of the United Lutheran Church in America from 1955 until the ULCA merged into the Lutheran Church in America and the LCA's pension program began operation in 1963. Pr. Berkheimer retired on June 30, 1976, and was succeeded by the Rev. Henry F. Treptow. Pr. Treptow came to the position of what was by then called executive secretary[6] from previous service on the staff of the ALC's Board of Trustees. He served through the conclusion of the ALC's life as a separate church body on December 31, 1987.

Overseeing the terms of the ALC pension and benefits program were nine members of the board who were elected to six-year terms at the ALC's biennial general convention.

Two plans—clergy and lay

The ALC of 1960 actually created two separate but similar pension plans—one for clergy and the other for lay church workers. The initial contribution rate by congregations or other salary-paying organizations for the pension and benefits of clergy was set at 12 percent "of the salary of the member." In the case of clergy who lived in parsonages, "salary" was defined as the fixed salary plus the equivalent of 15 percent of that amount. (That

---

[4] The pension unit in The American Lutheran Church originally was known as the "Division for Pensions." In a restructuring of the ALC's national office that was approved by the 1972 ALC General Convention, the unit was identified as a "service board" and was called, effective in 1974, the "Board of Pensions." For the sake of simplicity and clarity in this text, all references to the pension unit use the terminology of the ALC's later years, Board of Pensions.

[5] *Reports and Actions*, Second General Convention of The American Lutheran Church, Columbus, Ohio, October 21-27, 1964 (Augsburg Publishing House), p. 404. All of the minutes of ALC General Conventions were published by Augsburg Publishing House. Therefore, hereinafter, the publisher is not cited for the ALC's minutes.

[6] The title was shifted from "executive director" to "executive secretary" in a reorganization of the ALC's national office, as approved by the 1972 ALC General Convention and implemented in 1974.

calculation for those in parsonages was raised in 1969 from 15 percent to 25 percent and then to 30 percent in 1981.) For clergy not in parsonages, the contribution amount was based on the fixed salary plus the total of the housing allowance.[8]

Pastors were not required to make payments, but they could do so as additional contributions for their pension accounts.[9] Up to 20 percent of a pastor's salary could be diverted for a pension annuity, including the percentage allocated to the pastor's pension account from the congregation's contribution.[10] In addition, pastors who lived in parsonages were encouraged to urge their congregations to purchase on their behalf a tax-deferred annuity to serve as a "housing equity account," since they would lack the opportunity to build equity in a home. Eventually, that annuity could help pastors provide for their own housing in retirement.[11]

The contribution rate for the lay plan also initially was 12 percent of the individual's salary. Unlike the clergy plan, the lay participant was required to contribute three percent of the individual's salary and the employer, nine percent.[12]

For assets in both the clergy and lay pension plans, a balanced fund was used, with a combination of equities and fixed-income instruments. An interest-crediting rate was established annually by the ALC's Board of Pensions to determine the pace of growth of the fund for members.[13]

Of the 12 percent contribution rate in the mid-1960s, 8.5 percent was allocated for pension purposes, 1.5 percent for family-protection benefits, and 2 percent for major medical coverage.[14] The contribution rate was adjusted in succeeding years to cover costs, especially the increased expenses

---

[8] "Pension Plan for The American Lutheran Church," *Reports and Actions*, Constituting Convention of The American Lutheran Church, Minneapolis, Minn., April 22-23, 1960, p. 102.

[9] "The New Pension Plan for Clergymen," The American Lutheran Church, Minneapolis, Minn., 1961, p. 3.

[10] *1963 Annual Report: Pension Plan*, The American Lutheran Church, Minneapolis, Minn.

[11] *1982 Annual Report*, Board of Pensions of The American Lutheran Church, Minneapolis, Minn., p. 4.

[12] *Reports and Actions*, 1960, p. 109.

[13] *Reports and Actions*, Sixth General Convention of The American Lutheran Church, Minneapolis, Minn., October 4-10, 1972, pp. 683, 692-693, 701-702, and 853.

[14] *Reports and Actions*, Fourth General Convention of The American Lutheran Church, Omaha, Neb., October 16-22, 1968, p. 333.

for medical care. By 1982, 8 percent was devoted to pension accounts, 0.75 percent for reserve purposes, 0.75 percent for family protection benefits, and 6.5 percent for major medical, dental, and disability coverage, for a total contribution rate of 16 percent. That was raised to 18 percent by 1984 when 9 percent was allocated to pension accounts, 0.25 percent for protection benefits, and 8.75 percent for medical, dental, and disability coverage.[15]

The plan was amended in the early 1980s to specify that no less than 9 percent of the member's salary was to be submitted for the individual's basic pension account.[16] A higher amount could be allocated, however, by action of the Board of Pensions. In 1987, for instance, 12 percent was designated for the pension plan.[17]

New health insurance

Health-care coverage was a new element in the ALC's pension and benefits program. Within U.S. society, health insurance became an increasingly widespread phenomenon in the years following World War II. Even before that era, paying for medical care and especially hospital stays had become a concern.

As the demand for health care increased in the United States, new payment plans were developed. A precursor to Blue Cross was established in 1929 by a group of teachers in Dallas, Texas. They contracted with Baylor University Hospital for up to 21 days of hospitalization for a fixed annual rate of $6. Pre-paid hospital plans increased throughout the country, even during the Great Depression of the 1930s.

Because Blue Cross initially was a program of hospitals, the plan did not face the regular insurance requirements for reserves. As the program's popularity spread, physicians moved toward a similar pre-paid program that became known in 1946 as Blue Shield. Both Blue Cross and Blue Shield emerged because commercial insurance companies in the first half of the twentieth century had been reluctant to offer health insurance.

---

[15] *Reports and Actions*, Twelfth General Convention of The American Lutheran Church, Moorhead, Minn., October 17-23, 1984, p. 198.

[16] GC82.8.31, *Reports and Actions*, Eleventh General Convention of The American Lutheran Church, San Diego, Calif., September 6-12, 1982, p. 1165-1166. The increase of one percent in the minimum pension-contribution rate from eight percent to nine percent of defined compensation was made optional for 1983 and required, beginning January 1, 1984.

[17] *1987 Annual Report*, Board of Pensions of The American Lutheran Church, Minneapolis, Minn., p. 2.

That reluctance shifted to eagerness when companies saw that the risk of "adverse selection"—that is, coverage sought only by the very ill—could be avoided by offering health insurance only to groups of employed workers.

The trend toward health coverage for employees was helped by a 1949 ruling of the National Labor Relations Board. The board ruled in a dispute between the United Steelworkers Union and Inland Steel Company that the term "wages" could be understood as including pension and insurance benefits. Thus, when the union negotiated for wages, benefit plans also could be considered. That ruling was affirmed by the Seventh Circuit of the U.S. Court of Appeals[18] and later by the U.S. Supreme Court. The decision gave substantial impetus to employment-based health insurance. In addition, a 1954 revision in the Internal Revenue Service Code aided the trend. The change in the code meant that employer contributions to employee health plans were exempt from employee taxable income. By the end of the decade of the 1950s, nearly three-fourths of Americans were covered under some form of private health insurance.[19]

In 1945, President Harry S. Truman proposed to the U.S. Congress establishment of a national health-insurance program. A similar possibility had been suggested in 1935 for inclusion in the Social Security Act, but was withdrawn before consideration of the final legislation. An amendment to add health insurance to Social Security was introduced in 1943 and again in subsequent sessions until rejected finally in 1949.[20] The issue continued to be the focus of periodic debate throughout the remainder of the twentieth century and into the twenty-first century. Emerging from one period of that discussion was the Medicare legislation that was signed into law by President Lyndon B. Johnson on July 30, 1965. Part A of the Medicare program provided a compulsory hospital-insurance program in which individuals were enrolled upon reaching age 65. Part B offered subsidized coverage for the services of physicians.

---

[18] See Inland Steel Co. v. NLRB, 170 F. 2d 247, Seventh Circuit of the U.S. Court of Appeals, 1948.

[19] Melissa Thomasson, "Health Insurance in the United States," http://eh.net/encyclopedica/article/thomasson.insuranced.health.us, pp. 1-13.

[20] Provisions for national health insurance was deleted from President Franklin D. Roosevelt's proposal that led to the 1935 Social Security Act. The Murray-Wagner-Dingall bill was introduced in the U.S. Congress in 1943 and in subsequent congressional sessions in the 1940s. The measure, which ultimately was rejected in 1949, would have established nationalized health insurance for all U.S. citizens.

Within this context, the framers of the ALC pension and benefits program saw the need to include health-insurance coverage for pastors, other church workers, and their dependants, especially those facing catastrophic medical expenses.

Included "major medical coverage"

The ALC's major medical program covered those in active service. Eligible members initially were reimbursed for 80 percent of all covered medical expenses in excess of $300 during a benefit year. In its first biennium of operation, the program paid 423 claims for a total of $210,939—an amount reflecting the substantially lower medical costs in the 1960s versus the years of the early twenty-first century.

Initially, the ALC's medical program did not extend to retirees,[21] but the Board of Pensions was directed in 1962 to explore medical coverage for retirees.[22] Retiree coverage was inaugurated in 1965. The medical costs of those who had retired under the post-1961 ALC plan were covered by funds received through the two-percent medical contribution rate for active members. For those who had retired under predecessor plans, retiree medical coverage was provided by a $130,000 allocation in the ALC's benevolence budget.[23]

Beginning in the mid-1960s, participants in the ALC Major Medical Plan could elect to pay for the ALC supplemental program to cover unreimbursed medical expenses. The program was handled for the ALC by a commercial insurance company.[24] Often congregations purchased the supplement on behalf of their pastors. Eventually, the commercial supplemental program was terminated.[25] Instead, the ALC itself initiated in 1983 a supplemental plan of its own with key features of the earlier plan. The new plan covered 20 percent of the first $11,600 of expenses above the annual deductible of the Major Medical-Dental Plan.[26]

Effective February 1, 1977, dental coverage was added to the ALC major medical program. With the addition of dental coverage, the deductible was

---

[21] *Reports and Actions*, First General Convention of The American Lutheran Church, Milwaukee, Wis., October 18-24, 1962, p. 326.

[22] GC62.22.44, *Reports and Actions*, 1962, p. 331.

[23] GC64.27.133 and GC64.27.136, *Reports and Actions*, 1964, pp. 406-407.

[24] *Reports and Actions*, 1982, p. 984.

[25] *Reports and Actions*, 1982, p. 986.

[26] *1984 Annual Report*, Board of Pensions of The American Lutheran Church, Minneapolis, Minn., p. 6.

set at $250 per year per family ($150 for those over 65 who were covered under Medicare). After the deductible, 85 percent of the first $2,500 was paid by the ALC major medical and dental program in 1977, 90 percent from $2,500 to $10,000, and 95 percent above $10,000.[27]

Concern for "family protection"

A "family-protection benefit" was part of the ALC program from its beginning. For survivors of a member who died under the age of 40, the death benefit amounted to 18 months of what had been the member's salary up to the maximum of $7,500. The benefit decreased with the age of the member at the time of death: 40-49, 15 months up to $6,500; 50-59, 12 months, $5,500; 60-64, nine months, $4,500; 65-69, six months, $3,000; and 70 or older, three months up to $1,500 but no less than $500.[28]

Based on the initial experience with the program, the family-protection benefit was increased by the ALC's first general convention to 24 months salary up to a maximum of $12,000 as a death benefit for the survivors of a member through age 39. For ages 40 through 49, the benefit allowed for 18 months salary or a maximum of $9,000. The maximum amounts were adjusted upward in subsequent years. By 1980, for example, the maximum benefit for those who died under 40 was $24,000. For those 40-44, the benefit amounted to the equivalent of 21 months salary, up to $21,000; for those 45-49, 18 months, up to $18,000; 50-54, 15 months, up to $15,000; 55-59, 12 months, up to $12,000; 60-64; nine months, up to $9,000; 65-69, six months, up to $6,000; and 70 or more, three months, up to $3,000.[29]

In the ALC's program, seminary students were covered with a death benefit of $7,500.[30] The annual premium for seminarian coverage was $7.50.[31] Later, the option of a higher benefit of $15,000 was offered for an annual contribution of $15.[32]

Any changes to the ALC's pension and other benefits program required action by a majority vote of the ALC's biennial General Convention. At least 90 days notice of proposed changes was required. Precluded were any

---

[27] GC76.6.156, *Reports and Actions*, Seventh General Convention of The American Lutheran Church, Washington, D.C., October 9-15, 1976, pp. 767-768.

[28] *Reports and Actions*, 1960, p. 106.

[29] *Reports and Actions*, 1982, p. 354.

[30] *Reports and Actions*, 1962, p. 327.

[31] *Reports and Actions*, 1962, p. 469.

[32] Report and Actions, 1968, p. 339.

amendments that would "reduce the amount of . . . accumulations already to the credit of any member."[33]

Eligible for retirement benefits

Increases in the pensions of future retirees was helped not only by the higher contribution rate to their accounts in the mid-1980s, but also by growth in the salaries of pastors. The average salary for ALC pastors grew from $14,187 in 1976 to $25,516 in 1984, the equivalent of about $50,000 in 2008 dollars.[34] (That adjusted amount was similar but slightly less than the average salary of ELCA pastors in 2008.)

Plan members could begin to receive their pension at the end of employment at age 65. When commencing retirement benefits, "the entire accumulations to the credit of the member" were "applied as the actuarial equivalent . . . to provide an age retirement annuity for the member." The member could elect a "joint-life and survivor basis" for the pension payment, with 60 percent of the member's pension continued for his widow "if the marriage took place before the member" began his pension payments.[35] If the member did not have a spouse upon commencing the annuity, the member could "select another beneficiary" if the "single-life basis" for the annuity was not chosen. Once an option was selected, no change could occur after "the effective date of the age retirement annuity."[36]

A "minimum pension" for retirees was in place from the beginning of the ALC's program. For those who retired after January 1, 1961, a minimum pension of $1,200 per year was provided by the ALC. Adjustments were made to increase the minimum pension for those who had retired under the plans of the predecessor churches in order to match those of the ALC's plan, that is, $100 a month.[37] The 1968 ALC General Convention approved an increase in this base to $125 per month. To fund that increase, the ALC assumed the liability to be paid at $700,000 over a projected 26-year period from the benevolence budget.[38]

---

[33] *Reports and Actions*, 1960, pp. 107 and 114.

[34] *1984 Annual Report: Pension Plan*, The American Lutheran Church, Minneapolis, Minn., p. 8.

[35] The word, "his," was used in the documents at the time because The American Lutheran Church did not begin ordaining women until late 1970.

[36] *Reports and Actions*, 1960, p. 103.

[37] GC62.22.48, GC62.22.49, and GC62.22.50, *Reports and Actions*, 1962, pp. 328-329 and 339-340.

[38] *Reports and Actions*, 1972, pp. 111-112.

If a member died prior to commencing retirement benefits, a minimum pension was guaranteed for the surviving widow if the couple had been married for at least 25 years. If the couple had been married less than 25 years, the widow could receive the supplement for as many years as they were married, but for a period of not less than 15 years or until the children had reached age 18. Upon any remarriage, however, the supplement was discontinued.[39] If the member married after age 65 and died leaving a widow, the widow was not eligible for the supplement.[40] Provision for a minimum pension was in place in the event that the individual's accumulations distributed as an annuity to the widow would be insufficient for the support of the surviving spouse and children.

The definition of beneficiaries was clearly a relevant matter. In 1963, 25 pastors in active service died at an average of age of 58.3 years. In the same year, 47 retired pastors died at an average age of 79.9 years, and 36 widows of pastors died at an average age of 83.1 years.[41] Ten years later, deaths were reported of 15 pastors in active service with an average age of 52.1 years and 39 retired pastors with an average age of 77.5 years. Thirty-one widows of ALC clergy died in 1973 at an average age of 81.3 years.[42] Ages at mortality continued to vary from year to year. In 1980, for instance, 20 pastors died in active service at an average of 54.2 years, while 59 retired pastors died at an average age of 79 years and 34 widows of clergy died at an average age of 84.5 years.[43]

The minimum age at which a member was permitted to commence retiree pension benefits was adjusted from age 65 to 62, effective September 1, 1965.[44]

Annual "bonus" for retirees

For those receiving their regular pension as retirees in the ALC, an annual "bonus" boosted their overall retirement income. The ALC's

[39] *Reports and Actions*, 1960, p. 104.

[40] *Reports and Actions*, 1960, p. 105.

[41] *1963 Annual Report: Pension Plan*, The American Lutheran Church, Minneapolis, Minn.

[42] *1973 Annual Report: Pension Plan*, The American Lutheran Church, Minneapolis, Minn.

[43] *1980 Annual Report*, Board of Pensions of The American Lutheran Church, Minneapolis, Minn.

[44] Joint Council Resolution 65.7.18, *Reports and Actions*, Third General Convention of The American Lutheran Church, Minneapolis, Minn., October 19-25, 1966, pp. 648-650.

pension board initiated in 1964 a policy of paying a dividend to pensioners and surviving spouses. The dividend reflected the difference between the rate of interest assumed in determining the annuity at the time of retirement and the interest crediting rate for the year. The dividend for the preceding year was paid in a lump sum on or about July 1 of the following year. The amount of the "bonus" varied significantly. For 1981, it was unusually large, amounting to 50 percent of an individual's annual annuity.[45] Other years, it was more modest than that, but still significant. For example, paid for 1969 was a dividend equal to 21.12 percent of the individual's annual pension.[46]

Provision was made for individuals who were on the active roster but were temporarily without call or doing graduate work. They could continue their eligibility for family protection, disability coverage, widow's minimum pension, and major medical benefits by making contributions equal to four percent of an assumed annual salary in 1964 of $4,000.[47] That amount was adjusted upward in succeeding years.

A special fund, supported by the ALC's benevolence budget, was maintained for chaplains serving in the military as well as federal, state, or other governmental agencies. The purpose of the "Chaplains Fund" was to assure that clergy serving as chaplains would receive retirement and other benefits, in total, comparable to those paid to plan members who served in congregations or other entities of the church. The benefits to chaplains would be provided in the event that the chaplain, due to limited duration of service, did not qualify for a governmental pension.[48]

A "Good Samaritan Fund" was included in the ALC's program. The fund provided financial assistance to retired as well as active pastors and their widows who experienced "unusual expenses" due to "serious illness or other extraordinary circumstances." Special offerings took place in congregations during the season of Advent to support the fund.[49]

Interest on accounts

Interest of 3.5 percent was credited to the accumulation in member accounts in the pension plan for 1961 and also 1962. That rate was increased

---

[45] *Reports and Actions*, 1984, p. 200.

[46] *Reports and Actions*, 1972, p. 89.

[47] *Reports and Actions*, 1964, p. 399.

[48] *Reports and Actions*, 1962, p. 329.

[49] *Reports and Actions*, 1962, p. 330.

to 4.5 percent for 1963.[50] In 1964, the crediting rate was 6 percent and in 1965, 5 percent.[51] The credited percentage varied year by year: 1966, 6 percent;[52] 1967, 5.5 percent;[53] 1968, 5.25 percent;[54] 1969, 6 percent;[55] 1970, 6 percent;[56] 1971, 6.5 percent;[57] 1972, 7.5 percent;[58] 1973, 7 percent;[59] 1974, 7 percent;[60] 1975, 7.5 percent;[61] 1976, 7.5 percent;[62] 1977, 7.5 percent;[63] 1978, 7 percent;[64] 1979, 7.5 percent;[65] 1980, 8.5 percent;[66] 1981, 9 percent;[67] 1982, 10 percent;[68] 1983, 10.5 percent;[69] 1984, 10.5 percent;[70] 1985, 10 percent;[71] 1986, 11 percent:[72] and 1987, 11 percent.[73]

Adjustment in "vesting" period

The vesting period for the ALC pension program was adjusted, effective May 1, 1986, from five years to one year of contributions. The change occurred

[50] *Reports and Actions*, 1964, p. 399.

[51] *Reports and Actions*, 1966, p. 437.

[52] *Reports and Actions*, 1968, p. 333.

[53] *Reports and Actions*, 1968, p. 333.

[54] *Reports and Actions*, Fifth General Convention of The American Lutheran Church, San Antonio, Texas, October 21-27, 1970, p. 671.

[55] *Reports and Actions*, 1970, p. 670.

[56] *Reports and Actions*, 1972, p. 88.

[57] *Reports and Actions*, 1972, p. 88.

[58] *Reports and Actions*, Seventh General Convention of The American Lutheran Church, Detroit, Mich., October 9-15, 1974, p. 204.

[59] *Reports and Actions*, 1974, p. 204.

[60] *Reports and Actions*, 1976, p. 146.

[61] *Reports and Actions*, 1976, p. 146.

[62] *Reports and Actions*, 1976, p. 212.

[63] *Reports and Actions*, Ninth General Convention of The American Lutheran Church, Moorhead, Minn., October 18-24, 1978, p. 212.

[64] *Reports and Actions*, 1980, p. 224.

[65] *Reports and Actions*, 1980, p. 224.

[66] *Reports and Actions*, 1982, p. 248.

[67] *Reports and Actions*, 1982, p. 248.

[68] *Reports and Actions*, 1984, p. 199.

[69] *Reports and Actions*, 1984, p. 199.

[70] *Reports and Actions*, Thirteenth General Convention of The American Lutheran Church, Minneapolis, Minn., August 23-29, 1986, p. 216.

[71] *Reports and Actions*, 1986, p. 216.

[72] *1986 Annual Report*, Board of Pensions of The American Lutheran Church, Minneapolis, Minn.

[73] *Reports and Actions*, Closing Convention of The American Lutheran Church, Columbus, Ohio, April 29, 1987, p. 48.

for the transition to the ELCA's Pension and Other Benefits Program and also as a result of provisions in the Tax Reform Act of 1986.[74]

In the mid-1960s, 96 percent of the ALC's ordained ministers were members of the ALC pension and benefits program for clergy—a total of 4,980. At the same time, the ALC's Lay Workers Pension Plan had 843 members.[75] The percentage of clergy participation reached 98.4 percent by 1972,[76] and by 1978, 98.9 percent.[77]

When the Social Security program was opened in 1955 to participation by clergy, Lutherans churches welcomed that development. Initially, however, clergy had to opt to enter the program. That changed when Social Security coverage was made compulsory in 1968. Clergy could file a claim for exception, asserting conscientious objection on the basis of religious principles to receiving benefits from public insurance.[78] Some Lutheran clergy did so, although Lutheran theology really does not provide a basis for such an objection to government-sponsored coverage.

Question of "equal pensions"

"Equal pensions" became a hot topic of debate in some ALC conventions, just as had been the case in other church bodies, such as the United Lutheran Church in America in 1945. The same issue was raised in the Lutheran Church in America, and again later in the ALC as well as early in the life of the ELCA.

The issue of equalizing pensions was referred by a 1968 ALC convention resolution to the Board of Pensions for study. The resolution declared:

> WHEREAS, many pastors of The ALC receive very small pensions because they have served in small parishes or world missions; therefore, be it
>
> *Resolved*, that an equal pension, based on tenure, be given to all retired pastors of The ALC.[79]

The report submitted by the Board of Pensions to the ALC's 1970 convention highlighted the provision for a minimum pension for all

---

[74] *Reports and Actions*, 1987, p. 47.

[75] *Reports and Actions*, 1966, p. 436.

[76] *Reports and Actions*, 1972, p. 87.

[77] *Reports and Actions*, 1978, p. 211.

[78] *Reports and Actions*, 1968, p. 338.

[79] GC68.19.182, *Reports and Actions*, 1968, p. 344.

retired pastors. The response also disputed the equating of service in small parishes with limited pensions, claiming that "the primary reason a few retired pastors are receiving a small pension (or possibly none at all) is *not* because they 'served in small parishes or world missions' but rather because they did not avail themselves fully (or at all) of the pension plan offered them."[80] The report further declared:

> The church will always have these "loners" or "independent actors" within it. This is one of the prices we pay for our individual freedom. Certainly this freedom ought not be removed, but it then becomes necessary to ask two questions, namely:
>
> 1. Should pastors who have had the opportunity of participating in the pension plan but who elected not to do so expect the church to provide a pension for them in retirement?
>
> 2. Should the church feel under obligation to provide a pension for such pastors?[81]

Few pastors remain in lower salary brackets for their entire pastoral ministry, the report noted, just as few pastors are in higher salary brackets for all their years of service. Thus, the Board of Pensions concluded that "an 'equal pension based on tenure' does not appear to be a desirable feature for the pension plan."[82]

Neither the content nor the curt, crisp tone of the report met with favor at the ALC's 1970 convention. A resolution was approved that criticized the report as merely "a judgment by that board and not a detailed study citing research or the desires of either pastors or congregations." The convention instructed "the Board of Pensions to prepare a study on 'Equal Pensions' which includes the involvement of those who would be affected by equal pensions."[83]

This official rebuke was reflected in the subsequent report presented to the ALC's 1972 convention:

> The Board of Pensions presented the original study on this matter [in 1970] in all sincerity. Perhaps the area of misunderstanding as to the adequacy of the study arises in an endeavor to relate the philosophy of a pension plan with the practical operation of a pension plan.

---

[80] *Reports and Actions,* 1970, p. 683.

[81] *Reports and Actions,* 1970, pp. 683-684.

[82] *Reports and Actions,* 1970, p. 685.

[83] GC70.24.106, *Reports and Actions,* 1970, p. 682.

The board admits that in its study it dealt mainly with the latter. That was done deliberately and for good reason. The philosophic approach to a pension plan, that is, the kind of pension plan the church is to have, is not the prerogative of the Board of Pensions. The church has rightly retained this authority for itself. . . .

It may be of interest to note that none of the pension plans of the major Protestant denominations in the United States operate on a equal pension basis. It is particularly significant that neither of our sister Lutheran bodies follows such a procedure. If we are in earnest about closer ties with the Lutheran Church in America and The Lutheran Church–Missouri Synod, then a major shift in pension policy [to an equalized pension] . . . should be questioned very seriously.

Your board would submit that the question is not a reserve money-purchase pension plan versus an equal pension plan, but rather a reserve money-purchase pension plan with an adequate minimum pension support base versus an equal pension plan.[84]

Interestingly, the report did not appear to show the scope of research that had been demanded in the action of the 1970 convention. Nonetheless, the ALC's 1972 convention concurred in a resolution that had been recommended by the Board of Pensions:

WHEREAS, the Board of Pensions has studied the issue referred to it; and

WHEREAS, the board is firmly of the opinion that a change in the basic pension policy of the church is not advisable at this time; and

WHEREAS, the board believes that the minimum pension approach as a supplement to provide an adequate retirement pension is sound; therefore, be it

Resolved, that . . . the pension plan of the church be continued as a reserve money-purchase type plan; and, be it further

Resolved, that periodic review be made both of the adequacy of the minimum pension base and of the ability of the church to finance a higher base.[85]

---

[84] *Reports and Actions*, 1972, pp. 111-112.

[85] GC72.7.47, *Reports and Actions*, 1972, p. 897.

The issue of "equalized pension" was not the only question referred by the 1968 ALC General Convention to the Board of Pensions. Another 1968 resolution urged that study be undertaken "of the present and future financial condition" of the few "pastors in active service" who "are not members of the pension plan" and who "may be near retirement without adequate means of support."[86] At the same convention, a resolution was submitted that focused on the few pastors who did not participate fully in the pension plan prior to retirement and, therefore, did not meet "the eligibility requirements for a minimum pension." The resolution, which also was referred to the Board of Pensions, urged that such pastors be granted $50 per month "as a token of concern" and appreciation for their "faithful and diligent service for many years."[87]

The Board of Pensions reported to the 1970 ALC General Convention that "it would not be feasible for the church to provide financial assistance on a continuing basis to pastors who . . . elected not to participate in the pension plan."[88]

The resolution of 1968 on a $50 per month grant also drew a response from the Board of Pensions, noting the concern was "highly commendable" but not feasible to implement. Such an action "would be a basic departure" from the program, the board reported, adding that "it would not be advisable for the church to establish other criteria for any amount of minimum pension than those originally approved" for the pension plan. "All of the pastors *could* have participated in the pension plan of a predecessor church body and thus qualified for a minimum pension upon retirement. The fact that they failed to do so . . . is the *only* reason they are not now receiving a minimum pension."[89]

Recurring debate on "equalized pensions"

Notwithstanding debate on the topic in the late 1960s, the question of "equalized pensions" was raised again in a resolution at the 1980 ALC General Convention. The arguments in that 1980 resolution also would be made in somewhat varied forms more than a decade later in the ELCA. That 1980 ALC resolution declared:

> WHEREAS, pastors and lay workers who serve in smaller parishes generally receive smaller pensions, not because they are less faithful, but because they have smaller incomes; and

[86] GC68.22.189, *Reports and Actions*, 1968, p. 345.

[87] GC68.22.190, *Reports and Actions*, 1968, p. 346.

[88] *Reports and Actions*, 1970, p. 692.

[89] *Reports and Actions*, 1970, pp. 688-689. Italic emphasis is in the original text.

WHEREAS, our Lord values his servants by their faithfulness, not their incomes; and

WHEREAS, equal pensions would be fairer than the present unequal pensions, and would be a clear, concrete witness that we want to value our servants by the standards of the Lord, not those of the world; and

WHEREAS, a gradual process of equalization would affect least those nearest their pension years; therefore, be it

Resolved, that the Board of Pensions study the possibility of gradually equalizing pensions, and bring its report, with both pros and cons, to the next general convention.[90]

The 1980 ALC General Convention did ask the Board of Pensions to study "the possibility of gradually equalizing pensions." A report on the matter was to be submitted to the subsequent convention.[91]

In 1982, the ALC Board of Pensions recommended that the matter not be pursued. The response was based on advice from legal counsel, indicating that such an equalization plan likely "would not qualify for tax-favored treatment under Sub-chapter D of Chapter 1 of the Internal Revenue Code of 1954, as amended. . . ." Severely adverse tax implications for clergy could result.[92] Therefore, the Board of Pensions submitted to the convention a resolution that rejected equalization. That resolution of the pension board read, in part:

WHEREAS, the Pension Plan for Clergy and the Pension Plan for Lay Workers of The American Lutheran Church is an individually salary-based plan, recognizing the privilege of each of the 5,600 ALC employers, who sponsor workers in the plans, to determine their own salary levels; and

WHEREAS, low pension benefits among ALC workers since 1961 have been and are being augmented currently through the Level Minimum Pension and Vacancy Contribution Programs;[93]

---

[90] Reports and Actions, Tenth General Convention of The American Lutheran Church, Minneapolis, Minn., October 1-7, 1980, p. 1037

[91] GC80.7.165, Reports and Actions, 1980, p. 1037.

[92] "Letter from Mr. Hubert V. Forcier, Esq., Faegre and Benson, to the Rev. Henry F. Treptow, executive secretary, Board of Pensions," March 11, 1982, Reports and Actions, 1982, pp. 884-885.

[93] Under the ALC plan, a congregation without a regularly called pastor paid an amount equal to eight percent of the defined compensation of the previously called pastor during the vacancy. That contributed was credited to the Minimum Pension Fund.

currently $204.26 a month for retired clergy and lay workers; $122.55 a month for eligible surviving spouses; and through the Dividend Program since 1964, all earned annuitants, including minimum pensioners, for instance, received an annual dividend equal to 50 percent of their pension income during 1981; and

WHEREAS, it is the position of the Board of Pensions that such additional supplements, if desirable, should be made available by the church body through its legislative process; and

WHEREAS, the Board of Pensions, upon consultation with and the provision of a written opinion by its legal counsel, has been informed that "a level pension benefit unrelated to the ministers' compensation . . . would not quality for tax-favored treatment under Sub-chapter D of Chapter 1 of the Internal Revenue Code of 1954, as amended . . ."; therefore, be it

Resolved, that the Board of Pensions inform the General Convention of The American Lutheran Church that the consideration "of the possibility of gradually equalizing pensions" shall not be pursued further. . . .[94]

The 1982 ALC General Convention voted to receive the resolution of the Board of Pensions "as an adequate response to the 1980 General Convention action" on equalizing pensions.[95]

Reciprocal pension arrangements

Early in the life of the ALC, the Board of Pensions established reciprocal pension relations with the Board of Pensions of the Lutheran Church in America. Under the arrangement, members of the LCA ministerial pension and death benefit plan could transfer their ministerial standing and combined pension accumulations into the ALC's plan. Likewise, ALC pastors could shift into the LCA plan and carry with them their years of service for "satisfying waiting period requirements for eligibility" for disability, minimum widow pension, family protection, and major medical benefits.[96]

Like other church pension boards in the United States, the ALC's Board of Pensions sought and received a "letter ruling" from the Internal

---

[94] *Reports and Actions*, 1982, p. 1164.

[95] GC82.8.29, *Reports and Actions*, 1982, pp. 1164-1165.

[96] *Reports and Actions*, 1964, p. 399.

Revenue Service (IRS) regarding clergy housing. The request was made in the midst of various changes in the federal tax code. The IRS ruling granted permission for the board, under Section 107 of the IRS code, to designate as "housing allowance" a portion of the pension paid to retired ALC clergy from the basic pension account. During 1980 and 1981, the board designated 50 percent of the pension and dividend paid in each of those years for housing purposes. This meant that, to the extent that money was expended to provide housing, such funds did not need to be reported for federal income tax purposes. Then, following the pattern of other pension boards and IRS letter rulings, the board began designating up to 100 percent of the pension monies received by clergy retirees. Church pension boards were the sole entities that could designate housing allowances for retired clergy.[97] Clergy, however, could claim only the actual housing costs as a tax deduction.

Divestment debates

As was the case in many churches beginning in the 1970s and continuing in the ensuing years, intense debates erupted on the question of divestment from corporations doing business in South Africa (see also Chapter 5). The goal of those urging divestment was to oppose the practice of apartheid in that country and bring to an end rule by the White minority. In the ALC, the pressure built in the late 1970s to force a change in the investment policies. District conventions and the biennial general convention received hotly worded resolutions on the topic. Hours upon hours were consumed by floor debates. Representatives speaking on behalf of both the ALC's Board of Pensions and Board of Trustees emphasized the fiduciary responsibility of the church for the management of funds invested on behalf of future retirees. Those seeking a change of policy argued for a strong moral statement and clear action to oppose the oppression of South Africa's Black majority as well as the Black majority in South Africa-occupied Namibia.

The 1980 ALC convention voted to affirm "divestiture" as "the most legitimate strategy in opposing apartheid and the most effective consequence of a declaration of *status confessionis*" by the church.[98] At the

---

[97] *1987 Annual Report*, Board of Pensions of The American Lutheran Church, Minneapolis, Minn., p. 4.

[98] The term *status confessionis* means a matter inherent to the basics of the faith of the church. The call for divestment was submitted from the floor as a substitute motion and approved on a vote of 447-331 (*The Lutheran Standard*, October 28, 1980, p. 15) as GC80.4.56, *Reports and Actions*, 1980, pp. 983-984.

same time, the convention urged that such "disinvestment take place in a prudent manner that is consistent with legal requirements. . . ."[99]

Another important development in the divestment battles occurred at the same convention when a report was received on what was characterized as the "equivalency" principle. The report emphasized, "Only in those cases where economic considerations are equal—as between two or more securities issues under study—may the investment decision be based on social considerations."[100] The statement helped guide subsequent steps in the divestment saga.

On the basis of the "equivalency" principle, the ALC Board of Trustees in May 1981 adopted a resolution that said, ". . . in the buying and selling of securities, where, in the judgment of the Board of Trustees, the economic considerations are equal as between two or more securities issues under study, the Board of Trustees will, where applicable, choose in favor of the company not doing business in South Africa. . . ."[101]

The 1980 convention's call for divestment prompted the resignation of one of the members of the ALC's Board of Trustees, the board that had fiduciary responsibility for pension investments. Mr. Roger A. Severson, a Minneapolis banking executive, said that his conscience did not permit him to challenge the desires of the church "by refusing to act as we have been directed." Nor did his conscience allow him to follow the directive by engaging in "a series of improper and possibly wrongful acts and, by so doing, expose the church or its servants to significant legal and financial exposure." At the time of his resignation, he was serving as vice chair of the Board of Trustees.[102] Mr. Severson's letter of resignation reflected the dilemma that various trustees felt regarding their fiduciary duties for pension investments.

The "equivalency" principle, which had been reported to the 1980 convention, was affirmed in the subsequent biennium. The 1982 ALC General Convention voted to advise "the Board of Trustees that its efforts to divest stocks in corporations doing business in South Africa" was deemed "an adequate response to the 1980 American Lutheran Church General

---

[99] GC80.4.58, *Reports and Actions*, 1980, p. 985.

[100] *Reports and Actions*, 1980, p. 200. The dashes were added in this sentence for clarity in reading this quotation; they did not appear in the original text.

[101] *Reports and Actions*, 1982, p. 176

[102] "ALC trustee resigns in wake of convention divestment vote," *The Lutheran Standard*, November 25, 1980, p. 18.

Convention resolution (GC80.4.58), and to commend the board for its efforts."[103]

By August 1, 1982, the ALC's Board of Trustees reported holding 14 South Africa-related stocks, down from 27 two years earlier. The issue that had prompted "lengthy and sometimes rancorous debate" in earlier conventions was barely an issue by 1982, according to a report on the convention.[104]

Ready for new program

The scope and strength of the ALC's pension and benefits program were combined with those similar qualities in the pension and benefits program of the Lutheran Church in America to form a solid foundation for the start of the ELCA's Board of Pensions on January 1, 1988.

---

[103] GC82.11.116, *Reports and Actions*, 1982, p. 1213.

[104] *The Lutheran Standard*, October 1, 1982, p. 35.

CHAPTER 13

LCA Plan Wrestled With Mixed Practices Of Past

D r. Franklin Clark Fry—in his January 1957 letter on "the state of the church"—expressed regret that one large Lutheran church merger was not on the immediate horizon.[1] Two years earlier, the United Lutheran Church in America, of which Dr. Fry was then president, and the Augustana Lutheran Church had invited all Lutherans in North America to "consider such an organic union as will give real evidence of our unity in faith, and to proceed to draft a constitution and devise organizational procedures to effect union." The invitation promptly was rejected by The Lutheran Church–Missouri Synod and the Joint Union Committee of the American Lutheran Conference. That committee was preparing for the 1960 formation of The American Lutheran Church.[2]

Dr. Fry addressed with sadness the unfolding history of continuing divisions among Lutherans:

> Rails were laid that will run far into the future; their direction looks as if it is firmly set for a long time to come. New boundary lines were traced, crisscrossing in a deplorable and even sinful way over the broad Lutheran plains of this continent; substantial stone fences are being built on them, higher and higher.[3]

From that point in 1957, 30 years would pass before a new pathway would be charted for greater Lutheran unity.

Representatives of the Augustana Lutheran Church and the United Lutheran Church in America (ULCA) worked with counterparts from

---

[1] Johannes Knudsen, *The Formation of the Lutheran Church in America* (Philadelphia: Fortress Press, 1978), p. 11.

[2] E. Clifford Nelson, ed., *The Lutherans in North America* (Philadelphia: Fortress Press, 1975), p. 506.

[3] Knudsen, p. 11.

the American Evangelical Lutheran Church and the Finnish Evangelical Lutheran Church in the Joint Commission on Lutheran Unity. Emerging from the commission's efforts were plans for the Lutheran Church in America (LCA), which was constituted at Cobo Hall in Detroit, Mich., June 25–July 1, 1962. The LCA began operation on January 1, 1963.

From its start, the LCA was clearly more a church body and less a federation of synods than had been the pattern of the predecessor ULCA.[4] The unified, churchly heritage of the Augustana Lutheran Church was carried forward in that way. In many other respects, however, the LCA reflected the ULCA's ecclesial "culture."

At the time of the 1962 merger, the ULCA was the largest of the merging church bodies and had 5,125 ordained ministers and 2,495,763 baptized members in 4,677 congregations. The second largest was the Augustana Lutheran Church, with 1,353 ordained ministers and 629,547 baptized members in 1,268 congregations. In the Finnish Evangelical Lutheran Church were 105 ordained ministers and 36,274 baptized members in 153 congregations, while the American Evangelical Lutheran Church had 84 ordained ministers and 23,808 baptized members in 76 congregations.[5]

Key contributors in shaping the details of the LCA's pension and other benefits program were the Rev. George H. Berkheimer, then executive secretary of the ULCA's Board of Pensions, Mr. L. Edwin Wang, then executive secretary of the Augustana Pension and Aid Fund, and Mr. Robert J. Myers, then chief actuary of the Social Security Administration and a trustee of the ULCA's Board of Pensions.[6] Given his expertise, Mr. Myers served as the primary architect of the LCA's pension and benefits plans.[7] Throughout almost all of the quarter century of the LCA's operation, he was a trustee of the Board of Pensions and even served as the board's acting president in 1987 following Mr. Wang's retirement in the spring

---

[4] Knudsen, p. 39.

[5] *Yearbook, 1963*, Lutheran Church in America (Philadelphia, Pa.: Board of Publication of the LCA), p. 203.

[6] *Minutes*, First Meeting of the Subcommittee on Pensions of the Joint Commission on Lutheran Unity, George F. Berkheimer, secretary, July 24, 1957, p. 6. See also Knudsen, p. 115. Mr. Robert J. Myers was the chief actuary for the Social Security Administration from 1947 to 1970. He served as an LCA pension trustee from 1962-1968, 1970-1980, and 1982-1987.

[7] L. Edwin Wang, "Transcript of Oral History Interview," which was conducted by Franklin L. Jensen in Minneapolis on October 22, 1986, p. 10.

of that year. Mr. Myers also was elected at the constituting of the ELCA to serve an initial term, 1987-1991, on the board of trustees of the ELCA Board of Pensions.

Early in the deliberations that led to the LCA's formation, agreement was reached that responsibility for administering a pension program "shall be the prerogative of the general body." At the September 1957 meeting of the Joint Commission on Lutheran Unity, the decision was made "that the pension plan of the merged church shall be the money-purchase plan [with mandatory annuitization] on an actuarial basis." Contributions were to come from both the pastors and the congregations or organizations that they served.[8]

Unlike The American Lutheran Church of 1960 in which the four merging churches had contributory pension plans in place, only two of the four churches forming the LCA had such plans.

Augustana plan

The Augustana Pension and Aid Fund was a money-purchase plan that operated on an actuarial basis. The plan had minimum pension guarantees that had been funded completely by 1957. Eligible for participation in the contributory plan that began on January 1, 1938, were pastors, lay missionaries, and professors, teachers, and lay administrative officers at Augustana schools. The plan required member contributions of three percent of salary, plus a choice of methods for paying a death-benefit charge (an additional one-half percent salary assessment or a fixed sum determined by age for the premium cost of a $1,000 life policy paid up at age 65). The plan member's contribution was credited to the individual's account, but the congregation's or employer's contributions and interest earnings in excess of that allocated to the member's account were used to provide:

(1)   disability pensions of $1,200 a year to age 65;

(2)   basic pensions of $780 yearly to plan members with 30 years of service who were disabled or retired prior to July 1, 1956;

(3)   basic pensions of $600 yearly to plan members for 30 years of service who were disabled or retired after July 1, 1956 (on the assumption of coverage by Social Security);

(4)   basic pensions of $420 yearly to widows of plan members who were disabled or retired prior to July 1, 1956;

---

[8] Knudsen, p. 116.

(5)   basic pensions of $300 yearly to widows of plan members who were disabled or retired after July 1, 1956;

(6)   grants for children of deceased plan members of $100 yearly until age 18;

(7)   lump sum death benefits of $6,000 for plan members age 45 and under; $5,000 for age 46 to 51; $4,000 age 51 to 56; $3,000 age 56 to 61; $2,000 age 61 to 66; and $1,000 age 66 and above;

(8)   a waiver of pension assessment and death benefit premiums during a period of disability;

(9)   operating expenses paid from the congregation or employer contribution rate;

(10)   contribution to a contingencies fund; and

(11)   allocation of the balance from the contributions of congregations or employers in equal amounts to accounts of qualified plan members, but the allocation did not vest with the plan member. This represented a degree of socialization or equalization in pensions eventually paid.

The Augustana Pension and Aid Fund also included a "Relief Fund" financed from designated offerings. This fund provided financial assistance to plan members and their families in extraordinary need.[9]

ULCA plan

The Board of Pensions of the United Lutheran Church in America also operated a money-purchase plan on an actuarial basis. The plan, which was started on January 1, 1945, required a member contribution of four percent of salary, all of which was applied to the member's account. The plan also specified that congregations and employing organizations had to contribute eight percent of the plan member's salary, of which seven percent was credited to the individual's account, and the remaining one percent divided evenly between coverage of expenses of the fund and a contingency fund. Eligible for participation in the ULCA's plan were all clergy and all lay missionaries.

A separate lay pension plan existed for lay employees of ULCA church organizations, institutions, and congregations. That lay plan called for

---

[9] *Minutes*, Subcommittee on Pensions, July 24, 1957, pp. 1-3.

contributions by plan members of four percent of salary, less what the employee paid for Social Security coverage. Congregations or employing entities paid eight percent of salary less the employer's portion of the Social Security tax. A group life insurance plan for lay employees was provided. The benefit was based on the member's salary and ranged at the time of death from $2,000 to $7,000. The premium cost was shared at a rate of two-thirds from the employer and one-third from the employee per year.

The ULCA also operated a declining term Family Protection Plan, with death benefits ranging from $7,000 descending to $500, depending on age. Cost of that plan to members was $36 a year. Retired pastors paid $18 a year for coverage, as did seminarians.

The ULCA adopted a revised pension program as of January 1, 1957, which included provision for minimum pensions that were partially funded. A minimum annual pension of $1,200 was established in 1957 for clergy and missionaries who were on the pension roll as of June 30, 1956, including those who were part of the contributory plan begun in the mid-1940s and the non-contributory plan in place prior to that time. That minimum pension was to increase to $1,300 in 1959, $1,400 in 1960, and $1,500 in 1961. Widows of plan members received one-half the amount specified for the deceased spouse as a guaranteed minimum.

Further, a minimum annual pension of $900 was provided for all eligible retirees who were 51 years or older as of July 1, 1947, and who retired after July 30, 1956. The reason for the lower amount was the assumption of coverage under the Social Security program first opened in 1955 to clergy participation.

Widows of such plan members received $450 a year as a guaranteed minimum. For children, a grant of $100 a year was provided to age 18.

The pension benefit for those who had been part of the earlier non-contributory plan was financed from income earned on an endowment fund dating from the 1920s and 1930s and also from an annual appropriation from the ULCA's churchwide budget. That appropriation by the late 1950s was approaching $800,000 a year.

An Emergency Assistance Fund was supported by contributions from individuals and congregations and used to help pension plan members in extreme need.[10]

---

[10] *Minutes*, Subcommittee on Pensions, July 24, 1957, pp. 3-5.

The two other churches

The American Evangelical Lutheran Church—unlike both the Augustana and ULCA plans—did not have a reserve plan. Benefits of $1,000 a year were paid to eligible retired or disabled clergy with a spouse. For those without a spouse, the amount was set at $750 a year. The same amount was provided to surviving spouses age 60 or more or who had children under age 17. The plan required member contributions of two percent of salary but the members had no vesting rights. Earnings from investments, gifts, and church budget allocations supported the plan. The AELC program offered no lump sum death benefit to survivors.[11]

The Finnish Evangelical Lutheran Church (also known as the Suomi Synod) had started a contributory plan and then almost immediately abandoned it. Therefore, that church body did not have a reserve pension plan either. Benefits of $600 a year were paid to eligible retired or disabled pastors. For surviving spouses, benefits were paid for as many years as the deceased pastor had served while married or until all surviving children had reached age 18. No contributions were required of members. The plan was financed by annual dues levied on congregations and by income from investments, gifts, and bequests, as well as an appropriation from the church's budget. The plan did not provide for any lump sum death benefit for survivors.[12]

By mid-1961, there were 3,650 members in the ULCA's clergy and lay plans, 1,250 in the Augustana Pension and Aid Fund, 80 in the plan for clergy of the Finnish Evangelical Lutheran Church, and 50 in the plan of the American Evangelical Lutheran Church.[13]

First executive secretary

Almost the only executive secretary (later president) of the LCA Board of Pensions was Mr. Wang. He served from the time of his appointment in 1962 until he retired in the spring of 1987, only months before the LCA Board of Pensions was merged into the ELCA Board of Pensions. Mr. Wang had moved in 1956 from a highly successful career as an insurance executive on the West Coast to lead the Augustana Pension and Aid Fund in Minneapolis. As had been the case for the Augustana fund, the office of

---

[11] *Minutes*, Subcommittee on Pensions, July 24, 1957, p. 3.

[12] *Minutes*, Subcommittee on Pensions, July 24, 1957, p. 3.

[13] *Minutes*, "Pension and Death Benefit Plan Comparison," Subcommittee on Pensions of the Joint Commission on Lutheran Unity, August 15, 1961, p. 5.

the LCA's Board of Pensions was in Minneapolis. Some 4,500 square feet was leased on the second floor of what was then known as the Pillsbury building at 608 Second Avenue South.[14]

The new LCA board elected in 1962 had 21 members—16 from the United Lutheran Church in America, four from the Augustana Lutheran Church, and one from the American Evangelical Lutheran Church. Six board members were ordained ministers and 15 were laypersons. Among them was Mr. Myers, who had played such a significant role in the program's development.

Plans established for LCA

Both a clergy pension plan and a lay pension plan were established in the LCA. The individual pastor's pension contribution was set at four percent of the pastor's salary. For those in parsonages, the four percent contribution was based on the pastor's cash salary, plus 20 percent of that salary as the value of housing. (The amount was raised to 25 percent of salary in 1966.[15])

The congregation's contribution rate for pastors was eight percent, of which one percent was used for administrative expenses and the remainder credited to the pastor's retirement account. As was the case in predecessor church bodies, the costs of pension and other benefits were defined as an expense of the congregation and not a benevolence contribution.[16]

For the lay pension plan, the member's contribution rate was two percent of salary and the employer's rate was six percent.[17]

Special assistance for those in extreme need—a concern extending back to 1831 in the General Synod and, even before that, in the Ministerium of Pennsylvania to 1783—was to be budgeted by the church body. A churchwide budget allocation also was to underwrite the costs of the minimum pension and disability provisions. That was especially significant

---

[14] Willmar Thorkelson, "New Man at Pensions," *The Lutheran* magazine, July 11, 1962 (Philadelphia, Pa.: Board of Publication of the United Lutheran Church in America), pp. 20-21.

[15] *Minutes*, Third Biennial Convention of the Lutheran Church in America, Kansas City, Mo., June 21-29, 1966 (Philadelphia, Pa.: Board of Publication), pp. 153. All of the minutes of the LCA conventions were published by the Board of Publication. Therefore, the citation of the publisher is not included in subsequent footnotes on the minutes.

[16] *Minutes*, Constituting Convention of the Lutheran Church in America, Detroit, Mich., June 28–July 1, 1962, p. 157.

[17] *Minutes*, LCA, 1962, p. 173.

for retired pastors from the American Evangelical Lutheran Church and the Finnish Evangelical Lutheran Church. After all, those churches did not come into the LCA with funded reserves in contributory pension plans like those in the Augustana Lutheran Church and the United Lutheran Church in America.[18]

New health plan

Creation of the LCA's Ministerial Health Benefits Plan represented a significant step, just as had been the case in The American Lutheran Church, beginning in 1961 (Chapter 12). There had been, however, some health plans that preceded the LCA's formation. Twenty-seven different hospitalization and medical plans that varied greatly had been operative in the synods, conferences, and districts of the merging churches.[19] Initially, the clergy health-benefit premiums were paid through benevolence funds in the LCA. The pattern later was modified, with part of the payment being the participant's responsibility.[20]

The LCA's pension and ministerial health benefits program was adjusted and refined in the years subsequent to 1962. In fact, new circumstances and various legal requirements resulted in about 300 amendments being made over the next quarter century.[21]

The importance of increased participation in the LCA pension and other benefits program was emphasized in the 1960s. In both the predecessor Augustana Lutheran Church and the ULCA in the mid-1950s, only about two-thirds of the clergy were involved in the pension plan. To foster greater participation upon the formation of the LCA, health-benefit coverage was made contingent on participation in the pension plan. By the final year of operation for the LCA's Board of Pensions, 96 percent of LCA clergy were participating in the plan.[22]

A health plan for lay church employees was available too. Unlike the design of the ministerial health plan, employers paid the premiums for lay employee coverage.[23]

---

[18] Knudsen, pp. 116-117.

[19] W. Kent Gilbert, *Commitment to Unity: A History of the Lutheran Church in America* (Philadelphia: Fortress Press, 1988), p. 110.

[20] Wang oral history, p. 7.

[21] Gilbert, p. 110.

[22] Wang oral history, p. 5.

[23] Gilbert, p. 351. See also *Minutes*, Executive Council of the Lutheran Church in America, January 25-26, 1963, pp. 322-324.

Overall program

Operated on a self-insurance basis were the: (1) Ministerial Pension and Death Benefit Plan; (2) Lay Pension Plan; (3) Ministerial Health Benefits Plan; and (4) Ministerial Short-Term Disability Income Benefit Plan. Two benefit programs were operated through purchased insurance: (1) Lay Group Insurance Plan with group life and health insurance for lay employees and their dependents; and (2) Dental Care Insurance Plan for both ministerial and lay employees and their dependents.[24]

A clergy "family-protection" death benefit was supported by a $40 premium paid annually by the congregation or employing entity for clergy. The lump sum benefit ranged from $10,000 to $1,000 according to a declining term insurance schedule based on age. Initially, for those 25 and under, $10,000 was paid, with the amount decreasing $200 per year thereafter to $1,000 for those 70 or more at the time of death.[25] In 1966, the schedule was revised, with a death benefit for 25 and under set at $16,000, decreasing $500 a year to age 40 and then $250 a year to $1,000 for age 70 and above.[26] The maximum again was raised in 1968 to $18,600 for 25 and under, declining $500 a year to age 50 and then $250 thereafter to a level of $1,100 at age 70 and above.[27] Subsequently, the maximum was raised to $25,100, decreasing at a rate of $800 a year to age 40, then $600 a year to age 50, $300 a year to age 67, and remaining thereafter at $2000.[28] Then, effective January 1, 1973, the maximum was set at $31,900 for 25 and under, decreasing at a rate of $1,000 a year to age 40, $800 a year to age 50, $400 a year to age 67, and then remaining at $2,100 thereafter.[29] The amount continued to be adjusted, with a maximum on January 1, 1976, of $43,300 for 25 and under, decreasing $1,500 a year to age 40, then $1000 a year to age 50, $500 a year to age 67, and then remaining at $2,300.[30] Still later, the benefit was adjusted to $66,000 for those 25 and

---

[24] *Minutes*, Eighth Biennial Convention of the Lutheran Church in America, Boston, Mass., July 21-28, 1976, p. 647.

[25] Article XII, "Constitution of the Ministerial Pension and Death Benefit Plan," *Minutes*, LCA, 1962.

[26] *Minutes*, LCA, 1966, p. 151.

[27] *Minutes*, Fourth Biennial Convention of the Lutheran Church in America, Atlanta, Ga., June 19-27, 1968, pp. 140-141.

[28] *Minutes*, Sixth Biennial Convention of the Lutheran Church in America, Dallas, Texas, June 30–July 6, 1972, p. 97.

[29] *Minutes*, Seventh Biennial Convention of the Lutheran Church in America, Baltimore, Md., July 3-10, 1974, p. 213.

[30] *Minutes*, LCA, 1976, p. 97.

under, decreasing $2,400 a year to age 40, $1,200 a year to age 50, then $840 a year to 67 when the rate remained at $3,720.[31]

Added in 1968 was the provision for "short-term disability income" for members in good standing in the pension and other benefits program.[32]

Cost of health insurance

The cost of health insurance for pastors was covered by the LCA's budget at the equivalent of about $95 annually for each individual under the program. Eighty percent of the first $500 of hospital expenses was paid by the plan and 100 percent beyond that amount. The maximum hospital stay covered in any calendar year was 180 days, except for nervous disorders, where the maximum was 60 days.[33] The LCA allocated $572,800 in 1963 to cover the cost of the health insurance benefits.[34] The cost of the health insurance program grew rapidly in succeeding years and led to later adjustments. By 1973, the LCA's budgeted amount for clergy health plan coverage was $1,086,900. Clergy paid $901,894 in 1969 for health benefit coverage for their dependents, growing to $1,554,334 in 1973.[35] In many instances, the premiums for dependent coverage were paid by congregations on behalf of their pastors.

Reimbursement rates were adjusted in succeeding years. Even so, maximum out-of-pocket expenses per year were still $100 per person and $200 per family in the late 1970s.[36]

Looking back from the perspective of the early twenty-first century, the initial terms of the LCA ministerial health plan appear to have been a bargain. The maximum deductible per family for in-hospital benefits was $100 a year and for other medical expenses per family, $200 a year. Payment for an appendectomy, according to the initial fee schedule, was $150; treatment of a leg fracture, $75; delivery of a child, $75; prostate removal, $225; or blood transfusion, $38.[37]

---

[31] *Minutes*, Twelfth Biennial Convention, of the Lutheran Church in America, Toronto, Ontario, Canada, June 28–July 5, 1984, p. 672.

[32] *Minutes*, LCA, 1968, p. 428.

[33] Thorkelson, p. 22.

[34] *Minutes*, LCA, 1962, p. 164.

[35] *Minutes*, LCA, 1974, p. 711.

[36] *Minutes*, Ninth Biennial Convention of the Lutheran Church in America, Chicago, Ill., July 12-19, 1978, p. 503.

[37] *Summary*, "Benefits Provided by Health Benefits Plan of the Board of Pensions," Lutheran Church in America, circa. 1963, pp. 1-3.

The Dental Care Insurance Plan was added to the program, effective January 1, 1976, for both clergy and lay church workers.[38]

Factors in the health-benefits plans received ongoing attention throughout the 1970s and 1980s. For instance, eye-care coverage was requested by synodical memorials, but the Board of Pensions recommended that such coverage not be added to the clergy and lay health plans. The rationale given for declining the request was that "few Blue Cross–Blue Shield and insurance-company plans provide eye care coverage except for accident cases and cataract surgery." The LCA's Executive Council concurred with the board's recommendation.[39]

Pressure for expansion

Constant pressure existed for expanding the scope of coverage under the plan, in spite of escalating costs. For example, the Minnesota Synod memorialized the 1978 LCA biennial convention, urging that consideration be given to extended medical and nursing coverage for the plan's members. The Board of Pensions responded, underscoring the fact that coverage had been provided from the plan's start for "catastrophic medical care" costs.

> Ordinarily, "catastrophic medical care" costs are considered to be those which involve primarily extensive and expensive medical care as contrasted with fundamentally "board and lodging" costs. On the other hand, "custodial care" costs, which involve essentially moderately expensive board and lodging costs, and only minimum medical-care costs, have never been covered except to the extent of the applicable and allowable medical-care costs. . . . [The plan's] reimbursement for nursing-home and/or convalescent-home care is applicable only when solely for recuperative purposes and if such care is determined to be medically essential.[40]

In declining to add "extended nursing home coverage" to the health-benefits plans, the Board of Pensions also reported to the 1980 convention:

> Inasmuch as public assistance funds are available for the payment of costs for custodial-care purposes in excess of such

---

[38] *Minutes*, Executive Council of the Lutheran Church in America, February 18-20, 1976, p. 366.

[39] *Minutes*, Executive Council, LCA, February 18-20, 1976, p. 367.

[40] *Minutes*, Tenth Biennial Convention of the Lutheran Church in America, Seattle, Wash., June 25–July 2, 1980, p. 491.

persons' continuing retirement income, it would seem imprudent for the LCA to assume such an obligation. . . . If the payment of the cost of nursing-home care were to be shifted from Public Assistance funds to LCA congregations, would that not mean that some other needs now being met would have to be either cut back or eliminated?[41]

Escalating costs

Funding of the plan became an increasing concern as the costs escalated. The premium for clergy health-care coverage from the LCA budget grew from 3.2 percent of the LCA's benevolence income in 1963 to 8.1 percent in 1978. Projections anticipated significant increases in coming years, approaching by 1980 nearly $3 million a year.[42]

The cost question was not a new one. Even the LCA's 1962 constituting convention asked the Executive Council to present in 1964 an alternate proposal for financing the clergy health-benefit plan. Three options were offered: (1) by or through each synod; (2) directly by each congregation on behalf of the pastor; or (3) by the individual pastor. The Executive Council observed that while the congregation-funded plan was the best of the options, the preferred method was from the LCA's budget. The LCA's 1964 convention concurred with that recommendation.[43]

The LCA's Cabinet of Executives in 1970 encouraged "the Executive Council to consider sources other than the LCA apportionment receipts [benevolence budget] to support the health benefits plan" for pastors. The council replied that "of the various alternate plans of funding available, only the direct assumption of the cost by the immediate employer would appear to be worthy of consideration." Because that method previously had been rejected by the 1964 convention, no change in the funding method was proposed by the Executive Council.[44]

The issue was raised again by the LCA's Cabinet of Executives in 1971 when the cabinet urged that the Board of Pensions explore ways in which

---

[41] Minutes, LCA, 1980, p. 497.

[42] Minutes, Executive Council of the Lutheran Church in America, November 29–December 1, 1979, p. 359.

[43] Minutes, Second Biennial Convention of the Lutheran Church in America, Pittsburgh, Pa., July 2-9, 1964, pp. 101-102 and 426.

[44] Minutes, Fifth Biennial Convention of the Lutheran Church in America, Minneapolis, Minn., June 25–July 2, 1970, p. 182.

the clergy health plan could be "financed by employers and/or participants." The board responded with an extensive report on various means of funding, but supported retaining the system in place. The Executive Council, in response to that report, asked the Board of Pensions "to develop for further consideration a three-part package which would include pensions, death benefit insurance, and health insurance reflecting the following financing sources: 1) congregations, as primary source; 2) ministers, for required member portion of pension; and 3) the LCA for total health benefits for those members not currently employed in an LCA congregation or agency, and [for] a portion of the cost for those who are so employed."[45]

At about the same time, the LCA's Central Pennsylvania Synod submitted to the 1972 LCA convention a memorial that called for an evaluation of the entire medical-pension program of the Board of Pensions. The memorial, which advocated a voluntary program, was referred to the Executive Council for study.[46]

From the LCA Board of Pensions, the LCA Executive Council received a second study on issues of health-plan costs. No changes in the method of funding were recommended. The study did suggest, however, revision of the clergy health plan, adding some cost-sharing provisions. Amendments were requested from the board by the Executive Council that would place a ceiling on financing of the plan from the LCA budget at the 1974 level. Increased premium costs, under the revision, were to be paid by the employer.

The Executive Council sought the advice of the Conference of Synodical Bishops.[47] The conference indicated "that, in view of pending legislation in Congress concerning a national health insurance program, no major change in financing" the clergy health plan should be proposed at that time. The council accepted that advice and did not suggest changes to the 1974 convention.[48] (Obviously, discussion of legislation related to health insurance did not end in the mid-1970s, but continued decades later, especially in 1993-1994 as well as in 2009 and beyond.)

---

[45] *Minutes*, LCA, 1972, pp. 251-252.

[46] *Minutes*, LCA, 1972, pp. 52, 746, and 748

[47] Use of the title "bishop" began among North American Lutherans in the ALC in 1970, but it was not embraced officially by the LCA until 1980. "Bishop" is used here for consistency in terminology in this text for that synodical office. In the LCA's history in the 1970s, the name was Conference of Synodical Presidents.

[48] *Minutes*, LCA, 1974, pp. 218-220.

For a third time, the Executive Council asked the Board of Pensions in 1976 to submit alternate proposals for funding the clergy health plan or offer changes to the plan to relieve the impact of rapidly escalating costs on the church's budget. Under proposals for funding, consideration was given to (1) direct premium payments by congregations, (2) direct premium financing by congregations pooling resources through a group plan, (3) clergy paying their own premiums, and (4) a shared-cost arrangement by congregations and the LCA's budget. The cost-sharing approach was embraced and amendments to the plan were made effective January 1, 1979.[49]

Even in taking that step, questions remained. The Executive Council was informed that a consultant, Hewitt Associates, indicated that only the LCA and one other church body out of 15 church health plans included cost-sharing provisions. That procedure, however, was followed in the U.S. Medicare program, the consultant noted. Cost-sharing was anticipated as "the trend of the future in health benefit plans."[50]

Obligation of minimum pensions

The lingering issue of minimum pensions remained a concern. The roots of the issue stretched back into long-past promises in predecessor churches. Benevolence funds had to be allocated for maintaining the supplementary pension system to assure minimum pensions. In 1963, a total of $2,225,640 was devoted to that effort, including $1,061,700 from the benevolence budget and $1,163,940 from other sources.[51]

The minimum pension for those who retired prior to July 1, 1956, was $1,500. The amount thereafter was set at $900 annually on the assumption that pastors and lay workers who retired after that date were receiving Social Security benefits.[52] An increase in the minimum pension amount was embraced in 1966. The minimum pension for clergy without Social Security who had served in predecessor church bodies was raised by $500 to $2,000 per year. For those who were covered by Social Security, the amount was $1,200. The revised amount for widows of pastors was $1,200.[53] By 1973, $2,500 was the amount paid annually to each of the 61 pastors who

---

[49] *Minutes*, LCA, 1978, pp. 651-653.

[50] *Minutes*, Executive Council of the Lutheran Church in America, November 29–December 1, 1979, p. 363.

[51] *Yearbook*, 1963, p. 24.

[52] Thorkelson, p. 22.

[53] *Minutes*, LCA, 1966, pp. 746-747 and 772.

retired prior to July 1, 1956. At the same time, 419 widows in that category received $1,500 a year. Also in 1973, the 1,321 clergy listed as retired after July 1, 1956, were each receiving $1,500 a year and 760 widows, $900.[54]

Those entitled to benefits under previous plans were assured of continued support. They also were guaranteed that:

> . . . in no case shall reduction be made in a pension payment to (a) a member who was retired or eligible for retirement immediately before the effective date [of the new program,] or (b) a widow of such a member or of an individual who died before such date and was under the pension plan of one of the predecessor churches. . . . Any increase in amount of such a pension as a result of this benefit plan shall, however, be made on an actuarially equitable basis. . . .[55]

Keeping that promise of continued support was a significant challenge. The problem of low pensions was addressed frankly in a report to the LCA's 1966 biennial convention. Said Mr. Wang:

> If the LCA's predecessor churches had taken appropriate action in the establishment of adequate pension contribution rates 40 years ago, minimum pensions would not be a problem for the church today. It is obvious that measures taken by the predecessor churches in pension planning were "too little and too late."

> Many of the ministers who are now in retirement were responsible for voting time and again for some mission of the church at the expense of their pension benefits. Unfortunately, during earlier years, laymen in some of the antecedent church bodies did not take the initiative in these matters and see to it that over minister objections, adequate pension contributions were commenced and maintained for their ministers so that appropriate benefit levels could be achieved. This selfless "voting" on the part of ministers during their active years has resulted in pensions at or near the poverty level in their retirement years.

> Justice dictates that more adequate minimum pensions be paid to faithful servants of the church, most of whom have little

---

[54] *Minutes*, LCA, 1974, p. 713.

[55] Article XIII, "Constitution of the Ministerial Pension and Death Benefit Plan," *Minutes*, LCA, 1962, p. 153.

or no voice now to change their financial situation. Many of the persons on the board's pension roll served their church under economic circumstances which made it very difficult for them to save money apart from that which they placed in their pension plan. Salary levels for most of the retired ministers, during the early part of their careers, were unbelievably low.[56]

Mr. Wang addressed the matter again a decade later when discussion was under way on additional funding for minimum pensions. He wrote forthrightly:

> If the three former churches, other than Augustana, which consolidated to form the LCA had commenced their accumulation in individual accounts of pension contributions as early as did Augustana, much less supplementation would now be required than is the case [to meet minimum pension obligations]. Unfortunately, ULCA, the largest of the former churches, did not begin its contributory pension plan until February 1, 1945. Further, the two smallest such churches (AELC and Suomi)[57] did not accumulate pension contributions in individual accounts of ministers. Consequently, many ministers who retired in the early years following merger were entitled to only a minimum pension even though they had served their former church for a normal work span and met the necessary pension-participation requirements.[58]

Favorable investment returns had created a growing disparity between the pensions paid to retired Augustana and ULCA pastors and their widows versus the minimum pensions that were provided for those who had retired after service in the American Evangelical Lutheran Church and the Finnish Evangelical Lutheran Church.[59] The obligation for those minimum pensions remained, Mr. Wang said, in spite of past mistakes:

> A review of old convention minutes and reports seems to suggest that some . . . in authority-positions of the former churches

---

[56] *Minutes*, LCA, 1966, p. 772.

[57] These are references to the American Evangelical Lutheran Church and the Finnish Evangelical Lutheran Church, two of the four predecessor church bodies of the LCA.

[58] L. Edwin Wang, "Inadequate Pensions Payable to So Many Retired LCA Ministers and Surviving Widows of Retired LCA Ministers," Board of Pension of the Lutheran Church in America, December 14, 1977, p. 9.

[59] Wang, "Inadequate Pensions. . . . ," December 14, 1977, p. 16.

were successful in delaying the commencement of contributory pension plans beyond the time which might have been the case had "grass-roots" efforts for their cause not been stymied. As a consequence, is the LCA responsible for the earlier "transgressions," caused by well-meaning but poorly informed former church officials? Might not the church of today be considered to be responsible for such possible "transgressions" simply because the postponement of commencement of the pension plan is the primary reason for the low level of pension for so many retired ministers (and widows of ministers)?[60]

This problem of limited pensions arose from both late commencement of contributory plans and low compensation during active service. Later, in the Evangelical Lutheran Church in America, the primary source of the problem of low pensions was low compensation for many clergy during their years of active pastoral ministry (see Chapter 4).

Policy on reciprocity

As a matter of reasonable order, the question of reciprocity was addressed between The American Lutheran Church of 1960 and the LCA of 1962. Both pension boards agreed to such reciprocity. Specifically, the LCA Board of Pensions voted on November 2, 1962:

> That the process of determining eligibility for lump-sum death benefits, health benefits, non-contributory pensions and supplemental pensions for ministers who transfer from The American Lutheran Church to the Lutheran Church in America shall take into account the prior service of such ministers; service with The American Lutheran Church shall be counted as service in the Lutheran Church in America. Transfers from other Lutheran church bodies shall be considered on an individual basis at the time of transfer but with precedent.[61]

By the mid-1960s, 6,331 non-retired contributory clergy were enrolled in the pension plan while 935 retired and 41 disabled pastors were receiving benefits. In addition, 1,078 widows of clergy and 209 children were drawing benefits.[62]

---

[60] Wang, "Inadequate Pensions. . . . ," December 14, 1977, p. 15.

[61] *Minutes*, LCA, 1964, p. 142.

[62] *Minutes*, LCA, 1966, p. 744.

Investment allocations

Assets managed by the LCA Board of Pensions grew from $53.4 million in its first year of operation in 1963[63] to $158 million ten years later[64] and nearly $500 million in 1983.[65]

From the beginning, the investment approach was conservative with 58 percent in bonds, 16.5 percent in stocks, and the remainder in other income instruments. The bond return in 1965 was 4.74 percent and the stocks, 3.31 percent. As had been the case for investments in predecessor programs, a significant portion of the assets in the LCA program was placed in mortgages. In fact, mortgages accounted for 25.4 percent of the pension investments in 1965, showing a reported return of 4.96 percent.[66] Gains on stock investments in the early 1960s were allocated to the board's contingency fund.

In the United Lutheran Church in America, following introduction of the contributory pension plan, debate had been intense on the issue of equalization of benefits. The topic returned in the mid-1960s in the LCA when the New England Synod approved a memorial urging attention to "the merits of a pension plan which would provide a more equitable benefit for all members of the Ministerial Pension and Death Benefit Plan, based upon equal treatment by the church and not solely upon salary." After study, the Board of Pensions resolved that "the present pension plan should not be changed" in the way proposed by the New England Synod.[67]

Offer of both FIP and VIP

To provide greater flexibility, the option of a Variable-Income Pension (VIP) for both the ministerial and lay pension plans was opened July 1, 1967, by the LCA Board of Pensions, following approval at the 1966 LCA convention. Funds in the VIP plan were invested in equities. Continued at the same time was the original Fixed-Income Pension (FIP), which had a more conservative investment pattern.[68]

Creation of the VIP fund emerged from growing concern over whether the FIP fund could keep pace with inflation. Further, the Board of Pensions

---

[63] *Annual Report 1963*, Board of Pensions of the Lutheran Church in America, p. 4.

[64] *Annual Report 1973*, Board of Pensions of the Lutheran Church in America. The *Annual Report* in 1973 did not contain page numbers.

[65] *Annual Report 1983*, Board of Pensions of the Lutheran Church in America, p. 3.

[66] *Minutes*, LCA, 1966, p. 745.

[67] *Minutes*, LCA, 1966, pp. 746-747 and 772.

[68] *Minutes*, LCA, 1966, pp. 774-775.

had been receiving requests from members for quality investments that "they anticipate will provide them with more effective protection against inflation."[69]

In making the case for the VIP option, a report prepared by Mr. Wang at the request of the trustees declared:

> Common stocks are widely recognized as a suitable investment for pension plans which have provided a long-term hedge against the effect of inflation. Moreover, common stocks provide the only feasible means for pensioner and contributing members to share in the growth of . . . economies . . . predominantly based on private ownership.[70]

Thus, "variable-income pension plans invested entirely in common stocks, when properly coordinated with fixed-income pension plans, can and do provide combined benefits which tend to keep pace with the cost of living without fluctuating in amount so greatly as to impose hardships on pensions." Further, such a VIP option would allow the investment gain on common stocks to be used and distributed equitably among participants in the pension program.[71]

Clearly, the VIP option proved immediately popular, although members could allocate only the congregation's contribution to that fund. Even so, 60 percent of active plan members allocated all of the congregation's contribution to the VIP fund. At the same time, 30 percent divided three-fourths VIP and one-fourth FIP for congregation contributions, while nine percent specified half and half. Only one percent remained completely in the FIP option.[72]

Controversial complaint

A memorial from the LCA's Western Pennsylvania–West Virginia Synod in 1970 complained that the "present regulations of the Board of Pensions deny a pastor who leaves the service of the Lutheran Church in America the right to remove the total accumulation in his[73] pension

---

[69] L. Edwin Wang, "Variable-Income Pensions for the Ministerial Pension and Death Benefit Plan and the Lay Pension Plan," Board of Pensions of the Lutheran Church in America, May 6, 1966, p. 6.

[70] Wang, "Variable-Income Pensions. . . . ," May 6, 1966, pp. 11-12.

[71] Wang, "Variable-Income Pensions. . . . ," May 6, 1966, p. 45.

[72] Minutes, LCA, 1968, p. 419.

[73] The memorial was passed in the spring before the LCA convention in July 1970 approved the ordination of women to the pastoral ministry of Word and Sacrament.

account, except for closely defined exceptions." The memorial charged that the "regulations in effect allow the confiscation of funds which can be defined as part of a pastor's remuneration from his past and present congregations." With those assertions, the memorial asked that a study be initiated "with a view to liberalizing the present regulations of the Board of Pensions to allow the full portability of pension contributions. . . ."[74]

The response of the Board of Pensions—as reported to the LCA's sixth biennial convention in 1972—noted that the memorial actually appeared to be requesting "withdrawability," not "portability."[75]

> "Portability" refers to the right of a participant to transfer the cash equivalent of any pension benefits which have vested from (1) the employing organization from which he [or she] is severing employment to (2) another with which he [or she] is commencing employment.[76]

Further, the response of the Board of Pensions underscored good reasons "why 'withdrawability' should be limited," including precluding an individual from consuming "all, or even a large part, of the pension accumulations prior to the time . . . for [the] benefit payment to commence." Moreover, sponsoring organizations would find the withdrawals "unacceptable" because the contributions had been made with the understanding that they would provide eventually for a future income for the pastor in the event of disability or retirement and also care for the surviving spouse upon the death of the pastor.

> From the Board of Pensions' standpoint, unlimited withdrawability would present three problems that would have an adverse effect on all participants. Unlimited withdrawability would require much more liquidity of funds than is presently the case, thereby reducing the proportion of assets which could be invested on a permanent basis and consequently reducing the net investment yield otherwise available for crediting to participants. Unlimited withdrawability would make it necessary to . . . account for fixed-income-pension (FIP) accumulations on a unit

---

[74] *Minutes*, LCA, 1972, p. 690.

[75] *Minutes*, LCA, 1972, p. 698.

[76] *Minutes*, LCA,, 1972, pp. 696-697. As noted in a footnote of the report, "Such a transfer presumes that the pension plans ('old' employer and 'new' employer) are compatible and that appropriate credit will be given for the funds transferred from one employer to another."

rather than on a dollar basis or ... make appropriate adjustments to FIP-accumulation withdrawals to take into account fluctuations in market values which result form changes in the level of interest rates. In addition, unlimited withdrawability would destroy creditor-proof protection which presently exists.[77]

The board's response further noted that the second premise of the memorial was "faulty" in its use of the term "confiscation." The pension accumulations are not confiscated, but are held in trust for the members of the plan. Pension and other benefits are paid according to the terms of the plan when the member is entitled to receive them under the terms of the plans.[78]

Issue of clergy unemployment

Another issue in the early 1970s was clergy unemployment. Noting that some states required unemployment insurance for lay church workers, the LCA's Executive Council asked the Board of Pensions "to explore the feasibility of including religious organizations (and the clergy) in governmental programs of unemployment insurance."[79] In response, the Board of Pensions submitted a report that stated:

a. Unemployment insurance for ministers under the Social Security Act is not feasible either financially or politically.

b. Unemployment insurance for ministers, if provided, should be through a private plan with the following possible sources of financing:

1) Levy a small contribution rate on each congregation or employing organization. Small congregations in particular as well as those whose attitude is, "We would never let our pastor be unemployed," might well resist this additional assessment.

2) Add the premium cost to the budget of the LCA as was done with the Short-Term Disability Income Benefit Plan. The church must recognize, however, the increasing percentage of benevolence funds going into the several benefit plans which reduces the resources available for other phases of the church's program.

---

[77] *Minutes*, LCA, 1972, pp. 698-699. A footnote explained the "creditor-proof" references in this way: "Claims of creditors cannot be enforced against pension accumulations which are, by benefit-plan-constitution provision, non-withdrawable."

[78] *Minutes*, LCA, 1972, p. 699.

[79] *Minutes*, Executive Council of the Lutheran Church in America, October 18-20, 1972, p. 62.

3) Finance the cost from the Emergency Assistance Fund administered by the Board of Pensions. While such use of this fund would appear to be consistent with its purpose and currently its resources are at a fairly high level, a survey and analysis of potential cost and its impact on the fund should be made before responsibility is assigned here.

At that point, the matter was referred to the LCA's synodical bishops[80] and Division for Professional Leadership "for study and recommendation."[81]

Turbulent times for investment policies

The opening "salvo" in what would prove to be a time-consuming, multi-year struggle on investment policy came in a 1972 LCA document, "Social Criteria for Investments."[82] The LCA's sixth biennial convention that year had urged that "all churchwide agencies, synods, congregations, and church-related agencies and institutions" study that report and "share with the Board of Social Ministry their proposals in relation to the criteria set forth" in the report. They also were to present "their plans for fulfilling their investment responsibilities."[83] In turn, the Board of Social Ministry was to:

. . . provide to those churchwide agencies, synods, congregations and church-related agencies and institutions, which so desire, advice, counsel and assistance in implementing . . . [the] report on "Social Criteria for Investments."[84]

A meeting of the LCA's Office of Administration and Finance, which administered the Common Investing Fund, and the Board of Pensions—the two churchwide units with major investment responsibilities—was convened with representatives of the LCA's Division for Mission in North America. That division, as a result of a 1972 organizational reconfiguration, had inherited the portfolio previously held by the Board of Social Ministry. Subsequently, the respective governing boards of the Common Investing Fund and the Board of Pensions adopted the following resolution:

---

[80] Although not in official use in the LCA until 1980, the title is used here for consistency in terminology regarding this synodical office.

[81] *Minutes*, Executive Council of the Lutheran Church in America, January 31–February 2, 1974, p. 442.

[82] *Minutes*, LCA, 1972, pp. 590-596.

[83] *Minutes*, LCA, 1972, pp. 596-597.

[84] *Minutes*, LCA, 1972, p. 597.

That as a way to deal in good faith with the action by the 1972 convention of the church, which urged all agencies to share with the Division for Mission in North America "their plans for fulfilling their investment responsibilities," and in view of the division of responsibilities among several churchwide agencies, the Executive Council be requested to act upon this clarifying resolution:

(1)   The Division for Mission in North America shall be free to provide information about the social implications of investments to an appropriate staff official and an appropriate member of each of the boards of the investing agencies of the church.

(2)   The boards that hold responsibility for investments shall retain full discretion and power over their investments.

(3)   Rather than advocate divestment, the Division for Mission in North America shall develop procedures for its testifying to the church's view about moral issues within commercial corporate structures, similar to the procedures approved for testimony within governmental structures. Such procedures shall include at least the following provision:

When a clear moral issue, defined by official statement of the church, has emerged from the policy or practice of a commercial enterprise,

  a. Careful study and preparation, including conferences with knowledgeable persons related to the church's boards holding investment responsibility, shall precede any action.

  b. Private consultation with corporate management shall have precedence over public action.

  c. Public actions, such as those listed in the report on Social Criteria for Investments under "Strategies for Responsible Action," items 3, 4 and 5, shall require approval in each instance by the Executive Council, or by the officers of the church when timing would make Executive Council action impossible. The Executive Council shall have the power of decision over participation by representatives of the Division for Mission in North America in a meeting of the shareholders of a corporation in which an agency of the church holds equities.

The LCA's Executive Council in May 1973 received that resolution and voted to adopt it as the procedure to be followed by churchwide units in implementing the 1972 convention's "resolution related to the application of social criteria to investment policies."[85]

Unfolding struggle

That clearly was not the end of the debate on investment policies. An intense struggle would unfold in the next two decades on issues of fiduciary responsibility and social criteria on investments, especially in regard to opposition to apartheid in South Africa (see Chapter 5).

When the 1982 LCA convention approved a resolution that called for divestment from companies doing business in South Africa, Mr. L. Donald Woods, who had served as LCA treasurer since 1972, came to the podium and resigned.[86] Earlier in the convention, he had been re-elected treasurer on a 633-3 vote.[87] Mr. Woods, who was executive vice president of Mobil Oil Corporation, said that he would be "unable to remain, in good conscience, as an officer of the church."[88] He also said, "The convention has just made a clear witness of love for all those who suffer under apartheid in South Africa. . . . I share that with you. . . . The real key is how best to work for justice in South Africa. . . . You don't do it by abandoning people." He explained that Mobil's practice in South Africa was to pay Black and White workers equally, to train Black workers for better jobs, and to promote them to supervisory posts.[89]

The convention had voted to direct the Office for Administration and Finance "to act in a prudent manner consistent with legal requirements to exercise the option of divestment of securities of corporations which have direct investments in South Africa and the withdrawal of funds from banks which make direct loans" to South Africa. The resolution affected about $1 million in LCA funds invested in mutual funds, but did not apply to investments handled by the LCA's Board of Pensions.[90]

---

[85] *Minutes*, Executive Council of the Lutheran Church in America, May 2-4, 1973, pp. 230-231.

[86] *Minutes*, Eleventh Biennial Convention of the Lutheran Church in America, Louisville, Ky., Sept. 3-10, 1982, p. 304.

[87] "Treasurer Woods shocks delegates after divestment," *The Lutheran*, October 6, 1982, p. 7.

[88] "Divestment causes resignation," *The Lutheran Standard*, October 1, 1982, p. 23.

[89] *The Lutheran*, October 6, 1982, p. 7.

[90] *The Lutheran*, October 6, 1982, p. 7.

Two years earlier, divestment had been a hot issue at the ALC's tenth general convention. A policy was endorsed in the ALC that called for prudent divestment from all firms doing business in South Africa. Further, the ALC's 1980 resolution advocated an end to bank loans, sales of equipment to police and the military, and corporate withdrawal from South Africa.[91]

Proponents of immediate and complete divestment in both the LCA and ALC, at times, seemed unable or unwilling to understand that pension investments could not be treated as a tool of the social commitments or advocacy efforts of the churches. Mr. Wang as president of the LCA's Board of Pensions and the Rev. George Schultz as executive secretary of the ALC's Board of Trustees repeatedly made that point at successive conventions and in other meetings of the respective churches.[92]

Later, in an article reflecting on that period of controversy, Mr. Wang charged that "some headquarters officials and staff [during his tenure in the LCA] did not seem to understand or accept the differences between defined-benefit and defined-contribution pensions plans. They believed, mistakenly, that they had the right to interfere in the investment management of defined-contribution pension plan assets." They "assumed a position of 'divine right of authority' when it came to imposing corporate social responsibility . . . objectives on certain businesses."[93] The reference to "divine right" gives a clear indication of the intensity of the ongoing debate.

Mr. Wang declared, "Employer interference in the investment process of a defined-contribution pension plan is a breach of trust and should not be tolerated." He argued further, "Where the employer . . . provides a defined-contribution pension plan, pensioner-worker interests are jeopardized

---

[91] Action Number GC80.04.58, *Reports and Actions*, Tenth General Convention of The American Lutheran Church at Minneapolis, Minn., October 1-7, 1980, pp. 984-986.

[92] Subsequent to the Rev. George S. Schultz's retirement in April 1981, the Rev. David H. Rokke fulfilled that responsibility as executive secretary of the ALC's Board of Trustees through December 1987.

[93] L. Edwin Wang, "Corporate Social Responsibility Intrusions Adversely Impacted the Operations of the Board of Pensions [in the] Lutheran Church in America," unpublished article, 1994, p. 1. He observed in the article that "the words 'corporate social responsibility' sound reasonable enough," but "that extraneous matters were included under the CSR" banner that "served as a 'cover' for partisan political objectives. In other cases, the 'hidden agenda' involved an 'attack' on a certain industry or a particular business within an industry. In still others, the purpose, disguised or otherwise, seemed to be to advantage labor at the expense of management," pp. 1-2.

when . . . headquarters insists that its special interests . . . prevail over the prudent-investment process."[94]

He alleged that in the years immediately preceding formation of the ELCA, the LCA Board of Pensions "was blocked" by the LCA Division for Mission in North America (DMNA) "from establishing a third fund—a socially-oriented one—for pension plan participants who wanted to participate in such a fund." He charged that staff of DMNA opposed a social-purpose fund because the existence of such a fund would have given those with responsibilities for church-in-society issues less opportunity "to harass firms represented in the Board's . . . investment portfolios."[95]

Mr. Wang recalled, "Court decisions applicable to defined-contribution pension plans make it clear that such pension plan contributions are provided in lieu of wages and, therefore, such contributions and investment income thereon must be treated as the property of pensioners and workers—not the property of employers, as can be the case in defined-benefit pension plans."[96]

Wrote Mr. Wang, "Repeatedly, the senior investment officer and the president of the Board of Pensions explained . . . that since the LCA's pension plan was a defined-contribution" plan, the Board of Pensions "could not alter its investment responsibilities to accommodate special interests of the DMNA and its Church in Society" section.[97] He added:

> Regardless of the type of business employer (pension plan sponsor), the primary responsibility of a defined-contribution pension plan is to invest its assets for the "exclusive" benefit of its participants. The dedicated and highly principled directors and officers of the Board of Pensions devoted themselves fully to that purpose.[98]

That article by Mr. Wang reflected the harsh tone of the debates in the 1980s on divestment in corporations doing business in South Africa. In the midst of addressing those concerns in the early 1990s, leaders of the ELCA's Board of Pensions and also of the ELCA's churchwide organization faced litigation that consumed enormous amounts of time and involved

---

[94] Wang, p. 2.

[95] Wang, p. 4.

[96] Wang, p. 1.

[97] Wang, p. 4.

[98] Wang, p. 4.

significant legal expenses. The legal journey eventually ended largely where it began, but only after years of wrestling not only to protect the pension plan but also to uphold the First Amendment of the U.S. Constitution (see Chapter 6).

Emergence of social-purpose funds

Other issues were raised throughout the life of the LCA's Board of Pensions. For instance, the 1985 convention of the Pacific Northwest Synod memorialized the Board of Pensions "to create an additional investment option (AIO) in the LCA Pension Fund dedicated to investments which do not participate with firms involved in arms production and development."[99] The LCA Executive Council examined the concept and concluded that the start-up costs of separate funds "could not be justified in the limited life of the Lutheran Church in America." The matter of funds with certain social criteria was left to the ELCA's Board of Pensions.[100] Under the ELCA plan, social-purpose funds emerged as an attractive option for plan members. The Board of Pensions of the ELCA, thereby, served as a flagship for other church plans in the creation of social-purpose funds.

---

[99] *Minutes*, Closing Convention of the Lutheran Church in America, Columbus, Ohio, April 29, 1987, p. 202.

[100] *Minutes*, Thirtieth Biennial Convention of the Lutheran Church in America, Milwaukee, Wis., August 25-30, 1986, p. 754.

CHAPTER 14

Lessons from the Past
for the Present and the Future

Fear is not a solid foundation for wise decisions. President Franklin D. Roosevelt eloquently made that point in his first inaugural address. On Saturday, March 4, 1933, he warned that "the only thing we have to fear is fear itself."[1] Never mind that he may have borrowed the thought from Henry David Thoreau.[2] The declaration certainly was a timely one.

President Roosevelt spoke in a context that offered many reasons for fear. The country was in the depths of the Great Depression of the 1930s. By inauguration day, many banks were on the brink of collapse and thousands more already had closed. Thirty-eight states had declared bank "holidays," and withdrawals were limited in the other 10 states.[3] Unemployment at

---

[1] The Twentieth Amendment to the U.S. Constitution did not take effect prior to President Franklin D. Roosevelt's first inauguration. That amendment shortened the time between November presidential elections and the beginning of a president's new term following the election from March 4 to January 20 at noon (Eastern time). The amendment was proposed by the U.S. Congress on March 2, 1932, and was ratified by January 23, 1933, by the requisite number of states. As a result, President Roosevelt's second term began on January 20, 1937.

[2] Thoreau expressed that idea with the passage, "Nothing is so much to be feared as fear."

[3] Prior to President Franklin D. Roosevelt's inauguration, more than 5,000 banks already had failed. Early Monday morning, shortly after midnight on March 6, President Roosevelt declared that a "national emergency" had been created by "heavy and unwarranted withdrawals of gold and currency from our banking institutions." Therefore, he ordered all of the nation's banks to close their doors. The following Thursday, March 9, both houses of Congress passed the Emergency Banking Act, and the president signed it into law within nine hours of its introduction to the House of Representatives and the Senate. In President Roosevelt's first "fireside chat" on Sunday, March 12, he told his listeners that it was "safer to keep your money in a reopened bank than under the mattress." Further, he explained the reasons for the bank holiday and reported that on Monday, March 13, banks that had been certified as financially stable would begin to reopen in the 12 cities with Federal Reserve banks. The next day, banks would reopen in 250 more cities, with still more to follow. Of the nation's 17,308 banks, 11,878 were found to be sound and were authorized to reopen. Among the other 5,430 banks, 3,398 later were allowed to reopen after they had obtained adequate capital; the remaining 2,132 were closed permanently or merged with stronger banks (see Adam Cohen, *Nothing to Fear* [New York: The Penguin Press, 2009], pp. 3, 72-74, and 81; see also Milton Friedman and Anna Jacobson Schwartz, *A Monetary History of the United States, 1867–1960* [Princeton, N.J.: Princeton University Press, 1963], pp. 421-428).

its peak during that period climbed to 25 percent. Many of those listed as employed were only partially so, working for low wages with limited hours, yet glad to have a job. Farmers were losing their farms at a rate of 20,000 a month. In Iowa, one of the nation's primary agricultural states, one-seventh of the farms already had been lost to foreclosure by 1933. Automobile factories were operating at 20 percent of their capacity, and steel plants at only 12 percent. The Dow Jones Industrial Average from the prior peak on September 3, 1929, to its trough on July 8, 1932, declined 89 percent. The Dow average would not reach that 1929 peak again until 1954.

Seventy-five years after President's Roosevelt's inauguration in 1933, the second economic recession of the twenty-first century prompted widespread fear. That recession began in December 2007.[4] Credit dried up for individuals and businesses. Foreclosures on defaulting borrowers set new records. Unemployment grew. Week after week, numerous corporations cut thousands of jobs, exceeding a rate of 500,000 or more a month. In January 2009, for example, 741,000 jobs were lost, the biggest decline in a single month since October 1949.[5] The country experienced the longest streak of job losses since the 1930s. By the end of the first quarter in 2009, the jobless rate rose above 8.5 percent, a level not seen since the early days of President Ronald Reagan's Administration.[6] In subsequent months, the rate continued to climb, but generally at a slower pace of increase, reaching a national average of 9.5 percent by mid-year. More job losses followed in the second half of the year.

---

[4] The deep economic valleys since World War I generally are listed as follows for the United States: (1) the downturn of 1918–1921 in the aftermath of World War I; (2) the Great Depression from 1929 to 1939; (3) the post-Korean War recession of 1953–1954; (4) the recession of 1973–1975 and 21 percent inflation, which was prompted chiefly by the oil embargo and OPEC raising oil prices with the price of gasoline climbing 233 percent; (5) the recession of 1980–1982, also related to oil but with high interest rates and the prime rate climbing to 18.87 percent; (6) the recession of 1990–1991, which saw the failure of 653 banks and savings and loan associations; (7) the recession of 2001–2002 in the rupture of the technology bubble and the aftermath of the September 11, 2001, attacks; and (8) the recession of 2007 and beyond with the collapse of some investment banks and huge losses in others while housing prices and home construction plummeted and credit froze up for individuals and businesses. Economic downturns since World War II also occurred in 1949, 1957–1958, 1960, and 1970.

[5] U.S. Bureau of Labor Statistics, "The Employment Situation—March 2009," April 3, 2009, p. 1. In the 12-month period ending March 31, 2009, the number of unemployed persons grew by 5.3 million, an increase of 3.4 percent.

[6] Kelly Evans, "Jobless Rate Tops 8%, Highest in 26 Years," *The Wall Street Journal*, March 7-8, 2009, p. A1.

The Dow Jones Industrial Average had its worst months of its 113-year history in early 2009, down 8.84 percent in January and 11.7 percent in February.[7] The five-month period ending on January 31, 2009, saw a 31 percent decline in the Dow average—the sharpest slide since the five months that ended in December 1937.[8] By the end of February 2009, the Dow Jones Industrial Average was more than 50 percent off its record in October 2007.[9] Further, the worst performance in the 55-year history of *Fortune* magazine's annual listing of the 500 biggest U.S. companies was reported for 2008. Earnings fell nearly 85 percent from 2007 for those companies, dropping from $645 billion to $98.9 billion.[10] The economic slide was characterized as "a once-in-four-generations recession."[11]

President Barack Obama—upon taking office on January 20, 2009—warned that things would get worse before they got better. He urged quick action by the federal government, beyond the steps already under way, to create jobs and strengthen the economy. Some weeks later, he expressed the hope that "the pillars of recovery" had been put in place for renewed economic stability. "I don't think that people should be fearful about our future," he said, adding that people should not "suddenly stuff money in their mattresses and pull back completely from spending."[12]

Confronting the sliding economy, billionaire investor Warren Buffett said that the United States was experiencing an "economic Pearl Harbor." He acknowledged, however, that the nation's economic troubles, while severe, were not as bad as World War II or as deep as the Great Depression. A primary problem, he observed, was that people were in a cycle of fear. "We'll break out of it. It takes time."[13] In spite of his optimism about long-term prospects, however, he had to report that, in 2008, Berkshire Hathaway, Inc., an insurance and investment company, had its worst

---

[7] Peter A. McKay, "Dow Falls 119.15 Points, Losing 12% in February," *The Wall Street Journal*, February 28–March 1, 2009, p. B1.

[8] Annelena Lobb, "January Was Dow's Worst in 113 Years," *The Wall Street Journal*, January 31–February 1, 2009, p. B1.

[9] McKay, *The Wall Street Journal*, February 28–March 1, 2009, p. B1.

[10] "Rocky Year for the 'Fortune' 500," *U.S.A. Today*, April 20, 2009, p. B1.

[11] *The New York Times*, April 29, 2009, p. A20.

[12] "Reassurance on the Economy," *The New York Times*, March 8, 2009, p. 22.

[13] Associated Press report on an interview broadcast on "Dateline NBC," January 18, 2009. Mr. Buffet was the chairman and chief executive officer of Berkshire Hathaway, Inc., an investment firm based in Omaha, Neb., with a diverse mix of more than 60 companies, including insurance, banking, furniture, carpet, jewelry, restaurants, and utilities.

performance in the 44 years that he had served as chairman and chief executive officer.[14]

Market averages began to climb in March 2009. The Dow Jones Industrial Average moved above the 8,000 mark in early April for the first time in two months. Some notes of optimism emerged. Federal Reserve Chairman Ben Bernanke told Congress in May 2009 that he expected the economy to start growing again toward the end of the year, although the comeback could be weak and more jobs would disappear even after signs of recovery appeared.[15] Some experts characterized by the Associated Press as "financial wizards" predicted that, by the end of the year, companies would begin hiring workers, signaling the end of the worst economic downturn since the Great Depression.[16] Similar expectations were expressed in statements by various companies at the end of the first quarter in 2009.[17] Yet, in spite of some hopeful signs, economic anxiety persisted.

Officials of the Federal Reserve painted a picture in mid-2009 of "an unusual recovery" from the recession, with significant growth emerging in the economy even while high employment rates persisted and consumer spending remained sluggish.[18] Steady signs of recovery, however, were evident by autumn.[19] To aid in the recovery, the Federal Reserve maintained low interest rates in the belief that high unemployment and substantial unused factory capacity would keep inflation pressures "subdued for some time."[20]

Offering reassurance for the domestic and global markets in a mid-September 2009 speech, Mr. Bernanke said that the recession "very likely" had ended and recovery was under way. He indicated that moderate economic growth could be anticipated, but consumer confidence would take some time to heal, given the depth of the economic downturn.[21] His

---

[14] "Buffett Remains Upbeat Despite Berkshire Slide," Associated Press, February 28, 2009.

[15] Edmund L. Andrews, "Bernanke Sees Hopeful Signs But No Quick Recovery," The New York Times, online edition, May 6, 2009.

[16] David Pitt, "Recession Will End This Year, Experts Predict," Associated Press, March 24, 2009.

[17] Kelly Evans and Vanessa O'Connell, "Companies Spy an End to Declines in Earnings," The Wall Street Journal, April 22, 2009, p. A1.

[18] Brian Blackstone and Jon Hilsenrath, "Fed Prepares for Rising Unemployment Amid Higher Growth," The Wall Street Journal, July 16, 2009, p. A2.

[19] "Fed: Economy Stabilizing," Chicago Tribune, September 10, 2009, p. 28.

[20] Edmund L. Andrews, "Fed to Lower Safety Net, but Gingerly," The New York Times, September 24, 2009, p. B1 and B4.

[21] Stephen Labaton and Jeff Zeleny, "Fed Chief Sees End of U.S. Recession," International Herald Tribune, September 16, 2009, p. 16.

expectation of recovery from the recession was confirmed by the end of the third quarter in 2009 when the economy of the United States showed growth for the first time in a year.[22]

The path to that point, however, was littered with losses as a result of gigantic economic turmoil. Certainly, the ELCA's Board of Pensions did not escape the impact of the deep recession—a recession that was seen in retrospect as "one of the most harrowing periods in the history of modern finance."[23] Indeed, as Mr. Bernanke observed, "We came very, very close to a depression. . . . The markets were in anaphylactic shock."[24]

Reassurance amid fear

As the severity of the economic crisis became evident throughout the nation and world in 2008, the Board of Pensions of the ELCA sought to assure both active and retired plan members regarding the pension program. As part of that effort, President John G. Kapanke wrote:

> So many of us feel a range of emotions as turmoil in the financial markets continues to capture headlines. Confusion. Frustration. Uncertainty. . . . While no one can predict what's going to happen in the financial markets, I want you to know the ELCA Board of Pensions is staying the course to help you achieve financial security–for we believe in an investment philosophy that looks beyond today's news. . . . [We] base our decisions on the tenets of long-term investing. We carefully manage risk by making sure ELCA Retirement Plan investments are well diversified across and within asset classes. We avoid short-term market timing strategies that can lower your investment returns.[25]

He encouraged active members to review their asset allocations to determine that they were investing in appropriate ways for their long-term retirement needs. He added, "I believe people who stay focused on long-term objectives will prevail when it comes to their retirement needs."[26]

---

[22] Catherine Rampell, "U.S. Economy Started to Grow Again in Third Quarter," *The New York Times*, online edition, October 30, 2009.

[23] Dan Kadlec, "Don't Give Up Yet," *Time*, October 19, 2009, p. 35.

[24] Michael Grunwald, "Ben Bernanke: The 2009 Time Person of the Year," *Time*, December 28, 2009–January 4, 2010, p. 48.

[25] John G. Kapanke, "Letter to Plan Members," October 1, 2008.

[26] Kapanke, October 1, 2008.

Correction of market "bubble"

To help members understand the scope of the economic challenge, various steps were taken. Ms. Heather H. Williamson, a senior investment manager for the Board of Pensions, described the factors that had led to the economic downturn. She noted in a newsletter that any market "bubble" —defined as an "unsustainable price level"—eventually is corrected. Such was the case with the technology bubble in the early years of the twenty-first century. But the more recent credit bubble was even more complicated because of its broad impact on the global economy.

Ms. Williamson said that the "credit bubble" had been growing for almost two decades as a result of "easy and cheap access to credit." That had led to a hot housing market, driven in part by sub-prime loans. Blame, she said, might be placed on numerous participants in the financial services industry and regulatory agencies charged with their oversight. Foreclosures devastated various communities and forced families from their homes.

Institutions that facilitated the financial markets found themselves in serious trouble in 2008. Some large financial empires collapsed overnight when they lost access to credit. Others had to be sold to stronger operations. And large government guarantees were required to avoid deeper calamity.[27]

Amid the choppy economic waters, members of the investment staff of the Board of Pensions sought to chart a steady course, seeking to maintain a long-term perspective in spite of months of gloomy financial news. Even when signs suggested that the recession was nearing bottom, caution was exercised.

Caution for retirees

The massive consequences of the economic downturn caused grave concern on the part of leaders and trustees of the ELCA Board of Pensions. Mr. Kapanke wrote in mid-December 2008 to retirees and those about to retire, warning that the worldwide financial turmoil inevitably would affect the ELCA Participating Annuity and Bridge Fund. "The magnitude of the losses in 2008," he warned, "will have an impact on your annuity payments, although it is too early to know how much." Annuity payments might have to be reduced, he said. With a return to a positive market, "it will take time to bring us back to where we were at the beginning of 2008."

---

[27] Heather H. Williamson, "How Did This Happen?" *Planning Ahead*, a newsletter of the Board of Pensions of the ELCA, October 2008.

He concluded, "Even in these stormy days, . . . you can be certain . . . [that] we will continue to be faithful to your well-being for your lifetime."[28]

Mr. Kapanke was writing in the context of a long history. Throughout the two and a half centuries in which Lutherans in America have sought to provide for pastors, other church workers, and their families, the economic, legal, social, and religious challenges of operating a church pension program have been substantial. Yet, as Mr. Kapanke and other leaders of the Board of Pensions learned from history, fear must not be allowed to drive life's decisions, including those regarding pension policies and long-term investment strategies.

He emphasized that same long-term perspective when meeting with the Conference of Bishops in early March 2009. "We are in challenging times," he acknowledged. "We watched as flawed lending and borrowing practices in the housing market turned into an investment and banking crisis, which, in turn, caused markets to tumble on a global scale."

He reported that some congregation leaders, reflecting uncertainty on income, were asking if they could reduce or temporarily suspend retirement contributions for their pastors and staff. Some also were inquiring whether they could reduce their health-plan contributions or exclude coverage for family members by passing the cost to the pastor or staff member. A few even wondered if they could unbundle the plan by picking and choosing what benefits they would provide.[29]

Any "significant reduction in benefits or cost shifting could be devastating," Mr. Kapanke observed, in view of the fact that many clergy already are sacrificing on their salary levels.[30] He added:

> Our philosophy of benefits sets and maintains a standard to ensure that all in service to this church are treated equally. To this end, we tell . . . [congregation leaders that]:
>
> 1. Unbundling the program is not an option.
> 2. Our retirement plan sets and requires minimum contributions. Going below the minimums is also not an option.
> 3. Our health plan requires sponsors to pay the full contribution for a plan member, and strongly encourages but does not require

---

[28] John G. Kapanke, "Letter to Plan Members," December 2008.

[29] Kapanke, March 9, 2009, p. 6.

[30] Kapanke, March 9, 2009, p. 6.

sponsors to pay the full contribution for family members. We remind them . . . that the plan member is already sharing 20 percent of the cost of health benefits through deductibles, coinsurance, and copayments.[31]

Pointing to the broader horizon of the future, Mr. Kapanke declared:

These challenging times prove all the more why the Board of Pensions must stay focused on our long-term objectives in service to this church and those whom we serve. Our objectives require us to support the ministry of this church by providing strong health benefits and security in retirement. . . .[32]

Clearly, both the length and depth of the recession that began in late 2007 required heroic efforts to maintain a secure bridge of hope for both retirees as well as members in active service.[33] As an antidote to short-term decisions driven by fear, the ELCA Board of Pensions pursued prudence and creative vision for long-term goals.

Scope of the challenge

The 2008 *Annual Report* of the Board of Pensions underscored the dimensions of the economic challenge. Amid "one of the most dramatic and historic global economic downturns in modern financial times," markets tumbled worldwide. "The severity and rapidity of these investment declines, especially in the fourth quarter of 2008, cast the global economy into uncharted territory. This historic market downturn had a dramatic impact on pension plans throughout the country and abroad."[34]

Obviously, ELCA plan members were not "immune" from adverse investment market forces. Funds managed by the Board of Pensions offered

---

[31] Kapanke, March 9, 2009, p. 8.

[32] Kapanke, March 9, 2009, p. 2.

[33] How close did the United States come in 2008 and 2009 to a second Great Depression in 80 years? When asked that question, Ms. Christina Romer, the head of President Barack Obama's Council of Economic Advisors, answered, "Very close." An economic depression, she explained, is distinguished from a recession by the depth of its paralyzing fear—a fear of the unknown that prompts investors, businesses, and consumers to panic and flee from the markets. They cut spending and hoard cash; they sell stocks and avoid investments; they delay or avoid purchases; and they face frozen credit markets. Businesses also slice inventory and cancel capital development projects. Massive government efforts to stabilize the economy were required. Without such efforts, the severe recession could have been even more catastrophic (Robert J. Samuelson, "How We Narrowly Avoided a Depression," *Newsweek*, October 12, 2009, p. 25).

[34] *Annual Report*, 2008, Board of Pensions of the Evangelical Lutheran Church in America, p. 2.

clear examples of the sliding markets. While those funds performed well against their benchmark balanced funds, the declines in the 80 percent equity funds surpassed 35 percent, while the 60 percent equity funds were off slightly under 30 percent. The 40 percent equity funds decreased just over 20 percent.[35] In fact, "17 of the 20 ELCA investment funds posted double-digit negative one-year returns in 2008. . . ." Only the ELCA Bond Fund, ELCA Social Purpose Bond Fund, and ELCA Money Market Fund experienced gains for the year.[36]

Through brochures and correspondence as well as on the Web site, retirees and those contemplating retirement had been reminded periodically that:

> The goal of the Board of Pensions is to increase the amount of your lifetime monthly annuity income at approximately the rate of inflation over a period of years. Because the ELCA Retirement Plan offers a participating annuity, you "participate" in the fluctuations of the market to some degree.[37]

The depth of the recession underscored for members the reality of such participation. That became very clear in 2009.

Drastic step

As a result of market losses, the Board of Pensions took a drastic step. The ELCA Participating Annuity and Bridge Fund, out of which retirement benefits were paid, was closed to new investments on April 3, 2009. The investment losses of late 2008 and early 2009 had reduced substantially the funded ratio of the fund, thereby diminishing the expected future interest-crediting rates and annuity payments. The lowered value placed at a disadvantage those who invested in the fund under adverse conditions compared to those who invested under more normal conditions. Such "normal conditions" were defined as a funded ratio of 80 percent or higher.[38]

A reader of the 2008 *Annual Report* could see the harsh reality of the state of the Participating Annuity and Bridge Fund. At the end of 2008,

---

[35] *Annual Report*, 2008, pp. 2 and 6.

[36] *Annual Report*, 2008, p. 2.

[37] "ELCA Pension and Other Benefits Program: Retirement Information," Board of Pensions of the Evangelical Lutheran Church in America, January 1, 2005, p. 15.

[38] Action Number PN09.04.22, *Minutes*, Board of Trustees of the Board of Pensions, April 23, 2009, p. 3. The action of the management of the Board of Pensions in closing the ELCA Participating Annuity and Bridge Fund, after consultation with an ad hoc committee of the board of trustees, was confirmed in a special meeting of the full board of trustees, held by conference call.

the fund was $857 million below projected pension obligations.[39] That staggering number grew in the following months to nearly $1 billion at the end of February 2009 when the fund was $979 million below projected obligations, at a funded ratio of 61 percent.[40]

In 35,000 letters to plan members, various publications, and on the Web site of the Board of Pensions, annuitants were cautioned in early 2009 that "annuity payments may be reduced in the coming years as a result of market losses."[41]

As Mr. Kapanke told a special meeting of the trustees, the "significant gap between the net assets in the fund and the present value of the projected lifetime benefit obligations" had to be "closed to ensure the fund's long-term viability."[42] The situation did improve somewhat during the course of 2009; as of December 31, the deficit stood at 22 percent, a salutary improvement from the 39 percent deficit in early March 2009.

The investment "mix" for the ELCA Participating Annuity and Bridge Fund was 50 percent stocks, 45 percent bonds, including 10 percent of which were inflation-indexed bonds, and five percent real assets.[43] The funded ratio fluctuated with the market value of the assets in relation to the level of projected obligations.[44]

The catastrophic market plunge put the fund in tough territory. Unlike the market canyon in the 2001 recession that involved especially technology stocks, the plunge of late 2008 and early 2009 was global in

---

[39] *Annual Report*, 2008, p. 10.

[40] Normally anticipated over a span of years for the Participating Annuity and Bridge Fund was a pattern in which the funded ratio (assets divided by the annuity obligations) would be greater than 1.00 about half the time and less than 1.00 about half the time, usually staying with a range of 0.80 to 1.20. For the nine-year period ending in 2007, the year-end funded ratios ranged from 0.78 to 1.15, with an average of 0.95 for the years 2004 to 2007. Except for a brief period in late 2002 when the ratio dipped below 0.80, the funded ratio was within the expected range, until the monumental market downturn in late 2008 and early 2009.

[41] *Annual Report*, 2008, pp. 2 and 18.

[42] John G. Kapanke, "Special Meeting Notes," Board of Trustees of the Board of Pensions, September 21, 2009, p. 2.

[43] Stocks included 30 percent in U.S. stocks, 13 percent in non-U.S. stocks, and seven percent in alternative equities. For the bonds, 20 percent was invested in core bonds, 15 percent in high-yield bonds, and 10 percent in inflation-adjusted bonds.

[44] For the one-, five-, and ten-year periods ending August 31, 2009, the Participating Annuity and Bridge Fund had returns of -7.1 percent, +4.9 percent, and +4.6 percent, respectively, while a custom benchmark used for evaluation had returns for the same periods of -8.1 percent, +4.1 percent, and +3.7 percent.

scale and broad in its impact on most sectors of the U.S. economy.[45] As a result, members personally experienced the harsh reality of the market's sharp skid. Clearly, the assumed annual interest-crediting goal of 4.5 percent for the Participating Annuity and Bridge Fund could not be achieved in the immediate future. Painful steps would be required to sustain the fund.

The closing of the ELCA Participating Annuity and Bridge Fund represented a gigantic departure from the patterns of operation for the contributory pension plans of the ELCA and its predecessor church bodies. Contributory plans had been established for various Lutheran church bodies by the middle of the twentieth century.[46] The ELCA's pension plan carried forward many elements of those earlier contributory plans, including the granting of annuities for retiree pension benefits.

A nine percent decrease

Letters were sent on September 24, 2009, informing retirees that their monthly annuity payments would be decreased by nine percent, beginning January 1, 2010. Based on late 2009 projections, additional nine percent decreases could be anticipated in both 2011 and 2012.[47] Those actions were designed to bring the ELCA Participating Annuity and Bridge Fund to fully funded status by the end of 2012. As the letter stated:

> We have determined . . . to spread out this action over a multi-year period so the impact of reduced monthly annuity payments on members' monthly income and interest crediting rates will be less severe [than adjustments would be in a shorter period]. Members . . . will have better opportunity to adjust, as necessary, their monthly expenditures and other income sources

---

[45] In the first recession of the twenty-first century, losses were less severe than in the second recession (down 20 percent for the 24-month period ending September 2002 versus a 31 percent decline for the 17-month period ending February 2009. The recovery following the downturn that ended in 2002 was strong and sustained, with the Participating Annuity and Bridge Fund achieving average returns of more than 13 percent for the five years that ended September 30, 2007.

[46] The first Lutheran church body to inaugurate a defined-contribution plan was the Augustana Lutheran Church, on January 1, 1938. The American Lutheran Church was second on January 1, 1939, followed by the Evangelical Lutheran Church on February 1, 1941. The United Lutheran Church in America began such a plan in 1945. On February 1, 1952, the Lutheran Free Church established a defined-contribution plan. Likewise, on January 1, 1954, the United Evangelical Lutheran Church embraced such a plan.

[47] President John Kapanke told a group of retired pastors and spouses at Carefree, Arizona, on December 8, 2009, that this action was "the most challenging and painful decision that we have ever had to make."

over time. The alternative of addressing the funding gap in a single year, with a much larger monthly payment reduction, would potentially create greater hardship for most members.[48]

For those who had not yet annuitized, the Bridge Fund accounts were to be adjusted downward by 3.5 percent in 2010, with similar reductions anticipated in 2011 and 2012. That step, too, was deemed necessary to return the fund to stability.

With the reduction in annuity payments, the funded ratio of the Participating Annuity and Bridge Fund was estimated in early 2010 at 85 percent.

Some members wondered if the decrease in their pensions could have been avoided by more "conservative" investment practices. The 50-50 split between equities and other instruments in a balanced fund actually was seen as a stable approach for asset management—yet, at the same time, aggressive enough in the pursuit of the goal of a lifetime income for retirees with some degree of inflation protection.

Others asked if a contingency reserve should have been maintained to cushion against major market losses. A reserve of $750 million to $1 billion of the assets of members would have been required; that would have meant lower annuity payments to retirees over the years.

Caution had been exercised. The wisdom of history had been applied. Even so, retirees had to adjust to the prospect of receiving only 75 percent of their 2009 annuity income by 2013.

When the ELCA Participating Annuity and Bridge Fund was closed, research immediately got under way on options for future retirees, including annuity possibilities. In the meantime, those contemplating retirement who had assets in the 20 investment funds offered by the Board of Pensions could withdraw some money for retirement income along with their Social Security benefits.

After exploring a wide range of possible scenarios, the Board of Pensions took steps to provide two participating annuity funds by early 2011. One form reopened the established Participating Annuity Fund with its 50 percent equity asset mix in a variable annuity. The other was a new Participating Annuity Fund with about 20 percent in equities. The second, more conservative fund likely would experience a lower expected

---

[48] "Letter to Plan Members," Board of Pensions of the Evangelical Lutheran Church in America, September 24, 2009.

return than the first, but probably would have somewhat less risk of severe decreases in annual annuity payments amid volatile market cycles.

For purposes of calculating the initial annuity payment, the assumed investment return on both funds was set at 4.5 percent. For the "50e" balanced fund, the long-term expected return was estimated at 7.6 percent. The projected long-term return on the "20e" fund was 6 percent.

Because members—prior to annuitizing any assets for retirement benefits—could use any of 20 investment funds, including a money-market fund, what had been the "Bridge Fund" was not re-opened.

Plans called for annuitants in the previously existing "50e" Participating Annuity and Bridge Fund to have a one-time opportunity to shift into the "20e" Participating Annuity Fund, if they wished to do so.

The steep economic downturn in the great recession of 2007–2009 and the precipitous market slide of late 2008 and early 2009 presented significant challenges for the ELCA Board of Pensions and all other church as well as general pension funds.[49] What transpired became another dramatic part of the unfolding saga of Lutheran efforts to provide pension and other benefits for pastors, other church workers, and their families.

Lessons learned

Winston Churchill observed, "The farther backward you look, the farther forward you can see." Reflecting a similar awareness, Jean Jaurès, a French philosopher, advised that we should take from the past the fire, not the ashes.

Much has changed throughout the past decades in the form and operation of Lutheran pension programs. The underlying motivation has remained the same—specifically the support of and care for those who

---

[49] Both defined-contribution and defined-benefit plans were deeply affected by the recession. Stated in stark terms, the situation for defined-benefit plans could be described in this way: "The financial crisis has blown a hole in the rosy forecasts of pension funds that cover teachers, police officers and other government employees, casting into doubt as never before whether these public systems will be able to keep their promises to future generations of retirees. The upheaval on Wall Street has deluged public pension systems with losses that government officials and consultants increasingly say are insurmountable unless pension managers fundamentally rethink how they pay out benefits or make money or both. .... After losing about $1 trillion in the markets, state and local governments are facing a devil's choice: Either slash retirement benefits or pursue high-return investments that come with high risk" (David Cho, "Steep Losses Pose Crisis for Pensions: Two Bad Choices for Funds, Cut Benefits or Take Greater Risks to Rebuild Assets," *The Washington Post*, online edition, October 11, 2009).

serve Lutheran congregations, synods, churchwide ministries, agencies, and institutions.

As we ponder two and a half centuries of Lutheran pension and aid programs, what lessons have been learned along the way? Truly, some ashes are evident as we review the operation of certain programs in the past. What is more evident is the fire that inspired the original creation of Lutheran pension and aid programs. The dedication required for their development and operation shines even more dramatically as we look back from the perspective of the early twenty-first century.

Mindful of the unfolding history of Lutherans in America, we see how fear was crippling at various stages in the saga of church pension programs. Fear hobbled imagination and strangled courage. To avoid being captured by fear, leaders needed to practice wise caution informed by both deep knowledge and wide vision. They needed to hear the call to step forward with courage for the sake of current pastors and other church workers as well as those in future generations. Often, that is exactly what transpired.

The record, however, also shows this: Fear occasionally clouded judgment in the operation of various Lutheran pension plans. The limited range of investments chosen at times seemed to reflect such fear. For instance, serious problems were created by the concentration of investments in farm land by the Augustana Lutheran Church's pension and aid fund (see Chapter 9) or in urban real estate by the pension program of the United Lutheran Church in America (see Chapter 10).

Anxiety driven by the fresh memory of the market crash of the Great Depression prompted the pension programs of various Lutheran churches to limit their range of investments in the 1940s and beyond. Some of that hesitation was fed by the assumption that a deep economic downturn would follow the end of World War II, as had been the case following World War I.[50] Suspicion persisted in regard to equities into the 1950s and even the 1960s. So fixed-income assets were highly favored, instead of the pursuit of diversified portfolios.

The Board of Pensions of the ELCA now offers a wide variety of investment options from which members may select. The 20 different

---

[50] The post-World War I downturn affected primarily market prices for farmers, although manufacturing for a time also was hurt. As the manufacturing and urban economy began to roar in the mid-1920s, farmers did not benefit from the upturn. The farm economy lagged throughout that decade and then was hit even harder by the droughts, dust storms, and low market prices of the 1930s.

funds (see Chapter 1) are designed to enable members, depending on their age and risk tolerance, to pursue more aggressive or more cautious approaches in their asset allocations. Even within the various types of funds, the crucial investment principle of diversification is followed. As Mr. Curtis G. Fee, vice president and chief investment officer of the Board of Pensions, explained, "Our diversification . . . helped to avoid significant concentration in any one holding or sector of the markets," in contrast to some other financial institutions.[51]

Deferred compensation

Each new generation runs the risk of forgetting the lessons learned in previous generations. At various times in the history of Lutheran pension plans, leaders had to emphasize that the pension program was not a matter of charity. They insisted that the cost of the pension and other benefits program was to be understood as an operational expense of congregations and other church employers. The cost was not to be viewed as part of a congregation's benevolence contribution.

That understanding still requires periodic emphasis by bishops, synodical staff members, and others in working with congregations as they call pastors, diaconal ministers, deaconesses, or associates in ministry. Congregations are not doing a favor for a pastor or church worker in contributing to that person's pension fund. They are fulfilling an obligation in meeting part of their operational costs as healthy, mission-oriented congregations.

The pension of a pastor or other church worker in retirement constitutes a form of deferred compensation. That principle was embraced by Lutheran churches in view of the historically low salaries of pastors and other church workers, particularly in comparison with some other professions.

Crucial lay leadership

Another learning from history is this: Certain lay men and women were crucial in the creation, development, and operation of the ELCA Board of Pensions and all of those church pension programs that preceded it. For instance, Mr. George A. Huggins of Philadelphia influenced various church bodies to establish "money-purchase" pension plans (see Chapter 7). Without his knowledge and wisdom, we can only wonder what would have been the history of church pension plans. All evidence suggests that—if it

---

[51] Curtis G. Fee, Investment Update Memorandum," Board of Pensions of the Evangelical Lutheran Church in America, September 19, 2008, p. 2.

had not been for his visionary insight and expert guidance—the pension saga of churches could have been a terribly sad story. Now the only regret can be that the churches did not move more quickly in the twentieth century to funded plans.

Consider the efforts of Judge Henry N. Graven of Greene, Iowa (see Chapter 11). He was convinced of the need for a church pension plan, even when few others shared his sense of urgency. He believed the failure of a church body to establish such a plan was unfair to pastors and reflected a lack of respect for the office of the ministry of Word and Sacrament. Through his untiring efforts, the American Lutheran Church embraced a contributory plan in 1939, just one year after the Augustana Lutheran Church embarked on a similar plan. Judge Graven continued throughout the 1940s and 1950s to serve on the pension board of the American Lutheran Church until that church body merged with others in 1960 to form what also was known as The American Lutheran Church.

Recall the highly significant work of Mr. Robert J. Myers, who was the chief actuary of the Social Security Administration from 1947 to 1970. He was the primary architect of the pension and benefits program of the Lutheran Church in America (see Chapter 13). He also was a trustee of the Board of Pensions of the United Lutheran Church in America, then of the LCA's Board of Pensions for almost a quarter century, and for four years, from 1987 to 1991, of the ELCA's Board of Pensions. He served as acting president of the LCA's Board of Pensions in the final months of 1987 following Mr. L. Edwin Wang's retirement as president. Mr. Myers died at the age of 97 on February 13, 2010.[52]

In the initial decades of the ELCA, the conscientious leadership of Mr. Kapanke as president of the Board of Pensions can be remembered with admiration and gratitude. He led the development and operation of the ELCA's program of pensions and other benefits through challenging times into constructive new directions.

Dozens of other persons could be cited (see Chapter 7 and Appendix One for examples). Various individuals, in their time, rendered crucial and visionary leadership for the development of Lutheran pension plans.

The lesson of history is clear: The wisdom, courage, and vision of one person or of some key leaders can shape a wholesome and welcome future.

---

[52] Emma Brown, "Robert Myers, 97: Longtime actuary for Social Security Administration," *The Washington Post*, February 22, 2010, p. B4.

Stewards of a precious legacy

Both the trustees and staff of the ELCA Board of Pensions serve as stewards of a precious legacy of service—a legacy that stretches back to simple efforts in small grants to those with special needs and extends to the present in the broad and well-developed program of pensions and other benefits.

Trustees and staff understand that they must seek to be guardians against unintended consequences. At the same time, they serve as guides for helping to shape a wholesome future for plan members in regard to their pension needs and other benefits. In so doing, they carry out their respective responsibilities with utmost prudence and untiring dedication.

Trustees must exercise diligence in governance, seeking always to practice wisdom in policy setting and decision making. Staff must ensure that trustees have ample information and broad understanding of issues as the trustees carry out their duties.

Fiduciary duty is not a simple matter. One of the lessons of history is that decisions that were made some 50, 60, 70, or more years ago—or, in some cases, delayed far too long—had an impact decades later. To offer an example, decisions made in the Augustana Lutheran Church, the Evangelical Lutheran Church, and the Lutheran Free Church in about 1940 meant that 45 years later—in 1985—those who had served in the Evangelical Lutheran Church and Lutheran Free Church were receiving about one-fourth less in retiree benefits than those who had been pastors in the Augustana Lutheran Church. That was happening a quarter century after those church bodies had ceased to exist through the mergers of 1960 and 1962.[53] Clearly, governance requires great vision and wisdom. At the same time, trustees, leaders, and staff members must exercise untiring dedication to their respective duties.

The lessons of history demonstrate that both trustees and staff of Lutheran pension and other benefits programs—as has been the case for the ELCA Board of Pensions—must be mindful of the past while having an ear attuned to the present and an eye focused on the future. Their decisions must be informed as fully as possible by historical perspective and current information as well as a thorough analysis of trends. At the same time, they must be cognizant of the future and the long-term implications of decisions and developments. A particular decision made in 2009 may well have implications for what happens not just in 2010 but even 2020 and beyond.

---

[53] L. Edwin Wang, "Letter to the Rev. Reuben T. Swanson," Board of Pensions of the Lutheran Church in America, January 9, 1985, p. 1.

"Connective tissue"

When Presiding Bishop Mark S. Hanson of the ELCA met with staff of the Board of Pensions in May 2008, he characterized the work of the board as similar to the connective tissue in the human body. The Board of Pensions serves a connective role in exercising the care of the church for those who serve within ELCA congregations, synods, churchwide ministries, institutions, and agencies.

In speaking of connective tissue, Presiding Bishop Hanson was reflecting an awareness of the interdependent nature of congregations, synods, and churchwide ministries as expressions of the ELCA. The work of each expression is shaped by the ELCA's six primary purposes. Those purposes are to: (1) worship God; (2) proclaim God's saving Gospel; (3) carry out Christ's Great Commission; (4) nurture members in the Word of God; (5) serve in response to human need; and (6) manifest the unity of the people of God.[54] Within those six purposes, the Board of Pensions exercises its particular responsibilities and, indeed, serves as part of the connective tissue of the church body. In so doing, leaders of the Board of Pensions devote conscientious attention to the board's role as a churchwide unit—that is, to being one part of the ELCA's various churchwide ministries.[55]

This connective awareness flows throughout the history of the one, holy, catholic, and apostolic Church. Remember the Apostle Paul's description of the Church as the body of Christ (e.g., Romans 12:4-5 and 1 Corinthians 12:12-27). Lutherans in North America have manifested such an understanding in various ways. Even the motion made by the Rev. Dr. Samuel S. Schmucker in that 1831 meeting of the General Synod (see Chapter 8) shows a connective sense of mutual care and commitment. Dr. Schmucker urged that the synod establish a fund "for the relief of superannuated ministers . . . and their widows and orphans."

Little could Dr. Schmucker have imagined the grand saga that would unfold as Lutherans in America created an amazing story of vision and care for pastors, other church workers, and their families. Even now, the narrative of courage and commitment continues to unfold. With the coming of each new day, we discover there is more to the ongoing story of the Board of Pensions of the ELCA. For that, the people of the Evangelical Lutheran Church in America can be truly grateful.

---

[54] Provision 4.02., *Constitution, Bylaws, and Continuing Resolutions of the Evangelical Lutheran Church in America* (2007 edition), p. 21.

[55] Provision 17.61. through continuing resolution 17.61.A05., *Constitution, Bylaws, and Continuing Resolutions of the Evangelical Lutheran Church in America* (2007 edition), pp. 135-138.

Board of Trustees of the Board of Pensions

Initial development

The Articles of Incorporation for the Board of Pensions of the Evangelical Lutheran Church in America were executed by Mr. Arnold R. Mickelson on Thursday, February 26, 1986. Mr. Mickelson of Minneapolis served as coordinator for the Commission for a New Lutheran Church, the group of 70 persons who were elected by the conventions in August 1982 of The American Lutheran Church (ALC) in San Diego, Calif., the Lutheran Church in America (LCA) in Louisville, Ky., and the Association of Evangelical Lutheran Churches (AELC) in Cleveland, Ohio. The commission was responsible for developing the plans and governing documents for the formation of the Evangelical Lutheran Church in America (ELCA).

The Articles of Incorporation for the Board of Pensions of the Evangelical Lutheran Church in America were filed in Minnesota and a Certificate of Incorporation was issued on Monday, March 2, 1987, by Secretary of State Joan Anderson Growe.

The organizational meeting of the initial board of trustees of the Board of Pensions was held on Sunday, March 29, 1987, to fulfill certain legal obligations, including the adoption of corporate bylaws. Elected as initial officers of the new corporation were: LCA Bishop James R. Crumley Jr., president; ALC Presiding Bishop David W. Preus, vice president; and AELC Presiding Bishop Will L. Herzfeld, secretary and treasurer.

At that initial meeting, an agreement and plan of merger of the Board of Pensions of the LCA into the Board of Pensions of the ELCA was approved. The actual effective date of that merger was January 27, 1988, with the Board of Pensions of the ELCA being the surviving corporation. The ALC's pension and benefits operation was part of the corporation of the ALC and, therefore, became part of the ELCA on January 1, 1988. That also was true for the Association of Evangelical Lutheran Churches.

Elections upon constituting of ELCA

At the constituting of the Evangelical Lutheran Church in America in Columbus, Ohio, April 30–May 2, 1987, 18 members of the board of trustees of the Board of Pensions were elected. As part of the process at that time, three additional trustees were elected by the Church Council June 1-3, 1987, in accord with bylaw 17.01.19. in effect at the time in the *Constitution, Bylaws, and Continuing Resolutions of the Evangelical Lutheran Church in America* (1987 edition).[1]

Elected were: (1) Pr. **Jeanette H. Bauermeister**, St. Louis, Mo. (term 1987-1991); (2) Ms. **Mildred M. Berg**, Brooklyn, N.Y. (term 1987-1993); (3) Ms. **Marlene K. Bonds**, Baton Rouge, La. (term 1987-1989); (4) Mr. **W. Michael Carter**, Irving, Texas (term 1987-1989); (5) Pr. **Mario F. Castaneda**, Houston, Texas (term 1987-1991); (6) Pr. **Daniel Chu**, Federal Way, Wash. (term 1987-1991); (7) Ms. **Patricia Tillberg Hasselmo**, Tucson, Ariz. (term 1987-1991); (8) Pr. **Robert E. Karsten**, Columbus, Ohio (term 1987-1989); (9) Pr. **Theodore L. Menter**, Port Huron, Mich. (term 1987-1989); (10) Mr. **Bartley E. Munson**, Appleton, Wis. (term 1987-1993); (11) Mr. **Robert J. Myers**, Silver Spring, Md. (term 1987-1991); (12) Mr. **Richard Niebuhr**, Aberdeen, S.D. (term 1987-1989); (13) Ms. **Mary Olson**, Chicago, Ill. (term 1987-1993); (14) Mr. **Fred B. Renwick**, Manhattan, N.Y. (1987-1993); (15) Ms. **Elizabeth A. Storaasli**, Duluth, Minn. (term 1987-1991); (16) Pr. **Reuben T. Swanson**, New York, N.Y., and subsequently Omaha, Neb. (term 1987-1993); (17) Ms. **Martha C. Ward**, Des Moines, Iowa (term 1987-1989); and (18) Pr. **Jerald L. Wendt**, Whitewater, Wis. (term 1987-1993).[2]

The three persons elected by the Church Council in June 1987 were: Mr. **Ulysses Bell**, Elizabeth City, N.C. (term 1987-1989); Ms. **Mary Nelson**, Chicago, Ill. (1987-1991); and Ms. **Wanda D. Neuhaus**, York, Pa. (1987-1993).[3] This was done in keeping with bylaw 17.01.19.,[4] which assigned at

---

[1] Trustees in this listing are designated as lay (Mr. or Ms.) and clergy (Pr.). No professional or academic titles are used for those possessing advanced, specialized, professional, or academic degrees, such as M.D., J.D., Ph.D., Ed.D., or D.Min.

[2] *Minutes of the Constituting Convention of the Evangelical Lutheran Church in America,* Columbus, Ohio, April 30–May 3, 1987, pp. 90-91.

[3] *Minutes,* Church Council of the Evangelical Lutheran Church in America, June 1, 1987, Exhibit E, p. 7.

[4] This bylaw was renumbered 17.01.20. by the 1989 Churchwide Assembly (*1989 Reports and Records: Minutes,* First Churchwide Assembly of the Evangelical Lutheran Church in America, Rosemont, Ill., August 23-30, 1989, p. 727).

that time to the Church Council the election of three positions "in order to insure that . . . board have within their membership persons with the expertise and experience essential to the fulfillment of the work of the board."[5]

Two persons resigned from the board of trustees late in 1987 or early in 1988. They were Martha C. Ward (original term 1987-1989), who accepted a position as health-claims manager with the Board of Pensions, and Jeannette H. Bauermeister (original term 1987-1991), who accepted a position with the Foundation of the ELCA.

At its spring meeting in April 1988, the Church Council elected two persons to fill those unexpired terms. Elected were Ms. **Kathryn A. Swanson**, Thousand Oaks, Calif., (term to 1989) and Mr. **Allan R. Nelson**, Cromwell, Conn. (term to 1991).[6]

Subsequent elections

Of the initial board, the service of five ended in 1989. They were Ms. Marlene K. Bonds, Mr. W. Michael Carter, Pr. Robert E. Karsten, Pr. Theodore L. Menter, and Ms. Kathryn A. Swanson. In preparation for the 1989 Churchwide Assembly, the assembly's Nominating Committee declined to put forward the names of Ms. Kathryn A. Swanson and Pr. Theodore L. Menter.

At the 1989 Churchwide Assembly (terms 1989-1995), the only incumbent trustee who was re-elected was (1) Mr. **Richard Niebuhr**. Incumbent Mr. W. Michael Carter was defeated by (2) Mr. **Floyd O. Arntz**, Cambridge, Mass.; incumbent Ms. Marlene K. Bonds, by (3) Ms. **Sandra G. Gustavson**, Doraville, Ga.; and incumbent Pr. Robert E. Karsten, by (4) Pr. **Viviane Thomas-Breitfeld**, Milwaukee, Wis. Also elected to six-year terms in 1989 were (5) Ms. **Linda J. Brown**, Moorhead, Minn., and (6) Mr. **Theodore S. Rosky**, Louisville, Ky.[7]

In November 1989, (7) Mr. **Ulysses Bell** was elected by the Church Council to a regular term (1989-1995).[8]

Early in 1990, Mr. Niebuhr resigned from the board of trustees. Subsequently, at the April 1990 meeting of the Church Council, Mr. **Noel I. Fedje**, Fargo, N.D., was elected to fill the remainder of the unexpired term to 1995.[9]

---

[5] *Minutes of the Constituting Convention of the ELCA*, Exhibit C, 1987, p. 280.

[6] CC88.04.37, *Minutes*, Church Council, April 1988, p. 62.

[7] *1989 Reports and Records: Minutes*, pp. 772, 773, and 890.

[8] *Minutes*, Church Council, November 1989, p. 36.

[9] *Minutes*, Church Council, April 1990, p. 53.

The 1989 Churchwide Assembly adopted a new bylaw with the number 17.01.19. to define the beginning of terms of those elected to boards. The second half of that new bylaw said, "The commencement of terms of office of persons elected to regular terms by the Churchwide Assembly or Church Council on the board of the ELCA Publishing House and the board of trustees of the Board of Pensions shall be specified in the bylaws of these separately incorporated entities."[10]

The 1991 Churchwide Assembly of the ELCA amended bylaw 17.01.20., renumbered as 19.51.01., to eliminate the election of three members of the board by the Church Council. The revised bylaw read: "The Churchwide Assembly shall elect all members of each division board, the board of the Publishing House of the ELCA, and the Board of Pensions. The Nominating Committee [for the Churchwide Assembly] shall seek to ensure that these boards have within their membership persons with the expertise and experience essential to the fulfillment of the work of the board."[11]

Further, bylaw 16.51.34., renumbered 17.61.03., was amended by the 1991 Churchwide Assembly to read: "This board shall have a board of trustees composed of 21 persons elected to one six-year term with no consecutive reelection and with one-third elected each biennium as provided in Chapter 19. In addition, the trustees of this church shall include persons with expertise in investments, insurance, and pensions, and six persons who are participants in the plans, at least one of whom shall be a lay plan participant or lay recipient of plan benefit and at least one of whom shall be an ordained minister who is a plan participant. The Conference of Bishops shall elect one bishop to serve as an advisory member of the Board of Pensions."[12]

---

[10] Commencement of the terms was addressed in the board's bylaws (see "Summary of Church Council Minutes, April 1990," *1991 Reports and Records*, Vol. 1, Part 2, Second Churchwide Assembly of the Evangelical Lutheran Church in America, Orlando, Fla., August 28–September 4, 1991, p. 863). An amendment of the board's bylaws (Article 4, Section 4.2) was approved by the Church Council at the council's April 1990 meeting to read, "The terms of trustees elected by the Churchwide Assembly shall commence at the commencement of the first meeting of the Board of Trustees following the close of the Churchwide Assembly at which they are elected and shall expire at the commencement of the first meeting of the Board of Trustees in the year in which their successors are elected. The terms of trustees elected by the Church Council shall commence at . . . the close of the Church Council meeting at which they are elected and shall expire at . . . the commencement of the first meeting of the Board of Trustees in the year in which their successors are elected."

[11] *1991 Reports and Records: Minutes*, p. 308.

[12] *1991 Reports and Records: Minutes*, p. 432.

Following passage of those amendments, the 1991 Churchwide Assembly in Orlando, Fla., elected seven persons to six-year terms on the board of trustees. They were: (1) Ms. **Barbara L. Bauer**, Boise, Idaho; (2) Mr. **Ralph J. Eckert**, Dillon, Colo.; (3) Pr. **Kenneth C. Feinour Jr.**, Allentown, Pa.; (4) Ms. **Carolyn S. Nestingen**, St. Paul, Minn.; (5) Ms. **Shellie Reed**, Golden Valley, Minn.; (6) Mr. **David A. Russell**, Allentown, Pa; and (7) Pr. **Wilson Wu**, Monterey Park, Calif.[13]

Elected by the 1993 Churchwide Assembly in Kansas City, Mo., to six-year terms were: (1) Ms. **Mary Alice Bjork**, Salem, Ore.; (2) Mr. **Irving R. Burling**, Waverly, Iowa; (3) Mr. **William R. Halling**, Bloomfield Hills, Mich.; (4) Ms. **Carla P. Haugen**, Darien, Conn.; (5) Ms. **Emma Graeber Porter**, New York, N.Y.; (6) Pr. **J. Christian Quello**, Appleton, Wis.; and (7) Ms. **Ruth E. Randall**, Lincoln, Neb.[14] Mr. Burling resigned from the board on July 21, 1997. Elected by the Church Council to fill the two remaining years of his unexpired term was Mr. **Jon B. Christianson**, St. Paul, Minn.[15]

At the Churchwide Assembly in 1995, which met in Minneapolis, the following persons were elected to six-year terms: (1) Ms. **Ruth H. Beagles**, St. Croix, Virgin Islands; (2) Mr. **Willis I. Else**, Hudson, Ohio; (3) Mr. **Earl L. Mummert**, Harrisburg, Pa.; (4) Ms. **Janet Huber Neff**, Havertown, Pa.; (5) Mr. **John K. Roberts**, Gretna, La.; (6) Ms. **Lisa K. Stump**, Des Moines, Iowa; and (7) Mr. **Robert J. Thimjon**, Sioux Falls, S.D.[16]

The 1997 Churchwide Assembly in Philadelphia elected to six-year terms: (1) Pr. **James S. Aull**, Columbia, S.C.; (2) Ms. **Brenda A. Grandell**, Brooklyn, N.Y.; (3) Ms. **Gwen W. Halaas**, Minneapolis, Minn.; (4) Pr. **Larry C. Kassebaum**, Mesa, Ariz.; (5) Ms. **Barbara A. Swartling**, Bainbridge Island, Wash.; (6) Mr. **Michael B. Unhjem**, Fargo, N.D.; and (7) Mr. **Gregory R. White**, Salem, Ore.[17]

---

[13] *1991 Reports and Records: Minutes*, Exhibit B, pp. 570 and 802-803.

[14] *1993 Reports and Records: Minutes*, Exhibit B, Third Churchwide Assembly of the Evangelical Lutheran Church in America, Kansas City, Mo., August 25–September 1, 1993, pp. 672-673.

[15] Mr. Christianson was elected to the unexpired term at the Church Council's November 14-16, 1997, meeting (*Minutes*, p. 36).

[16] *1995 Reports and Records: Minutes*, Exhibit B, Fourth Churchwide Assembly of the Evangelical Lutheran Church in America, Minneapolis, Minn., August 16-22, 1995, pp. 731-733.

[17] *1997 Reports and Records: Minutes*, Exhibit B, Fifth Churchwide Assembly of the Evangelical Lutheran Church in America, Philadelphia, Pa., August 14-20, 1997, pp. 969-971.

Subsequently, Mr. Unhjem and Mr. White resigned from the board and were replaced, respectively, by Mr. **Kenneth G. Bash**, Scottsdale, Ariz., and Mr. **David Alvarez**, Guaynabo, Puerto Rico, who were elected at the April 17-20, 1998, meeting of the Church Council to fill the unexpired terms.[18] Ms. Halaas resigned in August 2001 to lead the churchwide ministerial health and wellness program. Elected in April 2002 to fill her unexpired term was Pr. **Jon R. Lee**, Dallas, Tex.

At the 1999 Churchwide Assembly in Denver, Colo., the following were elected to six-year terms: (1) Mr. **Jon B. Christianson**, St. Paul, Minn.; (2) Mr. **Bradley C. Engel**, Burlington, Wis.; (3) Ms. **Nancy J. Haberstich**, Lincoln, Neb.; (4) Ms. **Sarah C. Murphy**, Dayton, Ohio; (5) Ms. **Karen E. (Shaaf) Southward**, Columbus, Ohio; (6) Ms. **Jane C. von Seggern**, Atlanta, Ga.; and (7) Pr. **Lawrence W. Wick**, Woodstock, Ill.[19]

In Indianapolis, Ind., at the 2001 Churchwide Assembly, elected to six-year terms were: (1) Mr. **T. Van Matthews**, Greenville, S.C.; (2) Mr. **Kenneth G. Mertz II**, Middletown, Pa; (3) Mr. **Harry C. Mueller**, St. Louis, Mo.; (4) Ms. **Vivian Jenkins Nelsen**, Minneapolis, Minn.; (5) Ms. **Mary S. Ranum**, Circle Pines, Minn.; (6) Mr. **Joseph A. Swanson**, Racine, Wis.; and (7) Ms. **Yvonne Wells**, St. John, Virgin Islands.[20] Ms. Nelsen resigned from the board in November 2005. Because of the decision of the 2005 Churchwide Assembly to reduce the size of churchwide boards between 2005 and 2009 from 21 members of 15 members, her unexpired term to 2007 was not filled.

At the 2003 Churchwide Assembly in Milwaukee, Wis., elected to six-year terms were: (1) Ms. **Charlotte E. Carlson**, Northfield, Minn.; (2) Mr. **Emried D. Cole Jr.**, Baltimore, Md.; (3) Ms. **Louise P. Evenson**, Lafayette, Calif.; (4) Pr. **Jon R. Lee**, Dallas, Texas; (5) Mr. **Warren R. Luckner**, Lincoln, Neb.; (6) Mr. **James R. Penner**, Helena, Mont.; and (7) Pr. **Marcia B. Strahl**, Chadwick, Ill.[21] Pr. Strahl resigned before being seated on the board. Elected by the Church Council to fill her term was Pr. **Kathleen O. Reed**, Natick, Mass.[22]

---

[18] Church Council Minutes, April 18-20, 1998, pp. 14-15.

[19] *1999 Reports and Records: Minutes*, Exhibit B, Sixth Churchwide Assembly of the Evangelical Lutheran Church in America, August 16-22, 1999, p. 659.

[20] *2001 Reports and Records: Minutes*, Exhibit B, Seventh Churchwide Assembly of the Evangelical Lutheran Church in America, Indianapolis, Ind., August 8-14, 2001, p. 494.

[21] *2003 Reports and Records: Minutes*, Exhibit B, Eighth Churchwide Assembly of the Evangelical Lutheran Church in America, Milwaukee, Wis., August 11-17, 2003, pp. 441-442.

[22] *Minutes*, Church Council, April 16-18, 2004, p. 26.

The 2005 Churchwide Assembly, meeting in Orlando, Fla., elected to six-year terms the following: (1) Ms. **Ivy S. Bernhardson**, Bloomington, Minn.; (2) Ms. **Mary K. Gobber**, Lincoln, Neb.; (3) Ms. **Lois A. O'Rourke**, Madison, Wis.; (4) Mr. **David D. Swartling**, Bainbridge Island, Wash.; and (5) Mr. **James D. Swinford**, Indianapolis, Ind.[23] Mr. Swartling resigned effective December 31, 2006, to accept employment with the Foundation of the ELCA. (At the 2007 Churchwide Assembly, he was elected secretary of the ELCA.) Ms. Bernhardson resigned on May 30, 2007, upon appointment as a Hennepin County (Minn.) judge.

In Chicago, the 2007 Churchwide Assembly elected to six-year terms: (1) Ms. **Kelly L. Birch**, Chicago, Ill.; (2) Ms. **Ruby M. Joy**, Jamaica, N.Y.; (3) Mr. **Michael J. McCoy**, Ellison Bay, Wis.; (4) Mr. **Roger A. Sayler**, New Canaan, Conn.; and (5) Mr. **Greg K. Smith**, Freeport, Grand Bahamas.[24] Ms. **Ingrid S. Stafford**, Evanston, Ill., was elected at the November 2007 meeting of the Church Council to fill the unexpired term to 2011 of Judge Bernhardson. At the same time, Mr. **Bruce D. George**, Westborough, Mass., was elected to the unexpired term to 2011 of Mr. Swartling.[25] Ms. Birch resigned April 14, 2009, due to overseas employment.[26] Named by the Church Council in November 2009 to the unexpired term of Ms. Birch was Mr. **Cecil D. Bykerk**, Omaha, Neb.

At the 2009 Churchwide Assembly in Minneapolis, elected to six-year terms were: (1) Mr. **Kevin D. Anderson**, Gaithersburg, Md.; (2) Ms. **Lisa Ann Kro**, Plymouth, Minn.; (3) Ms. **Kathleen K. Mooney**, Cold Spring, Minn.; (4) Ms. **Jill A. Schumann**, Gettysburg, Pa.; and (5) Pr. **Jeffrey D. Thiemann**, Walnut Creek, Calif.

Chairs of board

Ms. **Mildred M. Berg** was elected on June 29, 1987, as the first chair of the board of trustees of the Board of Pensions.[27] She served for six years as chair and was succeeded by Mr. **Ralph J. Eckert** (1993-1997), Ms. **Emma**

---

[23] *2005 Reports and Records: Minutes*, Exhibit B, Ninth Churchwide Assembly of the Evangelical Lutheran Church in America, Orlando, Fla., August 8-14, 2005, pp. 577-578.

[24] *2007 Reports and Records: Minutes*, Exhibit B, Tenth Churchwide Assembly of the Evangelical Lutheran Church in America, Chicago, Ill., August 6-11, 2007, p. 431.

[25] *Minutes*, Church Council, November 9-11, 2007.

[26] *Minutes*, Board of Trustees of the Board of Pensions of the ELCA, April 23, 2009, p. 2.

[27] Mildred Berg was elected on the third ballot at the first regular meeting of the board of trustees of the Board of Pensions on a vote of Berg, 14, and Reuben Swanson, 5 (*Minutes*, PN87.06.09). At that meeting, the rules required a two-thirds vote for election.

Graeber Porter (1997-1999), Mr. **Earl L. Mummert** (1999-2001), Mr. **Kenneth G. Bash** (2001-2003), Mr. **Bradley C. Engel** (2003-2005), Ms. **Mary S. Ranum** (2005-2007), Mr. **Emried D. Cole Jr.** (2007-2009), and Ms. **Lois A. O'Rourke** (2009-present).

Advisory members

Serving as advisors to the Board of Pensions on behalf of the Conference of Bishops have been: Bishop Harold S. Weiss, Northeastern Pennsylvania Synod (1987-1991); Bishop Glenn W. Nycklemoe, Southeastern Minnesota Synod (1992-1995); Bishop Ronald K. Hasley, Northern Illinois Synod (1996-1998); Bishop Kenneth R. Olsen, Metropolitan Chicago Synod (1998-2001); Bishop Robert D. Berg, Northwest Synod of Wisconsin (2001-2007); and Bishop James A. Justman, East-Central Synod of Wisconsin (August 1, 2007–present).

The representatives of the presiding bishop to the Board of Pensions have been: Pr. Morris A. Sorenson Jr. (September 1987–October 1991); Pr. Lowell G. Almen (November 1, 1991–October 31, 2007); and Mr. David D. Swartling (November 1, 2007–present).

The treasurers of the Evangelical Lutheran Church in America also have been advisors: Mr. George E. Aker (1987-1991); Mr. Richard L. McAuliffe (1992-2001); and Ms. Christina Jackson-Skelton (2002-present).

Provision for Board of Pensions in the Governing Documents

Commitment to providing a pension and other benefits program is declared in the *Constitution, Bylaws, and Continuing Resolutions of the Evangelical Lutheran Church in America.* Provision 11.21. specifies, in part, that:

> In fulfillment of the purposes of this church, the churchwide organization shall:
>
> . . .
>
> e. Foster interdependent relationships among congregations, synods, and the churchwide organization to implement the mission of this whole church.
>
> . . .
>
> m. Provide pension and other benefits plans for this church.[1]

Further, provision 17.61. and following offer a more detailed outline of the responsibilities of the Board of Pensions:

> 17.61. This church shall have a church pension and other benefits plans unit. This Board of Pensions shall be incorporated. The president of the corporation shall serve as its chief executive officer.
>
> 17.61.01. The Churchwide Assembly shall:
>
> a. approve the documents governing the ELCA Pension and Other Benefits Program that have been referred by the Church Council; and

---

[1] Provision 11.21., *Constitution, Bylaws, and Continuing Resolutions of the Evangelical Lutheran Church in America* (2007 edition), pp. 85-86.

b. refer any amendments to the ELCA Pension and Other Benefits Program initiated by the Churchwide Assembly to the Board of Pensions for recommendation before final action by the Church Council, assuring that no amendment shall abridge the rights of members with respect to their pension accumulations.

17.61.02. The Church Council shall:

a. review policy established by the board and take action on any policy that would change significantly the documents establishing and governing the ELCA Pension and Other Benefits Program.

b. approve any changes in the ELCA Pension and Other Benefits Program when there is to be:

1) a significant increase in cost to the employers or members; or

2) a significant increase or decrease in benefits to the members.

c. refer any amendments to the ELCA Pension and Other Benefits Program initiated by the Church Council to the board for recommendation before final action by the Church Council, assuring that no amendment shall abridge the rights of members with respect to their pension accumulations.

d. refer, as it deems appropriate, proposed amendments to the ELCA Pension and Other Benefits Program to the Churchwide Assembly for final action.

17.61.03. The Board of Pensions shall have a board of trustees composed of 15 persons elected for one six-year term with no consecutive reelection and with one-third elected each biennium as provided in Chapter 19.

a. The board of trustees of the Board of Pensions shall include persons with expertise in investments, insurance, and pensions, and four persons who are members of the plans, at least one of whom shall be a lay plan member or lay recipient of plan benefits and at least one of whom shall be an ordained minister who is a plan member.

b. The presiding bishop shall serve as an advisory member of the board of trustees, with voice but not vote, or shall designate a person to serve as the presiding bishop's representative as provided in constitutional provision 13.21.[2]

c. The Conference of Bishops shall elect one bishop to serve as an advisory member of the board of trustees with voice but not vote.

d. The treasurer of this church shall serve as an advisory member of the board of trustees with voice but not vote.

17.61.04. The board shall organize itself as it deems necessary.

17.61.05. Constitutional provision 16.12.[3] and bylaws 14.21.02.,[4] 14.21.07.,[5] 16.12.11.,[6] and 16.12.14.[7] shall apply to this board.

---

[2] Provision 13.21.l., *Constitution* (2007 edition, p. 93) reads: "This church shall have a presiding bishop who . . . shall . . . [s]erve as an advisory member, with voice but not vote, on all committees of this church and all boards or committees of churchwide units, or designate a person to serve as the presiding bishop's representative."

[3] Provision 16.12., *Constitution* (2007 edition, p. 114) reads: "Each unit shall be responsible to the Churchwide Assembly and will report to the Church Council in the interim. The policies, procedures, and operation of each unit shall be reviewed by the Church Council in order to assure conformity with the governing documents of this church and with Churchwide Assembly actions."

[4] Bylaw 14.21.02., *Constitution* (2007 edition, p. 100) reads: "The Church Council shall review the procedures and programs of the churchwide units to assure that churchwide purposes, policies, and objectives are being fulfilled. Each unit shall recommend policy and develop strategies in its particular areas of responsibility after consultation with other units of the churchwide organization and affected synods, congregations, agencies, and institutions.

a. Policies related to the day-to-day functioning of the unit or to the specific responsibilities of the unit that have no implications for other units, congregations, synods, agencies, or institutions may be approved by the unit, subject to ratification by the Church Council.

b. All other policies shall be submitted to the Church Council for approval."

[5] Bylaw 14.21.07., *Constitution* (2007 edition, p. 101) reads: "Consistent with applicable personnel policies, churchwide units will have staff persons, some of whom shall be executive staff and others of whom shall be support staff. In conformity with this church's commitment to inclusive practice, churchwide units will assure that staff include a balance of women and men, persons of color and persons whose primary language is other than English, laypersons, and persons on the roster of ordained ministers. This balance is to be evident in terms of both executive staff and support staff consistent with the inclusive policy of this church."

[6] Bylaw 16.12.11., *Constitution* (2007 edition, p. 114) reads: "Each program committee, which normally shall meet two times each year, shall function as specified in this church=s constitution, bylaws, and continuing resolutions regarding its responsibilities in relation to a particular unit of the churchwide organization."

[7] Bylaw 16.12.14., *Constitution* (2007 edition, p. 114) reads: "Proxy and absentee voting shall not be permitted."

17.61.06.   The president shall be elected by the board of trustees of the Board of Pensions to a four-year term in consultation with and with the approval of the presiding bishop of this church. Nomination of a candidate for president shall be made jointly by the presiding bishop and the search committee of the board. The board, together with the presiding bishop, shall arrange for an annual review of the president. The president shall be eligible for reelection. The board shall establish the salary of the president with the concurrence of the presiding bishop. The president may be terminated at any time jointly by the board of trustees of the Board of Pensions and the presiding bishop of this church, following recommendation by the executive committee of the board of trustees.

17.61.07.   The specific responsibilities of the Board of Pensions shall be enumerated in continuing resolutions. Such continuing resolutions may be amended by a majority vote of the Churchwide Assembly or by a two-thirds vote of the Church Council. Should the board disagree with the action of the Church Council, it may appeal the decision to the Churchwide Assembly.

17.61.A05.   *Responsibilities of the Board of Pensions*

The Board of Pensions of the Evangelical Lutheran Church in America shall:

  a.   *manage and operate the Pension and Other Benefits Program for this church and plans for other organizations operated exclusively for religious purposes, and shall invest the assets according to fiduciary standards set forth in the plans and trusts.*

  b.   *provide pension, health, and other benefits exclusively for the benefit of eligible members working within the structure of this church and other organizations operated exclusively for religious purposes.*

  c.   *provide summary plan descriptions outlining all benefits to be provided as a part of the ELCA Pension and Other Benefits Program.*

d. report to the appropriate committee of the Church Council on the financial effect of changes to the ELCA Pension and Other Benefits Program.

e. report to the Churchwide Assembly through the Church Council, with the Church Council making comments on all board actions needing approval of the Churchwide Assembly.

f. maintain appropriate communication with other units of this church.

g. be self-supporting, except for certain ELCA minimum pensions and post-retirement health benefits of certain ELCA retirees, with all costs being paid from the administrative and management charges to the employers and members utilizing the plans and from investment income.

h. manage its finances in a manner that assures an efficient and effective administration of the plans for pension and other benefits. The board shall maintain its own accounting, data processing, personnel, and other administrative functions essential to the ongoing work of this organization.

I. not be responsible, nor assume any liability for, health-insurance programs provided by colleges and universities of this church through voluntary employees' beneficiary associations or similar arrangements.

j. manage and operate those portions of The American Lutheran Church and Lutheran Church in America plans requiring continuation in this church.

k. provide an appeal process with the Board of Pensions to enable members in the plans to appeal decisions.

l. make editorial and administrative changes and routine modifications to the ELCA Pension and Other Benefits Program, as well as changes required to comply with federal and state law.

m. set contribution rates for the ELCA Survivor Benefits Plan, the ELCA Disability Benefits Plan, and the ELCA Medical and Dental Benefits Plan, and establish interest crediting rates for the ELCA Retirement Plans.

n. manage assets, as requested, for the ELCA and other organizations operated exclusively for religious purposes.

17.61.B05.

> The Corporate Social Responsibility Committee of the Board of Pensions shall receive advice and counsel from the Advisory Committee on Corporate Social Responsibility formed by the appropriate churchwide unit and within the context of fiduciary responsibility for ELCA assets make appropriate recommendations to the board.[8]

---

[8] *Constitution* (2007 edition), pp. 135-137.

LUTHERAN ROOTS IN THE U.S.A.

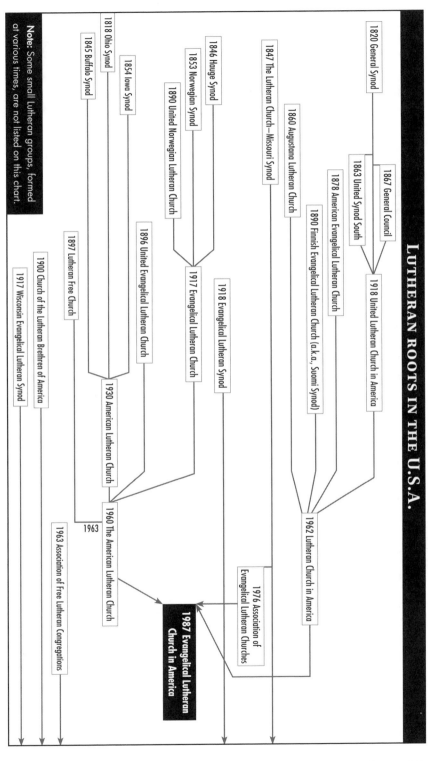

1820 General Synod

1818 Ohio Synod

1845 Buffalo Synod

1846 Hauge Synod

1853 Norwegian Synod

1890 United Norwegian Lutheran Church

1847 The Lutheran Church—Missouri Synod

1860 Augustana Lutheran Church

1854 Iowa Synod

1867 General Council

1863 United Synod South

1878 American Evangelical Lutheran Church

1890 Finnish Evangelical Lutheran Church (a.k.a., Suomi Synod)

1918 United Lutheran Church in America

1897 Lutheran Free Church

1896 United Evangelical Lutheran Church

1917 Evangelical Lutheran Church

1918 Evangelical Lutheran Synod

1900 Church of the Lutheran Brethren of America

1917 Wisconsin Evangelical Lutheran Synod

1930 American Lutheran Church

1963

1960 The American Lutheran Church

1962 Lutheran Church in America

1963 Association of Free Lutheran Congregations

1976 Association of Evangelical Lutheran Churches

1987 Evangelical Lutheran Church in America

Note: Some small Lutheran groups, formed at various times, are not listed on this chart.

Chart • 341

Index

Name

Subject